BEYOND SIGHT

Engaging the Senses in Iberian Literatures and Cultures, 1200–1750

EDITED BY RYAN D. GILES AND STEVEN WAGSCHAL

Beyond Sight

Engaging the Senses in Iberian Literatures and Cultures, 1200–1750

UNIVERSITY OF TORONTO PRESS
Toronto Buffalo London

Toronto Buffalo London
www.utorontopress.com

ISBN 978-1-4875-0003-0

Library and Archives Canada Cataloguing in Publication

Beyond sight : engaging the senses in Iberian literatures and cultures, 1200–1750 / edited by Ryan D. Giles and Steven Wagschal.

(Toronto Iberic)
Includes bibliographical references and index.
ISBN 978-1-4875-0003-0 (cloth)

1. Spanish literature – History and criticism. 2. Senses and sensation in literature. I. Wagschal, Steven, 1967–, editor II. Giles, Ryan D. (Ryan Dennis), editor III. Title. IV. Series: Toronto Iberic

PR275.S46B49 2017 860.9'3561 C2017-903715-3

University of Toronto Press acknowledges the financial assistance to its publishing program of the Canada Council for the Arts and the Ontario Arts Council, an agency of the Government of Ontario.

Canada Council for the Arts
Conseil des Arts du Canada

Funded by the Government of Canada
Financé par le gouvernement du Canada
Canada

Contents

Part Five: Sensing the Urban

Illustrations

Acknowledgments

This project had its beginnings in a symposium entitled "Sensory Worlds," which we organized at Indiana University, Bloomington, in October 2013. We thank the speakers as well as the faculty colleagues and graduate students in attendance for their participation in making it a worthwhile and stimulating venture.

We are appreciative of logistical and financial support for the Symposium provided by the College of Arts and Humanities Institute (CAHI). We are also indebted to the Institute for Advanced Study (IAS) for a collaborative research grant, which was awarded to us at a crucial time in the production of this book.

We would like to express our gratitude to doctoral student Christina Cole, who carefully assisted with the preparation of the manuscript. We are especially thankful for the patience and support of our families over the past three years.

Finally, we would like to thank Suzanne Rancourt, executive editor at the University of Toronto Press, for her guidance throughout this project, as well as the three anonymous readers of the manuscript, who offered many excellent suggestions that significantly helped improve this volume.

Ryan D. Giles and Steven Wagschal

BEYOND SIGHT

Engaging the Senses in Iberian Literatures and Cultures, 1200–1750

Introduction

RYAN D. GILES AND STEVEN WAGSCHAL

One visitor to Iberia who left a particularly vivid account of his travels was the Enlightenment thinker and future president of the United States John Adams. On his 1779 voyage to France to carry out a diplomatic mission, Adams found himself stranded on the Galician coast after his frigate, the *Sensible*, took on water and had to be docked to await lengthy repairs. Adams elected to make the journey by land, across northern Spain, so that much of his journey followed the old *Camino* route to Santiago – albeit in reverse.

Adams's narrative not only records visual impressions, but strikingly describes the sounds, smells, tastes, and feel of eighteenth-century Iberia. His descriptions convey varying attitudes of curiosity, fascination, disapproval, and disgust. For instance, he hears the Spanish language as "harmony to the ear," in contrast to "our language [which is] insipid and disgusting to them [...] less sonorous, and infested with very dissagreable sibillations" (12.20).[1] At times the chanting of monks pesters him like droning, swarming insects, but on other occasions is heard as beautiful music. The New Englander later enjoys the rhythms of a *fandango* song and dance. He is awakened by the smell of "the verdure in the gardens and fields," the fragrances of "rich soil" and "very large" turnips and onions boiling in a pot, but also the reek of run-down inns filled with smoke and soot, where travellers share the filthy straw floors with livestock (12.14). Adams dwells on gustatory impressions, describing the pure waters of Asturian snow melt and how Spanish ladies savoured chocolate, sugar, and cakes. He repeatedly praises the "wines of the country [...] good and wholesome [...] red and white [...] the Sherry, Alicante and Navarre [...] the oldest and best" – although he was once offered a more questionable vintage: "the wine was very sour" (1.6). But what especially appeals to Adams's palate are the produce, fish, and above all the cured hams, "most excellent and delicious," raised on "chestnutts" and a "peculiar kind of acorns growing upon old pasture oaks, which were very sweet" (12.19). At the same time the reader can appreciate the feel of the warming sun on the coast, where Adams finds children "with necked legs and feet" standing on "stones in the mud," followed by the sensation of the freezing highlands and the scourge of fleas, lice, and bedbugs (12.14). His written account of Iberia is, in a word, saturated with non-visual, sensory images. It is this often underappreciated range of imagery that concerns us in this volume. Its essays deal with the auditory, olfactory, gustatory, and tactile experiences of Iberian writers and thinkers and span from the heyday of the medieval *Camino* to Santiago to the century in which Adams made his accidental journey.

In spite of the "sensory turn" that has characterized studies in the humanities and social sciences over the past decade, very little scholarly attention has been directed to literary and cultural representations of non-visual sensory experiences – and much less to the Iberian Peninsula and in its colonies.[2] Our purpose in this broad-ranging collection is to explore many of the ways in which Iberian writers crafted images to describe sensory perceptions of the Old and New Worlds, both real and imagined, from the Middle Ages to the early modern period. Previous research by Hispanists interested in the senses has tended to focus on visual representations and ekphrasis.[3] Here we want to consider how medieval and early modern texts produced, activated, and continued to indulge the other senses (hearing, smell, taste, and touch) – from a multitude of perspectives, including literary and cultural history, philosophical aesthetics, and contemporary approaches to cognition. Our aim is to delve into the uses and meanings of these sensations in relation to material culture, employing other approaches that have developed over the past decade, including affective and cognitive studies and theories of embodiment in literature and culture. The essays show how the four non-visual senses, though underappreciated in most previous scholarship, are central to understanding Iberian authors and thinkers during the pre- and early modern periods. Furthermore, the collection has been envisioned as engaging with the growing field of Iberian Studies, conceived of as a dynamic interrelationship among cultures and languages, which are better understood in their plurality rather than in isolation.

Emphasizing non-visual sensual representations, while still considering the power of sight, bridges various areas of interdisciplinary research. The essays engage a portion of the vast historical array of philosophical, medical, artistic, and cognitive conceptualizations of the senses. Both Plato and Aristotle set the stage for thinking about a hierarchical relationship among the senses. For the former, sight was the "noblest" (*Republic* bk 6: 256); for Aristotle, "above all others the sense of sight" is loved (*Metaphysics* A.1:689), and it was long ago recognized that some animals were superior to humans in the use of certain senses (e.g., Aristotle noted, correctly, that dogs had superior olfaction).[4] The senses were understood in classical and medieval times as part of complex cosmological cycles. They were considered in relation to the Seasons, the Elements, the Constellations, and the

Ages of Man, as well as to the four humours. Sight and hearing have often been conceptualized as distance senses, more closely associated with reason and even the divine. Isidore of Seville used distance in order to rank the senses; thus, sight was superior to hearing, which was superior to olfaction (Juttle 65). Touch and taste, as contact senses – for the body needs to come into direct contact with perceived objects – constituted a more direct connection to material culture. They were important for an understanding of the body and animal nature and, eventually, for recognizing the relation of the senses to the feelings and emotions of human beings; along with sight, each of the other four senses was symbolized by a different animal in many medieval illustrations.[5]

Aristotle and later thinkers theorized correctly that most sensation occurred in the brain, to which the various sensory organs transmitted information. However, there was considerable debate as to what role the nose had in this process, and it is the one sense that does not fit neatly in their hierarchies. For Aristotle olfactory sensation took place in the nose itself – just as sight occurs in the eyes – but for a majority of later thinkers from antiquity through most of the seventeenth century, including Galen and eventually the important Renaissance anatomist Vesalius, the nose was merely a conduit or "hollow tube" through which smells travelled to reach the brain where dedicated lobes (still known today as the "mamillary bodies," since Avicenna had thought they looked like a woman's breasts) sensed the smells (Palmer 62).

In the Renaissance, anticipating Descartes, the Valencian humanist Joan Lluis Vives's *De anima et vita* is the first work to explore in detail the fundamental relations between the senses and the arousal of emotional states, something that many current psychological and cognitive studies examine. Hedonic emotional states, as well as the unpleasant, anhedonic ones, including the emotion of disgust, are often aroused quite directly by some of the so-called lesser senses, especially olfaction and gustation. *Beyond Sight* will show how these sensory contexts are crucial to understanding cultural and literary encounters from these periods. Indeed, the hierarchy of the senses is somewhat unstable across cultures when studied scientifically in the twenty-first century. As cognitive linguists have recently demonstrated through a cross-cultural comparison of action verbs in thirteen languages, the sense of sight dominates language across cultures and appears to be universally considered the most important sense; while the importance of sight seems stable in this study of languages from nine different language families (including Indo-European, Mayan, and Niger-Congo), the position of the other senses in the hierarchy varies significantly (San Roque et al. 49–52).[6] The essays in *Beyond Sight* will demonstrate a similar instability in their prominence across time, in which different senses, especially sound or smell, can take on a particular importance in changing socio-historical contexts.

During the Middle Ages, poetic representations of the sensorial plane forged synaesthetic gateways to transcendence and the ineffable. Authors engaged in discourses of sacramental and purportedly miraculous seeing, hearing, tasting, and touching were central to efforts at affirming the faith, as were denials and deceptions of the senses. Such writers and their readers could be said to belong to what Barbara Rosenwein has described as "emotional communities," which are brought together by shared "values," "assumptions" and "accepted modes of expression" (24). She makes a distinction between larger and subdivided communities, considering how these interrelate and interact with "textual communities" and, more specifically, conventions of genres such as hagiography, which might predetermine the way emotional relations could be represented, promoted, or discouraged and for what purposes, be they ideological, didactic, or aesthetic (25–7). Members of these emotional communities might adapt from one set of expectations to those of another group, in terms of what emotional responses are to be emphasized or are idealized and in what contexts.

The first section of the book, "Sensing Religion," delves into all of these issues. It features two essays that study the importance of smell in the construction of saintliness and religious difference. It begins with "The Breath of Lazarus in the *Mocedades de Rodrigo*," in which Ryan Giles examines a crucial episode from the medieval legend of the Cid's youthful deeds, when the hero encounters a leprous beggar. Rodrigo offers charity to the stranger and experiences a prophetic dream. The ailing leper, now described as fragrant and dressed in white, speaks in Rodrigo's ear, identifying himself as St Lazarus, sent by Christ to blow a fever into him, and in so doing to assure the hero's victory in battle. Giles shows how the repellent, feverish flesh and breath of the leper challenged medieval Christians to reconfigure their senses and thereby perceive the fragrance of their Saviour's redeeming Passion. The young Cid follows the example of saints and crusaders who drew on the model of *Christus quasi leprosus* to wage spiritual as well as military battles, conquering the stench of sin and death through the Passion and Resurrection of Christ's anointed, sweetly fragrant flesh.

Víctor Rodríguez-Pereira, in "*Sabrosa olor*: The Role of Olfaction and Smells in Berceo's *Milagros de Nuestra Señora*," then turns to Marian miracles collected by the medieval poet Gonzalo de Berceo in his *Milagros de Nuestra Señora*. The framed tales are preceded by an allegory that tells how the poet-pilgrim enters a garden with singing birds in trees, the sounds of a flowing river, and fragrant flowers. This sensory space freshens both the body and the mind, linking the sense of smell to an understanding of the meaning of Mary's holiness. The same idea is explored later, when a cleric devoted to the Virgin dies and a flower grows out of his mouth, filling the air with a delicious smell, so that sensory reception is again linked to sanctifying grace. However, in the miracle that immediately follows it another cleric sings the five Joys of the Virgin – a song that, according to the poet, will protect Christians from being led into sin by their five bodily senses. Rodríguez-Pereira places Berceo's writing in the context of medieval ways of understanding bodily senses, in particular smell, found in the works of theologians and hagiographic writers. His study demonstrates how Berceo draws on the danger of the olfactory as a pathway of deception and corruption, or as a means of revealing a higher truth that is conducive to salvation.

Subsequent sections of the volume investigate the role of the mind in processing sensory information, as early modern writers engaged with a growing range of smells and tastes. They developed modernizing approaches to understanding the tangible and intangible, and ways of taking in and thinking about a range of urban sound- and smell-scapes. Renaissance and early modern humanists and travellers shed new light on experiences of pungent, bustling ports and city centres, and the exotic musical performances of empire.

In this context Part II, "Cognition and the Senses," offers an exploration of the period from the standpoint of scientific debates on the role of the senses in cognition, drawing on academic and popular treatises along with literary texts. In "The Internal Senses in *Don Quixote* and the Anatomy of Memory" Julia Domínguez considers the influence of early modern medicine in the masterwork of Spain's best known author, Miguel de Cervantes. Her study examines numerous books on the subject from the fifteenth to the late sixteenth centuries with which Cervantes and his more well-read contemporaries would have been familiar. Not only do characters in the novel often suffer from pain, but a multitude of symptoms and ailments of different parts of the body are described, including neurological problems centred on the insanity of the main character, who frequently has difficulty correctly sensing and perceiving the world around him. This affliction is related to problems with what were called the interior senses or rational faculties of imagination, understanding, and memory, according to Renaissance neuropsychology. Specifically, Domínguez finds that the interior sense of memory, related to Quixote's reading of chivalric novels, infringes on and impedes his ability to perceive what is taken in. Turning to medical literature, with which Cervantes was apparently familiar, along with other contemporary, Aristotelian theories, the essay sheds light on how Don Quixote's interior sense of memory serves as a constant filter, bringing to mind what is remembered from books in a way that interferes with exterior sensation.

In "Taste, Cognition, and Redemption in *Guzmán de Alfarache*," Robert K. Fritz studies the particularly important role that the sense of taste, in light of historical and contemporary theories of cognition, plays on both narrative and rhetorical levels in Mateo Alemán's picaresque masterpiece (Part One, 1599; Part Two, 1604). This cognitive historicist essay relates the aspects of flavour perception to a divisive topic in the critical literature regarding Alemán's novel, namely, whether or not it primarily promotes a Post-Tridentine Catholic world view or is instead about the ultimate impossibility of redemption from the rogue's sinful origins. Applying principles of embodied cognition from George Lakoff and Mark Johnson (1999), alongside Patrick Hogan's notion of the downward projection of neurobiological structure (2003), Fritz argues that gustatory metaphors in *Guzmán de Alfarache* reflect the process of evaluative conditioning by which the brain flavour system learns flavour preferences and aversions. These metaphors contribute to the articulation of a Christian message of redemption by implying that innate hedonic reactions can be conditioned and reconditioned to favour either virtue or vice, suggesting that through the exercise of free will and the aid of divine grace, human sinfulness can be redeemed.

In this section's final essay, "The Aesthetics of Disgust in Miguel de Cervantes and María de Zayas," Steven Wagschal explores early modern notions of disgust in the work of royal physician Luis Lobera de Avila (1480–1551) and that of earlier-mentioned humanist Joan Lluis Vives (1492–1540) as well as current thinking on the emotion in philosophical aesthetics (Korsmeyer 2011) and cognitive studies (D. Kelly 2011). He compares techniques associated with the evocation of disgust in Cervantes's *Don Quixote*, *The Persiles*, and other works and in three novellas by María de Zayas. Wagschal analyses, from a cognitive historicist perspective, the association among certain sensory perceptions (often involving foul smells), the evocation of the emotion of disgust, and constructed social categories in the writing of these authors. He explains how these two literary authors employ a range of disgust elicitors, including bad breath and rotting flesh, but do so quite differently. Despite often employing similar literary techniques, Cervantes and Zayas typify two divergent approaches to the elicitation of aesthetic disgust in the reader.

Processes of early modern sensorial effects on human and social bodies lead to questions that are focused more on the relationship between individual experiences of hearing, touching, smelling, and tasting, as well as on understanding the inner life of the mind and the cultivation of inner desires in Renaissance and early modern culture. Such questions are addressed in Part III, "Perception," which explores the representation of direct sensory perception, with an emphasis on the connection between perceiving and emotional states.

In the first of these essays, "Sight, Sound, Scent, and Sense: Reading the *Cancionero de Palacio*," E. Michael Gerli studies imagery that accompanies a lyric poem in this early Renaissance manuscript. The verses of "Contrast d'amor" (Contrast of Love) metaphorically convey the tempestuousness or storminess of a love affair and include a polychrome, richly historiated capital L in the form of a unicorn. Gerli finds that, for an audience schooled in the lore of the unicorn, it is evident that there is an entirely different, olfactory dimension meant to be elicited when the verse is combined with this image of a mythical beast that can be tamed only by the scent of a virgin. As he shows, medieval schoolmen described this attraction as an excess of warm humours dilating the heart and the nasal passages of the unicorn. Perceiving the rich aroma that emanates from between the virgin's thighs, the animal is overcome with pleasure and lays its head upon her lap, fading into a blissful sleep. The illustration calls to mind the material emanations of the female body, whose fragrant sway cannot tame the violent winds of love that continue to beleaguer the speaking voice in the poem. The illustrations of the *Cancionero de Palacio* thus helped amplify the cognitive universe of its readers, opening up new understandings that transcended the written word and materiality of the text alone.

Subsequent essays in the section turn from this fascinating, but lesser-known, songbook to ways of understanding problems with perception in learned and popular medical literature that was more widely circulated in early modern Spain. In "Treating Sensory Ailments in Early Modern Domestic Literature," Carolyn A. Nadeau considers the question of what happens when one or more of the physical senses ceases to function as it should. If any of the senses was damaged, how would the loss be treated in order to restore harmony between the physiological and the psychological? This essay addresses these questions by considering the ongoing debate in the late fifteenth and early sixteenth centuries between those who followed traditional Galenism and those who considered more innovative Galenic practices. Nadeau finds that the latter approach, espoused by physicians serving in the courts of Charles V and Philip II, began to base their principles on observation and followed the new anatomy and clinical approaches to better understand concepts of health and sensory perception. The essay then turns from medical treatises to prescriptive domestic literature from late fifteenth- to early sixteenth-century Spain as it seeks to understand strategies for maintaining the physical faculties and for curing sensory deprivation brought on by injury or illness. These works approach the higher and lower senses in different ways: for sight and hearing, remedies are curative and treat the individual only after a problem has occurred; touch and taste are both curative and, more often than not, preventative. Nadeau also examines the ingredients used in these remedies in order to understand the connections between the material world and the human body and, in doing so, to contextualize academic and popular approaches to natural medicine and the physical senses from the period.

In the next essay, "Cervantes's Exemplary Sensorium, or the Skinny on *La española inglesa*," Charles Victor Ganelin identifies sensory perceptions and depletions as a central preoccupation in Cervantes's *Novelas ejemplares*. He points out how characters cannot be fully comprehended without consideration of the senses at play, as evidenced by descriptions of clothing, which are accorded far greater detail than the people wearing them. The richness of garments seduces the eye, but also compels touch, with texture almost crossing the threshold between text and reader. Similarly, sight cannot prove identity, but neither can sound; only touch against the skin can provide assurances. Throughout the novellas Ganelin locates qualifying statements that action will be carried out by all five senses, yet frequently only one of them is the deciding factor, working in conjunction with perceptiveness. This essay explores how the *Novelas ejemplares* demonstrate a *sensorium* reflective of the multivalent role that the senses played across the arts and, of course, in the wider conception of early modern representation. Cervantes's ingenious *sensorium* holds a new mirror up to nature and questions old ways of social control and culture formation. This essay shows how the *Novelas ejemplares* clamour for a pervasive need to understand the senses, the language used to evoke them, and the cultural manifestations that call them forth.

Cervantes, of course, lived during a time of imperial, transatlantic ambitions on the Iberian Peninsula – ambitions and expectations that had been conditioned by earlier legends of empire, as well as contact with the indigenous peoples of the Americas; exotic sensory experiences and performances; impressions of pungent, bustling ports, and new, distant, urban spaces. Contributions in Part IV, "Sensing Empire," investigate the phenomena of widening, even global sensory realms, as writers imaginatively perceived and evoked smells and tastes in new ways. Its essays examine the vibrant role that sensual descriptions play in imperial aspirations and colonial encounters, from a prescriptive medieval account musing on Alexander the Great's conquests to much later accounts of colonizers in which the sounds of indigenous and African identities seem to drown out the privileged visual descriptors of Europeans.

Emily Francomano's "The Senses of Empire and the Scents of Babylon in the *Libro de Alexandre*" shows how this thirteenth-century classic work explores the rich allegorical possibilities of Babylon as a multivalent biblical *figura* and creates a synaesthetic ekphrasis of the city as part of its poetic integument. Francomano examines the poet's continual appeals to the senses, finding that the description of Babylon is the most sensual and rhetorically synaesthetic episode of the *Alexandre*: the poet's audience is invited not just to *see* its majestic architecture, healthy and well-dressed inhabitants, and the abundant gems and worldly goods traded there, but also to listen to its birdsong and minstrels, to smell the plethora of spices ground in its mills, and to taste and feel the salubrious water streaming from its fountains. Moreover, this essay demonstrates how the synaesthetic ekphrasis of Babylon extends beyond the five corporeal senses to appeal to the inner, rational senses of *Alexandre*'s audience, while also inviting its audience to consider the relationships between sensory perception and allegorical sense in the poem's meditation upon the rise and fall of Alexander the Great.

In "Portuguese Scenes of the Senses, Medieval and Early Modern," Josiah Blackmore next examines a selection of testimonies of sensorial delight in Portuguese writings from the medieval through early modern periods. He begins with a contemplation on speech as one of the "senses of the mouth," to follow C.M. Woolgar's formulation in a well-known letter on the finding of Brazil by the Portuguese scribe Pero Vaz de Caminha (c. 1500). The essay looks at how coastal and maritime realms are privileged, idyllic scenes of sensorial experience and plenitude, and how a Portuguese imaginary related to water and nautical movement evolves from medieval lyric to early modern maritime imperial expansion, culminating in the work of Portuguese Renaissance poet Luís de Camões (c.1524–80). Blackmore's work turns up unexpected and profoundly revealing links between touch and the workings of the heart and mind, as well as between carnal union and an early modern, maritime gnosis of an expanding globe-space.

Henry Berlin's essay, "Eucharistic Thought and Imperial Longing in Portugal from Amadeus da Silva's *Apocalypsis Nova* (1502) to António Vieira's *História do Futuro* (1663–1667)," begins by examining a part of Amadeus da Silva's important *Apocalypsis Nova* (1502) that deals with the Eucharist. In this text he seeks to explain how the metaphysics underlying the Angel Gabriel's account of the Eucharist is deeply relevant to the millenarian perspective of the *Apocalypsis*. If the work as a whole is structured by the question of presence and absence, this part of the text analyses the ability or inability to perceive real divine presence in the Eucharist – questions raised, in part, by what is felt, smelled, tasted, and heard during the sacrament. Despite Christ's real corporeal presence, the accidents of the bread and wine are, Gabriel explains, theologically necessary conventional signs – mediated perceptions that, until Christ's final return and the end of the world, are viewed in the perspective of Portugal's imperial fortunes. Berlin's study then turns to António Vieira's unfinished, but influential *História do Futuro* (c. 1663–7), in which Vieira predicts the advent of a new, glorious era of Portuguese history. During this "Fifth Empire," Christ will return, exerting not just spiritual but temporal control over the entire globe through Portugal's kings. In this way the essay explains how ideas in these texts about the Portuguese empire's place in sacred time and history relate to theological notions of Christ's bodily being made sensorially present in the Eucharist and in the end of days.

The book then moves from the stakes of maritime exploration of the known world, to indigenous and colonial Portuguese cultural encounters in America. Lisa B. Voigt's "Festive Soundscapes in Colonial Potosí and Minas Gerais" demonstrates how musical performances in the context of public festivals were intended not only to produce sonic harmony but also to represent religious harmony, piety, and order. Specifically, Voigt focuses on the music, drumming, and other sounds represented in eighteenth-century accounts of ceremonial entries, which describe the entry of the archbishop into Potosí on his way to Lima and festivities surrounding the entry of the bishop into a new diocese created in the mining region of Minas Gerais. The essay highlights the representations of subaltern musical performance – Indians in Potosí, blacks in Mariana – as well as the instances of cacophony and sonic disharmony. Music (and festivals) may have been understood as an effective means of indoctrinating and acculturating those who were new to the Catholic faith, whether indigenous or African, but the instruments, tunes, and rhythms of musical performances in festivals echoed other traditions and identities and served other goals. Furthermore, these examples point to the importance of attending to the soundscapes of festivals, even when the accounts that describe them emphasize their visual dimensions.

Finally, Part V, "Sensing the Urban," turns to the Old World to explore representations of increasingly overloaded senses in the early modern court and city. In "Celestial Visions and Demonic Touch: García's Inventions in *La verdad sospechosa* Frederick A. de Armas examines the many falsehoods and fabrications in the play that are replete with images that evoke the senses. As the stories are heard, characters listening would be struck not just by the visual, but also by the tactile elements. Thus, hearing, sight, and touch are manipulated so as to make the lies seem tangible, while smell and taste also appear at times to buttress the other three. The wondrous materiality of García's imagined scenes evokes the saturation of all five senses in the urban spaces of seventeenth-century Spain. At court, newness was avidly sought and the senses became overloaded, risking an imbalance of the humours and illness caused by excessive input, which might in turn affect the senses. The connective link between inventions, the senses, the four humours, and the four elements, de Armas argues, allows the audience to understand García's excessive, mendacious and sensory fabrications. The element of fire, connected to García's choleric disposition, exacerbates his imagination and leads him to trick and deceive. As de Armas shows, it also leads him to imagine fiery things, from the stars in the heavens to the more demonic fires of gunpowder. His verbal magic seduces through hearing and creates wonderment; while it seeks to show the brilliance of the sky and of his mind, it also hides the anxieties of a cosmos that no longer conforms to ancient authorities and a self that wills to turn away from sight to the lower senses. As de Armas shows, through the magic of his voice he can instil a desire for the lowest of senses and, although he claims to desire a celestial being, García hides his cravings for forbidden touch.

In the final essay of the collection, Enrique García Santo-Tomás's "Motherhood Interrupted: Sensing Birth in Early Modern Spanish Literature" asks why childbirth became a pivotal tool for early modern Spanish writers, as he engages in a sustained dialogue between the history of medical practices and literature that evoked all of the senses. García Santo-Tomás examines the changing history of the use of female and male midwives and the reliance on wet nurses as symptomatic of the role of men in baroque society. He examines images of birthing in an urban milieu – as Iberian cities like Madrid and Seville experienced a demographic explosion throughout the sixteenth and seventeenth centuries – focusing in particular on works by Cervantes, Alonso Jerónimo de Salas Barbadillo, and Francisco Santos. The essay finds that mothers of all guises, in fact, abound in the cultural representations of baroque Spain, but when motherhood is reflected, sensory experiences and their stakes are always problematic and reveal tensions related to the masculinization of women's medicine. Santo-Tomás explores fictional accounts of sensing and perceiving scenes of parturition that reveal the fruitful potential of a type of image that, surprisingly, has received little attention. This meditation on sensory meanings attached to childbirth in early modern Iberia brings to a close the volume's broadly conceived collection of essays.

As the sections and chapter summaries attest, this collection approaches literary and cultural representations of the senses over the *longue durée* and through the expansive spaces of Iberian empires, real and imagined. Essays delve deeply into the smells and tastes of holiness and the sacred, disease and corruption, and premodern approaches to interpreting and allegorizing exotic and dangerous sensory experiences, when nothing less than salvation is at stake. The pages that follow provide insights into the significance of other senses in late medieval manuscript culture and into the role of sensory cognition in the creation of moral character during the early modern period. Also explored are failures and treatments of the nose and ears, the aesthetic, literary possibilities of disgust, and connections between the skin and tactility with religious, political, and gender identities in the creation of fiction. No less important in the chapters of this volume are wilful sensory deceptions in both Old and New World contexts, senses of communion and musicality as imperial conceptions of control and resistance, sensual experiences and representations of maritime exploration, and the birth and rebirth of baroque cultural productions. While they are divided into five sections, there is necessarily a significant overlap between and among the essays. Indeed, while the scope of this project might appear quixotically ambitious in temporal, spatial and thematic terms, we are confident that the results have broken new ground in the interdisciplinary study of the senses that extend beyond sight.

NOTES

1 Citations are made by the month and day (in that order) given for entries in Adams's diary and autobiography.

2 For instance, Mark Smith, *Sensing the Past: Seeing, Hearing, Smelling, Tasting, and Touching in History* (Berkeley: U of California P, 2007); Stephen G. Nichols, Andreas

Kabitz, and Alison Calhoun, eds, *Rethinking the Medieval Senses: Heritage / Fascinations / Frames* (Johns Hopkins UP, 2008); and Katharine A. Craik and Tanya Pollard, eds, *Shakespearean Sensations: Experiencing Literature in Early Modern England* (Cambridge UP, 2013), among others.

3 See especially the monographs and collections of Frederick de Armas, including *Cervantes, Raphael and the Classics* (Cambridge, New York: Cambridge UP, 1998), *Writing for the Eyes in the Spanish Golden Age* (Lewisburg, PA: Bucknell UP, 2004), *Ekphrasis in the Age of Cervantes* (Lewisburg, PA: Bucknell UP, 2005), and *Quixotic Frescoes*.

4 Dogs indeed have far superior olfactory perception than humans in what, according to recent scientific literature, is referred to as "orthonasal olfaction," which is what most lay people generally refer to as "smelling" or "sniffing." In this regard some dogs can detect odours in a small fraction of the substance concentration compared with humans – hence the use of dogs, for instance, to sniff out illicit substances such as drugs or explosives. However, humans are more discerning than dogs at a particular kind of smelling, which is known as "retronasal olfaction" and is a kind of olfaction that importantly forms part of the experience of taste or flavour (see G. Shepherd 19–27). There is still some scientific debate on the relative strengths of human orthonasal olfaction versus that of other animals. In "Mechanisms of Scent-tracking in Humans" Jess Porter et al. tested whether humans would be able to perform "scent-tracking" in an open field in the way that dogs and other macrosmatic animals can, and they found that humans are able to do so and that they improve with practice over time. The two species were tested on different substances (chocolate for humans, pheasants for dogs), and while the research found that humans can scent-track, the paper refers to dogs as having "greater scent-tracking ability."

5 For instance, in Thomas de Cantimpré's *Liber de naturis rerum*, the five senses are symbolized by a lynx (vision), a boar (hearing), a monkey (taste), a vulture (smell), and a spider (touch) (4,I,194; qtd in Nordenfalk 1).

6 This study affirms the "visual dominance hypothesis" for homo sapiens and its findings are "contrary to the relativist predictions of Aikhenvald and Storch (2013)" (San Roque et al. 49).

PART ONE

Sensing Religion

1 The Breath of Lazarus in the *Mocedades de Rodrigo*

RYAN D. GILES

The *Mocedades de Rodrigo*, concerning the youthful deeds of the Castilian hero later known as the Cid, is a mid-fourteenth-century poem that draws on epic traditions that are also present in earlier chronicles. It has been preserved in a single manuscript and has received increasing attention over the years from prominent scholars. Both Alan Deyermond and Samuel Armistead, for example, published important studies of the *Mocedades* that have shed light on its composition and purpose. These and other critics have been particularly interested in the existence of an earlier, oral *gesta* and also have considered how the *Mocedades* seems to promote the late medieval diocese of Palencia.[1] Although most Hispanomedievalists are well acquainted with the story told in the *Mocedades*, this prequel to the classic *Cantar de mío Cid* may be less familiar to other scholars. The narrative first recounts the genealogy of the hero, who descends from the first nobles of Castile. Because the version that has been preserved was adapted by a Palencian cleric, it adds an account of how heroic Castilians played a role in the founding and supporting this diocese. We are then told how, at an early age, Rodrigo kills his father's enemy. To re-establish peace the king orders him to marry the victim's daughter, Jimena. Rodrigo's initial refusal to fulfil this obligation sets the stage for a series of battles in which the young warrior defeats Christian and Moorish foes on the Peninsula and beyond the Pyrenees.[2]

One of the least understood episodes in the poem comes after Rodrigo completes his pilgrimage to Santiago, just before a victorious duel and followed by further military action.[3] Travelling in cold, rainy weather, the young warrior and his 300 knights encounter a leprous beggar, who asks for help crossing the Duero. Although his knights express their disgust, spitting and backing away from the leper ("todos escopían e ívanse d'él arredrando") (v. 638), Rodrigo takes the stranger by the hand, covers him with a green cape, and carries the sick man across the river Duero on a mule. The two then take refuge under a rocky outcrop near the riverbank and, after falling asleep next to the beggar, Rodrigo experiences a prophetic dream.[4] The ailing leper, his diseased state described as being a "malato" and "gapho," speaks in Rodrigo's ear, identifying himself as St Lazarus, sent by Christ to "blow" a "fever" into him (a "resollo" and "calentura") and in doing so assures the hero's victory in battle (vv. 644–5, 649). Apart from a possible association with the life of Martin of Tours or other, similar legends, Deyermond observes that, by the end of the thirteenth century the Cid was accredited with the founding of a Palencian church and leprosarium dedicated to Lazarus. This saint was viewed by medieval Christians as a healed leper and protector of those who suffered from this disease.[5] Armistead compares the leper's breath to the epic tradition of heroes' feeling the heat of battle fury, and both scholars consider further details found in the early fourteenth-century *Crónica de los reyes de Castilla,* which seems to have incorporated a traditional *gesta* concerning the Cid's youth.[6] Here, Rodrigo also is said to have shared food with the leprous beggar, and he asks the figure of Lazarus, who appears before him in white "vestiduras [...] '¿quién eres tú que tal claridat e tal olor traes?'" (clothing [...] "who are you that is so bright and has such a smell") (Montaner 155).[7]

My purpose in this essay is to consider how differing sensory perceptions and experiences of the disease, in particular what Rodrigo refers to as "tal olor," can shed further light on the meaning of the episode. Specifically, I will show how the repellent, feverish flesh and breath of the leper challenged medieval Christians to reconfigure their senses and thereby perceive the fragrance of their Saviour's redeeming Passion. My findings build on the work of scholars such as John K. Walsh and Geoffrey West, who have shown how hagiographic rhetoric influenced epic writing in medieval Spain. At the same time we will see how being divinely chosen to suffer from the contagious disease was associated with a tradition of monastic knights' taking up and dying for the Cross as they waged war against the enemies of Christendom. Not only was the premodern leper seen through and defined by a status of exclusion that Michel Foucault famously described as a manifestation of divine punishment and grace (5–7), the outcast's significance in the medieval imaginary was at the same time dependent on potentially blessed, corporal interactions with non-lepers that often revolved around perceptions of and reactions to his smell.

The evocation of "tal olor" in the *Mocedades* can be interpreted in at least two different ways. On the one hand it might allude to the saintly smell of resurrection in keeping with the Gospel story of Lazarus of Bethany, and on the other it could suggest the residual odour of the leper as the living dead. The fragrance of sanctity was often compared to honey, flowers, a sweet smell of herbs emanating from the tomb of virtuous Christians.[8] Of course, just as the senses enable the human being to perceive a sign of transcendence, they were also employed by the Devil to lead the sons of Adam into sin. Whereas all Rodrigo's men are repulsed by the wretched beggar, the hero's acts of charity seem to have enabled him to discern the sweet fragrance of holiness.

According to medieval preachers, the nose was just as likely to deceive sinners as the eyes. For instance, Jacques de Vitry tells the story of an attractive, perfumed youth who was perceived by angels to be giving off a spiritual stench as a result of his sins (Beriou and Touati 123–4). Yet the reek of a corpse left behind by a redeemed soul went unnoticed by the same celestial beings. During the Mass incense was used as an olfactory symbol of prayer ascending to heaven, giving a foretaste of the fragrance of the divine.[9] Christ's anointed body was accordingly described as emitting a perfume, or what Walter Mapp describes as "an odor of sweetness that drew the heart to it" (Rawcliffe 134). On the other hand, foul bodily smells, and specifically the reek of the leper's diseased flesh and breath – apparently provoking Rodrigo's knights to spit and back away – were linked with the sulphurous torments of Hell and the demonic misuse of the senses.[10] In some cases, the leper or leprosarium could even represent the collective guilt of humanity, an idea that is expressed in the popular and influential twelfth-century *Policratus*, where John of Salisbury speaks of a "general leprosy that affects us all" (46). Therefore, the revulsion of Rodrigo's 300 knights could speak to a more generalized culpability or propensity to sin. They prove unable to overcome their sensory repulsion, much less to recognize their own spiritual leprousness or associate themselves with the suffering of another.

In fact, the disease and associated bad smells were especially linked with hypocrisy.[11] Jesus exposed those who boastfully praised God as stinking hypocrites, bearing the stench of the tomb. This attitude can be seen in illustrations of the personified Church holding her nose (see Rawcliffe 123).[12] Comparable iconography can be found in depictions of Lazarus being summoned by Christ from the tomb while awaiting figures hold their noses as if they still expected him to emerge as a decomposed cadaver, in keeping with Martha's warning that her brother's body has been entombed long enough to smell (John 11.39). Late medieval manuscript illuminations include onlookers – sometimes identifiable as Jews, merchants, or Christian sinners – covering their noses as the cadaver somehow emerges from the tomb. In this case their gesture of disgust appears to suggest that they are tempted to disbelieve, and so they fail to overcome the misleading, instinctual reaction of the body's senses. Such onlookers are prevented from perceiving the spiritually purified smell of Lazarus risen from the dead. They rely solely on exterior senses, as opposed to the soul's sensory transcendence of death and decay, being revealed – paradoxically – through the corruptible matter of Lazarus's body, in accordance with Carolyn Walker Bynum's recent study *Christian Materiality*.

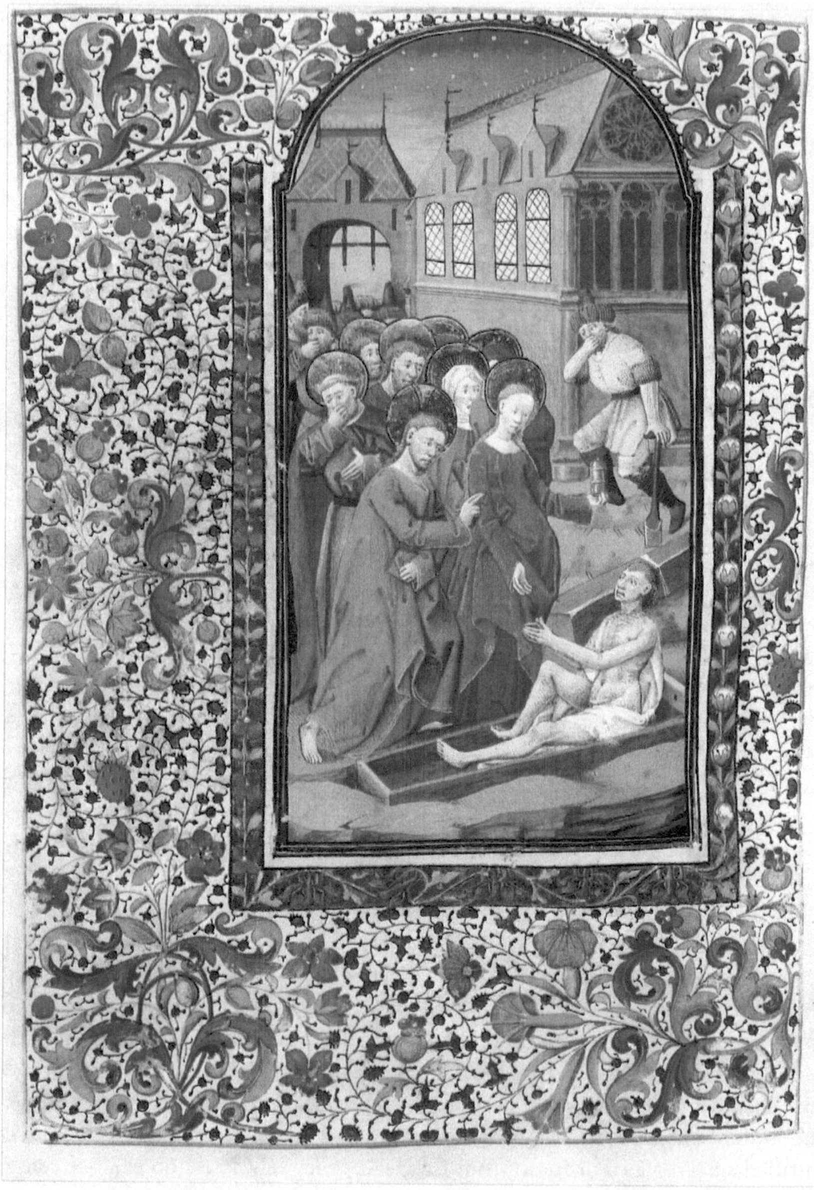

Figure 1.1 The Raising of Lazarus. Fifteenth-century French prayer book. Heures de Rolin-Lévis, à l'usage de Paris, fol. 222v, detail. Photo credit, Erich Lessing / Art Resource.

Undoubtedly, these connotations are implicated in the leper's self-identification in *Mocedades* as Lazarus, the messenger of Christ, as well as the reaction of Rodrigo's men. Medievals imagined Martha's brother to have died of leprosy before having his life miraculously restored and rising from the grave in a white shroud (sometimes resembling bandages) with his flesh purified, in accordance with the "vestiduras blancas" (white clothing) depicted in the *Crónica de Castilla*. This event seems to influence Rodrigo's story insofar as the beggar lies down with his host as a sufferer of leprosy, but arises from his sleep free of the disease.

The figure was conflated in hagiography with another character from the Gospels, Lazarus the beggar, who, like Job, is afflicted with a disease that rots his skin and leaves him covered with sores. In Christ's parable the beggar sits outside the gates of a rich man, but is denied charity (Luke 16.19–31). In the next life, he will be welcomed into heaven, whereas the avaricious are condemned to the depths of Hell. Thus, Rodrigo's pious display illustrates an awareness of the eternal danger inherent in refusing to care for the sick, especially lepers. Ironically, the infernal destination of uncharitable sinners was imagined as reeking of bodily decay – in other words, smelling like a medieval leprosarium (cf. note 10). This very real odour was caused by the patients' festering lesions (both oral and on their extremities); dirty bandages; the foul, stagnant water in which they bathed; in addition to the spoiled food that was often donated to them. Like Job, lepers who lived a righteous existence of atonement could attain a state of grace, since God had marked and elected them to undergo a redeeming trial. In recent years this phenomenon has been studied in depth by Carole Rawcliffe, who has brought together an abundance of relevant primary sources. For example, she discusses a popular sermon by Jacques de Vitry, called "Ad lepros et alios infirmos" (To Lepers and Others Who Are Sick), that recalls the ten lepers healed by Jesus, associating them with the Decalogue, as a Christianizing fulfilment of Mosaic law (57).[13] Following this logic, the single leper cured after the Sermon on the Mount (Mark 1.40) was thought to represent Adam, whose inherited Original Sin could be healed in the body of the Church. For this reason, sermons urged Christians to go to confession "as soon as they detected the first symptoms of spiritual leprosy," so they might return from the state of isolation that Hugh of St Victor called the "leprosy of vice" and "the contagion of sins, as by leprosy" (Rawcliffe 127). Christ's curing of lepers in the Gospels was also reimagined in new miracle stories. According to one, a pious leper entered the empty basilica of St Denis to pray, lamenting that "nobody will dare to speak to me, because I have polluted breath" (Rawcliffe 114). Reminiscent of the leper in the later *Mocedades*, his breath is revealed instead to be especially efficacious when Jesus recognizes the purity of his prayer and immediately heals him.

Once again, this episode can be compared to Job's reeking skin being miraculously healed by God. The long-suffering Old Testament patriarch, who suffered from leprosy, according to medieval lore, was widely known through Gregory the Great's *Moralia in Job*.[14] Medieval writers cultivated a topic of *Christus quasi leprosus*, partly on the basis of their interpretation of Job's misery as a prefiguration of the Passion. The idea of "Christ-as-leper" first emerged from St Jerome's translation of a verse in Isaiah thought to prophesize the coming of Christ: "Surely he hath borne our infirmities and carried our sorrows: and we have thought him as it were a leper [*quasi leprosum*]" (53.4). As Rawcliffe has pointed out, this tradition linked the lacerated skin of the leper to wounds inflicted on the Saviour's body (62).[15] We will see how it further illuminates the significance of Lazarus's being identified as a direct messenger of Jesus in the *Mocedades*.

Notable examples of the *quasi leprosus* topic include a sermon by Gregory the Great that urges believers to perceive Christ's presence in the sight and smell of the leper's body: "what can be more abject in the flesh of man than the flesh of the leper, harrowed by swollen sores and suffused with nauseous exhalations? But see that he has appeared in the aspect of a leper; and He who is revered above all has not scorned to appear despised beneath all" (Rawcliffe 63).[16] It has been shown how Rodrigo's men fail to understand the hero's charitable actions towards a stinking "gafo" in *Mocedades* story. Their misperception can be implicitly extended to the auditory realm. Lepers typically carried rattles, bells, or clappers to attract almsgivers, producing a sound that would have warned of their presence and at the same time caught the attention of Rodrigo and his knights when the "malato" begs for "piedad" (mercy) (vv. 636–7). The confinement of lepers during the Middle Ages was at times incomplete and sporadic and could be enforced with "laxity," to the extent that sufferers (some of whom were imposters) could be seen and heard begging outside populated areas (Magner 126).[17] In fact, medieval preachers may have employed lepers' noisemakers as an auditory reminder intended to move their listeners to compassion for these and other sick Christians, who had been divinely chosen to serve as symbols of Christ's suffering.[18] In this way sensory appeals could be used to negotiate and reinforce what Barbara Rosenwein has called "emotional communities," which included the "dead and the living" (62).

It is also significant that the appearance of the beggar in the *Mocedades* seems to represent the interests of a leper house that, as Deyermond has shown, was probably attached to the parish of "San Lázaro" in Palencia and, according to a fourteenth-century legend, had been founded by the Cid.[19] Being isolated in the leprosarium, similar to monks in a monastery, medieval lepers often combined the mortification that characterized their disease with a requirement of strict prayer regimes. They were seen as undergoing a sort of purgatory on earth, or sacrificing themselves through a living death. Visions of Purgatory from the period often indicate a reek that emanates from souls' being purified. The hideous condition and repugnant smell of lepers was thought to free them from the seductions of beauty and sensuous living, what Bernard of Clairvaux calls a "divine gift" (Rawcliffe 55). Thus, the odour in the *Mocedades* legend, comparable to Lazarus pungently emerging from the tomb, could be interpreted as a blessedly foul smell or a stench that is sweetened by redemption through Christ. Such an olfactory reinterpretation was certainly a challenge. Sources from the period frequently describe the stomach-turning smell of leprosaria and other places where lepers gathered. For example, a legend collected in the fourteenth-century *Fioretti di San Francesco* (Little Flowers of St Francis), features a leper who warns "I will that you wash me all over, for I stink so foully that I cannot abide myself," before being cured by the saint (Boeckl 84–5). These leprosaria were located outside the city walls, typically near water sources for bathing, not unlike the place where Rodrigo first encounters the "gafo" on banks of the Duero. In some cases, rotten meat and fish, as well as rancid lard were sent to the lepers as an act of charity, since their malodorous flesh was, in the words of Rawcliffe, "already riddled with the disease," making them supposedly "able to eat it with impunity" (79). Visitors sought to imitate the saints by carrying out acts of mercy and sometimes they experienced sensory miracles. They were challenged to approach olfactory perception in Pauline terms – in other words, to smell their surroundings by means of the spirit as opposed to merely the flesh.[20] I would suggest that "tal olor" together with the leper's "resollo" in the *Mocedades* and *Crónica* could evoke just this kind of reimagining discernment of a sanctified fragrance in the breath of the "gafo."

These meanings did not escape later writers who drew on medieval legends of the Cid's youth, building on accounts preserved in romances or ballads in addition to historiographic sources. In the early seventeenth-century play *Las Mocedades de Rodrigo* Guillén de Castro wrote a scene in which the hero's charity for the leper broadly alludes to the tradition of saints such as those I have been discussing. While his soldiers react with repulsion ("'asco tengo' [...] 'vomitar querría'") to the sickly "gafo," Rodrigo prayerfully commends the power and heavenly fragrance of Lazarus's breath: "¡Qué olor tan dulce y suave / dexó su divino aliento!" (163–4).[21]

Saints were said to have patiently overcome the repulsion caused by this stinking illness and thereby illustrated virtue and holiness, as in the lives of Elizabeth and the canonized bishop, Hugh of Lincoln, both of whom humbled themselves to wash the ulcerated feet of lepers. According to legend, the latter was even able to kiss leprous flesh, in the tradition of St Martin, since the "sweet perfume of Christ" made him "impervious to the vile odours that made others retch" (Rawcliffe 135).[22] An insistence on artificially disguising bad smells was, at the same time, on occasion described as a "sin of the nose," indicative of a refusal to attend to the sick and poor due to their stench. Such sinners instead chose to delight in the scents of perfumed flesh, ripe fruits, and other olfactory temptations of this world. The lepers themselves, or materials that had come into contact with them, such as wash water or bed linens, are described as smelling noxious to sinners but sweet to the saints, since holiness made their noses especially sensitive to inner truth. Hagiographers imagined them detecting a lingering fragrance of Christ, in spite of an exterior perception of lepers as overwhelmingly foul smelling.[23] It has already been noted how St Martin, patron saint of soldiers, exemplified "heroic compassion" for a beggar as well as a leper who inspired disgust in others (Rawcliffe 144). On St Louis's visits to leprosaria, the crusader personally brought food, like Rodrigo insisting on sharing food with the leper in the *Crónica* (Gaposchkin 44, 200). Some legends reflect the topic of *Christus quasi leprosus* and involve anagnorisis, in which a sufferer of the disease is revealed to be Jesus. In other words, the leper is recognized not just as pious or saintly, as in the case of the messenger Lazarus in *Mocedades*, but as the Son of God. Examples include Gregory the Great's life of the holy monk known as Martyrius, and the better-known case of Francis of Assisi, who resolved to become a mendicant after recognizing a leprous beggar as Christ (Gobry 40). This convention follows a form of anagnorisis first used in the Gospels, when disciples recognize a stranger (*peregrino*) as the resurrected Christ, after breaking bread with Him (Luke 24.13–35).

Importantly, medieval visitors to the leper hospitals were also challenged to overcome fears of contagion, as they spiritually recalibrated their senses to perceive Jesus dying for their sins in the bodies of the sick. From the standpoint of premodern medicine the leper's smell was believed to have potentially deleterious effects on the body's humours. By the mid-thirteenth century physicians influenced by Arab science proposed that a miasmic smell exhaled and otherwise emanating from the sick could enter the body as airborne particles and cause contagion.[24] Such pollution could be counteracted by fumigation, for instance, the burning of aromatic plants, a practice thought to offer medicinal and protective effects against different kinds of illness, including the plague.[25] The humoral imbalance or *dicrasia* of leprosy was primarily the result of a choleric "adustion," causing the body to overheat like a furnace with an abundance of poison that could not be sufficiently expelled through exhalation and other forms of elimination (Rawcliffe 72). Putrefaction would take place, as it were, from the inside out, due to an unexpelled excess of black choler spreading its burning malignancy. This theory was heavily influenced by the *Canon* of Avicenna, which was translated in Toledo during the twelfth century by Gerard of Cremona and cautioned doctors to avoid "air corrupted … because of proximity to lepers" (Rawcliffe 92). Once again, odours were crucial to the contagion of disease, since they could transmit pathological bodily qualities through the air: "whereas clean and bracing air invigorated the entire body, promoting a sense of happiness and equilibrium, noxious vapours […] had the opposite effect" (Rawcliffe 91). Although acceptance of a miasmic transmission of leprosy can be traced back to the mid-thirteenth century, Galen had already warned that the breath of ill patients was dangerous to physicians. Similarly, early Muslim physicians like the ninth-century Ibn Qutayba cautioned that "the leper gives off an odour so strong that it causes anyone who long remains in his presence or eats with him to fall ill" (Rawcliffe 92). Thus, inherent in the feverish heat of the breath of the "gafo" – the *calentura* of the *resollo* – is a contagious smell of disease and death. Yet this air will not sicken Rodrigo, but rather fortifies him, presumably as a result of his charitable acts and saintly recognition of the leper's true *olor* as that of the body's resurrection.

For medieval audiences the fever given to Rodrigo also could be expected to confer a kind of fierceness in battle, as Armistead suggests. Lazarus was not only the protector of lepers, but also the patron saint of a knightly and monastic order that sponsored hospitals in Jerusalem and Acre as well as leprosaria throughout western Europe.[26] It was founded by a first wave of crusaders who had contracted the disease in significant numbers and has been studied most thoroughly by David Marcombe. The seal of the order fittingly displays a priestly figure holding a cross – perhaps indicative of notions of Christ's wounded body on the cross as *quasi leprosus* – together with a leper holding a rattle, his face covered with lesions (Marcombe 5).

Knights of the order took up the cross by deploying their repulsive condition as a sort of pious weapon to fight against the Saracens, a militant imitation of Christ as "the most despised and rejected of men" (Marcombe 8).[27] Their hospitals in the Holy Land, not unlike those in Europe, not only were places of quarantined separation – due to the disgust lepers inspired, and growing fears of contagion – but also functioned somewhat like a monastery, to the extent that brothers wore tonsures and habits and committed themselves to a regimen of communal prayer, following the Augustinian rite. The first masters were inspired by the example of a saintly monk named Alberic, who had taken a vow of poverty and dedicated his life to lepers at the newly founded Jerusalem hospital. Dressed like John the Baptist, "clad in a goat-hair shirt and wearing his hair and beard in an outlandish style," Alberic was known to engage in public self-flagellation as a means of drumming up charity for the leprosarium (Marcombe 8–9). He purportedly fed himself on the leftovers of lepers, made their soiled beds, carried the most crippled among them on his back like St Christopher, and – similar to other holy workers – made a habit of kissing their flesh. In the *Mocedades* and *Crónica* we have seen how Rodrigo engages in comparable, though less extreme, acts of mercy by carrying the leper across the river and eating and lying down with him. According to Gerard of Nazareth's account, Alberic also washed their feet with water that he carried to the hospital. The buckets became "mixed with blood and discharge," but he overcame his initial reaction of "nausea" by immersing "his face and, horrible to say" drinking large quantites of the disgusting fluid (Marcombe 9).[28] This pious legend, written in the twelfth century, seems to have influenced a tale by Juan Manuel in which a leprous nobleman decides to go on pilgrimage to Jerusalem. His vassals become nauseous from washing his sores, but then prove their loyalty by drinking "daquella agua que estava llena de podre et de pustuellas que salían de las llagas" (from that putrid water that was full of pus coming from his lesions) (229–30). After first spitting in disgust like Rodrigo's men, they become remorseful and imbibe the polluted water. The legend of Alberic can also be compared to a scene in another fourteenth-century text, the *Vita* of Catherine of Siena, composed by the Dominican Raymundus de Vineis. Not unlike the loyal vassals in the *Conde Lucanór*, Catherine was said to have imbibed the pus from a nun's cancerous breast. Like the saintly monk whose story seems to have inspired Juan Manuel, she does this as a means of overcoming her worldly disgust having received a vision in which she is nourished from the wound in Christ's side. From the standpoint of audiences, as well as participants in this sort of medieval piety, their initial reaction of disgust could be made to yield a greater pleasure. As Carolyn Korsmeyer puts in in her transhistorical study of the aesthetics of aversion: "the conversion of the disgusting into the delicious. Certain encounters with what we might consider particularly profound eating transform an initially aversive experience into something significant and savorable" (72).

Scholars have pointed out that, like the count in Juan Manuel's story, aristocratic lepers in the Order of St Lazarus – many of them former Templars – continued to enjoy the privileges of their elevated class, in spite of their repugnant affliction.[29] Numerous sources speak of diseased warriors from the order continuing to fight and die in large numbers, in hopes of preserving Christian rule over the Holy Land during the twelfth and thirteenth centuries, in what has been called: "a last line of defence [...] the 'living dead' mobilised in a desperate attempt to ward off the inroads of the infidel [...] moulded by notions of chivalry and the special relationship between God and his chosen sufferers" (Marcombe 13).[30]

This context helps explain how the hot breath of the leper revealed to be Lazarus in the *Mocedades* becomes linked with Rodrigo's readiness for battle against his enemies, comprising Saracens as well as tyrannical Christians. While the leper's seemingly ambiguous odour is feared to be contagious by his knights, in accordance with contemporary medical theories, the young Cid follows the example of saints and crusaders who drew on the model of *Christus quasi leprosus* to wage spiritual as well as military battles. This story shows not only how the young Cid's characterization draws on hagiographic conventions, but more important, how his epic persona can be understood in the context of an emotional, sensory community of warrior saints and redeemed sinners. The long-standing topic of the leper, which has concerned me in this study, encouraged believers to follow Christ by conquering the stench of sin and death through the Passion and Resurrection of His anointed, sweetly fragrant flesh. Medieval Christians contemplated the meaning of leprosy in hopes of overcoming the pungency of sin and decomposition, by breathing in the sweet *olor* of transcendent renewal through the resurrection of the material body. Just as Paul and the Church Fathers urged believers to follow the spirit as opposed to what was understood as the dead letter of the law inscribed in the flesh, medieval Christians who sought to imitate the saints were expected to perceive life in what their carnal senses told them was the oppressive and seemingly inescapable smell of death.

NOTES

1 The manuscript is housed at the Bibliothèque Nationale in Paris (ms. Español 12). In recent years Leonardo Funes has completed a critical edition of the poem, and Matthew Bailey has edited a volume of essays as well as a bilingual edition. Citations and translations are from Bailey's edition.

2 Before the text abruptly ends the young hero makes an excursion north and defeats the French in battle, humiliating their king by refusing to pay tribute and even standing in opposition to the Holy Roman Emperor and the pope.

3 This duel with a count settles the question of whether Calahorra belongs to Aragon or Castile.

4 The topic of supernatural dreams and visions is, of course, characteristic of medieval epic as a whole and can be compared to the visit of the angel Gabriel in the *Cantar de mío Cid.*

5 Deyermond first links him to the monastery of San Pedro de Cardeña through the *Cantar* and later to the Diocese of Palencia in the *Mocedades*. He notes parallels with the life of St Martin, the patron of soldiers, who famously offered half of his cape to a beggar, and was also said to have healed a leper. Deyermond views the episode as a product of pseudo-hagiographic traditions attached to the young Cid. See also John K. Walsh's classic study of the cult of saints and other religious expressions in the Spanish epic.

6 Armistead discusses accounts of heroic fevers written in Old English, Gaelic, and Germanic, comparing these to the power of the hot breath of Lazarus in this episode – and later in the narrative, when Rodrigo asks for a wine sop to hasten the return of the "calentura" promised to empower him in combat. The critic compares this to a late medieval *romance*, known as "La fuga del rey Marsín," in which another character experiences what is described as psychosomatic "corajes" (furies), prior to going to battle against the Moors – a condition not unlike the battle fury that overcomes heroes in earlier traditions (72–3).

7 Alberto Montaner has studied different versions of the story and includes an appendix of primary texts. This retelling was later copied in the *Crónica general de España de 1344* (see Armistead 69). As Deyermond puts it, Rodrigo's devotion is "in marked contrast to his behaviour in most of the poem, but the contrast is even more marked if we recall the fear and horror with which leprosy was viewed in the Middle Ages" ("Epic" 113). On the other hand, as Armistead points out, "se miraba como un acto de piedad destacada y de lo más ejemplar" (was seen as a marked act of piety and especially exemplary) (72).

8 In hagiography this fragrance is often encountered when the incorrupt saint is being interred or exhumed. Examples of smelling holiness can be found in Berceo's *Milagros de Nuestra Señora*: the flowery scent coming from this Marian devotee's mouth (112c) recalls the poet's earlier vision of paradise in his famous introduction (3a). A later instance of a delicious, heavenly smell defying death occurs in Alfonso X's *Estoria de España*, when the Cid is visited by St Peter (634). Rebeca Sanmartín has studied later representations of the bodies of visionary Spanish women, even in death, exuding a pleasant fragrance (chap. 1).

9 In pilgrimage centres, including Santiago de Compostela, censers would be used to cover the odour of the many, often sickly, unwashed, and impoverished visitors, and represent the therapeutic holiness of the place and the sweet presence of Christ and the apostle entombed there. The meaning attached to incense hearkened back to the traditional offerings of the three kings, which according to the medieval play, *Auto de los reyes magos*, represented celestial kingship (Surtz 13–18).

10 Such corrupted air is vividly described in the early fourteenth-century infernal *Visión de Filiberto*: "connortosos olores [...] creo que non te huele ahora tan bien [...] acabando su vida en pecado mortal et en los viçios e plazeres del mundo [...] atápanse [...] como de cosa que fiede muy mal [...] él que ayer era bivo ya podreçe" (pleasurable smells [...] I believe now do not smell so good [...] finishing their life in mortal sin and in the vices and pleasures of the world [...] they cover themselves [...] as if from something that reeks very badly [...] he that was alive yesterday is already rotting) (Octavio de Toledo 52, 59–60). In keeping with other interpretations of bad smell, the *Visión* also links this stench with the mouth speaking fallen words as a result of Original Sin. My translation.

11 The sweet fragrance of hypocrisy and mortality are compared to the smell of a rotting apple in the *Libro de buen amor*: "El amor sienpre fabla mentiroso [...] lo que semeja non es [...] las mançanas [...] más ante pudren que otra, pero dan buen olor" (love always speaks mendaciously [...] it is not what it seems [...] applies rot sooner than other [fruit] [...] but are pleasantly fragrant) (sts 161–4). My translation.

12 Accordingly, leprous sores and lesions were likened by Isidore of Seville and Gregory the Great to "heresy that defiled the body of the Church" (Rawcliffe 111). The truly devoted were thought of as making offerings to God that emitted a pleasant scent, even if others found them to be foul smelling.

13 The sermon exegetically refers to the impure status of Old Testament lepers' being purified by the New Convenant.

14 On Job's status as a patron saint of lepers, see the study by Lawrence Besserman. In Spain, during the late fourteenth and early fifteenth centuries, Pero López de Ayala translated and reworked parts of the Gregorian gloss into Castilian.

15 In fact, when tending to lepers, the religious sometimes imagined themselves imitating the Virgin Mary caring for the crucified body of her Son (142).

16 An even better-known example can be found in Chaucer's *Canterbury Tales*, when the Parson cautions that treating deformed lepers with scorn constitutes an assault on Christ (308).

17 As Lois Magner points out, they could also be found in public places, including markets, sounding their noisemakers, exchanging money, after pointing to objects they wished to purchase (in order to avoid spreading contamination through their mouth) (126). An example of a phony leper using the expectation of charity to dupe a nobleman and his knights can be found in the thirteenth-century romance concerning an outlaw named Eustace the Monk (see Kelly, Knight, and Olgren 680).

18 The voices of lepers were typically ruined by the disease. Eventually, the course of the disease could not only render them mute, but destroy their capability for sensory perception by afflicting the eyes, nose, and ears, not to mention crippled hands denoted by the Spanish word "gafo" used in the *Mocedades*. The sound of the rattle the leper still managed to clutch must have signalled a kind of living, breathing *memento mori*.

19 Deyermond observes that the current location of the Gothic St Lazarus parish in Palencia would have been outside of the city during the later Middle Ages, not far from a branch of the *Camino de Santiago* – although no river is nearby ("Epic" 112).

20 For example, the arrival of Theobald of Champaign at a leprosarium was said to have transformed the scent in the air from a reek to a sweet smell (Woolgar 128).

21 An ecclesiastical contemporary of the dramatist, Alonso de Villegas, commented on the smell of Lazarus in his *Flos sanctorum*, linking Martha's initial anticipation of and sensitivity to the "mal olor" with those who are overly scrupulous and overreact to the perceived faults of others: "dan mil arcadas, hazen ascos y melindres" (they retch a thousand times, are revolted and peevish) (5).

22 Other men and women also aspired to holiness by kissing leprous flesh, for example, in the life of St Matilda told in the *Chronica majora* of Matthew Paris (Huneycutt 104–5).

23 The holy, though often depicted as particularly sensitive to smells, were seen as protected from the repelling effects of foul odour, as if their presence and closeness to Christ had filled the air with a smell of spices or incense, powerful enough to cover the polluted reek of those being nursed in the leprosarium.

24 This danger is discussed in the *Siete Partidas* (no. 4.2.7), with regard to marital relationships in which one partner has contracted leprosy and moves into a leprosarium, warning that close contact can lead to contagion. In the case of unrepentant lepers, their smell could potentially compromise the state of the soul – for as one medieval preacher warns, "leprosy makes the soul spiritually very foul" (Rawcliffe 46).

25 This strategy of warding off miasmic contamination was perhaps most famously employed by the pope in Avignon when the Black Plague struck in the mid-fourteenth century.

26 A leper hospital was established in the newly conquered city of Jerusalem, through a land grant given in 1142 (Marcombe 7).

27 The order included knights – often noblemen from the Templars – who were officially required to join the Order of St Lazarus by 1260 after they had contracted leprosy in the East. The most famous leper of the crusader period is the Christian king of Jerusalem, Baldwin IV. Importantly, the order also included healthy sponsors and attendants (see Marcombe 11; Rawcliffe 54). The Third and Fourth Lateran Councils restricted lepers from living in proximity to the healthy, and it is likely that sick and healthy brothers remained in separate quarters (Boeckl 48–9). The green colour of the order might even be conveyed in the *Mocedades* by the sharing of Rodrigo's "capa verde" (green cape) (v. 640).

28 The hospital in the Holy City was located on a road that led from the Mount of Olives to the River Jordan. Thus, the spectacle of monastic lepers and the seemingly grotesque charity of their devotees would have been witnessed by a large number of travellers, to include wealthy and even royal sponsors such as Almalric I, as well as regular almsgivers. The hospital was re-established outside the city walls of Acre, after Jerusalem was retaken by Muslim forces in 1187 (Marcombe 11).

29 "A knight suffering from leprosy remained a knight and his scars and spots did not bring him any closer to other lepers of common birth" (Marcombe 11).

30 The last remaining leprous warriors in Acre died in battle when the sultan of Cairo attacked the city in 1291. By this time the order had moved most of its operations into leper houses in France and elsewhere in western Europe (see the first chapter of Marcombe's study). It is even possible that members were involved in the early founding and endowment of what Deyermond conjectures to be a hospital of "San Lázaro" in Palencia, documented after the fall of Acre. The establishment of this leprosarium was soon after attributed to the Cid, as mentioned earlier.

2 *Sabrosa olor*: The Role of Olfaction and Smells in Berceo's *Milagros de Nuestra Señora*

VÍCTOR RODRÍGUEZ-PEREIRA

Gonzalo de Berceo (1196–1259) was a cleric from the area near the monastery of San Millán de la Cogolla, located within what is now the autonomous community of La Rioja (northern Spain), where he was probably born, and most certainly was raised. In addition to several clerical positions he held in the monastery of San Millán, Berceo was also a prolific writer whose vernacular works consisted of five lives of saints, three poems written in honour of Holy Mary, one poem about Mass, and another about signs that would be seen in the End Times. Although the range of his writing is substantial, Berceo's most popular work today is the *Milagros de Nuestra Señora* (*Miracles of Our Lady*) (c. 1246–52), a collection of miracles performed by the Virgin Mary, most of them taken from known Latin sources. As one would expect, the bibliography about the *Milagros* is broad in scope and extensive. Most studies have focused on the linguistic aspects of Berceo's poetry in addition to his literary or rhetorical sources, biographical information about the author, and the place of the *Milagros* in the development of Marian tradition throughout thirteenth-century Europe.

However, less attention has been given to Berceo's use of sensory images, or issues concerning the senses in medieval culture and how this context relates to the works of the Riojan poet. One critic who considered aspects of this was Joaquín Artiles, who listed and commented on references to sensory images in a large number of passages from all of Berceo's works. Though Artiles identifies references to the senses and images related to the five senses, he argued that vision is the most prominent of the senses within Berceo's poetry. Moreover, when listing colour images found throughout Berceo's poems, Artiles argued that Berceo's use of colour lies in a middle point between the almost entire absence of colours in the *Cantar de Mio Cid* (*Song of my Cid*) (c. 1195–1207), and the "cromatismo del *Libro de Alexandre*" (the chromatics of the *Book of Alexander*) (c. first half of the thirteenth century) (151).

Another literary device discussed by Artiles, related to visual images, is that of synaesthesia. The term has been used mainly to describe a neurological human phenomenon in which stimulations of a sensory organ lead to experiences through another sense. For instance, it manifests itself in some people through a vivid association between numbers and colours. However, literary intersections of sensory images could be the product of an author's perception and experience of the world, or an artistic resource intended to stress an idea or image so as to make it have a deeper impact on the works' audience. Examples can be found in Berceo's work, especially when he refers to the smells as "*sabrosa olor*" (flavourful smell), or "*dulce olor*" (sweet smell) (Artiles 157). In addition, Artiles lists instances in Berceo's work in which images pertaining to different senses overlap, grouping them in four clusters: taste-sound, taste-smell, taste-visual, and taste-touch images (159–60). Though Artiles's comprehensive work enumerates many of these images in the works of Berceo, he does not engage in a more thorough study of their deeper implications or connections between the poetry and the author's cultural context. In his work, examples of images pertaining to the other senses, such as smell, touch, and hearing, are not fully explored by the author.

In these pages I will study the role of olfactory imagery in Berceo's *Milagros* in relation to ways of understanding the senses among medieval thinkers and the use of sensory images in hagiographic narratives. In my view Berceo's use of olfactory images not only fulfils an aesthetic or artistic purpose, but also sheds light on the role of saints and Holy Mary as intercessors between God and humanity. Medieval thinkers like Thomas Aquinas pointed out that olfaction is a problematic sense, and he placed it in an intermediate point between vision and touch or taste. Ultimately, the sweet smell of saints and Mary that Berceo explores in his poetry points to the broader place of *mester de clerecía* (the cleric's craft) poetry in thirteenth-century culture.

Medieval attitudes towards sensory perception were anticipated, to a certain extent, by writers of late antiquity, who often made a connection between good smells and what is morally correct, and between foul smells and the opposite. This connection was often transferred to other areas of society, and often smells functioned as social markers, indicating an individual's social class. Foul smells frequently were linked with foot soldiers, peasants, and the homeless, while pleasant fragrances were associated with the wealthy (Classen, Howes, and Synnott 33). Moreover, smells were also important in areas that we would find surprising today, such as warfare. For example, incense was commonly used to indicate surrender in Roman times, a tradition that probably gave us the common idea of the "smell of victory" (Classen, Howes, and Synnott 39). And, of course, smells were an integral part of social gatherings and events, such as banquets rich in different fragrances, and perhaps were used to counter the foul smells of improvised bathrooms placed around the rooms in a tradition that dates as far back as Pliny's *Historia Naturalis* (*Natural History*) (Classen, Howes, and Synnott 14).[1]

Although some ancient approaches to smells persisted during the Middle Ages, Christianity during these centuries seemed to have a much more problematic relationship with olfaction. Christian conceptions of sin and evil, as they are linked to corporeality and the material, created anxieties about the body and everything that was remotely sensorial, an attitude that was particularly prevalent during the development of early medieval monasticism. Overpowering passions and desires entailed a kind of denial of the body, insofar as the senses could provide pathways to sin through it. Moreover, in certain cases like that of count Gerald of Aurillac, medieval asceticism entailed a constant cleansing of all bodily fluids, especially those provoked by "nocturnal illusions," in order to keep the body clean of all visual and olfactory traces of sin (Odo of Cluny 123).

Earlier Christians had even eschewed the use of incense for cultic purposes, since it had formed part of pagan temple rituals. Incense had also been used to pay tribute to deified emperors, a highly political custom that might have seemed outrageous to early Christians. Thus, during the first centuries of Christianity the practice of burning incense in religious ceremonies was forbidden. For Athenagoras and Justin Martyr, for example, the laws of the New Testament are specific: God requires only prayers, not physical offerings (Cuthbert and Atchley 81–2). Moreover, for other Church figures, such as Tertullian and Origen, using incense was a non-Christian practice that originated among the peoples of the Arabian Peninsula and should be rejected (Cuthbert and Atchley 83–4). Although the Magi were believed to have brought an offering of incense to the infant Christ, as a symbol of his divinity, the Gospels do not describe this gift being burned as part of their worship of the new Saviour. Nevertheless, Christianity eventually absorbed the practice of burning incense, and after the sixth century incense became widely popular in churches, allowing the potentially unpleasant smells of worshippers and pilgrims to be masked and offset.

Fragrances also had practical and even medical uses during medieval times, perhaps motivated by beliefs concerning the pernicious qualities of certain smells for the human body. The links between fragrances and smelling and sustaining the human body had precedents dating back to ancient writers such as Pliny, who located in India a race called the Astomoi who could live for long periods of time "only on the air they breath and the scent they inhale through their nostrils" (7.26). The idea that fragrances could feed the body helped shape the belief that aromatic smells were thought to protect against diseases, and the belief that foul smells could cause them. For this reason, during the plague burning certain aromatic trees and herbs such as juniper and rosemary was customarily recommended to protect against contagion. In addition, doctors recommended covering the nose with a pouch containing a mix of fragrant herbs or plants and, if nothing else, carrying an apple that one could smell while walking through infected areas (Ziegler 73). At the same time fragrant smells were used to cure more minor or common illnesses and conditions such as headaches, upset stomach, or gynecological cramping. Some medieval medical literature even recommended placing aromatized vapours around a woman's genitalia in order to make a displaced uterus move back to its appropriate location (Classen, Howes, and Synnott 126).

However, this was not the only approach to the senses, and specifically olfaction, during the Middle Ages. Alongside practical and medicinal uses of fragrances, Christian theology developed a literature of the senses that reflects on the role of the bodily senses in the context of human salvation. There were two approaches to the senses in medieval spirituality as it relates to Berceo and by extension to other clerical writers of the period. One of these is embedded in theological discourses on the body, whereas the other is rooted in popular beliefs of sanctity.

Thomas Aquinas (1225–74) exemplifies the first of these approaches through his explanation of the five senses as passive powers of the soul that need the body in order to abstract impressions of worldly phenomena. Yet some senses are more important or useful than others on account of their capacity for "spiritual immutation," that is, their capacity to acquire knowledge of things in the world while enduring the least amount of physical change on the sensing organ and the object of sensation (Campbell 169). Thus, for Aquinas the primary sense is sight, whereas hearing and smell are paired and classified as intermediary, and touch and taste are the least important. The reason for Aquinas's structure is that a sense is more useful in apprehending reality (and consequently conducive to knowledge of God) according to its proportion of spiritual and natural immutation. Natural immutation happens when a change is effected in either the sensing organ or the object sensed. Consequently, according to Aquinas's reasoning, sight is the most useful sense precisely because there is no transmutation in the eye, for example, upon seeing a colour (Aquinas I.78.3).[2]

Sight is followed by hearing and smell because the latter entail a natural change in the object sensed, but not in the sensing organ. That is, a natural process occurs in the object that emits the smell or sound, but no contact is necessary and therefore no natural change. Finally, Aquinas locates taste and touch at the bottom because of their pure materiality and need for contact, which leads to natural immutation in both the sensing object and the subject.[3] For Aquinas a physical sense is more effective the less it needs natural immutation to facilitate knowledge of reality. This happens best when no physical change in the object or the subject takes place, thus making sight privileged, in the same way that the human soul seeks God not through physical contact but through immaterial contemplation. However, Aquinas does not study olfaction as succinctly as he does the other senses, perhaps on account of its problematic theological role.

An example of the second type of Christian discourse of olfaction is exemplified by, among others, St Bonaventure in his account St Francis's life, contained in the *Legenda maior S. Francisci* (The Greater Legend of St Francis) (c. 1260–3). In the fifth chapter of this text there are four episodes narrating miracles performed by the saint. Each sense-related miracle is clearly linked to the four properties of the body once reborn after physical death. In this way touch is linked with *habitus* (habit), taste with *subtilitas* (subtlety), hearing with *agilitas* (quickness), and sight with *claritas* (brightness). Yet the sense of smell is left out of this ascendant structure of the senses. Although one would be tempted to think that this meant the sense of olfaction was not important to St Bonaventure, chapter fifteen gives the sense of smell a much more prominent role, as it features the events of 1230, when St Francis's body is exhumed and transported to another church. Much to everyone's astonishment, the body of the saint is said to emit a sweet fragrance that draws believers to seek Christ: "ut per odorem salvificum affectus traheretur fidelium ad currendum post Christum" (so that through the redemptory smell the faithful would be drawn to run towards Christ) (Astell 127). The sweet smell of the saint's corpse has the purpose of showing all believers God's powers, so that they would seek Him more. Thus, smell becomes an intermediary agent that links humanity to sanctity. Smell also has a prominent redemptory function in another work by Bonaventure, the *Itinerarium mentis Deum* (Journey of the mind to God) (c. 1259). Unlike Aquinas's seemingly troubled relationship with smell, for Bonaventure it is, in fact, an important sense because it helps the human faculty *discretio* (discernment) to distinguish between good and evil, echoing a similar comparison that had been around since pseudo-Denys, Hugh of St Victor (Astell 107). These examples show that Christianity had a more problematic relation with the "other senses," such as smell, than with sight and hearing. Perhaps because of its ineffability, the impossibility of apprehending (or difficulty of preserving) smells, olfaction seemed to be more troubling for a religion that avoided the body, considered a path to perdition, as much as Christians praised it for its intellectual capacities.

It is this concern for the usefulness, futility, and dangers of the senses with regard to the attainment or loss of salvation that characterizes Berceo's *Milagros*. In the first part of the work the famous allegorical introduction, Berceo (or a "literary" version of himself that functions similarly to an Everyman) goes on a pilgrimage until he finds a fragrant garden, following the medieval topic of the *locus amoenus* (delightful place):

Yo maestro Gonçalvo de Verceo nomnado
yendo en romería caesçí en un prado,
verde e bien sencido, de flores bien poblado –
logar cobdiçiaduero pora omne cansado. (st. 2)

I, Master Gonzalo de Berceo,
while on a pilgrimage happened to pause in a meadow
green and untouched, full of flowers –
a desirable place for a weary man.[4]

The garden overloads the reader with sensory images, most likely to convey the effects of this natural scenario in the human body to his listeners. A weary Berceo describes many fruits of different kinds that recall the sense of taste (st. 4), the delightful sounds of nature that the poet describes as "dulces e modulados" (sweet and modulated) (7), and a soft grass that recalls the sense of touch (11). However, two kinds of sensory images seem to be most important in this introduction and its relationship to the rest of the text: primarily olfactory images and, to a degree, gustatory images. The third stanza introduces the reader to the sense of smell through the description of flowers that emit a marvellous fragrance that "refrescavan en omne las carnes e las mientes" (they were refreshing to the spirit and to the body) (st. 3b). However, a fuller development of olfactory imagery comes in the fifth stanza:

La verdura del prado, la olor de las flores
las sombras de los árbores de temprados savores
refrescáronme todo e perdí los sudores:
podrié vevir el omne con aquellos olores.

The greenness of the meadow, the fragrance of the flowers,
the shade of the trees of soothing aromas
refreshed me completely and I ceased to perspire:
anyone could live with those fragrances.

Smell here not only fulfils an olfactory function, but has alleviating and perhaps even palliative properties. Fragrances can sustain the body the way food does, but this is so because in introductory stanzas of the *Milagros*, much as in the medieval allegorical tradition, nothing is merely what it seems to be. This is the reason for

Berceo's warning to his audience in stanza 16: "palavra es oscura, esponerla queremos: / tolgamos la corteza, / al meollo entremos" (what we have just said / is an obscure parable and we wish to explain it. / Let us remove the husk and get to the marrow). Nature was not only a place in the minds of most medieval writers, but also a cultural construct and a space to perceive (and eventually come to terms with) symbols of God that humanity was expected to explicate hermeneutically (Curtius 320). In stanza 19 Berceo exemplifies this when he states that this vibrant garden of delights symbolizes the Mother of Christ:

> En esta romería avemos un buen prado
> en qui trova repaire tot romeo cansado:
> la Virgin Gloriosa, madre del buen Criado
> del qual otro ninguno egual non fue trobado.
>
> On this pilgrimage we have a good meadow
> in which any weary pilgrim will find refuge:
> the Glorious Virgin, Mother of the Good Servant,
> the equal of Whom has never been found.

Following Berceo's explanation of the deeper meaning hidden behind the garden's motifs, nature (trees, flowers, rivers, and leaves) becomes a symbol of Mary's qualities. In stanza 31 Berceo explains that the fragrant flowers covering the fields, which are the source of the sweet smell of the garden, are identified here not only with the Mother of God herself, but more specifically with her names: "las flores son los nomnes que li da el dictado / a la Virgo María, madre del buen Crïado" (The flowers are the names the book gives / to the Virgin Mary, Mother of the Good Servant) (31c). In this way smells are connected to the Virgin ontologically through the names that all Christians use to identify her. If, as was the case for medieval intellectuals, one can achieve knowledge of a thing and capture the essence of its meaning through its name (an approach exemplified by Isidore's *Etymologies*, among many other encyclopedic works), one could get to know Mary through the sweet smells associated with her name.

This connection between Mary and the bodily senses is reinforced in the fourth miracle, "El galardón de la Virgen" (The Virgin's Reward). The miracle tells the story of a man whose intense devotion to the Mother of Christ prompted him to compose a song in her praise. Eventually, the cleric falls victim to an unmentioned disease (st. 123a), which ultimately causes his death (st. 128cd). The Virgin comes to take his soul to heaven, an act that is witnessed by other clerics around him (st. 131). In addition to the importance of this miracle to popular Christian traditions as they pertain to the devotion of Mary, it exemplifies medieval views of bodily senses as a conduit for sin and perdition as well as virtue and redemption. From the very beginning of the poem the listener is presented with the senses indirectly:

Apriso cinco motes, motes de alegría
que fablan de los gozos de la Virgo María;
diziégelos el clérigo delante cada día,
avié ella con ellos muy grand placentería. (st. 118)

He learned five phrases, all phrases of joy
that speak of the Joys of the Virgin Mary;
the cleric recited these before her each day
and She was very well pleased with them.

The cleric sings daily five verses on the Joys of Mary that are said to be deeply pleasing to her. Medieval Christianity originally posited seven Joys, although other writers eventually expanded the number to fifteen. The five Joys mentioned in Berceo's poem are the Annunciation ("que el angel credist") (who believed the Angel); her virginity ("que virgo conçebist") (who as a virgin conceived); the Nativity of Christ ("que a Christo parist") (who bore the Christ Child); and the passing from the old Law to a new one ("la ley vieja çerresti e la nueva abrist") (the old law You closed and the new one You opened) (st. 119). In this way the number of Joys is reduced to five, in keeping with the number of verses that the cleric composed for Mary, which in a later stanza are connected to the five bodily senses:

Por estos cinco gozos devemos ál catar:
cinco sesos del cuerpo que nos facen peccar,
l' ver, el oír,el oler, el gostar,
el prender de las manos que dizimos tastar. (st. 121)

In these five Joys we must understand more:
five bodily senses that make us sin:
sight, hearing, smell, taste,
and that of the hands which we call touch.

The Joys of the Virgin primarily symbolize the grace bestowed on Mary by God. However, in an expression of pious devotion the cleric draws a parallel between the five Joys and the bodily senses. Admittedly, in Christianity's view the body leads to sin – including the Original Sin of Adam and Eve, which can be redeemed only through the incarnation of Christ in the womb of the Virgin Mary. But although this miracle stresses the inevitability of sin through the senses, it also proposes another use of the senses, not as pathways to sin, but rather as the spiritual faculties that can be reliable in the avoidance of sinful acts, enabling Christians to escape perdition:

Si estos cinco gozos que dichos vos avemos
a la Madre gloriosa bien gelos ofrecemos,
del yerro que por estos cinco sesos facemos
por el sancto ruego grand perdón ganaremos. (st. 122)

If these five Joys that we have named
we offer freely to the Glorious Mother,
for the error we commit due to these five senses
we will earn pardon through Her holy intercession.

Using the senses to sing in praise of Mary, the cleric's song about the five Joys acquires healing qualities that restore the soul from sins caused by the senses, thus linking the operation of the senses with salvation through the mediation of the Virgin. In so doing, the miracle about the Virgin's reward reinforces Her image as both holy and human.

Although this double image of Mary goes back as far as the fifth century, a particular proliferation of tales concerning her connective redemptory position between Humanity and God took place during the thirteenth century. Perhaps in an effort to build a compassionate, human figure that could have the effect of circumventing the increasing bureaucracy of the Church's soul-saving business, the miraculous Virgin progressively took a motherly, thus human, aspect in pictorial arts.[5] Moreover, in popular music She was being compared to flowers and springtime smells, as well as other sense-related images. Of course, flowers were very strong symbols of life, renewal, beauty, and resurrection in the High Middle Ages. In fact, in lay and religious discourses comparing a woman to a flower meant elevating her as a daughter or imitator of the Blessed Mother. Thus, composers further humanized the Virgin by describing her as fragrant and flower-like, making her more accessible and immediate (Rothenberger 320).

Incidentally, flowers and sweet fragrances also point to Christian anxieties about death and the punishment of bodily corruption that humanity continues to endure as a result of the Fall in the Garden of Eden. Perhaps in response, Christianity adopted the custom of embalming bodies with sweet fragrances of spices and flowers in order to give the deceased some solace – anticipating not only salvation of the soul, but also the resurrection and heavenly restoration of the body. Marian tales describing her as smelling of ambrosia, flowers such as lilies and roses, and spices such as myrrh, are most fruitfully read in the context of Christian notions of spiritual and material transcendence over the corruptibility of the human body. Allocating such holy fragrances to Mary, which in the Old Testament had been exegetically attributed to Christ (Gen. 27:27, "the smell of my son is the smell of a field which the Lord has blessed"), endows Mary with attributes that transcend corruptibility, but still anchors her humanity (Warner 99).[6]

The anxiety over bodily decay and the smell that covers it as a sign of a martyr's grace bestowed by God provides a clarifying context to the third miracle in Berceo's collection, "El clérigo y la flor" (The cleric and the flower). It tells the story of a cleric who led a dubious life, "ennos vicios seglares feramient embevido" (and deeply absorbed in worldly vices) (101). However, like most of the protagonists in Berceo's collection, the cleric was also respectful and devoted to Mary. Consequently, at the moment of his death the cleric is buried outside town, on account of his sins. In response Mary intercedes for the cleric, appearing in another cleric's dream, ordering him to bury her devotee in the same place as all other believers. Much to everyone's surprise, when the body is exhumed,

> Issiéli por la boca una fermosa flor
> de muy gran fermosura, de muy fresca color;
> inchi'é toda la plaza de sabrosa olor
> que non senti´én del cuerpo un punto de pudor. (112)

> There issued from his mouth a lovely flower –
> of very great beauty and very fresh color.
> it filled the entire place with a wonderful fragrance;
> they did not smell any foul odor from the body.

The body of the saint, which at that point should have decomposed, emits instead a sweet smell that covers the entire town. Miraculously, the smell comes from a flower in the corpse's mouth. In addition, the following stanza comments on how well preserved the saint's tongue was, so much so that it looked like the inside of an apple (113ab). As previously mentioned, Christianity's use of fragrances as symbols of the freely given love of God for His creation are related to fears about the human body's postmortem decay. In addition, it has been mentioned that the sweet smell of dead and living saints was a common convention in hagiographic literature. In keeping with Berceo's retelling of the cleric and the flower, the presence of a fragrant smell upon the discovery of a martyr's corpse or its exhumation in order to relocate the body or any relics available can be found in several earlier lives of saints. Not surprisingly, theologians, monks, clerics, and other Church figures often used these olfactory events in order to promote the cult of saints.

Gregory of Tours, for example, narrates a similar event that took place around 590 CE in which a basilica was built for a martyr called Mallosus, whose relics were thought to be lost. However, the martyr appeared to the deacon of Metz in a dream, announcing that the martyr's body was buried under the church (Roch and Uytfanghe 267). When the corpse was found, a sweet fragrance spread everywhere. It is this fragrant smell that moved others to believe in Christ: "et ait: 'Credo in Christo, quod ostendit mihi martyrem suum'" (and he said: "I believe in Christ, because he has shown me his martyr") (Roch and Uytfanghe 268). Moreover, similar Latin stories were penned on the Iberian Peninsula, most of them composed around the ninth and tenth centuries. The *Vitas patrum emeretensium* (Lives of the Fathers of Merida) (c. 600–800 CE), authored by the mostly unknown Paul, the deacon of Mérida, narrates the story of a monk who repents of a life of gluttony and excesses before dying. A few years later, when the Guadiana River flooded the city, the monastery was destroyed almost completely and the tomb of the monk opened. Much to everyone's surprise, the tomb emitted a sweet smell of fruits ("nectareus odor erupit"), showing the extremely well-preserved body of the saint: "Ipse vero integer et incorruptus reppertus est" (Truly, the body was discovered, whole and preserved) (Roch and Uytfanghe 265).

The appearance of sweet smells upon discovering a saint's corpse can also be connected to common early Christian analogies between prayers and incense. These analogies feed from the dispersive character of smells and apply it to prayers, which are taken to ascend to the heavens like incense. The monk and theologian Beatus of Liebana (730–800 CE), for example, wrote of Christ as the incense burner through which a Christian's prayers ascend to God (Guiance 136). In this view the connection between saints, Mary as *mediatrix*, and fragrances takes on a much stronger meaning for the context on which Berceo composed the *Milagros*. As discussed earlier, olfaction was described by Aquinas as an intermediary – as opposed to a primary – sense, due to its susceptibility to natural changes. On the other hand, St Bonaventure metaphorically described olfaction as an especially appropriate tool to discern good and evil. These trends could have informed the kind of Latin source material Berceo used to compose his collection of miracles. For example, an anonymous twelfth-century bestiary (vastly influenced by the *Physiologus*) explains that the panther falls into a deep slumber after eating, which usually lasts for three days. On the third day, upon waking up, the panther emits a "very sweet smell from its mouth, like the smell of all-spice" that makes all beasts gather around it (White 14). The panther's sweet breath is then compared to the voice of Christ, which attracts all peoples to Him, regardless their beliefs. During the centuries when Christianity was spreading rapidly throughout Europe, the dispersive, corruptibly human, physical character of smell took a central role in popular Christian discourses of conversion and Christian salvation.

It is possible that medieval authors did not ignore these notions regarding olfaction, both theological and popular, when composing their works. Berceo, like other *mester de clerecía* poets, were fully aware of their intermediary cultural and intellectual role between the lay world of Castilian speakers and the Latin, clerical setting of the monastery. Most of the works produced by the *mester* poets are translations and reworkings of hagiographic, moralizing, and didactic literature available mostly in less accessible languages such as Latin. The composer of the *Libro de miseria de omne*, for example, expresses this concern directly in the introduction to the poem. In the first verses the poet explains that the work in which it is based, Innocent III's *De miseria humanae conditionis* (On the Misery of the Human Condition) has been overlooked and forgotten because it was composed in Latin and thus was not accessible to a wider audience (3b–d). A similar self-awareness can be found in the introductory verses of works such as *Libro de Alexandre* and *Libro de Apolonio* (*The book of Apollonius*). The composers of these poems expressed either directly or indirectly that their works aim to both translate and reinterpret previous works that in their view should be heard, memorized, and put into practice.

Several modern critics have argued that the cultural role of the *mester de clerecía* poets was that of intermediaries between the lay world of church attendees and the spiritual, intellectual values in which they wrote their works. In fact, Julian Weiss recently argued that Berceo's omission of Chartres as the location where "El clérigo y la flor" displaces the tale from its ecclesiastical centre, thus challenging the Church's stance on serving as the only intermediary in the confessional process (36). Consequently, it is not surprising that a poet like Berceo made hagiography the aim of his corpus and, in the case of the *Milagros*, the Virgin's mediation in favour of the less learned members of his society. Moreover, it seems only logical, considering the intermediary role between cognition and the reality of the senses, that smell, specifically, takes prominence in Berceo's text – a text that itself stands on the threshold between the clergy and the laity. Like the senses, the Virgin serves as a *mediatrix* (intercessor) between believers and the Divine, similar to Berceo's performance within a poetic genre that serves as a *mediatrix* between intellectual and popular cultures. As we have seen, at the beginning of the poem the audience finds Berceo in the garden, imbued with the smells of the fragrant flowers, which are interpreted by the poet as a symbol of Mary's names. This sets the scene for his later olfactory mediations, in which the poet translates into a more accessible discourse the perfume of Marian *flores* (flowers), or miracles, for a wider audience to both learn and enjoy. The *Milagros* functions like a thurible whose incense sweetens and converts the corporal smell of sin brought into the church by the pilgrims and penitents into the sweet smell of redemption.

NOTES

1 See Pliny, *Historia Naturalia* Bk XIII. Excessive fragrances would not have been well received in these times, perhaps due to the association of certain fragrances such as cinnamon, myrrh, and frankincense with their origins in the East (Classen, Howes, and Synnott 14).

2 "Est autem duplex immutatio, una naturalis, et alia spiritualis. Naturalis quidem, secundum quod forma immutantis recipitur in immutato secundum esse naturale, sicut calor in calefacto. Spiritualis autem, secundum quod forma immutantis recipitur in immutato secundum esse spirituale; ut forma coloris in pupilla, quae non fit per hoc colorata." (Now, immutation is of two kinds, one natural, the other spiritual. Natural immutation takes place by the form of the immuter being received according to its natural existence, into the thing immuted, as heat is received into the thing heated. Whereas spiritual immutation takes place by the form of the immuter being received, according to a spiritual mode of existence, into the thing immuted, as the form of color is received into the pupil which does not thereby become colored.) Translations from the *Summa* are by the Fathers of the English Dominican Province (719).

3 "Visus autem, quia est absque immutatione naturali et organi et obiecti, est maxime spiritualis, et perfectior inter omnes sensus, et communior. Et post hoc auditus, et deinde olfactus, qui habent immutationem naturalem ex parte obiecti. Motus tamen localis est perfectior et naturaliter prior quam motus alterationis, ut probatur in VIII Physic. Tactus autem et gustus sunt maxime materiales, de quorum distinctione post dicetur. Et inde est quod alii tres sensus non fiunt per medium coniunctum, ne aliqua naturalis transmutatio pertingat ad organum, ut accidit in his duobus sensibus" (Now, the sight, which is without natural immutation either in its organ or in its object, is the most spiritual, the most perfect, and the most universal of all the senses. After this comes the hearing and then the smell, which require a natural immutation on the part of the object; while local motion is more perfect than, and naturally prior to, the motion of alteration, as the Philosopher proves [Phys. viii, 7]. Touch and taste are the most material of all: of the distinction of which we shall speak later on [ad 3,4]. Hence it is that the three other senses are not exercised through a medium united to them, to obviate any natural immutation in their organ; as happens as regards these two senses) (Ia.78,3; Fathers of the English Dominican Province [719])

4 All English translations from the *Milagros* are taken from Berceo, *Miracles of Our Lady.*

5 It is important to remember that the period in which Berceo composes his *Milagros* was characterized by efforts to formalize, centralize, and unify the Church as an institution (Flory 2). Problems caused by uncontrolled, unregulated priests engaged in simony and concubinage had to be addressed directly Gregory VII (r. 1073–85) increased centralization and sought to enforce chastity for all priests and prohibit

simony. Pope Urban II (r. 1088–99) continued to develop these reforms and to address problems with the organization of the Church and its priesthood, while promoting orthodox doctrines concerning the meaning of the Virgin birth of Christ, as it relates to His Passion and Resurrection.

6 See Warner for more examples of Mary as a flower and the association of fragrances to Her, especially chapters 6 and 8.

PART TWO

Cognition and the Senses

3 The Internal Senses in *Don Quixote* and the Anatomy of Memory

JULIA DOMÍNGUEZ

To speak of external senses in the time of Cervantes invites us also to explore theories of the inner senses and, in particular, the prevailing understanding between the fourth century and the seventeenth century of how human cognition worked. During Cervantes's time, it was held that information coming from the outside world through sensory perception was interiorly processed in the brain. Although this volume focuses on the non-visual external senses, in Cervantes's time such an approach inevitably implies a strong connection to the inner senses. And, as I show below, when examining the textual references to these processes, it becomes clear that what Don Quixote's senses capture are subdued by the function of the internal ones. As is well known, Miguel de Cervantes's seminal novel, *Don Quixote,* is a work that features a main character whose mental illness leads him to perceive reality in such a way that he experiences life differently than those around him do. More specifically, Alonso Quijano goes mad reading chivalric works, decides to don old armour, take on a squire, and seek adventures so as to make right the wrongs and injustices of the world. The most significant problem for the knight, however, is how he internalizes his readings of books of chivalry, which colours his awareness of reality. His perception is most altered in moments of great alienation, as happens frequently in the novel. Yet, as I show below, these temporary alterations in his process of perception are caused by disruptions in what was commonly called the inner senses, rational human powers or faculties known at the time as imagination, intellect, and memory. The existence and function of these inner senses conform to a well-known neuropsychological model in the Renaissance, inherited from the classical tradition, which described the interaction between the inner and external senses and how they were affected by the act of perception. This process of cognition, based on the teachings of Galen and Aristotle, was thought to be located in the ventricles of the brain where input from the outside world captured by the external senses was combined. In fact, as Josep Lluís Barona Vilar states, there were different points of view in the mid-sixteenth century regarding the functioning of the sensorial organs. Furthermore, no consensus existed as to whether or not sensations were verified in the sensorial organs or directly in the brain. According to the famed physician Francisco Valles: "one must now consider if what we have said is true: whether vision takes place in the eyes, smell in the nose, hearing in the ears, or if all of these sensations occur in the brain which transfers colours through the eyes, sounds through the ears, smells through the nose, tastes through the tongue, and touch throughout the skin as is the opinion of some philosophers and, among physicians, Juan Manardo, a learned man" (qtd in Barona Vilar 214–15).[1] In the pages that follow, first I describe the inner senses within the framework of the neuropsychological understanding of the time. Next I analyse the relationship of memory to the sensory and cognitive process in *Don Quixote*. In the novel the writer addresses memory as one of the inner senses from both the medical and the philosophical traditions by emphasizing the value of memory as a mental capacity and leaving aside the rhetorical tradition, where memory played a very important role as well.[2] Finally, I will analyse the close relationship between imagination and memory as a key to understanding the protagonist's behaviour.[3]

The Inner Senses

Since ancient times, the major thinker on the inner senses (imagination, intellect, and memory) was Aristotle. In and through various writings, the philosopher took up the question of what comprised the inner senses, their meaning and significance, how they functioned, and what their value was for human behaviour. He also studied their close relation to the external senses in the processes of perception and cognition. There is no specific term for what Aristotle considered the inner senses in the third book of *De anima* or in *De memoria et reminiscentia*, nor does he differentiate them from the five external senses (sight, smell, taste, hearing, and touch) mentioned in his second book of *De anima*. Subsequent philosophical texts from the Latin, Arabic, and Hebrew used the term "interior senses," highlighting their physical location within the brain.[4] Throughout the centuries the number of inner senses or faculties of the soul has varied considerably – usually between three and seven – and they were based on the interpretation of the aforementioned Aristotelian texts as well as through later analyses of their functions.[5] By the time Cervantes writes *Don Quixote* (Part One in 1605 and Part Two in 1615) the number of inner senses is generally reduced to three: imagination, memory, and intellect, as postulated by many erudite scholars on the subject, such as Juan Huarte de San Juan (see 1988 ed.).

Based on the Aristotelian tradition, the primary function of the three was to process the images captured by sensory perception, which took place in the brain's ventricles.

According to the influential Greek physician, Galen of Pergamum, the brain was divided into cerebral chambers or ventricles, where these faculties or inner senses were developed in close relation to the five external senses. One follower of Galenic tradition, Gregor Reisch, explained the theory of the ventricles in detail in his *Margarita Philosophica* (1503). Although only one of the many examples of how the structure of the brain was conceived, it was the prevailing method for understanding the brain's physiology through the eighteenth century.

Since Galen and the school of medicine from Alexandria – formed by influential figures such as Hippocrates, Herophilus, and Erasistratus – the inner faculties in the ventricles were believed to be located in the anterior, middle, and posterior areas of the brain. In each of these ventricles a series of processes occurred that hierarchically and systematically structured perception and cognition. This complex process was carried out in part by the bodily fluids or "spirits," which were understood to be the physiological base of the ventricular theory. Stated simply, the bodily fluids obtained from the heating process carried out in the liver passed through a refining process in the heart before being transformed into animal fluids in the brain. These fluids filled the sensory and motor nerves and facilitated the connection of sense organs and the ventricles of the brain, bringing the exterior and interior senses together. Perhaps this is why Don Quixote's niece and maid gave Don Quixote "cosas confortativas y apropiadas para el corazón y el celebro" (the appropriate comfort food for the heart and the brain) (II.1:625).

According to Galenic theories, the *sensus communis* or common sense area was located in the first ventricle of the brain, where sensory perceptions converged in the imagination (*imaginativa*). Kemp and Fletcher explain the main function of the common sense as follows: "The common sense discriminated modalities of perception from each other, such as whiteness from sweetness [...]. It also compared and summed information received (often known in the terminology of the day as *species*) from the different sense modalities" (563). Once in the *imaginativa* perceptions of the external senses were received and mental images (*phantasmata* as Aristotle called them) were created in correspondence with the information coming from the exterior environment. The imagination was therefore the intermediary faculty between sensory impressions and the intellect. From the first ventricle impulses passed to the middle ventricles, where the intellectual faculty was located (also called *cogitatio* and *estimatio*). In this second ventricle concepts containing information from the outside were elaborated, or, put another way, sensory data images collected in the *imaginativa* were processed. Finally, in the posterior ventricle, the cavity where memory was located, the images were stored.

According to the neuropsychological model of the time, therefore, the five acknowledged exterior senses transmitted signals to the inner senses. In his treatises *De Anima* and *De memoria et reminiscentia* Aristotle placed great importance on how mental images are associated with the external senses and later held in memory. An image – previously formed in the *imaginativa* during sense perception – is thus an interior design of absent objects recorded forcefully in memory. In his *Examen de ingenios para las ciencias* (Examination of Men's Wits) (1575), Juan Huarte de San Juan summarizes the process:

> Porque así como el escribano escribe en el papel las cosas que quiere que no se olviden y después de escritas las toma a leer, de la misma manera se ha de entender que la imaginación escribe en la memoria las figuras de las cosas que conocieron los cinco sentidos y el entendimiento y otras que ella misma fabrica. Y cuando quiere acordarse de ellas, dice Aristóteles que las torna a mirar y contemplar.

> Just as the scribe writes on paper the things he does not want to forget, and he reads them after they are written, in the same way imagination writes on memory the figures of the things the five senses and the intellect learned and others that it creates itself. And when it wants to remember them, says Aristotle, it returns to look at them and contemplate them.[6]

It should be noted that, after Aristotle and Galen, followed by Huarte, memory was considered less important than the other two inner senses. But memory still played an essential role in cognition. The process of cognition was based on the interaction with the immediate reality filtered through the memories stored in the memory ventricle. Memories have the ability to alter both perception and cognition, mainly due to the connection between the internal and external senses. An example of the process can be viewed in Gerard of Harderwyck's *De sensu*, found in his *Epitomata* (1496):

> The upper two heads show the usual divisions and labeling. The one on the left is said to represent the teachings of Galen and Avicenna and has four compartments: "sensus comunis," "phantasia," "cogitativa," and "memorativa." The first ventricle has two parts and contains the first two of these faculties. The one on the right has five: "sensus comunis," "imaginativa," "estimativa," "phantasia," and "memorativa," and is said to accord with the tenets of St. Thomas Aquinas and Albertus Magnus. The lower figure is of greater interest for it depicts not only the cranial divisions but also various sensations, special and peripheral, impinging upon the first cell to form the "sensus comunis." (Rpt. in Clarke and Dewhurst 17)

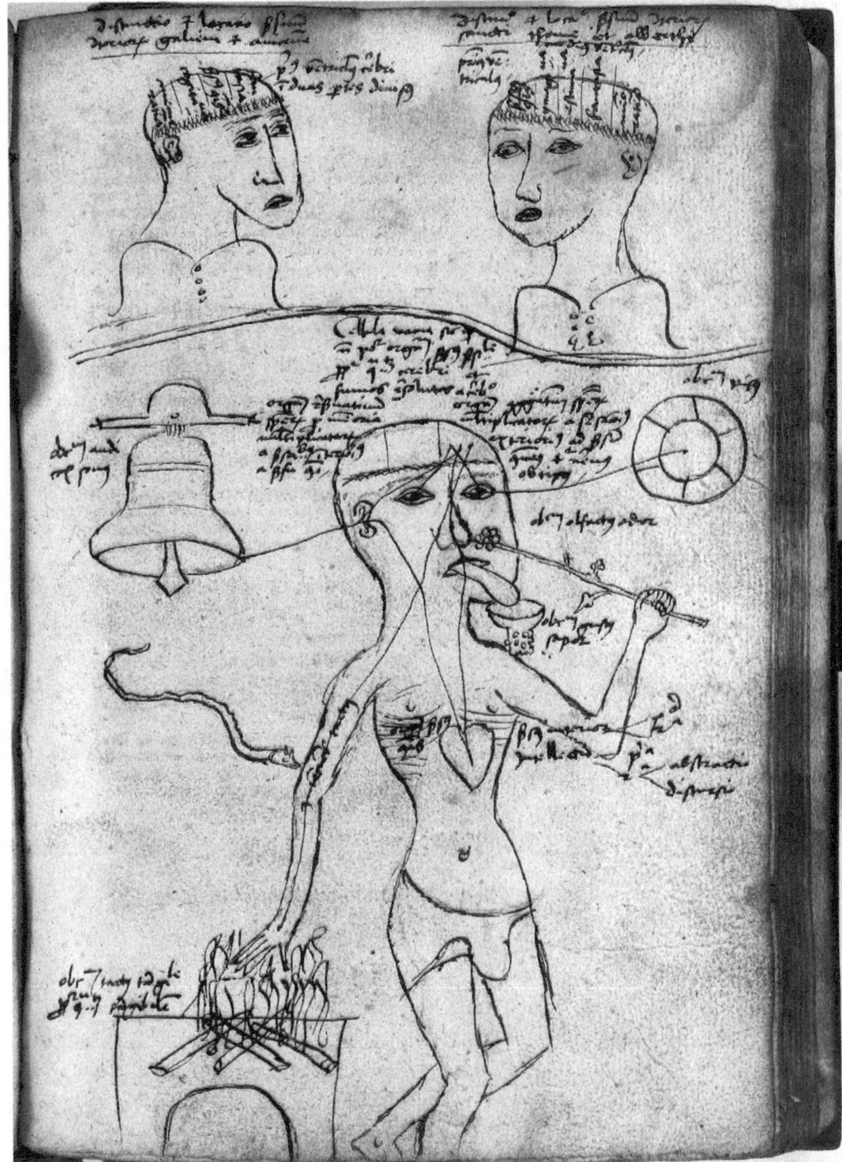

Figure 3.1. Cognitive process depicted in *De Sensu. Epitomata* of Gerard de Harderwyck (1496). Wellcome Library, London, detail.

Galenic Humoral Theories: Memory in the Sensory and Cognitive Process in *Don Quixote*

Don Quixote was written during a time of great interest in the psychology of man and the study of the human mind as suggested by Louise Fothergill-Payne: "If during the Middle Ages it was enough that the man was a composite of body and soul, now it turns out that this rational animal is divided by the painful conflict between reason and appetite, which is subject to a variation of moods" ("La percepción" 69). Cervantes seems to have been familiar with the prevailing ideas regarding the mind and its connection to perception through the five senses of the body. This discernment is especially evident when one considers his adept description of some characters' bouts of madness that can be understood as perceptual disturbances closely related to the malfunction of the inner senses. Indeed, one need only consider his exacting depiction of many cases of insanity such as Don Quixote himself or the main character in the *El licenciado vidriera* (The Glass Licentiate) to corroborate the idea that Cervantes had at least some familiarity with the impact of the inner senses on the individual. The author's awareness of period medicine could have come from his family (his father was a *cirujano*) and friends such as Alonso Ponce de Santa Cruz and Alonso López Pinciano.[7] On the other hand, he may have been acquainted with many influential and popular medical treatises related to the neuropsychological disciplines of the time.

I am not the first to suggest that Cervantes's *Don Quixote* is an excellent source for understanding prevailing medical theories of the day. When asked to recommend a list of books to prepare his medical students, Thomas Sydenham (1624–89), the physician and professor of medicine widely known as the "English Hippocrates," pointed to Cervantes's novel as requisite reading: "Read *Don Quixote* it is a very interesting book; I read it often" (qtd in García Barreno 176). William Osler, considered the father of modern medicine, offered similar advice to his medical students (qtd in Palma and Palma 248). Even Sigmund Freud and Santiago Ramón y Cajal were reported to have been influenced by Cervantes's work.[8] This documented interest in the novel by renowned physicians and psychologists suggests that the well-known story of Don Quixote may have been marked or influenced by the medicine of the time. According to Daniel Eisenberg, Miguel de Cervantes's own library apparently held 214 volumes, including well-known medical treatises of his time, such as the *Libro de las quatro enfermedades cortesanas* (Book of the four courtesan' diseases) (1544) by Luis Lobera de Ávila (1480?–1551), *Práctica y theórica de cirugía en Romance y Latín* (Practice and Theory of Surgery in Romance and Latin) (1584) by Dionisio Daza Chacón (1513–96), *Practica in Arte Chirurgica Copiosa* (Practice in the Abundant Surgical Art) by Giovanni de Vigo (1450–1525), *Dioscórides* (Dioscorides) (1555) by Andrés Laguna (1499–1560), the *Tratado nuevamente impreso de todas las enfermedades de los riñones, vexiga, y carnosidades de la verga*

(Newly Printed Treatise of All the Diseases of the Kidneys, Bladder and Fleshiness of the Penis) (1586) by Francisco Díaz, and *Examen de ingenios para las ciencias* (Examination of Men's Wits) by Juan Huarte de San Juan (1575).[9] In addition to these prominent works in his possession, Cervantes may have been familiar with a great many other medical authors of the period: Francisco Vallés Covarrubias (1524–92); Antonio Gómez Pereira (1500–88), *Antoniana Margarita* (1554); Andrés Alcázar (1490–1585), creator of one of the first treatises of neurosurgery *De vulneribus capiti* (1582); Miguel de Sabuco and Alvarez (1525–88) and the study of emotions by his daughter Olivia Sabuco of Nantes, *Nueva filosofía de la naturaleza del hombre* (New Philosophy of the Nature of Man) (1587); the famed anatomist Juan Valverde de Amusco (1525–64), *Historia de la composición del cuerpo humano* (History of the Composition of the Human Body) (1556); Piedrahieta Juan Bravo (1527–1610), author of one of the first treatises on physiology and the functioning of the senses of taste and smell, *De saporum et odorum differentiis* (1592); and Juan Luis Vives (1492–1540), *De anima et vita* (1538), in which he considered emotions as possible elements of destabilization of the intellect. These titles represent the many important volumes of medical treatises and studies that Cervantes could have known in addition to those mentioned by Eisenberg above. Unfortunately, Eisenberg's reconstruction of Cervantes's library is not without some speculation on his part. For example, nothing in the historical record can completely corroborate Eisenberg's inventory of books, and it is well known that Cervantes's personal finances were usually problematic, making it difficult to believe that the struggling author could have purchased so many important tomes. Still, the evidence suggests that Cervantes did own some books of medicine and psychology, which invites us to explore the extent to which he understood the prevailing medical theories of the day.

There is textual evidence for Cervantes's appreciation for medicine – and science more generally. In chapter 18 of the second part of *Don Quixote*, the reader encounters the famous passage where the knight describes the necessary qualities and knowledge that anyone who engages in the "science" of chivalry should possess, including those related to the medical profession:

> La de la caballería andante [...] es una ciencia [...] que encierra en sí todas o las más ciencias de mundo a causa que el que la profesa ha de ser jurisperito y saber las leyes de la justicia distributiva y comutativa, para dar a cada uno lo suyo y lo que le conviene; ha de ser teólogo, para saber dar la razón de la cristiana ley que profesa clara y distintamente, adonde quiera que le fuere pedido; *ha de ser médico, y principalmente herbolario, para conocer en mitad de los despoblados y desiertos las yerbas que tienen virtud de sanar las heridas, que no ha de andar el caballero andante a cada triquete buscando quien se las cure.* (II:18; my emphasis)[10]

> The science of chivalry [...] is one [...] that contains within itself all of the other sciences of the world because he who professes it must be a legal expert and know the laws of distributive and commutative justice in order to give each person what is his due and what suits him; he must be a theologian in order to know how to advocate for the Christian law that he professes clearly and distinctly wherever he is asked; *he must be a physician and primarily an herbalist, in order to know in the middle of uninhabited lands and deserts the herbs that have the virtue to heal wounds so that the knight does not have to seek someone to cure him all the time.*

Healing through herbs of various kinds was common practice at the time. The preventive medicine inherited from the Galenic tradition recognized, first, the prevention of diseases through a healthy lifestyle, then the use of herbs for the treatment of diseases, and finally surgical intervention as a last resort. This would explain the episode in which the knight talks about the physician Andrés Laguna and his popular illustrated translation and commentary on Dioscorides's *Materia medica,* published with the title *Annotationes in Dioscoridem Anazarbeum* (Annotations on Dioscorides of Anazarbeus) (1554): "Tomara yo ahora más aína un cuartal de pan o una hogaza y dos cabezas de sardinas arenques, que cuantas yerbas describe *Dioscórides,* aunque fuera el ilustrado por el Doctor Laguna" (Right now I would rather have a piece of bread or an entire circular loaf and two sardine heads than all the herbs the *Dioscorides* describes, even if it were the edition illustrated by Doctor Laguna himself) (I: 18). Laguna's *Dioscorides* was considered one of the most influential books about therapeutic medicine in the history of Spain. As the citation attests, since Cervantes knew of the text, he probably understood something of the Greco-Roman medical tradition and its pharmacological application. This medical work is one of the many reflecting the debt to the Hippocratic-Galenic tradition, and it is very likely that Cervantes was familiar with it thanks to the many medical treatises that existed at the time.

In fact, in addition to the countless occasions where the characters suffer pain, the novel describes numerous and varied medical, dermatological, digestive, urinary, eye, infectious, and neurological conditions and their symptoms.[11] Neuropsychology is prominently featured in several references. Many characters in the novel suffer conditions related to neuropsychological malfunctions such as tremours or shaking, insomnia, hallucinations, and fainting, among many others.[12] Moreover, in the novel Cervantes refers to the brain or brains (*celebro, cerebro, sesos, cerbelo*) more than a dozen times (García Barreno 170). Generally, these references to the brain reflect poor function that emphasizes the internal sense of the intellect – usually as a sign of folly such as the seminal description of the knight whose excessive reading was the root of his madness: "y así, del poco dormir y del mucho leer, se le secó el cerebro de manera que vino a perder el juicio" (and what with little sleep and much reading, his brain dried so that he lost his judgment) (I: 1).

The protagonist's momentary – but frequent – losses of judgment cause him to suffer disturbances in the perception of external reality. In short, what Don Quixote experiences externally often contradicts what his readings have taught and consequently recorded in his memory, as affected by his inner senses. Such a characterization coincides with seventeenth-century scientific understanding, which included a special concern for the problem of perception in addition to an interest in human psychology. The study of perception and psychology centred on the dichotomy between seeming and being, appearance and reality, deception and disappointment, which was an epistemological problem closely related to the functioning of the five external senses and their correspondence with the three inner ones (Fothergill-Payne, "La percepción" 69). Don Quixote typifies the malfunction of all of them.[13] The knight's temporary insanity is caused by dyscrasia or humoral imbalances that alter his process of external perception. In particular, a disorder of the three inner senses of imagination, intellect, and memory – guided by his faulty readings – causes a malfunction in the five external senses. When a hierarchical imbalance of functions results, the senses are confused and, in Don Quixote's case, he begins to "toma unas cosas por otras, y juzga lo blanco por negro y lo negro por blanco" (take one thing for another, and judges white for black and black for white) (II: 10). But, which factors actually provoked this alteration of the senses?

The answers lie in what was believed to be the brain's structure and chief functions. During the Renaissance the physiology of the brain's ventricles and the organ's proper functioning was related to the theory of humours developed by Galen (following the Hippocratic conception).[14] Galen conceived the human body as a system composed of a combination of the four basic elements (water, fire, earth and air), whose mixture in variable proportions gave rise to four secondary elements or humours (blood, phlegm, yellow bile, and black bile or melancholy). According to the Galenic model, the combination of these four fluids within the human body led to pairs of opposite qualities (hot-wet, cold-wet, hot-dry and cold-dry, respectively). The humours were characterized by their "flow ability, the capacity to mix (krasis) and the fact that variable proportions of the four elements would result in different qualities: hot-cold and wet-dry" (Borges Guerra, Moreno, and León del Río 71).[15] It was understood that out of the various possible combinations of humours and qualities then arose different temperaments (sanguine, choleric, melancholic, and phlegmatic) with their respective emotional characteristics. When the qualities were balanced, the subject was in a state of eucrasia, or good health. However, when the humours were disproportionately mismatched (dyscrasia) and some qualities prevailed over others, emotional imbalances or diseases resulted, yielding a situation that a physician should treat.

The predominance of a certain mood causes the differences of wit, and according to this hypothesis, madness itself can be regarded as a special model of ingenuity. So the different neuropsychiatric disorders assumed at the time, such as mania, melancholia, and frenzy, are due to a change in the patient's brain temper, a temperament that would reverse when the patient was cured (López Muñoz et al. 492).

One of the leading authorities on the humoral imbalance was the physician and writer Juan Huarte de San Juan. As Spanish medicine gained importance during the sixteenth century – especially in terms of the study of brain function – Huarte de San Juan played a unique role in terms of both medical theory and its impact outside of medicine. Since Cervantes apparently held a copy of Huarte de San Juan's major treatise, *Examen de ingenios* (1575), in his own library, the physician likely influenced the novelist. In the treatise Huarte de San Juan followed a particular neuropsychological model to explain the main differences between people based on their physical differences.[16] According to the author, for the proper functioning of human mental faculties, a number of essential conditions must exist: "Good mix of humoral elements, good skull shape, good quantity of brain, and the existence of four distinct and separate ventricles, each one in the proper place in the brain" (Borges Guerra et al. 67).[17] For Huarte de San Juan a properly functioning brain required both the appropriate physical features and the correct balance of the Galenic humours. In fact, he clearly viewed disease as an imbalance among the four humours, resulting in the strengthening of one and the weakening of another:

> Si el hombre cae en alguna enfermedad por la cual el celebro de repente muda su temperatura (como es la manía, melancolía o frenesía) en un momento acontesce perder, si es prudente, cuanto sabe, y dice mil disparates; y si es nescio, adquiere más ingenio y habilidad que antes tenía. (305)

> If the man falls into a disease in which the brain suddenly changes its temperature (such as mania, melancholia, or frenzy), if he is prudent at the time this happens, he loses everything he knows and says a thousand follies; and if he is a fool, he will obtain more intelligence and skill than he had before.

Physicians of the time used the classical Galenic theory of humours and temperaments to explain the causes of disease. For example, a lack of humidity would provoke instability in the humours, yielding choleric and melancholic temperaments such as those that plague Don Quixote throughout the novel. This imbalance in the protagonist's temperament helps explain his great capacity for invention and imagination as well as an excellent memory, as Sancho notes: "pareciéndole que no debía haber historia en el mundo ni suceso que no lo tuviese cifrado en la uña y clavado en la memoria" (it seemed to him that there was no history nor historical event in the world that his master did not have written on his fingernail or nailed into his memory) (II: 486).

According to Galenic humoral theory, among the four humours the most negative was black bile or *atrabilis*, which was thought to be cold and dry, which attacks the brain and affects the inner senses such as memory and damages its functions. The negative impact of excessive black bile was melancholy. At the same time the melancholic humour also had a special propensity to develop imagination leading to great bouts of intelligence and genius. "It [had] its role in the humoral balance. It [had] a force that incited diverse functions: from whetting the appetite in the stomach to adding wit to the brain. That is why the melancholic individuals or *atrabilarios* [were] intelligent, lively, with flashes of genius; while they also [were] unstable and disconcerting" (Paniagua 18).

The positive and negative nature – or hybridity – of this humour was historically important. During the period thinkers followed Plato's initial description of black bile in *Ion*, in which the philosopher saw a close connection of insanity to superior wit – *ingenium excellens cum mania* (superior wit accompanied by insanity) (qtd in Huarte 202). The humour therefore was believed to be responsible for both disease and the gift of intellect, poetic skill, or enthusiasm for the divine. Plato's defence of genius appeared in his *Phaedrus*. Later, in the Renaissance, some Neoplatonists, such as Marsilio Ficino (1433–99) in his *De vita libri tres*, stated that melancholy was a mental state that provided a special facility for all creative activities and highlighted the work of memory and imagination in literary creation. In the anonymously written (often attributed to Aristotle) *Problemata Physica XXX*, the doctrine of genius also is associated with the melancholic humour black bile: "Why men who stood out for their wit, in philosophical studies, in the governance of the republic, in the composition of poetry, or in the arts, all show having been melancholic?" As the *Problemata* indicates, such creativity typically is allied with melancholy and linked to the imagination, but not to the intellect. Whereas intellect displays good temperance, the imagination exhibits intemperance. Moreover, according to Huarte, when an individual suffers a brain injury, he is likely to suffer bouts of madness and display erratic behaviour: "en un momento hablan cosas de ingenio y habilidad, y en otro dicen mil disparates" (at one moment they say things full of wit and ability, and at another moment they say thousand absurdities) (216).[18] Hence, a hybrid character who is choleric-melancholic was thought to suffer great behavioural inconsistencies, leading observers to believe that the victim was sometimes crazy and sometimes not so crazy. As a result, anyone suffering from melancholy exhibited different variants ranging from madness to genius. The choleric-melancholic imbalance clearly can be seen in the "partial intemperance" of Don Quixote (Serés 357n31). The knight suffers from a fluctuation caused by these two humours, which sometimes leads his mind to either view the world with great lucidity or create an alternative reality based on his bookish memories. This explains why the rest of the characters ask themselves over and over why such an intelligent man sometimes can be so crazy. The answer, of course, is related to his infatuation with his bookish chivalric memories, which has helped create the madness he suffers.

A similar intemperance occurs with another humoral quality, heat. It was generally held that heat and dryness energize imagination and lead writers and artists to create great artistic works. For Alonso López Pinciano, for example, heat is one of the key elements in poetry: "The instrument of this faculty is heat with dryness, which are companions of poetic fury, whose cause is a very convenient sense for writing poetry" (49). For his part, Huarte writes that heat and dryness intensify creative imagination: "Porque el amor calienta y deseca el celebro, que son las calidades que avivan la imaginativa" (For love warms and dries the brain, which are qualities that fuel the imagination) (408). When considering the qualities of heat and melancholy, then, Huarte de San Juan characterizes melancholic individuals as gifted with great imagination and memory. In *Don Quixote*, in times of heat and dryness the knight's "frenesía" or "mania" is overwhelmingly related to his previous readings of chivalric romances: "de manera [decían los que lo conocían] que como no le toquen en sus caballerías, no habrá nadie que no le juzgue sino por de muy buen entendimiento" (those who knew him said that as long as you do not touch upon his chivalric adventures, no one would judge him to not have good sense) (I: 2). Unfortunately for Don Quixote, the knight's melancholic character or *atrabilis* gains greater strength towards the end of his life. His choleric temperament has injured his imagination which has been further amplified through sleep deprivation, fasting, and excessive concentration:

> Llenósele la fantasía de todo aquello que leía en sus libros, así de encantamentos como de pendencias [...]; y asentósele de tal modo en la imaginación que era verdad toda aquella máquina de aquellas soñadas invenciones que leía [...] se le secó el cerebro, de manera que vino a perder el juicio. (I: 1)

> His head was filled up with so much fantasy including enchantments and penances from the books he read [...]; and he came to believe in his imagination that all of the fabrications and dreamed-up inventions he read about were real. [...]. His brain dried up in such a way that he ended up losing his mind.

According to Huarte, a melancholic's fiery imagination serves to help "memory and reminiscence and provides figures and sentences that makes him talk without cause to anyone" (458).

In the previously mentioned work commonly attributed to Aristotle, the *Problemata Physica*, and also in his *De memoria et reminiscentia*, the philosopher was one of the first to add the physical and psychological factors of melancholy and relate them to memory. In the work the author emphasizes the melancholic and its propensity for love, thus combining the Platonic idea of melancholy in love that the influential humanist philosopher Marsilio Ficino will later pick up. In the case of Don Quixote the mixture of Platonic and melancholic love helps explain the altered relationship between the internal faculties of the soul and his external senses in which he benefits from an exalted imagination and higher-than-usual memory capacity that is separated only occasionally from the intellect. Such a view is supported by Aristotle in his *De memoria et reminiscentia*:

> People whose humors are out of balance are sometimes better at remembering or recollecting than when they are in balance. Those who are melancholic are too fluid to retain images well and remember uncontrollably. The reason for recollecting not being under their control is because just as it is no longer in one's power to stop something when they throw it, so too is recollecting when he who tries to recollect sets up a process in which affection resides. (453a14)

For Aristotle the melancholic is incapable of properly recalling memories, due to an imbalance. Similarly, for the humanist Pedro Simón de Abril the images created by the *imaginativa* in the perception process and stored in the memory represent "'fábricas' y composturas, unas veces bien concertadas, cuando la sustancia del cerebro está bien dispuesta, y otras de disparates, cuando está mal dispuesta de alguna excesiva calidad" (inventions and adornments, sometimes well prepared when the brain's matter is ready or faulty when it is badly prepared because of some excessive quality) (qtd in Huarte 291n36). Quoting Galen, Huarte tells us that "cuando en la enfermedad se desbarata el temperamento y buena compostura del cerebro, muchas veces se pierden las obras del entendimiento y quedan salvas las de la memoria y las de la imaginativa" (when during a disease the temperament and the composure of the brain are disrupted, often the works of the intellect are lost and those of memory and *imaginativa* remain safe) (357).

After Aristotle both Hippocrates and Galen divided life into five ages and related each of them to a particular memory capacity: pueritia, pubertas, iuventus, aetas consistendi, *senectutis*.[19] These divisions later were followed by Huarte, who, paraphrasing Aristotle, stated the following with respect to the memory of the old: "La memoria de los viejos está llena de tantas figuras de cosas como han visto y oído en el largo discurso de su vida, y así quiriendo echarle más, no lo puede recibir, porque no hay lugar vacío donde quepa" (The memory of the old is full of so many things that they have seen and heard in the course of their long life, and they want to store even more, but they cannot do it because there is no available space where it can fit) (335). An obvious parallel can be made with Don Quixote, who no longer has memory space because it has been filled with assorted images that he retrieves time and again following Huarte's ideas (336). Indeed, the knight utilizes a refined associative capacity of reminiscence, which works non-stop with the imagination, but according to the theories of the time, it is detailed but limited.

Don Quixote's awareness of what is happening is powerfully affected by the *imaginativa*, which exerts a constant influence on what is perceived in the present. As Aurora Egido has noted, the many images the knight has stored in memory interrupt the appropriate awareness of the present: "The memory makes a constant filter between sensory perception and imagination, forcing it to represent what is remembered and not what the senses capture in the present" (12). In other words, the stored memories from his readings are activated and give free rein to his imagination in the process of the perception of reality; it is as if the hierarchy of what was believed to be the process of perception and cognition reversed its traditional order, starting instead with the memory. In fact, it was believed that in dreams or in moments of alteration or sickness "the order could be reversed so that the imagination, itself stirred by memories or other input for the later faculties, affected the common sense and even the sense organs" (Kemp and Fletcher 56), which explains Don Quixote's sensorial perception problems. Huarte similarly describes this process: "la memoria no es más que una blandura del cerebro [...] para recibir y guardar lo que la imaginativa percibe, en la misma proporción que tiene el papel blanco y liso con el que ha de escribir" (memory is only a softness of the brain [...] to receive and save what the *imaginativa* perceives, in the same proportion that it has the smooth white paper that has to write on) (363). Whereas imagination is thought to be of greater value, it is memory that provides the material with which the imagination functions. In Don Quixote's case, his memory allows him to constantly imitate his models.[20] Furthermore, according to Huarte, memory and imaginativa work together; memory stores information, but it is the imaginativa that writes on memory and then reads: "De manera que hacer memoria de las cosas y acordarse de ellas después es obra de la imaginativa" (recalling things and remembering them later is the work of the *imaginativa*) (364). The latter, as a result of the illness caused by the humoral imbalances, is what provides the pictures that will later be used in his adventures, adapting his bookish memories to reality and identifying it with the perceptions of the present.

Memory filters both sensory perception and imagination, depicting what is remembered, not what his senses capture in his present moment, thus blocking his sensory perception:

> a nuestro aventurero todo cuanto pensaba, veía o imaginaba le parecía ser hecho y pasar al modo de lo que había leído, luego que vio la venta se le presentó que era un castillo con sus cuatro torres y chapiteles de luciente plata, sin faltarle su puente levadiza y honda cava, con todos aquellos adherentes que semejantes castillos se pintan. (I: 1)

> to our adventurer all that he thought, saw, or imagined seemed to happen in just the ways he read, so that when he saw the inn, it was presented to him as a castle with four towers crowned with polished silver columns without forgetting the raised bridge and deep moat and all of the other necessary details that such castles are depicted to have.

The errant memory of Don Quixote is so powerful that the images perceived and the places that he transits pass immediately to be identified with the places and images stored in his mind (Egido 11). Don Quixote therefore certifies in chapter II that he imagines everything he sees, hears, touches, eats, and drinks. The adventure of the windmills, to mention just one of many, serves to confirm how the images stored in his memory supersede his reality, obfuscating the function of his external senses. We have seen previously, as Aristotle had indicated, that sensory data persist or reproduce in imagination or in memory. The common sense or "sensus communis," which served as an anteroom to the imaginativa, must be able to distinguish between new images and those that are already stored in the memory from previous experiences. This is where the problem of Don Quixote lies. Cervantes's protagonist identifies the past of his readings with present perceptions, since memory is designed for the past and Don Quixote uses it to imagine future adventures. Don Quixote does not see, or hear, or smell, or touch what is obviously in front of him, but rather he imagines constructs with the aid of the references that memory provides (Egido 18). But it is not only the external sense of sight that suffers from these alterations. There are several similar examples of Don Quixote's malfunctioning external senses. When he arrives at the inn, "llegó a la venta un castrador de puercos, y así como luego, sonó su silbato de cañas cuatro o cinco veces, con lo cual acabó de confirmar Don Quixote que estaba en algún famoso castillo y que le servían con música y que el abadejo eran truchas, el pan candeal y las rameras damas y el ventero castellano del castillo" (a castrator of hogs arrived at the inn and when the man played his cane whistle four or five times it confirmed for the knight that he was in some famous castle and that they welcomed him with music, and that his cod was really trout, his bread was the whitest, the wenches were ladies, and the innkeeper was the liege of the castle) (I: 3.54). Similar transformations in his judgment of the outside world can be seen in the episode of the fulling mills ("batanes") in which he equates the pounding of the hammers for some great evil. While the knight does not actually convert the hammers into some giant or malevolent force as in other instances, what is interesting is how the acute perception of his surroundings work to instil fear: "la soledad, el sitio, la escuridad, el ruido del agua con el susurro de las hojas, todo causaba horror y espanto, y más cuando vieron que ni los golpes cesaban ni el viento dormía ni la mañana llegaba, añadiéndose a todo esto el ignorar el lugar donde se hallaban" (the loneliness, the place, the darkness, the sound of the water with the whisper of the leaves all caused horror and fear and even more so when they saw that the hammering did not stop nor did the wind sleep nor did the morning arrive) (I.20:208). As much as Don Quixote misjudges the natural world, he fares no better with humans. For example, in his encounter with the maid Maritornes her repulsive body odour and breath seemed to him to be "suave y aromático" (smooth and aromatic), and her inadvertent touch incites in his mind the belief that he is being visited by a great and beautiful maiden. Finally, it is worth mentioning Don Quixote's "flight" atop the pegged horse, Clavileño, one of the more famous episodes, where the knight and his squire are blindfolded on a wooden horse and told they will fly to the heavens and touch the stars. Although the pair never leaves the ground, the heat spread from the great chimney bellows used by the palace servants to simulate their flight leads the knight to believe he is nearing the sun.

According to Kia Nobre, a neuroscientist at the University of Oxford, memory and perception processes are so closely related because memories have that ability to change the way in which reality is perceived by manipulating sensory information: "Memory is a set of things you chose in your environment at the time because you found them interesting or useful [...] memories are constantly changing the way we perceive the world [...]. Our attention is selective and amplifies and filters the information that comes from the outside world according to our own desires or purposes, creating a world hypothesis that, along with the memories we hold within us, guide and manipulate sensory information to create our particular reality."[21]

Not only is the attention of Don Quixote selective, but so is his memory, as he chooses from his readings whatever fits his needs at the time. As Ruth El Saffar once put it: "Cervantes can celebrate, in *Don Quixote*, and everything else he wrote, the tremendous, transformative powers of the imagination, showing again and again how the engagement in story – writing, listening to, telling – effects change in those who participate in it" (89).

To conclude, this masterwork of literature provides new insights for understanding the relationship between the external and the internal senses as they were understood during the Renaissance. The novel can be seen as a laboratory for the study of the Don Quixote's encoding, storage, and retrieval of memory and its influence on the external senses. He has a distinct way of perceiving and also a particular way of retrieving his memory experiences. In *Elements of the Episodic Memory* Endel Tulving emphasized the importance of the physical and cognitive environments to initiate retrieval (171) and "he has found memory retrieval to be most effective when it involves the same cues and context as those of the original information" (Nalbantian 261).

Whatever the knight finds in his adventures is a trigger for his chivalric reminiscences as directed by his stimulus-based memory process. Over and over again sounds, smells, and other sensory cues are the impetus for Don Quixote's memory retrieval. Once those experiences are stored in the third ventricle of memory, the sensory visual, olfactory, tactile, and auditory cues stimulate the involuntary recall of his bookish memories. The obvious connection between the external and the internal senses determines how Don Quixote understands his environment, just as his bookish memories influence both. To that end, and as a way of summarizing Don Quixote's confused sensory understanding of his world, perhaps no one does so quite like Sancho: "Siendo, pues, loco como lo es, y de locura que las más veces toma unas cosas por otras y juzga lo blanco por negro y lo negro por blanco, como se pareció cuando dijo que los molinos de viento eran gigantes, y las mulas de los religiosos dromedarios, y las manadas de carneros ejércitos de enemigos, y otras muchas cosas a este tono" (Being mad as he is, and suffering from a madness that usually takes some things for others and judges white for black and black for white just as when he said that the windmills were giants and the monks' mules were dromedaries and the flocks of sheep were armies of the enemy and so many other similar things of that nature) (II: 10.703).

NOTES

1 My translation: "Por eso hay que sopesar ahora si es verdad lo que hemos dicho, esto es que la visión se realiza en los ojos, la olfación en la nariz y la audición en los oídos: o si todas las sensaciones se realizan en el propio cerebro, y suben las especies de los colores a través de los ojos, las de los sonidos a través de los oídos, las de los olores por la nariz, las de los sabores por la lengua, las de las cualidades táctiles por toda la piel, como opinan algunos filósofos, y entre los médicos, Juan Manardo, hombre de no vulgar erudición."

2 Based on the legacy of classical antiquity, in Cervantes's time two different traditions that study memory prevailed. A rhetorical tradition, whose principal representatives

were Cicero, Quintilian, and the *Rhetorica ad Herennium*, examined artificial memory and techniques of mnemonics. The other tradition was linked to the medical philosophy that will be examined in this essay. The latter began to take on special relevance as a result of the treatises and studies whose objective was to examine the mind and memory. Memory was part of the rhetoric along with *inventio*, *dispositio*, *elocutio*, and *actio*. The memorization of an oral discourse depended on natural memory (*naturalis*) associated with the medical-philosophical tradition and artificial memory (*artificialis*) derived from the artificial-philosophical tradition.

3 For a more detailed study on the relation between memory and imagination see my article "The Janus Hypothesis in *Don Quijote*."

4 The terms "faculties of the soul" or "interior senses" have been replaced over time by "spiritual" or "cerebral" in the same way that "corporal" and "passive" are terms used to refer to "external senses." See the studies of Harry Wolfson and Ruth Harvey on this topic.

5 With the birth of modern scientific thought during the Renaissance, a new form of observing reality developed that abandoned medieval traditions, including scholasticism. Instead, scholars returned to the original sources of Plato, Aristotle, and physicians such as Galen and Hippocrates. Among those who have studied and commented on Aristotle's works were Averroes, Avicenna, Juan Damasceno, Isaac Israeli, Algazali, Maimonides, Alberto Magno, Saint Augustine, and Saint Thomas. See Wolfson's article on the subject.

6 My translation. For Huarte de San Juan the three faculties – memory, intellect, and imagination – were together located in each chamber or ventricle of the brain, a notion that departed from classical theory.

7 Although there is no evidence that Cervantes and Pinciano were friends, F. López Muñoz et al., following Alfredo Carballo Picazo and his work on Alonso López and his *Philosophía Antigua Poetica* on, believe so. López Muñoz et al. 490.

8 For other examples of citations on the medical knowledge of Cervantes see Palma and Palma.

9 For more information on the contents of Cervantes's library, see Eisenberg.

10 All translations of *Don Quixote* are mine.

11 For a detailed analysis of the presence of medicine and its context in the work see García Barreno.

12 For more information on this topic see José Alberto Palma and Fermín Palma, renowned physicians who study Cervantes's literary works from a neurological point of view in their article "Neurology and Don Quixote."

13 It is helpful to keep in mind that this alteration manifests itself in the principal actions of the chivalric novels: "those who knew him said that as long as you do not touch upon his chivalric adventures, no one would judge him to not have good sense" (I: 2).

14 It is generally believed that the origin of the four humours can be traced to Alcmaeon of Croton (c. 500 BCE) who affirmed that "the equilibrium among humidity, dryness, coldness, heat, bitterness, sweetness and the others, conserves one's health, but the domination of one alone produces sickness" (qtd in García Barreno 157). For his part, Philistion (c. 385 BCE) believed that sickness appears due to an excess or defect of one quality. After 400 BCE Hippocrates summarized these ideas in "On the Nature of Man."

15 The attribution of basic qualities to the humours was as follows: blood – heat and humidity; phlegm – cold and humidity; yellow bile – heat and dryness; black bile or melancholy – cold and dryness.

16 The title *Examen de los ingenios* or *Examination of Men's Wits* seems misleading for a neurophysiological treatise. In fact, the word *wit* actually referred to the faculties or inner senses (López Muñoz 494). In the work the physician – following Andreas Vesalius – introduces some variants, such as the existence of four ventricles and the location of the interior senses or faculties in each one.

17 During the Renaissance the study of human anatomy witnessed a revolution under the influence of significant figures such as Leonardo Da Vinci (1452–1519), Berengario da Carpi (1460–1530), Andreas Vesalius (1514–64), Costanzo Varolio (1543–75), Juan Valverde de Amusco (1525–87), and Realdo Colombo (1515–59).

18 As an example of melancholics who have the power to foresee, Huarte de San Juan cites the Hippocratic example of Democritus of Abdera (208), while Aristotle points to Hercules, Heracles, and the prophetic Sibyls and Bacchantes.

19 "Childhood, hot and wet; adolescence, tempered; youth, hot and dry; consistency, tempered by heat and cold, and ill-tempered by dryness; old-age, cold and dry" (Huarte 249).

20 In Don Quixote's case, his use of mimetic memory allows him to constantly imitate all that he has read: "He thus goes on living what he has read, trying to reproduce it to the extent possible including linguistic instances" (Egido 11).

21 My translation of a fragment from an interview on the Spanish television program *Redes*.

4 Taste, Cognition, and Redemption in *Guzmán de Alfarache*

ROBERT K. FRITZ

Mateo Alemán's *Guzmán de Alfarache* (Part 1, 1599; Part 2, 1604) consists of the pseudo-autobiographical reflections of a self-confessed *pícaro*, whose crimes have earned him a slave's seat on a galley ship in the Spanish navy. Guzmán relates episodes from his life describing the misfortunes which befell him as he drifted between cities in Spain and Italy, making a living in the employ of various masters or, when circumstances required, by begging, thieving, or gambling. Guzmán the narrator claims to have reformed himself and exchanged his wicked ways for a life of Christian righteousness, yet the authenticity of his repentance has been a divisive topic among critics, who tend to divide themselves into two camps: those who accept Guzmán's conversion as sincere and those who find it less than convincing at best and a cynical falsehood at worst. In general terms, critics such as A.A. Parker (*Literature*), Michel Cavillac, and José María Micó, who adhere to the straight interpretation, understand Guzmán to be the portrayal of a sinner predisposed to wickedness by original sin, yet whose free will enables him to redeem himself with the aid of divine grace (Vaíllo 451). In contrast, what I call the "cynical" critics, including Joan Arias (1977), Carroll Johnson (*Inside*), Benito Brancaforte, and Francisco Ramírez Santacruz, among others, all cast doubt on the straight reading. These cynical critics detect underlying heterodox ideologies in *Guzmán de Alfarache* which place the blame for human wickedness not on original sin but on the fundamental imperfection of creation itself. In my reading I rely on the insights of cognitive historicism to defend a view which fits into the first camp by focusing on the sense of taste. Significantly, the text depicts taste in evocative terms which often foreground physiological and cognitive aspects of characters' sensations. Recent work in the field of cognitive literary studies suggests that such depictions of sensory experiences can yield critical insights into a text because they reflect the embodied nature of human cognition from which meaning emerges. This approach not only offers insights into how taste metaphors create meaning in the novel, but also suggests ways in which early modern theories of embodied cognition influenced the development of science, religion, and literature in sixteenth-century Spain. In this regard, Guzmán's metaphorical language bears close examination since sixteenth-century models of human cognition explained human thought, emotion, and perception in terms of largely material, embodied processes. In the following cognitive-historicist interpretation of *Guzmán de Alfarache* I therefore argue that the descriptions of taste sensations and taste metaphors contribute to the literary articulation of a Christian message of redemption in which salvation is as much a matter of embodiment as it is a question of spiritual atonement.

A basic premise of cognitive historicism is that literary texts reflect cognitive processes common to all human beings as well as the particulars of the historical moment in which they were written. The field's growing body of scholarship represents an eclectic mix of approaches that adapt theories from cognitive and brain sciences to the study of literature from various eras and traditions. According to Lisa Zunshine, the goal of such studies is to "understand the evolving relationship between [...] the human mind and cultural artifacts, such as novels, poems, or paintings" (Introduction 3). The cognitive literary historian's methodology is to adapt and apply paradigms of cognitive architecture to the study of a literary text.[1] The architecture I employ to analyse taste in *Guzmán de Alfarache* is embodied cognition, the idea that the body's sensorimotor experiences of interactions with its environment serve as the basis for conscious thought and the creation of meaning.[2] As I will argue, however, cognition also depends on the organization and interpretation of sensorimotor information by higher-level cognitive functions, a factor of flavour perception that has important implications for the role of taste in *Guzmán de Alfarache*.

In brief, the theory of embodied cognition holds that the human mind analogically relates non-discursive sensorimotor experiences of material reality to more abstract and subjective modes of thought through primary metaphors. In *Philosophy in the Flesh* George Lakoff and Mark Johnson propose "that the very properties of concepts are created as a result of the way the brain and body are structured and the way they function in interpersonal relations and in the physical world" (37). The neurological mechanisms that operate beneath the level of awareness, the cognitive unconscious, conflate information from sensorimotor domains with higher levels of subjective experience (a process they call "cross-domain mapping") in order to produce primary metaphors. These metaphors, in turn, form the basic building blocks of conscious thought. Lakoff and Johnson claim that the cognitive unconscious is the "hidden hand that shapes our conscious thought" (15), without which we could not reason.[3] Despite its causal role in cognition, it is "the realm of thought that is completely and irrevocably inaccessible to direct conscious introspection" (12). Therefore, not only is the cognitive unconscious the causal basis of thought, it is also asymmetrical in that it operates "in one direction only, from the sensorimotor domain to the domain of subjective judgment" (55).[4] In short, inferences formed in the cognitive unconscious constitute the fundamental units of thought, which then flow into the conscious mind through neural connections, yet the cognitive unconscious itself is hermetically isolated from the influence of higher-level cognitive structures.

Sensorimotor metaphors manifest themselves linguistically in a variety of ways. The body's heavy reliance on vision for gathering information about the world (predetermined by our evolutionary heritage, which has made sight our strongest sense), for example, means that we often think of knowledge in visual terms. Hence many primary metaphors conflate the sensory domain of sight with the domain of thought: "knowing is seeing," "an aid to knowing is a light source," "being ignorant is being unable to see," and so on (238). Furthermore, when multiple primary metaphors from various domains are combined through conceptual blending they produce metaphors of increasing complexity that reflect aspects of the sensorimotor domain from which they derive.[5] Take, for example, this complex metaphor from *Guzmán de Alfarache*: "I saw clearly how adverse fortune makes men prudent. At that juncture I believed I had seen a new light that, as in a clear mirror, showed me the past, present, and future" (1: 264).[6] Here the primary metaphors of "knowing is seeing" and "an aid to knowing is a light source" blend to form a complex metaphor involving light, a mirror, and knowledge. Drawn from the sensory experience of passing from darkness into light, Guzmán's metaphor conceives of the insight afforded by experience as a new light that reveals previously little understood aspects of his life.

Like vision, taste and the associated physiological processes of eating and digestion constitute important sources of sensorimotor experiences for cross-domain mapping in *Guzmán de Alfarache*.[7] On the one hand, key moments in the plot hinge upon Guzmán's ability to distinguish good food from bad by its flavour alone. Ranging from delicious to disgusting, these vividly depicted gustatory experiences produce some of the book's most memorable episodes. On the other hand, metaphorical language frequently relates the temptations of a sinful life to an unrestrained appetite for sweet foods. In a prologue to Part 1 Alemán even employs gustatory imagery to encourage the reader to take an active approach to the interpretation of the text, writing, "You may moralize on the tale as it is offered to you: its margins have been left wide for you to fill. Should you find it either undignified or immoderate, it is because the subject of this book is the nature of a rogue. Revel in such things as these: for *splendid tables* should have delicacies for all *tastes*" (1: 112; emphasis added).[8] Scholars have accepted Alemán's invitation to this "splendid table" by filling the margins of the novel with the interpretations alluded to before. A careful analysis of the novel's taste metaphors, however, lends credence to the straight reading of Guzmán's life story as the sincere confession of a repentant sinner.

From the perspective of cognitive embodiment, the prologue's metaphorical conflation of the sense of taste with abstract concepts concerning aesthetic and moral judgment leads to significant interpretive insights. As Lakoff and Johnson explain, one of the complex metaphors used to describe a well-functioning mind is that of the healthy body. They write, "Just as a body needs the right kind of food – healthful, nutritious, and appetizing – so the mind needs the right kind of ideas, ideas that are true, helpful, and interesting" (241). Indeed, primary metaphors associated with eating frequently describe the acquisition of ideas in such terms: interest in ideas is appetite for food; good ideas are "healthful" foods; helpful ideas are "nutritious" foods; bad ideas are "harmful" foods; interesting, pleasurable ideas are "appetizing"; uninteresting ideas are "bland" foods; fully comprehending is "digesting" (241). These associations emerge from the cross-domain pairing between the sensorimotor domains of eating and digesting and that of learning new ideas and concepts. Alemán's metaphorical splendid table, for example, also includes "smooth, velvety wines that give good cheer as they aid in digestion" (1: 112).[9] Like fine wines, the entertaining elements of the novel aid in the digestion (i.e., learning) of its meatier subject matter related to morality and salvation. Cross-domain mapping thereby conflates digestion and flavour perception with the metaphorical consumption of didactic subject matter in the pleasant guise of leisurely reading material.

Furthermore, taste metaphors in *Guzmán de Alfarache* are remarkable in that they demonstrate the intimate relationship between language, thought, and the embodied sensorimotor experience of flavour perception. The novel's evocative depictions of taste stimuli suggest that Guzmán's taste metaphors emerge out of his sensorimotor experiences of the world much like the primary metaphors of Lakoff and Johnson's theories of embodied cognition. Nevertheless, the cognitive basis of Guzmán's metaphors departs from *Philosophy in the Flesh* in at least one significant way. In the following study, I posit that Alemán's use of taste metaphors reflects aspects of embodied cognition in which higher-level cognitive structures play an essential interpretive role in processing sensorimotor information from the cognitive unconscious, a phenomenon which Patrick Colm Hogan calls the "downward projection of structure." Specifically, the novel employs metaphors of flavour preference plasticity, that is, the ability of human flavour preferences to change over time as a consequence of activity and experience, to show that human nature is plastic and capable of change. These metaphors project the learned, high-level cognitive aspects of flavour perception onto abstract moral concepts concerning the acquisition of habits or ideas. The downward projection of structure implied by these gustatory metaphors indicates that human beings are capable of redeeming their wicked nature through the use of reason and discipline.

To appreciate the relation of Guzmán's taste metaphors to the intricacies of human cognition a brief description of flavour perception is in order. Properly speaking, the sense of taste is limited to the perception of salty, sweet, sour, bitter, and umami (savory), yet the overall experience of flavour perception is multimodal in that it combines input from a variety of sensory systems. Retronasal olfactory perceptions supplement the five simple tastes to create the sensation of flavour.[10] Food colour and mouthfeel, the tactile sensation of food in the mouth such as temperature and texture, also contribute to flavour perception. These perceptions are furthermore influenced by our behavioural state and they change, depending on whether we are hungry or full or even sad or angry (G. Shepherd 98). The complex physiological and psychological process of flavour perception therefore involves multiple aspects of our cognitive faculties besides the taste neurons of the tongue. While taste buds inform the brain that ice cream, for example, is sweet, retronasal olfaction determines whether or not it is vanilla or pistachio, and mouthfeel evaluates its consistency and temperature. The resulting flavour may be more pleasing if we are hungry or less so if we have just eaten a large meal.

The sensorimotor information is further enhanced by different parts of the brain responsible for memory, emotion, language, and higher-level cognitive processing involved in decision making, a network that Gordon Shepherd refers to as the brain flavour system (4). The neurological relationship of flavour perception to higher-level cognition and language processing supports Lakoff and Johnson's assertions regarding the importance of basic sensorimotor input to the creation of primary metaphors. John Prescott, too, observes a close correspondence between language and taste. He writes, "Sweetness is embedded in our language as a metaphor for positive experiences in general [...] [whereas] 'bitter' and 'sour' clearly reflect unpleasant emotions" (30). Such associations are a consequence of inborn hedonic and anhedonic reactions to these tastes which are common to all anatomically standard human beings.[11] A sweet taste elicits a pleasurable response because the body instinctively associates it with high-energy sugary foods, whereas bitter tastes may elicit disgust because they suggest the presence of toxins. Prescott observes, "The origin of this use of tastes to describe such everyday emotions lies in the universal role that tastes play as in-built arbiters of what is good and bad in those things that we consume" (30). In terms of embodied cognition, the hedonic and anhedonic flavour responses Prescott describes are projected onto more abstract experiences of pleasure and disgust to create primary metaphors.

This cross-domain mapping results in the kinds of complex taste metaphors found in *Guzmán de Alfarache*. Guzmán frequently compares positive hedonic experiences to sweet flavours such as honey, delectable fruits, almond pastries (*alfajor*), and syrupy compote (*almíbar*), whereas he compares unpleasant experiences to bitter flavours such as aloe (*acíbar*) and bile (*hiel*) or sourness, as when his master regarded him "with an expression such as one who has just tasted vinegar" (1: 326).[12] This figurative use of language not only is consistent with Lakoff and Johson's theory of embodied cognition but also reflects the neurological processes involved in taste and flavour perception described by Shepherd and Prescott.

However, the novel's complex metaphors related to taste are not limited to describing what is merely pleasant or unpleasant. In the narrative world of *Guzmán de Alfarache* what tastes sweet on the outside often hides within it an unexpected bitterness. Taste, then, also relates to the idea of *desengaño*, or disillusionment, a theme identified by a number of critics as essential to understanding the novel.[13] In this regard sweetness is revealed to be an illusory sensation, or *engaño*, that often hides some sort of corruption. Consequently, it is not unusual for Guzmán to speak of falsehood and truth in terms of sweetness and bitterness or other unpleasant tastes and sensations. Hypocrites, for example, "are like dates: they are sweet on the outside and speak in honeyed words, yet have hardness in their souls" (2: 263).[14] Regarding invitations to dine, he observes, "this business of guests is a fine mystery: I have always found that he who invites has a honeyed mouth and bitter hands. [Hosts] promise with sincerity and give with avarice; they invite with joy and eat with sadness" (1: 463).[15] This opposition between sweetness and bitterness offers further insight into the role of cognitive embodiment in Guzmán's figurative language. At the beginning of Part 2 he relates taste, truth, and falsehood through a series of puns on the word *pícaro* and the various meanings of the verb *picar*.[16] He tells the reader, "Either I tell you truths or lies. No, not lies [...]; I speak truths and they taste bitter to you. Their taste offends you because they smack of your offences" (2: 42).[17] Here he assumes the reader shares with the *pícaro* a preference for the false and appealing, eschewing bitter truths for sweet lies, and he takes for granted that his moral digressions will be taken as noisome distractions from his otherwise amusing stories. By means of yet another taste metaphor, Guzmán offers insight into the challenge of interpreting his multifarious approach to narration, remarking that he has deceptively concealed the bitter truths he wishes to convey by coating them with humour:

> I can already hear them tell you, reader, to cast me into a corner, because they grow weary listening to me. They have a thousand reasons. That since they are truly truths of which I treat they are not for amusement, but rather for enlightenment; not for waggery, but rather to be studied closely and then thoroughly remedied. Yet, lest the purgative disgust you with its foul odor and taste and you fail to take it, let us cover it with a bit of gold, something that looks appealing. (2: 377)[18]

In this passage Guzmán characterizes his moralizing as a medical purgative foul to the taste but good for the health. The purgative truths he offers are therefore concealed within the outwardly amusing tales of his antics, recalling Alemán's remarks in the preface: "Do as you read and read as you will; and don't laugh at the anecdote and miss the antidote" (1: 111).[19] The stories thus serve to entice the reader who by consuming them also guzzles down a healthy dose of sound advice from a repentant sinner. Guzmán is, after all, narrating his life from the sobering perspective of the Spanish galley to which he has been sentenced after running afoul of the law in Seville.

Yet another kind of taste metaphor that appears in *Guzmán de Alfarache* has to do with the acquisition of food and flavour preferences. This type of metaphor goes beyond the cross-domain mapping of inborn hedonic taste reactions to reflect the process of evaluative conditioning by which humans learn flavour preferences and aversions. According to Prescott, though the hedonic reactions to the five basic tastes are present from birth, the appeal of retronasal smells and, consequently, flavours, is learned from experience and is highly subjective (63–4). The brain flavour system also exhibits a high degree of plasticity in that flavour perceptions and preferences can change over time with repeated exposure to tastants and the contexts in which food consumption occurs.[20] In this way the brain flavour system learns to discriminate between closely related flavours and develop preferences for frequently consumed foods that do not produce adverse effects such as nausea on the body. Inborn hedonic taste reactions and frequency of exposure combined with accompanying contextual and behavioural factors contribute to the acquisition of flavour preferences. This process of evaluative conditioning explains why, even though the basic flavour of sweetness elicits a pleasurable response in the human brain, preference for the level of sweetness in a given food's flavour differs from person to person (Prescott 44). Such is the power of evaluative conditioning that even inborn negative reactions to certain tastes and flavours can be overcome. The natural aversion to the pain induced by the capsaicin molecules found in chili peppers, for example, becomes a pleasing flavour component for those conditioned by repeated exposure to spicy foods (G. Shepherd 131). Cultural background, family traditions, individual differences, memory, and conscious thought all therefore play a role in training the brain flavour system to interpret the raw sensorimotor information it receives from the neurons responsible for olfaction, taste, and touch.

Although cognition is a hierarchical process in which the deep, lower-level neurological structures of the cognitive unconscious shape the form and function of higher-level psychological processes, the foregoing account of the brain flavour system demonstrates that higher-level processes nevertheless play an essential role in organizing and interpreting sensorimotor information, illustrating Hogan's principle of the "downward projection of structure" (207).[21] Hogan explains that, even as the laws of neurobiology place limits on psychological structures, "patterns that appear at the level of psychology themselves define certain structural relations in neuroanatomy" (207). Thus, when the brain fires synapses or releases hormones, the mind must organize and interpret these complex neural events as, for example, anger or fear; otherwise they are mere shots in the neurological dark. The same holds true for the perception of flavours as appealing or disgusting. The hedonic aspects of flavour perceptions (as opposed to simple taste perceptions) are not biologically innate but instead constitute what could be considered in Hogan's terms "a contingent feature of secondary structure" and therefore "incompatible with all-consuming biological accounts" (207). Hogan further explains that, while the causal principles of neuroanatomy (e.g., the sensorimotor content of Lakoff and Johnson's cognitive unconscious) are conserved upward, "the selection and segmentation of brain events is a result of their interpretation in mentalistic terms" (208). This implies that while the cognitive unconscious is essential to conscious thought, it is not *the* causal factor. Rather, thought emerges from the interaction of the unidirectional upward flow of sensorimotor information and the downward projection of structure which organizes and interprets this information. In other words, the causal factors of cognition are not strictly asymmetrical but interactive, and the meaning of neurological events is emergent. The brain flavour system demonstrates these principles in that a number of cognitive structures (e.g., memory, language, behavioural state, decision making) must interpret raw gustatory sensations to produce flavour perceptions. In terms of downward projection, "the higher-level structure gives us the meaning in terms of which the lower level is interpreted" (209). These perceptions are highly subjective and contingent upon the personal sensorimotor history of any given individual. In this paradigm cognition is not the unidirectional, asymmetrical process described by Lakoff and Johnson, but a more symmetrical and emergent phenomenon in which the cognitive unconscious is essential but not causal.

In *Guzmán de Alfarache*, taste metaphors frequently foreground the contingency and plasticity of the brain flavour system to suggest that one's capacity for moral and aesthetic judgments are learned through embodied activity and experience. Both prologues which precede Part 1 discuss modes of interpretation in terms of taste. In the first prologue Alemán seems to anticipate a negative reception of his work by the vulgar public (*vulgo*), whom he addresses rhetorically with no little disdain.[22] He writes, "It is nothing new to me, although it may be news to you, oh antagonistic rabble [...] that you are so unworthy and ignorant, that you are so acerbic, envious, and avaricious; that you are so quick to defame, and so slow to praise" (1: 108).[23] He further compares the public to a mouse, writing, "You are but a field mouse; you eat the hard rind of a melon, bitter and foul, and upon reaching the sweet part you find it repulsively cloying" (1: 109).[24] The novel's first reference to taste thus equates a preference for unpleasant food with an inability to appreciate Alemán's literary endeavours or, in other words, to distinguish the good from the bad. Furthermore, this metaphor inverts the gustatory imagery employed in the aforementioned metaphors such as the gilded pill; that is, the outside of the melon is bitter and the inside is sweet instead of the other way around. Evaluative conditioning appears to have overridden the innate hedonic taste reactions of the metaphorical mouse's brain flavour system, and its flavour preferences have been entirely dissociated from nutritional content: the bitter, nutrient-poor rind is pleasing to the taste whereas the sweet, nutrient-rich inside is unpalatable. The inversion of the mouse's hedonic taste reactions would appear to obey the same principles by which the body's natural aversion to capsaicin can be overcome with conditioning. Just as the brain flavour system learns to perceive the burning sensation of capsaicin as pleasant, the mouse has learned through conditioning to prefer the bitter rind to the sweet fruit. The metaphorical implication is that though certain hedonic motivations are innate, they can be trained via secondary, contingent cognitive structures to desire either good things or bad things. By conflating the emergent, conditioned nature of flavour perception with literary tastes, Alemán insinuates that poor reading habits have inured the public to low-quality literary texts. The public enjoys these works simply because they have been conditioned to do so.

In contrast, the second prologue is dedicated to the wise reader (*discreto lector*) whom, writes Alemán, "I truly had in mind as I wrote this book" (1: 111).[25] Stating that he has crafted his work in such a way that only the careful reader will be able to interpret it correctly, he writes, "I tell you many things that I wish to tell you, and others have I written without writing them" (1: 111).[26] It is unclear why he feels compelled to dissimulate his message to the discreet reader, though he alludes vaguely to reasons which prevent him from addressing his topic more explicitly: "You will find that many things are mere sketches or outlines that I refrained from rendering in full colour for reasons which prevented me from doing so. Others are rather more retouched, for I shied away from giving chase and nabbing them, fearful and reluctant to commit some unintended offence" (1: 111).[27] The prologue therefore puts the reader on guard, suggesting that the book's contents should not be taken at face value. Though he offers little in the way of an interpretive key, Alemán cryptically tells the reader, "Gather up, collect this soil, take it into the crucible of consideration, put it to the fire of the spirit, and I assure you that the gold you find therein will enrich you" (1: 111).[28] The act of interpretation, then, is not one of passive reception, but of active consideration. In short, the episodes of the life of Guzmán must be processed by the reader's understanding in order to render their meaning fully intelligible. The prologue concludes with the reference to the "splendid table" cited previously.[29] The variety of material found in the text thus strives to offer something for everyone, whatever the reader's preferences: anecdotes, sermon-like digressions, intercalated novels, as well as the episodic adventures of Guzmán.[30] Like a good meal, there is something to appeal to everyone's tastes in this multifaceted work.

Among the plethora of taste references in *Guzmán de Alfarache*, several in Part 1 relate the learned nature of flavour preferences to the formation of one's moral fibre and the ability to reason. A character's diet, for example, can reveal much about his personality. In chapter 3 of Part 1, Guzmán leaves his home, describing himself as a "mischevious and pampered lad [...] fattened on rashers, buns and butter, and rose-scented honey" (1: 163).[31] In this depiction of a well-fed, spoiled youth, the emphasis on diet is important in that the details provide a basis for understanding fundamental aspects of Guzmán's character according to the principles of sixteenth-century medical theory.[32] Though radically different from twenty-first-century understandings of human nutrition and physiology, early modern medical science shares remarkable conceptual parallels with theories of embodied cognition with regard to its emphasis on the role of the body cognitive processes. In his 1575 *Examen de ingenios para las ciencias* (translated by Richard Carew as *Examination of Men's Wits* in 1594), for example, Huarte de San Juan (1988) writes that diet predisposes humans to behave in certain ways and even affects levels of intelligence. Quoting Plato, he asserts that "one of the things that was most detrimental to a man's wits and good conduct was poor instruction in eating and drinking. Thus, [Plato] advises that we give delicate and well-tempered foods to our children so that, as adults, they know to condemn bad things and choose the good ones" (364–5).[33] If, on the contrary, children consume unhealthy food on a regular basis, the brain and its reasoning faculties will fail to develop properly. Huarte de San Juan's suggestion that the sense of taste should be trained from a young age implicitly recognizes that evaluative conditioning plays a role in the formation of flavour preferences. Likewise, Juan Luis Vives writes in *De anima et vita* (1538) that, though a healthy body will naturally be repulsed by the taste of noxious substances and enjoy the flavour of healthy ones, the normal functioning of the sense of taste can be corrupted by illness or a regular diet of bad food (36). Sixteenth-century medical science thus understood the rudiments of flavour preference plasticity and the role of evaluative conditioning in the brain flavour system.

Of course, Vives and Huarte de San Juan conceived of these processes in terms radically different from those of modern-day cognitive scientists. They based their conclusions on the principles of humoral medicine and faculty psychology, the predominant models of human physiology and cognition of the sixteenth century. Though advances in medical science long ago discredited these models of cognition, I argue that they constitute a kind of cognitive architecture that explains human cognition in terms of embodiment. According to humoral theory, the body consists of four humours derived from the four elements, each with distinct properties: yellow bile, consisting of fire, is hot and dry; black bile, consisting of earth, is dry and cold; blood, consisting of air, is hot and wet; and phlegm, consisting of water, is wet and cold.[34] The humoral balance governs the proper functioning of the body on a physiological level and is influenced by factors such as diet and exercise. Faculty psychology complements humoral medicine by explaining human cognition in terms of the circulation of subtle, material spirits between the faculties of the brain: memory, imagination, and intellect. The quality of these spirits depends largely upon the humoral balance of the body. Food that is too warm and moist, for example, addles one's ability to reason because it renders the spirits in the brain too viscous to circulate properly.

Though the principles of faculty psychology originated in the writings of Aristotle and Galen, Thomas Aquinas's articulation of the theory harmonized the pagan concept and later Arabic interpretations with Christian doctrine.[35] Aquinas furthermore asserted that the body and soul did not exist in isolation from one another but were inextricably bound together. The reason relied on input from the five senses, without which mental processes had no content upon which to operate. Through the uptake and processing of sensory experiences, the mind developed abstract thought from the analogical comparison and recombination of *phantasmata* (miniature images drawn from sensory experiences and the memory) in the imagination. Ruth Harvey writes that in Aquinas's model "the whole process introduces the external world in all its detail to the incorporeal intellect, which deals in abstractions" (54). Aquinas's insistence on the human being's composite nature – a being of spirit *and* body – thus reasserted the debt the intellect owed to sensation (54). According to Aquinas, Harvey concludes, sensory experience was not only "necessary for man's development, but essential to his very nature ... his body is not a prison or a punishment, but a proper constituent part of his nature" (54). In this regard, the soul could not achieve salvation without the cognitive processes that emerged from the human body's sensory interactions with the world. Like Aquinas, Huarte de San Juan acknowledges the hybrid embodied nature of thought in the following terms: "to think that the rational spirit – residing in the body – can operate without a corporeal organ to aid it, goes against all natural philosophy" (121).[36] The embodied nature of thought serves as the basis for his broader argument that the differences between individuals' ability to reason depend on differences in their bodies: "And the reason [for the differences in men's wits] is that the rational spirit is manifested through the body and it does not operate except through the use of its corporeal instruments" (372).[37] In a sense, these explanations of the relation between physiology and cognition constitute a kind of proto-embodied cognitive stance insofar as the material state of the body has a direct effect on the cognitive faculties of the mind.

This embodied explanation of cognition prompted natural philosophers and physicians to look for material explanations for the various manifestations of human character and behaviour. Hence, sixteenth-century dietician Francisco Nuñez de Oria wrote that a child born with a healthy humoral balance and good character could be corrupted by a poor diet: "In this manner the nature of a child born with a well-tempered [humoral] complexion, but raised in idleness and pampered, and fed diverse and at times contrary dishes, is corrupted and he becomes spoiled and uncontrollable" (6).[38] On the other hand, inborn tendencies to vice can be corrected through a healthy diet. The dietician explains that this is because "from good food, good blood is generated; from good blood, good [humoral] complexion and constitution, from which proceeds a good intellect and good judgment, and therefore good conduct" (6).[39] He concludes that "fed and nurtured by wholesome, tempered foods, good conduct arises, as well as the desire to be chaste and to serve God; on the contrary, raising a child in much idleness and pampering, feeding him an abundance of dishes, leads to carnal desires and shameful things, which ends in the commission of atrocious and wicked crimes" (6–7).[40] Given that in sixteenth-century scientific discourse diet could lead to either virtuous behaviours or sin and vice, salvation was as much a matter of embodiment as it was spiritual.

It should therefore come as no surprise that Alemán, a student of medicine and the son of a physician, incorporated elements of these discourses into Guzmán's tale of redemption. Consider, for example, Guzmán's advice for healthy living: "Eat enough to live, for all is superfluous that exceeds that which is necessary, for it is not through [surfeit] that the rich man lives nor the poor man dies; but rather diversity and abundance in dishes is a disease, producing viscous humours which occasion grave mortal afflictions and apoplexies" (1: 293).[41] Descriptions of the things Guzmán eats therefore provide important information about his physical and moral disposition.

What, then, does Guzmán's description of his diet at the beginning of chapter 3 tell the reader? The rich foods he is accustomed to eating would have produced viscous spirits inimical to the proper functioning of his reason. The rashers are made from pork, which, according to sixteenth-century dietetics, is naturally very moist, greasy, and hard to digest.[42] The *mollete*, or bun, too, likely consisted of rich ingredients such as milk, butter, and eggs, which were considered detrimental to the subtlety of the spirits.[43] Nuñez de Oria is critical of such confections because they produce viscous humours: "In brief, all those confections made of eggs, butter, milk, flour [...] and pastries of pine nuts, walnuts, and hazelnuts, prepared with oil and many others of diverse kinds made with unleavened dough all engender viscous humors" (71).[44] Butter, of course, is made from cow's milk, which, according to Andrés Laguna's annotated translation of Dioscorides's *De materia medica* (1555), contains the most fat and viscous humours of any animal's milk (64). Furthermore, milk was believed to be a superfluity of twice-concocted blood which, when consumed, reverted back to blood, thereby increasing the moisture and heat in the body (Albala 75). Finally, the rose-scented honey also would have had a negative effect on the humoral balance of a young man like Guzmán. According to Nuñez de Oria, honey "is harmful to young men, for those with a choleric temperament, those who suffer from fever, and for those whose [humoral] complexion is hot, because it causes excessive heat in them and becomes intense choler and fever, especially in summer; it causes a very bitter humor" (298).[45] Given the negative humoral effect of Guzmán's diet, his characterization of himself as "given to vice" (*vicioso*) is possibly a reference to his poor humoral health. This suggests that the spirits of his cognitive faculties would be thick and lacking in subtlety, thereby inhibiting his ability to reason. What is more, according to Huarte, youth is indeed a factor in poor reasoning, since the moisture in a youth's body makes the spirits thick, unlike those of an older and, hence, drier man who reasons better because his spirits are more subtle (354). Guzmán's diet and age therefore offer an embodied basis for his moral decline because the humoral corruption of the body inhibits the proper functioning of his reasoning faculties and predisposes him to wickedness.

Indeed, throughout the novel Guzmán frequently experiences hunger and malnutrition, which, rather than weaken him physically, actually make him healthier and therefore more astute by correcting his initial humoral imbalance. As an experienced *pícaro* begging in the streets, Guzmán appreciates the health benefits of his particular vocation: "I ate only what was necessary, for my belly was never my god and man does not have to eat more than what is sufficient to live; and in excess it is brutality, for the beast only fattens itself by eating to satiety. In this way, eating with moderation, I neither dulled my spirit nor weakened my body; I did not engender bad humours" (1: 333).[46] As a homeless beggar, Guzmán's health thus improves significantly because he is deprived of the humour-thickening rich foods to which he was accustomed as a child. Dietetics and humoral theory – along with all their implications for embodied cognition – therefore constitute an explicit themes which are directly related to the question of Guzmán's life as a rogue and his eventual reform. Though humoral theory is utterly baseless in the light of modern-day scientific understandings of human nutrition and physiology, its preoccupation with the material, embodied origins of human behaviour and language lends itself to productive interpretive approaches informed by theories of embodied cognition.

Guzmán's vivid sensorimotor experiences of taste, for example, structure the way he thinks about life as well as the language he uses to describe it. Taste is central to key plot developments in Guzmán's early encounters with unscrupulous innkeepers in which his inability to reason will lead to some unfortunate taste-related mishaps. In these episodes the dishes he encounters provide no visual cues as to the precise nature of their contents; thus, taste alone must discern them. Though in both cases something does not taste right, faulty reasoning leads him to swallow his food anyway. In terms of embodied cognition, these episodes dramatize the processes by which gustatory sensorimotor experiences contribute to the emergence of Guzmán's abstract thought and metaphorical language.

The first way in which taste experiences influence Guzmán's abstract thought concerns the discernment of deception. Guzmán eats his first meal on the road at an inn where he is informed that there are only eggs to eat. In a proleptic description, Guzmán the narrator gives the reader a taste of what the young Guzmán has yet to discover about his repast: "that fiend of an innkeeper, either because of the excessive heat or because the fox had killed the hen, mingled the eggs that were ready to hatch with the good ones in a box so as not to incur a total loss" (1: 167).[47] Thus the reader knows what the young Guzmán does not: the innkeeper has mixed the good eggs with the bad. The ensuing description of the meal demonstrates that though his sense of taste detects that something is amiss, Guzmán's rational faculties are not able to correctly interpret the sensory information. A careful reading also reveals that his taste experiences correspond with various aspects of the brain flavour system described by Gordon Shepherd, beginning with his behavioural state. When the innkeeper offers Guzmán the omelette, his hunger is such that he is more interested in filling his belly than tasting the food. He recalls, "I was naive, my stomach empty, my intestines on guard and so empty that they were rubbing together" (1: 168).[48] He swallows the food "as a hog eats acorns" (1: 168), that is, without really tasting it.[49] He admits that despite his haste, "I felt the tender little bones of the unfortunate chicks crunch between my teeth, and it was as if they were tickling my gums" (1: 168).[50] Here the crunch of the tiny bones tells Guzmán that this omelette is unlike others he has eaten. Nevertheless, he is young, inexperienced, and hungry, and therefore incapable of using his sensory data to explain what the strange sensation could be: "It certainly struck me as odd, and even the taste was unlike that of the eggs which I was accustomed to eating in my mother's home; yet in my hunger and fatigue I paid no heed to such thoughts, figuring that it was a consequence of the distance I had travelled and that not all [eggs] were of the same taste and quality" (1: 169).[51] In this passage the combination of mouthfeel and taste inform Guzmán that something is not right, yet his poor reasoning fails to properly interpret his sensory experience. His attribution of the strange taste and feel to the foreignness of the land ultimately proves faulty but is sufficient for the moment to choke down the omelette, especially given his state of hunger. A hungry man, he observes, is indifferent to the sauces that season his meal.[52]

As the day wears on, however, Guzmán's imagination begins to serve up various explanations for the crunchy mouthfeel of the eggs, which he compares to the playing of castanets.[53] Here one sees glimpses of Guzmán's future discernment as the process of rational thought informed by his imaginative faculty considers the possible reasons for a crunchy omelette: "I kept mulling it over in my imagination; and the more I mulled it over, the more varieties of unfortunate possibilities came to mind and my stomach grew upset, for I never suspected anything less than disgusting, seeing [the eggs] so poorly prepared, the oil so black it seemed to be made of candle butts, the pan like a pig, and the bleary eyes of the hostess so muculent" (1: 173).[54] His imagination eventually arrives at the truth of the matter, that is, he reasons his way to a conclusion regarding the crunchy mouthfeel until "like a woman with child, eructations came and went from my stomach to my mouth, until there remained absolutely nothing in my body" (1: 173).[55] Such is the effect of the eggs that Guzmán declares, "And to this day it seems that I can still feel the poor little chicks cheeping there inside me" (1:, 173).[56] The taste experience becomes emblematic of the deceit that awaits him in the adventures to come. Furthermore, Guzmán's frequent recourse to taste and flavour metaphors throughout the novel demonstrate that the embodied nature of the incident structures the way he thinks about deceit as well as the language he uses to describe it.

A second way in which taste sensations influence Guzmán's abstract thought concerns the metaphorical relation of flavour preference plasticity and an individual's ability to discern the truth. His powers of taste perception are challenged once again in chapters 5 and 6 when he and a muleteer order dinner at yet another inn. The innkeeper offers to prepare a meal with what he claims is a recently slaughtered calf. The meat, however, is that of a mule foal which he recently slaughtered to prevent the authorities from discovering that he had allowed a horse and a donkey to interbreed.[57] Serving the foal in a sauce to Guzmán and the muleteer seems an expedient way to dispose of the evidence. Initially, Guzmán guzzles down the mule meat, unaware of what he is eating because, once again, his hunger has overwhelmed his sense of taste. It is only after he is somewhat satiated that he is able to detect that something is amiss: "It did not taste good to me and it smelled of rotten straw" (1: 192).[58] Meanwhile his companion the muleteer enthusiastically eats his fill. Guzmán remarks that the muleteer is incapable of detecting the trick because "he was born among savages, of brutish parents who trained his palate with cloves of garlic; and in matters of taste (never mind their goodness or cleanliness), rustic, vulgar folk seldom distinguish the good from the bad. Most of them lack perfection in their senses" (1: 191).[59] Guzmán's characterization of the muleteer's sense of taste recalls the mouse metaphor of the prologue, only in this instance he also describes the process of evaluative conditioning by which the muleteer learned to eat so indiscriminately. Moreover, he associates the sensory experience of taste with the ability to distinguish between good and bad in terms which foreground the embodied aspects of flavour preference acquisition. Guzmán, however, insists on attributing his own initial lapse in judgment to his behavioural state, adding, "But that I, who had been raised and spoiled by such civil, cleanly parents, should be fooled by the deception: great was my hunger and that excuse exonerates me [...]. Have you never heard that to a hungry man there is no such thing as bad bread?" (1: 192).[60] On the following day the innkeeper serves more of the same, and while the muleteer praises the dish, Guzmán observes, "but speaking the truth, it was bad and stated well who [the muleteer] was" (1: 196).[61] He arrives at this conclusion by way of an intuitive understanding that flavour preferences are learned over time through exposure. By means of this folk psychology, Guzmán is able to surmise the process of evaluative conditioning which resulted in the muleteer's lack of good taste, namely, a diet limited by his humble station in life and lacking in a variety of flavourful foods.[62] The episodes' rich gustatory imagery establishes a thematic relationship between flavour discernment and the ability to reason.

In this regard Guzmán's cognitive development as a *pícaro* is essentially embodied, for it is through his body's activity and experience in the world that he learns to think in abstract terms and speak in metaphors. Furthermore, many taste metaphors that appear in the text reflect the process of evaluative conditioning in a way that creates cross-domain pairings between learned food preferences and Guzmán's adoption of a picaresque lifestyle. The implications of these metaphors are important for a straight reading of the novel in that they allow for the plasticity of cognitive processes necessary for Guzmán's to redeem himself. At various points in the novel Guzmán insists that he was not born a *pícaro* but rather developed a taste for wrongdoing from repeated exposure to its rewards. The appeal of a wicked lifestyle was therefore not a fundamental, inborn character flaw but learned, just as one learns to prefer certain flavours over others. The plasticity of flavour preferences therefore constitutes the ideal metaphor for this morality tale: developing a taste for unhealthy food is in many ways a precursor for developing a taste for bad behaviours, since the humoral properties of the food one eats creates a predisposition to certain behaviours or character traits. Guzmán's use of taste metaphors supports this reading of the text by associating his gradual perdition with the process of evaluative conditioning. He admits, for example, that his transformation from spoiled child into a *pícaro* occurred over a long period of time as a consequence of repeated experiences: "I admit that in the beginning I was somewhat uneager, unwilling, and above all afraid; as a way of life utterly new to me, it suited me poorly and I took to it even worse, for all beginnings are difficult. But later I developed a taste for the syrupy-sweet life of a *pícaro* and I threw myself blindly into it" (1: 277).[63] Through its metaphorical association with a degenerate lifestyle sweetness (here a kind of syrup or *almíbar*) takes on a sinful connotation, especially given the fact that Guzmán turns a blind eye (literally, "*a cierra ojos*") to his wrongdoing. As a result of his success as a beggar, he adds later, "I developed a craving for my new vocation such that I simply couldn't be quit of it" (1: 386).[64] By connoting an unhealthy tendency to feed the appetites rather than one's hunger, the word *craving* (*golosina* in the original) implies that his new lifestyle was not so much a vocation as a vice.[65] Survival tactics born of necessity thus grew into addictive habits, which left him hungry for more. Guzmán's ill-gotten rewards offered an appealing alternative to the curse bequeathed to humankind by Adam, whom God expelled from Eden, declaring, "By the sweat of your brow you will eat your food until you return to the ground" (New International Version, Gen. 3.19). Alonso de Barros's characterization of Guzmán as "a son of leisure" (1: 115) in his prefatory *Elogio* to Part 1 thus seems apt.[66] Considered in this light, the *pícaro's* sin consists in his refusal to sweat for his food, a point made all the clearer by Guzmán's libertine praise of the "briviatic art" (1: 385), a way of life which not only frees him from work but liberates each of the five senses:[67]

> Who in the world today more licentiously and truly delights [in the five senses] than a poor man, or with more security or better taste? And since I've already said taste, I'll start with that one: for there is no pot from which we don't skim, no dish we don't try, nor any banquet from which we do not take our share. Whither does the poor man go that, if he is turned away from a house today, tomorrow he will not return there and receive alms? He visits them all, he begs in each, and enjoys the lot. He can tell you very well in which house the food is seasoned best. (1: 407)[68]

In Guzmán's cynical description of poverty, there is not only freedom from want but a freedom to indulge the senses, especially that of taste, by taking advantage of the generous alms of the better-off. It would therefore be in keeping with the novel's figurative use of taste to say that Guzmán savours his life as a *pícaro* because it enables him to indulge his appetites with minimal effort.

The connection between the taste of sweetness, wickedness, and evaluative conditioning is made all the more apparent by Guzmán's frequent theft of food, especially while he serves as a page in the home of a Roman cardinal. The cardinal stocks his residence with fruit, honey, and preserves to indulge his appetite for sweet foods. Guzmán and the other pages are frequently tempted to steal these delicacies from the table or larder. Describing the cardinal, Guzmán writes, "He was genteel and without a hint of malice, always pleasant, and acted in good faith without duplicity, though he was rather importunate and more than a little pensive" (1: 443).[69] This characterization of the cardinal is nevertheless suspect, given the established association between a rich diet and poor moral character elsewhere in the novel. In humoral terms the cardinal's consumption of sweets creates the suspicion that he is somehow morally wayward, considering that this diet likely produces the kinds of thick and heavy humours which lead to vice and sin. Yet any criticism of the cardinal's lifestyle is implicit and must be inferred. This covert criticism of a member of the clergy is perhaps one of the veiled topics Alemán alludes to in his prologue, which he dissimulates in order not to "commit some unintended offence."

The cardinal's sweets certainly have a deleterious effect on Guzmán, who had already acquired a taste for ill-gotten gains living in the streets. He writes that, in the house of the cardinal, "I later became what theretofore had never crossed my mind, that is, a glutton for sweets" (1: 438).[70] Here the embodied connection between sweetness and sin grows especially strong in that in order to eat the sweets Guzmán has to steal them. Not only does repeated exposure contribute to the development of a preference for sweets, but the brain flavour system also establishes links between the pleasing flavour and theft, the associated behaviour. Thus, Guzmán writes, "I went after sweets like a blind man his prayers. Those which my eyes chanced to glimpse were no longer safe in the coffer. My hands were eagles, and as the stag draws serpents from the bowels of the earth with its inhalations, so it was with me: for no sooner did I set my eyes upon something to eat than it surrendered itself into my mouth" (1: 438).[71] Guzmán therefore becomes adept at stealing the fruits and preserves that the cardinal keeps in a locked chest, such as when he steals the *zamboa castellana*, a kind of grapefruit. He recalls the delicious fruit, writing, "[it] seemed a glowing golden ember to the eye and its flavour was such that even today I can still taste it in my mouth: never in my life have I eaten anything better or seen its equal" (1: 440).[72] The memory of pleasure associated with the theft would have a lasting effect on Guzmán. He writes, "the wicked ways that I learned became indelible. It would have been easier to give up breathing than to get by without them. This was even truer of the childish antics I had already gotten the hang of and savoured" (1: 441).[73] In these passages the narrative descriptions of sweet taste combine with the figurative language used to describe how Guzmán acquires a taste for wrongdoing. Crime is sweet for Guzmán because he associates it with the hedonic sensations of sweet flavours, as the episodes in the house of the cardinal demonstrate. The same process of evaluative conditioning that creates a preference for sweet food thus is also in part responsible for conditioning him to live life as a *pícaro*. Guzmán is not therefore an inherently wicked person, but rather is conditioned to engage in wicked behaviour through his embodied activity and experience.

By the end of Part 2 Guzmán's stint in the galley provides a new kind of conditioning, which sets him on a path to Christian righteousness. According to the principles of cognitive embodiment and, importantly, the downward projection of structure, his conversion can be understood to emerge from the interaction of higher-level mental structures and the lower levels of sensorimotor experience. Exposed to the discomforts of the ship and the constant threat of theft and mistreatment at the hands of the other galley slaves, Guzmán soon regrets the wicked behaviours that led to his deplorable fate. Though unpleasant, the conditions on the galley are propitious for the improvement of his humoral health and eventually that of his spirit. The food, for example, consists of little more than dry, hardened biscuits, and the strenuous physical work of rowing expels moisture from his body. According to the principles of humoral medicine, the combination of simple fare and exercise cleanses the body of viscous humours, thereby improving the cognitive faculties of the brain. Huarte de San Juan, for instance, observes the following regarding the health of galley slaves: "there is no better remedy for the health than to expose the body to all weather: hot, cold, humid, and dry. And thus Aristotle asks why it is that those who live on galleys are healthier and have better colour than those who live in malarial lands" (368).[74] Those who live exposed to the weather, he explains, grow accustomed to all conditions such that they develop immunity to the harmful effects of sudden changes in the air. Before the advent of microbiology, the quality of the air was indeed believed to be responsible for disease, as evidenced by the word malaria itself (*mal-aria* or *bad air*). The healthy change appears to restore Guzmán's ability to reason well and he credits divine providence for this blessing in disguise, writing that sometimes God clouds the understanding of men like him so as to lead them into circumstances in which they must "acknowledge their sin and in time with clear vision know him, serve him, and be saved" (490).[75] Unlike Guzmán's previous bouts of health when he lived hand to mouth in the streets, the galley environment prevents him from applying his rational powers to anything but the contemplation of his predicament. Eventually, Guzmán realizes the error of his ways and begs God's forgiveness: "Do you see, Guzmán, the summit of the mountain of misery where your shameful sensuality has gotten you? You are now high enough that you could jump into the abyss of hell or with ease raise your hand and reach heaven" (505).[76] After a tearful night spent pondering these matters, Guzmán reasons his way to salvation: "Wake from this dream once and for all. Turn and see that, although it is true that your sins brought you here, use these punishments so that they bear fruit. You looked for wealth to employ; look for it now so as to purchase eternal bliss" (505).[77] When he awakes, he feels a change has taken place: "I found myself changed, not myself, nor with that old heart from before. I gave thanks to the Lord and I implored him to take me in his hand" (506).[78] Given that Guzmán the narrator has insisted on his repentance throughout the novel, his decision to reach for heaven at this juncture should come as no surprise to the reader. The scene is, rather, a rendering of the conditions that result in the conversion, a capstone that contributes to the narrative and thematic unity of Guzmán's life story in which the narrator and protagonist collapse into one entity for the remainder of the book. Furthermore, the scene is a dramatization of the downward projection of structure that changes the way Guzmán experiences the sensorimotor information channelled into his conscious mind via the cognitive unconscious. In the context of the galley, Guzmán's learned hedonic impulses are susceptible to the discipline of higher-level cognitive processes such as memory, emotion, and discursive reason. In this case Christian salvation discourse constitutes the conscious interpretive paradigm by which Guzmán mentally organizes his life experiences, thereby enabling him to moderate behaviours conditioned through hedonic responses to his environment. Guzmán's salvation and, consequently, the straight reading of the novel emerge from the interactions of embodied processes and higher-level cognitive functions of the conscious mind.

Moreover, this interpretation of conversion as an instance of downward projection of structure is consistent with an appetite-related metaphor Guzmán uses to characterize the human condition. He writes that the human soul is composed of two parts, one rational and divine and the other of natural corruption (434). The opposing tendencies of each create an infernal war between the appetite and reason. The appetite, he writes, "persuades us with that which best conforms to our nature, with that which we find the most appealing, such that we find pleasure in engaging in it and desire to acquire it" (434).[79] The reason, on the other hand, is "like a teacher, who, to correct us well, always carries the whip of reprehension on his person, scolding us for the bad things we do" (434).[80] While one could interpret this opposition of reason and appetite as an example of mind-body dualism, Guzmán's description of a composite soul instead suggests a Thomistic, hybrid human being in which embodiment is an essential aspect of its nature. In this respect Guzmán's reason and appetite reside entirely within the body. The teacher is thus a metaphorical representation of the downward projection of structure from conscious mental faculties. While the appetite arises from hedonic impulses, the rational faculties of the conscious mind organize and structure behavioural responses to the environment according to discursive mental content which, in Guzmán's case, happens to be the discourse of Christian salvation.

Yet Guzmán's conversion is not entirely unequivocal, and his recidivism demonstrates the persistence of hedonic behaviours structured by embodied cognition. Guzmán finds his old habits hard to break, explaining, "Later I tried to confess frequently, reforming my life, cleaning my conscience, a course I followed for some days. Yet I was made of flesh. With each step I stumbled and fell many times;

yet, with regard to my bad conduct, I remained much improved from that point onward" (2: 506).[81] Guzmán's candour regarding his continued failings would appear to be an endearing expression of humility, confirming that, though he is of flesh, his heart, at least, is in the right place. Furthermore, his statements are consistent with his frequent digressions on morality throughout the narrative, as well as his insistence that his confessions be taken as examples of how *not* to live one's life, as in his introduction to Part 2: "I declare [...] that this general confession that I am making, this public show of my life that I depict for you, is not for you to imitate me, but rather that, once known, you can correct your own faults" (2: 42).[82] These elements of the text form the basis of the straight reading of the *Guzmán* as a didactic tale of Christian repentance and salvation. Furthermore, it is a tale in which sixteenth-century science serves faith by showing that salvation must be embodied by properly caring for and disciplining the body. It is a hopeful vision of human nature in which the means of salvation are at everyone's disposal. Considered from either the perspective of sixteenth-century medical science or twenty-first-century theories of embodied cognition, taste is therefore an apt metaphor for Guzmán's tale of perdition and redemption.

NOTES

1 Patrick Colm Hogan writes that "'cognitive architecture' is just the way cognitive scientists refer to what makes up the human mind" (30). This architecture encompasses the structures, processes, and contents involved in shaping and organizing information from our environment.

2 Barbara Dancygier points out that recent studies in cognitive linguistics offer experimental support for the major claim of cognitive linguistics that "meanings emerge out of the basic levels of embodiment" (25). In empirical terms, embodied cognition therefore holds promise as a stable architecture upon which to base cognitive literary studies.

3 Lakoff and Johnson assert that most "thought is unconscious, not in the Freudian sense of being repressed, but in the sense that it operates beneath the level of cognitive awareness, inaccessible to consciousness and operating too quickly to be focused on" (10). According to their theory, the cognitive unconscious is the causal factor of conscious thought.

4 Even so, Lakoff and Johnson explain that "universal conceptual metaphors are learned; they are universals that are not innate" (57). Insofar as flavour perceptions are concerned, I argue, food preferences and the resulting learned metaphors are far from universal in that they are highly subjective and vary from person to person. Furthermore, higher-level cognitive structures must organize and interpret the flow of information transmitted from gustatory imagery to give it meaning, a process

Patrick Colm Hogan refers to as the "downward projection of structure," which implies an element of symmetry not found in Lakoff and Johnson's theory of embodied cognition.

5 Lakoff and Johnson adapt the concept of blending from a series of publications by Gilles Fauconnier and Mark Turner (Fauconnier and Turner "Conceptual Integration" and "Conceptual Projection"). Fauconnier and Turner have since developed the concept further in *The Way We Think*.

6 All translations are my own."Vi claramente cómo la contraria fortuna hace a los hombres prudentes. En aquel punto me pareció haber sentido una nueva luz, que como en claro espejo me representó lo pasado, presente y venidero" (2010 ed.).

7 Taste and flavour perception is a motor as well as sensory experience in that the mouthfeel of food is related to the movements of the cheeks, jaws, and tongue. Chewing also releases the volatile molecules from food that are perceived as flavour (G. Shepherd 153).

8 "En el discurso podrás moralizar según se te ofreciere: larga margen te queda. Lo que hallares no grave ni compuesto, esto es el ser de un pícaro el sujeto deste libro. Las tales cosas, picardea con ellas: que en las mesas espléndidas manjares ha de haber de todos gustos." *Picardear* can be read as a pun on *pícaro* implying that part of the fun of dining at Guzmán's splendid table is that it may lead one to feel a bit roguish oneself. The *Diccionario de la Real Academia Española* defines *picardear* as, among other things, to teach someone to do or say roguish things or to acquire bad habits. A suggestive synonym offered in the dictionary is *resabiarse*, the reflexive form of *resabiar*: to taste food or drink or to delight in pleasant things. I have translated *picardear* as *revel* because of its hedonistic connotations as well as its orthographic similarity to the word *rebel*. Compare with James Mabb's 1622 translation of the passage: "Such things as these (which are not very many) sport theyself a while with them, jest & play the wagge, and afterwards shake hands with them" (n.p.).

9 "vinos blandos y suaves, que alegrando ayuden a la digestión."

10 Retronasal olfaction is largely responsible for the perception of flavour in the mouth. Olfactory sensory neurons located in the nasopharynx detect the volatile molecules released from masticated food to produce the sensation of flavour when one chews with the mouth closed or exhales. Orthonasal olfaction, on the other hand, is responsible for the perceptions of the scents we detect by inhaling. Both retro- and orthonasal olfactory sensations – flavour and smell – are produced in the olfactory cortex. For a thorough description of this process see Gordon Shepherd's *Neurogastronomy*.

11 Research has demonstrated that these reactions to sweet and bitter tastes are relatively independent of culture and diet in adults and are present at birth (Prescott 31).

12 "mi amo me hizo un gesto de probar vinagre."

13 Carlos Blanco Aguinaga, for example, writes that the novel reveals the world to be full of lies and deceit through what he terms a dogmatic realism of disillusionment (316). Gonzalo Sobejano, too, writes that disillusionment is a cardinal motif in *Guzmán de Alfarache* (728) and stands in absolute opposition to *engaño* or falsehood.

14 "Son como los dátiles, lo dulce afuera, la miel en las palabras y lo duro adentro en el alma."

15 "Esto de huespedes tiene misterio: siempre hallé en el que convida boca de miel y manos de hiel. Con franqueza prometen, con avaricia dan, con alegría convidan y con tristeza comen."

16 According to the *Diccionario de la lengua española*, *picar* can mean, among other things, to nibble on something, to irritate the palate, to sting, or to provoke someone with words and actions. The context of this passage, rich in taste metaphors related to morality, suggests a pun that draws on all of these connotations. I have attempted to convey this play on words in my translation.

17 "O te digo verdades o mentiras. Mentiras no [...]; digo verdades y hácensete amargas. Picaste dellas porque te pican."

18 "Ya le oigo decir a quien está leyendo que me arronje a un rincón, porque le cansa de oírme. Tiene mil razones. Que, como verdaderamente son verdades las que trato, no son para entretenimiento, sino para el sentimiento; no para chacota sino para con mucho estudio ser miradas y muy remediadas. Mas, porque con la purga no hagas ascos y la dejes de tomar por el mal olor y sabor, echémosle un poco de oro, cubrámosla por encima con algo que bien parezca." Describing the trope of the gilded pill (*píldora dorada*) in his 1611 dictionary, *Tesoro de la lengua castellana o española*, Sebastián de Covarrubias observes that apothecaries coated pills in gold to conceal the taste of the bitter aloes within. The proverbial gilded pill could thus refer to anything whose outward appeal masked an unpleasant secret (Micó, I: 167n17).

19 "haz como leas lo que leyeres y no te rías de la conseja y se te pasa el consejo."

20 This plasticity is due in part to the body's ability to regenerate taste and smell neurons from stem cells throughout adult life (G. Shepherd 200).

21 I am indebted to Professor Hogan for his helpful explanations of this concept, an original insight which appears in his volume *Cognitive Science, Literature, and Arts*.

22 In *La novela picaresca española*, Francisco Rico notes that books with two prologues, one condemning the vulgar public (*vulgo*) and another praising the wise reader (*discreto lector*), are quite common (91n). For more on the rhetorical address to the *vulgo*, see Green.

23 "No es nuevo para mí, aunque lo sea para ti, oh enemigo vulgo ... lo poco que vales y sabes, cuán mordaz, envidioso y avariento que eres; qué presto en disfamar, qué tardo en honrar." Like the English word *acerbic*, the Spanish word *mordaz* connotes both an unpleasant taste and biting criticism.

24 "Eres ratón campestre, comes la dura corteza del melón, amarga y desabrida, y en llegando a lo dulce te empalagas."

25 "verdaderamente consideré cuando esta obra escribía."

26 "Mucho te digo que deseo decirte, y mucho dejé de escribir, que te escribo." Here Alemán's meaning is ambiguous. Mabb translates the passage thus: "I have much to say unto thee, and desire to doe, yet may not tell it thee. I have written unto thee, yet have I left out much of what I would have written" (n.p.). I preserve the paradoxical phrasing of the original in my translation to suggest that it is a caveat to read between the lines of Guzmán's tale.

27 "Muchas cosas hallarás de rasguño y bosquejadas, que dejé de matizar por causas que lo impidieron. Otras están algo más retocadas, que huí de seguir y dar alcance, temeroso y encogido de cometer alguna no pensada ofensa."

28 "Recoge, junta esta tierra, métela en el crisol de la consideración, dale fuego de espíritu, y te aseguro hallarás oro que te enriquezca" (1: 111). While the reference to the extraction of gold from earth in a crucible (that is, transmutation) may suggest an alchemical reading, metaphors comparing the purification of gold and spiritual purification also appear in various verses of the Bible: Psalms 12.6, Proverbs 17.3 and 27.21, and Ezequiel 22.18. See Pierre Darnis for a Paracelsan-alchemical interpretation of the *Guzmán*.

29 According to Jeanneret, the trope of the banquet was important to early modern writers in that during a meal "[man] shares his pleasure equitably between sense and senses: he brings into balance the desires which are normally disjoined [...] [N]ot only does [the banquet] celebrate the union of man and nature and of man and society, it also symbolizes the integration of body and spirit" (32). One finds echoes of this trope in Alemán's prologue to the wise reader.

30 In her study of early modern Spanish miscellanies, Asunción Rallo Gruss states that the sheer variety of content in *Guzmán de Alfarache* leads one to ask whether or not it would have been considered a miscellany in its own right in the sixteenth and seventeenth centuries (165).

31 "muchacho vicioso y regalado [...] cebado a torreznos, molletes y mantequillas y sopas de miel rosada."

32 Regarding the use of medical discourse in *Guzmán de Alfarache*, Francisco Ramírez Santracruz writes that descriptions of characters' bodies and health are so detailed that they are comparable to clinical histories of patients suffering from an illness (153).

33 "una de las cosas que más echaba a perder el ingenio del hombre y sus buenas costumbres era la mala educación en el comer y beber. Por tanto, aconseja [Platón] que a los niños les demos alimentos y bebidas delicadas y de buen temperamento, para que, cuando mayores, sepan reprobar lo malo y elegir lo bueno." Translations of Huarte and Núñez de Oria are my own.

34 Mary Thomas Crane observes that the perceptually grounded principles of humoral medicine "are clearly similar to the 'conceptual metaphors' that George Lakoff and Mark Johnson see as structuring human thought and language" (107). Humoral

medicine provided explanations of processes in the body that could not be seen or felt in terms of analogical comparisons with what could be directly experienced: heat, cold, wetness, and dryness.

35 Though many early modern Spanish descriptions of faculty psychology refer only to the intellect, memory, and imagination, Aquinas divides the faculties into five: the *sensus communis*, the imagination, the *cogitativa* or *ratio particularis*, memory, and *fantasia*. Ruth Harvey describes the full process in detail in her volume *The Inward Wits* (53–7).

36 "porque pensar que el ánima racional – estando en el cuerpo – puede obrar sin tener órgano corporal que le ayude, es contra toda la filosofía natural."

37 "Y es la causa, ser el ánima racional acto del cuerpo, y no obrar sin aprovecharse de sus instrumentos corporales."

38 "Que ansí el niño que de su complexión nasce templado, pero por criarse en ociosidad y regalo, y con manjares diversos, y a las vezes contrarios, se corrompe su naturaleza y se haze vicioso y desenfrenado."

39 "del buen manjar, se engendra buena sangre, de buena sangre, buena complexión y contextura, de donde procede el buen entendimiento y buen juyzio, y dende buenas costumbres."

40 "apascentandose y criandose de buenos y templados alimentos, proceden las buenas costumbres, y el dessear ser castos, y servir a Dios, por el contrario, de criarle en mucho ocio y regalo, mucha abundancia de manjares, procede el desseo de luxuria y cosas torpes, de donde se cometen atroces y fascinorosos delictos."

41 "Come con que vivas, que fuera de lo necesario es todo superfluo, pues no por ello el rico vive ni el pobre muere; antes es enfermedad la diversidad y abundancia en los manjares, criando viscosos humores y dellos graves accidentes mortales y apoplegías."

42 Ken Albala writes that though Galen described pork as highly nutritious, later Christian authors noted "its phlegmy, gross [i.e., thick or viscous], and corruptible substance" and Renaissance authors "refuted the idea that readers should eat it regularly" (70). Cold and moist, pork requires "hot and dry correction" (90), without which the body's own natural heat may be insufficient to digest it, resulting in "gross blood, crass humors, and dull spirits" (92–3).

43 Covarrubias (1987) describes a *mollete* as "el pan regalado y blando" (553), that is, a roll probably prepared with lots of butter or milk. In his edition of *Guzmán de Alfarache* (2010), Micó notes that in modern Spanish Guzmán's *mollete* would likely be called a *bollo*, that is, a kind of bun or pastry (163).

44 "En fin todas aquellas composturas que se hazen de huevos, manteca, leche, harina ... y tortadas de piñones, nuezes, avellanas, conficionadas con azeyte, y otras muchas cosas hechas de massa sin levadura, de diversas figuras, todas engendran gruesos humores."

45 "es dañosa para los mancebos, para los coléricos, para los que padecen calentura, para los calientes de complexión, porque causa en ellos incendio, y hazese colera y calentura agudas, especial en tiempo de estio, causa un humor muy amargo."

46 "Comía lo que me era necesario, que nunca fue mi dios mi vientre y el hombre no ha de comer más de para vivir lo que basta, y en excendiendo es brutalidad, que la bestia se harta para engordar. Desta manera, comiendo con regla, ni entorpecía el ánimo ni enflaquecía el cuerpo; no criaba malos humores."

47 "que a la bellaca de la ventera, con el mucho calor o que la zorra le matase la gallina, se quedaron empollados, y por no perderlo todo los iba encajando con otros buenos." Interestingly, Andrés Laguna writes that eggs fertilized by a rooster are the healthiest (149).

48 "Halléme bozal, el estómogo apurado, las tripas de posta, que se daban unas con otras de vacías." I have translated "de posta" as "on watch" from the expression "estar de posta" (to be on watch or guard duty). There is some debate among Hispanist scholars as to the meaning of this expression in this context. See Micó 168n26.

49 "como el puerco la bellota"

50 "sentía crujir entre los dientes los tiernecitos huesos de los sin ventura pollos, que era como hacerme cosquillas en las encías."

51 "Bien es verdad que se me hizo novedad, y aun en el gusto, que no era como los otros huevos que solía comer en casa de mi madre; más dejé pasar aquel pensamiento con la hambre y cansancio, pareciéndome que la distancia de la tierra lo causaba y que no eran todos de un sabor ni calidad."

52 "Tan propio es al hambriento no reparar en salsas" (1: 169). Hunger related proverbs recur throughout the *Guzmán* and emphasize that flavour perception is often contingent upon a body's state of satiety.

53 "aquel tañerme castañetas los huevos en la boca" (1: 173).

54 "Fui dando en esta imaginación, que, cuanto más la seguía, más géneros de desventuras me representaba y el estómago se me alteraba; porque nunca sospeché cosa menos que asquerosa, viéndolos tan mal guisados, el aceite negro, que parecía de suelos de candiles, la sartén puerca y la ventera lagañosa." The description of the food as black recalls Shepherd's observation that colour plays a role in flavour perception.

55 "[como] mujer preñada, me iban y venían eruptaciones del estómago a la boca, hasta que de todo punto no me quedó cosa en el cuerpo."

56 "Y aun el día de hoy me parece que siento los pobrecitos pollos piándome acá dentro." This passage is reminiscent of Andrés Laguna's anecdote about spoiled eggs in his annotations of Dioscorides's *Materia médica*: "aquellos [huevos] que allí comí (lo qual no digo para alabarlos) eran muy vellacos, y dessabridos: y aun me parece que desde entonces regueldo a ellos, y que me pian pollicos en el estomago" (149).

57 As Samuel Gili y Gaya notes in his edition of *Guzmán de Alfarache*, such cross-breeding had been forbidden since the rein of Enrique III in order to preserve the pure bloodlines of horses. The innkeeper's crime was punishable by the confiscation of the donkey and a fine of 10,000 *maravedís* (138n6).

58 "No me supo bien, olióme a paja podrida."

59 "nació entre salvajes, de padres brutos y lo paladearon con un diente de ajo, y la gente rústica, grosera, no tocando a su bondad y limpieza, en materia de gusto pocas veces distingue lo malo de lo bueno. Fáltale a los más la perfección en los sentidos."

60 "Mas que yo, criado en regalo, de padres políticos y curiosos, no sintiese tal engaño, grande fue mi hambre y esta excusa me disculpa [...]. ¿No has oído decir que a la hambre no hay mal pan?"

61 "pero hablando verdad, ello era malo y decía bien quien era."

62 Hogan defines folk psychology as "a set of pragmatic ideas, which are only partly explicit, and which have been developed over a period of time in order to deal with daily life. Thus it does not define a cognitive architecture systematically and precisely" (32).

63 "te confieso que a los principios anduve algo tibio, de mala gana y sobre todo temeroso; que, como cosa nunca usada de mí, se me asentaba mal y le entraba peor, porque son dificultosos todos los principios. Mas después me fui saboreando con el almíbar picaresco, de hilo me iba por ello a cierra ojos."

64 "puso golosina el oficio nuevo para no dejarlo."

65 Covarrubias defines *golosina* as "la frutilla, o cosa dulce, que no se come tanto por mantenimiento, como por gusto" (441) and a *goloso* as "él que busca manjares de mucho gusto para el paladar, atendiendo mas a esto que a dar buen mantenimiento al estomago" (441).

66 "un hijo del ocio"

67 The *Oxford English Dictionary* provides the following definition of *briviatic*: "Of vagrants or medicants" (n.p.). The entry adds that the word entered English usage with Mabb's translation of *Guzmán de Alfarache*. In a footnote Micó defines *arte bribiática*, the original Spanish expression, thus: "el arte de los holgazanes y de los pícaros profesionales que vivían de la mendiguez" (385n7).

68 "¿Quién hay hoy en el mundo, que más licensiosa ni francamente goce [de los cinco sentidos] que un pobre, con mayor seguridad ni gusto? Y pues he dicho gusto, comenzaré por él, pues no hay olla que no espumemos, manjar de que no probemos ni banquete de donde no nos quepa parte. ¿Dónde llegó el pobre, que si hoy en una casa le niegan, mañana no le den? Todas las anda, en todas pide, de todas gusta y podrá decir muy bien en cuál se sazona mejor."

69 "Era hombre donoso, sin punta de malicia, todo del buen tiempo, hecho a la buena fe, sin mal engaño, salvo que era importuno y más de un poco imaginativo."

70 "di en una cosa después, que jamás me había pasado por el pensamiento, y fue en goloso."

71 "Íbame tras la golosina, como ciego en el rezado. Las que mis ojos columbraban, en el erario no estaban seguras. Mis manos eran águilas; y como el ciervo con el resuello saca las culebras de las entrañas de la tierra, así yo, poniendo los ojos en las cosas de comer, se me rendían viniéndoseme a la boca."

72 "[e]ra un ascua de oro a la vista y después me supo, que hasta hoy lo traigo en la boca: nunca mejor cosa ni su semejante vi en mi vida."

73 "las malas mañas que aprendí, me quedaron indelebles. Así pudiera sustentarme sin ello, como sin resollar; y más aquellas niñerías, que ya les había tomado el tiento y me sabían bien."

74 "Ni hay mejor remedio para la salud que hacer el cuerpo a todos los vientos, calientes, frios, húmidos y secos; y, así, pregunta Aristóteles que es la causa que los que viven en las galeras están más sanos y tienen mejor color que los que viven en tierra paludosa."

75 "es que le ciega Dios el entendimiento, para por aquel camino traerlo en conocimiento de su pecado y a tiempo que con clara vista lo conozca, le sirva y se salve."

76 "¿Ves aquí, Guzmán, la cumbre del monte de las miserias, adonde te ha subido tu torpe sensualidad? Ya estás arriba y para dar un salto en lo profundo de los infiernos o para con facilidad, alzando el brazo, alcanzar el cielo."

77 "Acaba de recordar de aquese sueño. Vuelve y mira que, aunque sea verdad haberte traído aquí tus culpas, pon esas penas en lugar que te sean de fruto. Buscaste caudal para hacer empleo: búscalo agora y hazlo de manera que puedas comprar la bienaventuranza."

78 "halléme otro, no yo ni con aquel corazón viejo que antes. Di gracias al Señor y supliquéle que me tuviese de su mano."

79 "Que, como [el apetito] nos persuade con aquello que más conforma con la naturaleza nuestra, con lo que más apetecemos, y esto sea de tal calidad que nos pone gusto el tratarlo y deseo en conseguirlo."

80 "y por el contrario la razón es como el maestro, que, para bien corregirnos, anda siempre con el azote de la reprehensión en la mano, acusándonos lo mal que obramos."

81 "Luego traté de confesarme a menudo, reformando mi vida, limpiando mi conciencia, con que corrí algunos días. Mas era de carne. A cada paso trompicaba y muchas veces caía; mas, en cuanto al proceder en mis malas costumbres, mucho quedé renovado de allí adelante."

82 "Digo [...] que aquesta confesión general que hago, este alarde público que de mis cosas te represento, no es para que me imites a mí; antes para que, sabidas, corrijas las tuyas en ti."

5 The Aesthetics of Disgust in Miguel de Cervantes and María de Zayas

STEVEN WAGSCHAL

In his 1530 treatise on proper customs and habits for gentlemen who wish to distinguish themselves, *Banquete de nobles caballeros*, Luis Lobera de Avila (1480–1551), royal physician to Charles V, recommends brushing one's teeth in order to prevent bad breath: "Assimismo se lave la boca, y las limosidades de los dientes, porque de no hazerlo, se seguiria hedor en el aliento, y corrupcion en los humores y perturbacion en el celebro. Assimesmo se laven despues de comer, e despues de cenar" (Also, the mouth should be cleaned, and tartar on the teeth, because if not, a stench of the breath would follow, as would corruption in the humours and disturbance in the brain. Also, they should be cleaned after dinner and after supper) (18).[1] These routines are explicitly linked by Lobera with "limpieza de nobles hombres" (cleanliness of noble men), a kind of cleanliness that, among other outcomes, will avoid bad breath and be a mark of distinction. Therefore, it is one of the practices in which a gentleman should engage: "Esto de limpiar la boca y dientes, y peynar la cabeca, con cabello y sin ello y lavar la cara y ojos, y manos y cortar las uñas, se haga continuo, por que de no hacerlo se signe [*sic*] mucho daño. Y es limpieza de nobles hombres, y *los haze differir de otros de no tanta suerte*" (Cleaning one's mouth and teeth, and combing one's head with or without hair, and washing one's face and eyes and hands, and cutting one's nails, should be done continually, because not doing these things would result in much harm. And it is cleanliness of noble men, and *it makes them stand out from others who are not as fortunate*) (19; emphasis added).[2] Teeth-brushing for Lobera is a part of what today we would call "good personal hygiene." One of the ills that would afflict the nobleman without such care is a stench that would pursue him, which others would detect and experience disgust over. This would lead to their appraisal of the man as not clean and, hence, not noble.

This type of association between stench, disgust, and social class is found in many literary works. This chapter examines several literary representations of disgusting objects and situations in the work of Cervantes and Zayas, investigating the manner in which they are presented and the reactions that are prescribed to the reader, which shed light on two tendencies in contemporary studies of disgust. First I will discuss some early modern theoretical understandings of the response of disgust; next I will turn to some current cognitive and philosophical theories of disgust; and finally I will analyse and compare examples from these two early modern Spanish authors, drawing some conclusions about the poetics of disgust in the early modern period and more broadly on the use of disgust aesthetically.

An Early Modern Theoretical View

Lobera de Avila's statements on hygiene clearly demonstrate an appreciation of the relationship between olfactory sensation, the emotion of disgust, and, implicitly, socio-economic or moral judgments. For humanist Joan Lluís Vives (1492–1540) "offensio" (*de offensione*) was a negative emotion triggered by any sensory stimulus that is discordant from that which is pleasing to a particular sense (*De anima et vita* 3.11:586), and it has been translated variously in Spanish and English as "disgusto," "disgust," and "irritation."[3] While not encompassing all of what the modern notion of the emotion would entail, Vives's concept as explained clearly shares elements of disgust, and, among the emotions dealt with in his treatise, this one is clearly the closest to what we would call by that name today. According to Vives, one can experience ocular disgust at lines that are not straight and sounds that are disharmonious; with respect to what were considered the lesser senses Vives is more vague. For instance, smells that provoke the emotion are simply defined analytically as "odores certos" (certain smells) (586). Vives's understanding of the emotion is broad and engulfs reflections on falsehood and poor reasoning. He first speaks about general principles (discordance and disharmony), but he later specifies that there are innumerable varieties of this emotion and, with considerable disdain, remarks that various individuals have held singular kinds of idiosyncratic disgust (examples include becoming disgusted at the sound of a pig's squeal or at the sight of the way another man moves his hands). Feeling "offensio" too readily is worthy of contempt, and some people use this reaction as a replacement for their lack of wisdom as they censure all practices. Along these lines Vives suggests that feeling "offensio" is often a sign of weakness and inexperience (593).

In his description of the visceral effects of the emotion Vives focuses on mental processes such as anger and irritation. The minimal affect is "aversion" (*aversatio*), which he calls minimal because this negative feeling is eliminated easily for him by separation from the offending object: "infimum autem aversatio, quum offensio aversione sola et separatione placatur" (the lowest aversion, since it abates by itself and with separation from what is offensive) (594). Vives does not mention a related, key element of disgust that is plain in Lobera de Avila's explanation of "hedor" (stench), involving the visceral feeling beyond aversion that incorporates nausea and even vomiting. In his chapter on taste, however, Vives distinguishes between things that are, by nature, repugnant to taste, due to their noxious or toxic qualities (1.7:146), which is more akin to Lobera's notion. Olfaction is treated in a separate chapter and is explicitly related to taste for Vives, as he draws a connection that is borne out by current scientific studies: "Ita hic sensus magnam habet cum gustu non solum confinitatem, sed et congruentiam; nam cuique, quae bene sapiunt, bene olent" (So this sense has great affinities and congruencies with taste, for what tastes good, smells good, and vice versa) (1.8:150). The sense of smell exists in order to protect animals from ingesting harmful foods and to encourage them to ingest healthful ones (150). Nature, for Vives, seems perfect in this regard. Yet it can be perverted by humans with custom and upbringing. Thus, Vives points out that the best smell of all used to be that of the spring harvest – "Olim nihil habebatur suavius quam odor messis, odor campi verni" (At one time there was nothing more enjoyable than the smell of the harvest, of the fields in spring) (150) – but now, it would seem that court or city life has perverted that experience. Disgust makes people turn away "ad primum velut mali gustum" (at the first bad taste) (3.11:594) so as to help avoid developing a taste for such things.

Modern and Contemporary Theories of Disgust

This early modern exploration of smell, taste, and disgust can be compared fruitfully with modern and contemporary theorization, which can shed light on the insights of early modern authors and help to elucidate which elements of described emotional responses are culturally constructed and which are transhistorical. In the nineteenth century Charles Darwin came to the conclusion that disgust is a universal human emotion that can be found in all societies accompanied by a common physical facial reaction. The disgust expression involves wrinkling the nose, constriction of the nostrils, opening the mouth, and partially sticking out the tongue, the last of which seems like an attempt to repel the offending object. Importantly, this facial expression, known as the "disgust gape," communicates to other humans that there is something wrong with the food being consumed by the person who is experiencing disgust.[4]

In the twenty-first century cognitive and philosophical theory on disgust is highly informed by the late-twentieth-century work of pyschologist Paul Rozin, who delineated eight categories of "core" disgust elicitors, which are followed by

Figure 5.1 *Man receiving treatment for his ailments. Feldtbüch der Wundtartzney* of Hans von Gersdorff (Strassburg: Schott, 1517). Lilly Library, Indiana University, Bloomington, detail.

Figure 5.2. *Man Vomiting.* Flemish drawing by P. Boone (1651). Wellcome Library, London, detail.

philosopher Carolyn Korsmeyer in her recent study *Savoring Disgust*: "1. Contaminated foods; 2. bodily products such as vomit, pus, mucus, sexual fluids and excrement; 3. related violations of hygiene codes; 4. lower order animals such as vermin; 5. violations of the bodily envelope such as wounds or evisceration; 6. perverse sexual activities; 7. signs of death and decay; 8. violations of the moral social code" (qtd in Korsmeyer 32). While the particular objects that satisfy the requirements for provoking disgust may change at times and among cultures, theorists contend that they will always fall into the same broad categories (e.g., while what "stinks" may vary from culture to culture, that certain foodstuffs are considered "stinky" is pan-cultural).[5]

For Rozin, Korsmeyer, and other current thinkers, disgust is markedly more physiological than it was for Vives, since in its extreme form the physiological reaction is accompanied by nausea and vomiting – whereas Vives adduced only an "aversion." The response may be triggered by any sensory stimulus, but most frequently it is one of smell or taste, two of the so-called lesser senses.[6] Like touch, taste requires physical contact between the object that is perceived and the subject who perceives. From the standpoint of the history of philosophy – going back to Aristotle – these contact senses are the most bodily and most base, precisely because they require contact with or proximity to the body for perception, unlike the so-called higher senses – typically sight and sound – which better perceive input from afar. Insofar as smell and taste are chemical senses that require contact with the body, disgust is now thought of in evolutionary terms as a mechanism that works to protect the body from the ingestion of harmful items (as Vives partially understood it), one that typically "follows encounters with spoiled food, sewage, and slime; slugs, maggots, and lice; infected sores, gangrened flesh, and decomposing corpses" (Korsmeyer 5).

Korsmeyer focuses on core or material disgust, drawing on psychological studies, especially Rozin's. As she puts it, "All of these [aforementioned] and some other sensory stimuli will [...] prompt unqualified visceral disgust and may include unpleasant involuntary responses, including the gag reflex, nausea, and even vomiting" (5); "[the] heart rate slows, and blood pressure drops – [...] [there is a] pause in the recoil, [and] a tendency to dwell, albeit with loathing, over the disgusting object" (19). Importantly, this visceral disgust "is aroused in situations entangled with moral, social, or religious precepts, and part of its meaning will derive from those values" (5).

Whereas Vives is most concerned with aversion as a feeling that can be easily abated through self-discipline, I am more interested in exploring the phenomenology and cognitive implications of the experience, in keeping with Korsmeyer and other contemporary theorists. Given the palpable physiological recoil and the subject's lingering upon an object of the emotion, how might an author harness literary or cultural representations of disgust? In which way can a social condition or situation be paired with the visceral reaction of primary (core) disgust? Even more interesting, perhaps, are there instances in which an author relies merely on the immediate aversion without pairing it with a social or moral element? This immediate aversion is exemplified by Korsmeyer as being like the experience "when one recoils from the reek of decomposing flesh before actually recognizing what it is" (23).

Empirical neurological studies demonstrate that the recognition of disgust in others (when a person sees in certain contexts another person make the typical "disgust gape" associated pan-culturally with experiences of disgust, as explained above) occurs in the insula and the basal ganglia regions of the brain. Since the insula is also involved in direct taste aversion as well as the perception of nauseating tastes (upon actual ingestion), research seems to indicate, therefore, that we actually feel at least part of the disgust that we perceive others to be experiencing. We might think of this recognition and potential experience of disgust as a kind of empathy with persons or with characters experiencing disgust in an aesthetic experience. The character or voice that a reader or viewer is to imitate in the experience of this kind of empathic disgust can be called a "mimetic correlate" (Korsmeyer 108).

The Epistemic Value of Moral Disgust

Rozin's eighth category of core disgust – "violations of the moral social code" – is controversial. Is the response of disgust to certain *prima facie* morally wrong actions a core universal response or is it more culturally conditioned than the other seven categories? For Korsmeyer the last category may at times be only a metaphorical extension, not brought about by a sensory trigger (not "core").[7] But she insists that it is a separate core category and that there is significant overlap between core and moral, as when, she explains, disgust is brought about "by human agency with violent purpose" (33). In such cases the experience of disgust is considered not metaphorical but direct. Korsmeyer, following William Ian Miller, whom she cites, believes that there is such a category of triggers in the world that, in an unmediated manner, elicit a disgust response: these triggers consist of "harms that sicken us in the telling, things for which there could be no plausible claim of right: rape, child abuse, torture, genocide, predatory murder and maiming" (Miller 36; qtd in Korsmeyer 33). However, while maiming, torture, and the other horrific activities listed by Korsmeyer and Miller may provoke disgust, I would suggest that it may not be because these activities belong in a separate category based on their immorality, but rather because they also pertain to one of Rozin's preceding seven categories (e.g., maiming partakes of "violations of the bodily envelope"; genocide shows "signs of death and decay").

However, even if there is such a distinct category, it does not follow necessarily that it holds privileged moral epistemic status, as Korsmeyer's quote implies ("sickens us [...] no plausible claim of right"). Indeed, there are two basic positions on this issue; some theorists would like to heed the disgust responses and grant them privileged epistemic status, while others maintain that we should be sceptical, since such responses are highly fallible with respect to moral insight.

While I am in agreement with Korsmeyer on the immorality of all of the examples she adduces in the citation above, I am not convinced that one's experience of disgust when faced with them is probative of their immorality. For one, in many historical cultural contexts disgust at the lower classes, disgust at interracial marriage, and so on were widespread and socially sanctioned, yet these practices and groups are not morally problematic.

For philosopher of cognitive science Daniel Kelly there is yet another more important reason for not privileging the moral epistemic value of disgust. In *Yuck!: The Nature and Moral Significance of Disgust* Kelly provides a case against such moral epistemic value grounded in evolution. In his simplest formulation the disgust response evolved in *homo sapiens* to protect individuals from the ingestion of bad or possibly contaminated foods, while also serving a social communication function of alerting others to avoid such foods. From Kelly's point of view, whenever the disgust response is evoked with respect to a moral issue or situation, it can never have any epistemic value because core physiological disgust is about core issues of disgust (food, etc.), and thus the response has been "co-opted" in such instances. For Kelly such moral associations (whether they end up agreeing or not with contemporary morals or mores) are pernicious to morality in part because they can be co-opted for nefarious purposes and are always beyond the parameters of the original mechanism.[8]

Kelly divides thinkers into two camps based on their view of the moral epistemic value of disgust, placing himself in the second group.[9] First, there is the "deep wisdom" camp, which holds that the disgust response is valuable to intuitions about morality; second, there are the "skeptics" who do not believe this to be the case (145–6). For Kelly disgust is not a reliable source of "special, supra-rational information about morality"; we need to be "extremely skeptical of any variation of the idea that disgust deserves some kind of special epistemic credit, that the emotion is a trustworthy guide to justifiable moral judgments, or that there is any deep ethical wisdom in repugnance" (152). The reason is fallibility and the potential for co-opting such a reaction as a means of determining ideas of immorality: "Disgust should not be regarded as an appropriate response even to ethically questionable activities or practices, and by similar reasoning, that because moralization, in the technical sense, can easily slide into dehumanization and demonization, it should be regarded as morally problematic itself" (152).[10]

Disgust in the History of Aesthetics

In the history of aesthetics, disgust in particular has usually been treated as a bodily response that is incompatible with an intellectually based pleasure, and for this reason disgust has been held to be an un- or anti-aesthetic response, unlike other negative emotions of fear, terror, and pity, which have been thought to be bound up with tragic or sublime aesthetic experience and can be balanced, overcome, or transformed. For Kant, for instance, all aesthetic experience ends the minute disgust is aroused, because it disrupts the disinterested cognitive free play at the basis of aesthetic experience, paradigmatically, of the beautiful. Something of this idea already exists in Aristotle's proscription, in the *Poetics*, on showing too much gore on stage. This proscription is also found in Hume's "Of Tragedy." Basically, disgust has been regarded in this tradition as a bodily response that is incompatible with an intellectually based pleasure.[11]

Recently, however, several aestheticians have made a case for disgust as compatible with aesthetic engagement. Scholars of horror films – especially aesthetician Noël Carroll – for example, see disgust as an integral part of aesthetic engagement with this genre. Korsmeyer argues the case more generally for aesthetic disgust, which she defines as "the arousal of disgust in an audience, a spectator or a reader under circumstances where that emotion both apprehends artistic properties and constitutes a component of appreciation" (88). After the moment of lingering typical of the disgust response in the viewer or reader, other effects can be aroused, that is, other emotions and parts of aesthetic experience can be harnessed. As Korsmeyer puts it, "aesthetic disgust holds open-ended possibilities of tenor and valence from dismal to hilarious, melancholy to erotic. The visceral response is crucial, but it too varies from slight twinge to horrified nausea" (137). While Korsmeyer calls this later component of the emotion by the same name of aesthetic disgust, it may also contain other feelings and experiences, just as, say, if we imagine (or recall) an episode of jealousy that may be complex and heterogeneous and may change over time: our feelings might begin as a kind of anxiety, turn to frustration, lead to anger, then move back to doubt, and so on. That is, an emotion is not necessarily a unified experience or feeling.[12] Some artistic uses of disgust seem in line with the Deep Wisdom view of the emotion and some are more in line with the Sceptical view. In what follows I will analyse several examples and make a case for the way in which the texts try to evoke disgust and in which ways they are more or less aligned with these two views on the epistemic value of this emotion.

Cervantes

Despite aesthetic proscriptions on disgust, literary authors have evoked it as an aesthetic phenomenon and employed it in various contexts since at least classical times.[13] In addition to parodic and carnivalesque episodes, medieval Christian texts often employ disgust elicitors to demonstrate how a character may overcome the disgust impulse for holy ends, while early modern works evoke disgust in a variety of ways, especially for derision of characters, societal critique, and humour.

There are typical elicitors of disgust scattered throughout Cervantes's work, including the smelly violations of hygiene codes, bad food, bodily fluids or products, and violations of the bodily envelope. In *Don Quixote* 2.10, for instance, the peasant who Don Quixote is led to believe is the enchanted Dulcinea, reeks of garlic; in fact, Don Quixote believes her transformed into a peasant in part because of the odour she exudes: "le quitaron lo que es tan suyo de las principales señoras, que es el buen olor, por andar siempre entre ámbares y entre flores" (112) (they had to [...] deprive her of that prime characteristic of all noble ladies, namely, their lovely scent, which they acquire naturally, spending so much of their time among perfumes and flowers) (401).[14] Don Quixote's perception and appraisal of the woman's bad smell, in lieu of his experience of her absent yet assumed good smell, is set up in opposition to a medieval Christian tradition continued in the early modern period, in which inner beauty was supposed to shine olfactorily despite disgusting outward appearances.[15] Later, on the eve of Sancho's governorship, Don Quixote warns him never to eat garlic, lest this smell reveal his peasant nature to his future subjects through their experience of olfaction (2.43:361). Furthermore, in the multisensorial description of the peasant Maritornes (1.16:203–4), the reader learns that her breath smells like "ensalada fiambre y trasnochada" (garlic and stale salad)[16] and that she would induce vomiting in almost any man.[17]

Nonetheless, as I will demonstrate, such disgust elicitors in Cervantes only infrequently evoke disgust in the reader or a character and do so in varying degrees. Moreover, while Cervantes sometimes offers a moral critique of characters, he tends to eschew the pairing of disgust response with (potential or perceived) moral aberration.

For Korsmeyer the eviscerated human heart is a species of "violation of the human envelope," and can be one of the most profound disgust triggers in life and art. It has been used as an element that effectively creates a sense of horror in films, for instance, in the film *Angel Heart* (Parker, Marshall, and Kastner). In Cervantes's hands, however, the eviscerated human heart evokes little or no disgust in characters or in the reader.[18]

In *Don Quixote* the way in which the scene involving an eviscerated heart is recounted limits significantly the potential disgust impact, reducing it to something only vaguely, if at all, disgusting. In fact, the image is made to be quite innocuous before it has any power to provoke the emotion. First, it takes place in the Cave of Montesinos in what is generally considered a dream sequence; thus, it is not an actual event.[19] Second, the evisceration is retold, within Don Quixote's narration of his dream experience, by another character. Third, Cervantes introduces the image in a removed past tense and prefaces the first mention of the heart with doubt about the veracity of the tale that Don Quixote will hear. These multiple layers of mediation raise a significant ontological doubt about the event, one that is mentioned within an already dubious narration, which is probably a dream or hallucination: "Apenas me dijo que era Montesinos, cuando le pregunté *si fue verdad* lo que en el mundo de acá arriba se contaba: que él *había sacado de la mitad del pecho*, con una pequeña daga, *el corazón* de su grande amigo Durandarte" (2.23:212; emphasis added) (He had no sooner told me that he was Montesinos than I asked *if it were true* that, as they said out in the world above, using a tiny dagger *he had cut his* great friend Durandarte's *heart right out of his chest*) (469). In the next sentence Cervantes makes this already highly mediated narration absurdly comical by the introduction of the discussion of which of two very similar implements were used to remove the heart, that is, whether it was a *daga* or a *puñal*, as if this question were of prime import: "Respondióme que en todo decían verdad, sino en la daga, porque no fue daga, ni pequeña, sino un puñal buido" (212–13) (I told him that that was indeed what was said, except for the dagger, for it was said to have been neither a dagger nor tiny but a knife sharper even than a carpenter's awl) (469). This evisceration of the heart is coupled with another potential disgust trigger mentioned in the passage: the idea of rotting flesh. But before the reader can be disgusted by it, Montesinos tells Durandarte directly, now in the present, that the heart has been salted so that it will not stink: "En el primero lugar que topé, saliendo de Roncesvalles, eché un poco de sal en vuestro corazón, porque no oliese mal" (216) (I took some salt, in the first village we came to once we'd left Roncesvalles, and sprinkled it over your heart, to keep it from stinking) (471).[20] In Cervantes's hands, then, the eviscerated heart is not foul. Here Cervantes does not use a mimetic correlate who experiences disgust, that is, there is no character in the text who finds this disembodied heart disgusting, and it arouses here only the most mild form, if any at all, of physiological disgust. The process of doubt and mediation has decreased the potential emotional impact on the character and the reader before the emotion has been experienced.

In Cervantes's posthumous *The Trials of Persiles and Sigismunda* (1617) another image of an eviscerated heart may evoke some terror, but only hypothetical disgust. Early on in the novel, Taurisa, one of the many intradiegetic narrators, explains that on the Barbarous Island all male visitors are sacrificed so that their hearts may be used as part of an elaborate test to determine who should rule the island's people:[21]

> persuadidos, o ya del demonio, o ya de un antiguo hechicero a quien ellos tienen por sapientísimo varón, que de entre ellos ha de salir un rey que conquiste y gane gran parte del mundo; este rey que esperan no saben quién ha de ser, y para saberlo, aquel hechicero les dió esta orden: que sacrificasen todos los hombres que a su ínsula llegasen, de cuyos corazones, digo, de cada uno de por sí, hiciesen polvos, y los diesen a beber a los bárbaros más principales de la ínsula, con expresa orden que, el

que los pasase sin torcer el rostro ni dar muestra de que le sabía mal, le alzasen por su rey. (1.2:57)

being persuaded either by the Devil or by an ancient sorcerer they consider the wisest of men [...] that from among them a king will come forth who will conquer and win a great part of the world. They don't know who this king is that they await, but, in order to find out, the sorcerer gave them the following order: they must sacrifice all the men who come to their island, grind the hearts of each of them into powder, and give these powders in a drink to the most important barbarians of the island with express orders that he who should drink the powders without making a face or showing any sign that it tasted bad would be proclaimed their king. (21)

Similar to the narration about Durandarte's heart, there is considerable distancing from the reader and characters which diminishes any experience of disgust. First, in the passage, the hearts under discussion are hypothetical rather than actual hearts. Second, there is no mimetic correlate for the reader: the only ingestion that is imaged directly, and hypothetically, is that of an unknown future king, who not only never ingests the heart powder but if he were to do so, he would specifically *not* feel the emotion of disgust. If he were to feel it, then he would have to be able to suppress his response sufficiently to hide any semblance of its experience, making this barbarian a would-be hero for Vives in his ability to avoid feeling the emotion. It is intriguing to note that here Cervantes seems aware of the universality of the disgust gape, well before Darwin's observation in the nineteenth century. Indeed, Taurisa relates specifically, about these "bárbaros" from a far-off "isla septentrional," that they too would grimace at something they found disgusting and would do so in a manner that would be completely recognizable to Southern Europeans: "sin torcer el rostro ni dar muestra de que le sabía mal [...]" (1.2:57) (without making a face or showing any sign that it tasted bad) (21).[22] As explained above, recognition of the disgust response by others is a way for the feeling to be communicated and experienced. Likewise, the absence of such a grimace and of any mimetic correlate in the text diminishes the possibility of the feeling of disgust in the reader.

Another of the disgust elicitors, which involves the rotten smell of "ensalada fiambre y trasnochada" (garlic and stale salad), is only hypothetical from a strictly phenomenological stance. The scene's extradiegetic narrator seems mildly disgusted by Maritornes (1.16), but Don Quixote, as mimetic correlate, is not. Indeed, the entire scene describes not what any character feels, but instead what Don Quixote misperceives and what a normal human being would have been expected to feel, but never did.[23] Don Quixote misperceives the Asturian servant's odour because he believes her to be a princess; such princesses, according to his logic of class, could never smell bad. The narrator points out that the odour emanating from her mouth hypothetically should have induced vomiting in any man who was not a muleteer: "pudieran hacer vomitar a otro que no fuera arriero [...]." (which would have made anyone but a muledriver vomit) (1.16:203–4). Not only is Maritornes maligned for her class and sex, but so are all muleteers, who, simply because of their lower-class social standing (and possibly their race),[24] are aberrant, given that they would not vomit in the presence of an object of sensory disgust that, according to the narrator, should make all species-typical men experience the most serious outcome of the disgust experience, that is, vomiting. In addition to the bad smells that she exudes, which are never perceived by Don Quixote, the sight of her and the feel of her apparently ought to provoke disgust as well. While the text certainly associates social class with notions of bad smell and disgust, Cervantes does not facilely co-opt the disgust mechanism in a character or reader for a moral end. Indeed, the absence of a mimetic correlate who experiences disgust makes this plain.

Beyond Dulcinea *encantada* and Maritornes, there are other peasant women with bad breath, including La Arguello in Cervantes's novella *La ilustre fregona* (The Illustrious Kitchen Maid), who is from the lower classes, works at an inn, is not young or beautiful, but is lusty. La Argüello sets her eyes on the much younger Lope-Diego, a catch of much higher status than Maritornes's muleteers: "Habla más que un relator y que le huele el aliento a rasuras desde una legua; todos los dientes son postizos, y tengo para mí que los cabellos son cabellera; y para adobar y suplir estas faltas, después que me descubrió su mal pensamiento, ha dado en afeitarse con albayalde, y así se jalbega el rostro, que no parece sino mascarón de yeso puro" (165) (She's more talkative than a court reporter and her breath reeks a mile off of the lees of bad wine. All her upper teeth are false and I reckon her hair is a wig. To cover and make up for these flaws, after revealing her loathsome intentions to me, she has taken to painting herself with white lead, and she daubs it on her face in such a way that it's like a grotesque mask made of nothing but plaster) (91).[25] This is the opinion not only of Lope-Diego, but also of his buddy: "'Todo eso es verdad,' replicó Tomás" ("You're right about all that," answered Tomás) (165). Like Maritornes, La Argüello suffers from bad breath, but the two women reek of different things. Here La Argüello's breath stinks of "rasuras" a mile a way. These are the "heces del vino," that is, the lees or dregs of wine – associating her, literally, with the bottom of the barrel.

Men are not immune to stinkiness. In scenarios similar to that of La Argüello two men provoke mild disgust when they are judged much too old for the women they are married to in Cervantes's interludes "El viejo celoso" and "El juez de los divorcios." In the latter the husband suffers from various illnesses and complains too much, but worst of all is his foul breath, which can be smelled from a significant distance:[26] "estar obligada a sufrirle el mal olor de la boca, que le güele mal a tres tiros de arcabuz" (99) (I have to put up with the stench of his breath – it stinks to high heaven) (14).[27] In the former the disgustingness of the old man is depicted largely through the humorous words of the servant Cristinica, who complains of having to empty his urine out of the basin, of having to apply his many medications to his body, of his illnesses and his many complaints, combining olfactory, tactile, and auditory insults. She mocks the old man's speech in her derision: "'Daca el orinal, toma el orinal; levántate Cristinica, y caliéntame unos paños, que me muero de la ijada; dame aquellos juncos, que me fatiga la piedra.' Con más ungüentos y medicinas en el aposento que si fuera una botica; y yo, que apenas sé vestirme, tengo de servirle de enfermera. ¡Pux, pux, pux, viejo clueco, tan potroso como celoso, y el más celoso del mundo!" (258) (Bring me the bedpan, empty the bedpan; get up Cristinica and fetch me hot cloths, my belly's killing me." Or, "Where are my pills? My kidney stone's playing me up." There are more salves and potions in his room than you'd find in an apothecary's shop. As for me, I'm scarcely old enough to dress myself, yet I have to nurse him. Cluck, cluck, cluck, he coddles his aches and pains like an old broody hen! I don't know which makes him more impotent, his hernia or his jealousy!) (133–4).[28] However, Cristinica never says she is disgusted and does not seem to have a strong aversion to emptying out the bedpan or applying the ointments (she continues to do her job); indeed, she seems more angry than anything. These are mildly disgusting elicitors that are coupled with a light moral criticism of the winter-spring wedding.

Overall, the images of bad breath, urine, and ugliness in these scenarios are not strong disgust elicitors, but mild ones. They evoke a little disgust, coupled with mild social or moral criticism, of arranged marriages, of old men who wed young women, of older women who seek out younger men. In the case of Maritornes, I would argue that she would not be an object of derision were it not for Don Quixote's confusing her with a beautiful princess. The point of the scene describing her seems mostly in order to depict Don Quixote as out of touch with reality.

In contrast to these weak elicitors with a little disgust, when Cervantes uses strong disgust elicitors, like the eviscerated heart, he generally does not couple them with moral characteristics, or if he does, then the description is highly mediated. But there are two passages with full-blown disgust-aversion responses in a character who serves the role of mimetic correlate. In the well-known anecdote about the elixir or *bálsamo* that has a delayed effect of food poisoning in *Don Quixote*,[29] the disgust begins after Don Quixote vomits, although the vomit is not immediately identified by Sancho. When Don Quixote throws up, Sancho lingers on this sensory input, experiences a broad emotional reaction with a cognitive component, and only after does he vomit: Cervantes lays out Sancho's experience in the past tense but in a rather unmediated way. The trigger is of Rozin's "bodily product" type (number 2 in his schema of core disgust elicitors). Ironically, the reader knows what the trigger is before the squire does: "Llegóse Sancho tan cerca, que casi le metía los ojos en la boca, y fue a tiempo que ya había obrado el bálsamo en el estómago de don Quijote, y al tiempo que Sancho llegó a mirarle la boca, arrojó de sí, más recio que una escopeta, cuanto dentro tenía, y dio con todo ello en las barbas del *compasivo escudero*" (1.18:225; emphasis added) (Sancho came closer, virtually putting his eyes into Don Quijote's mouth, and that being the moment when the balm had had its chance to work on his master's stomach, his mouth erupted swifter than any rifle, just as Sancho bent over, and emptied the entire contents of Don Quijote's stomach all over the *sympathetic squire*'s beard) (102). At first, then, Sancho doesn't know what the substance is, and during this time the narrator makes a point of mentioning Sancho's *compassion.* This feeling might trigger our own empathy for him, as he tries to make sense of what is going on: "'¡Santa María!,' dijo Sancho, 'y ¿qué es esto que me ha sucedido?'" (225) ("'Holy Mother of God!' cried Sancho. 'What's happening to me?'") (102). He answers his own question, but incorrectly, as the reader already knows: "Sin duda este pecador está herido de muerte, pues vomita sangre por la boca" (225) (This sinner is surely mortally wounded, because he's vomiting blood from his mouth) (102). But it is not blood. Sancho picks up on this as he reflects on the properties of the substance that is all over him: "reparando un poco más en ello" (225) (when he examined it more closely) (102). He thinks about the colour, taste, and smell, lingering on these features if only for a moment, trying to find an adequate concept, in a brief moment of reflective (aesthetic) judgment that results soon enough in complete and immediate revulsion: "echó de ver en la color, sabor y olor, que no era sangre, sino el bálsamo de la alcuza, que él le había visto beber" (225) (it became apparent from the colour, taste, and odour that it wasn't blood but just the magic balm, which he'd seen Don Quijote drinking) (102). This brings on the full feeling of nausea and the vomit response of complete disgust: "y fue tanto el *asco* que tomó, que, revolviéndosele el estómago, vomitó las tripas sobre su mismo señor" (225; emphasis added) (and this so *disgusted* him, that it made his stomach turn over and he vomited out his guts all over his master) (102). The narrator and Sancho have lingered on the aesthetic properties of the vomit, for which Sancho did not have a correct concept; soon his senses and judgment are able to determine precisely what they are. His intellect, calling into play his memory of having seen his master drink the *bálsamo* earlier, centres on the concept of vomit. But now that the lingering is over, the narrator ends the disgusting moment with a funny description, ironically describing Sancho and

Quixote as attractive: "y quedaron entrambos como de perlas" (225) (which left them both perfectly matched) (102).

There is also one scene of strong core physical disgust that leads to strong moral disgust in a character: in this well-commented-on scene, in *El coloquio de los perros* (The Dialogue of the Dogs) Berganza expresses his disgust about the witch Cañizares.[30] When she first tries to give him a kiss – he a dog, she a witch – he explicitly feels disgust and recoils at the prospect of physical contact with her: "si la dejara me besara en la boca; pero tuve asco y no lo consentí" (336) (if I had let her she would have kissed me on the mouth; but the idea repelled me and I wouldn't allow it) (127). The reader must infer that his disgust response is due to her physical appearance combined with her moral disposition, since just a few lines earlier Berganza had explained that "fuese la gente maldiciendo a la vieja, añadiendo al nombre de hechicera el de bruja, y el de barbuda sobre vieja" (336) (the people went away cursing the old woman, calling her a witch as well as a sorceress, and an old hag as well as an old woman) (125). In this story of talking dogs, who at one time may have been human and transformed by witchcraft, it is worth noting that Berganza's disgust response is typical of humans rather than canines. Indeed, as described above, the disgust recoil in humans is typically from an olfactory or gustatory experience that leads to an avoidance of noxious or contaminated substances. Importantly, aversions to such objects are not typically experienced by dogs, who are well known to seek out and enjoy the smell of conspecifics' urine, roll around in the smell of rotting flesh, and engage in coprophagia or the eating of faeces. If there is a disgust mechanism in species-typical canines, it is certainly nothing like that of *homo sapiens*. Yet Berganza feels disgust in quite a human way. Later, when the witch covers her naked body with ointment that she believes will allow her to transport her spirit, he feels anger and again disgust. The description at this point is aimed at evoking disgust in the reader, Berganza being the mimetic correlate who sees the world as a human, privileging sight:

> que me dio gran temor verme encerrado en aquel estrecho aposento con aquella figura delante, la cual te la pintaré como mejor supiere: Ella era larga de más de siete pies; toda era notomía de huesos, cubiertos con una piel negra, vellosa y curtida; con la barriga, que era de badana, se cubría las partes deshonestas, y aun le colgaba hasta la mitad de los muslos; las tetas semejaban dos vejigas de vaca secas y arrugadas; denegridos los labios, traspillados los dientes, la nariz corva y entablada, desencasados los ojos, la cabeza desgreñada, las mejillas chupadas, angosta la garganta y los pechos sumidos; finalmente, toda era flaca y endemoniada. Púseme de espacio a mirarla y apriesa comenzó a apoderarse de mí el miedo, considerando la mala visión de su cuerpo y la peor ocupación de su alma. Quise morderla, por ver si volvía en sí, y no hallé parte en

> toda ella que el asco no me lo estorbase; pero, con todo esto, la así de un carcaño y la saqué arrastrando al patio; mas ni por esto dio muestras de tener sentido. (344)

> I was really frightened to find myself shut up in that small room with that figure in front of me which I shall describe to you as best I can. She was more than seven feet long; she was all bone, covered in a black, hairy, hard skin; her stomach, which was like sheepskin, covered her private parts, and hung down to her thighs; her teats looked like two bladders of dried up and wrinkled cows; her lips were blackened, her teeth closed tight, her nose was hooked and misshapen and her eyes protruded; her hair was disheveled, her cheeks sunken, her neck thin and breasts flaccid; in short, she was thin as a rake and like the devil himself. I began to look at her more carefully, and suddenly I was gripped by fear, seeing the evil appearance of her body and even worse, considering the occupation of her soul. I decided to bite her to see if she would come to, but I could not find a part of her which did not repel me; even so, I grabbed her by her heels and dragged her into the yard, but not even this made her give any sign of recovering her senses. (135–7)

Despite his feeling of disgust, Berganza is able to overcome the aversion and he successfully bites her. This scene is one of the scariest and least humorous in all of Cervantes. But it should be remembered that mediation is at its highest here, because the story we are reading is of talking dogs who do not seem canine and whose story is related through a syphilitic, perhaps delusional narrator, Ensign Campuzano.

Zayas

We can productively contrast these evocations of disgust with examples found in other literary works of the early modern period. For purposes of comparison I select a few passages from María de Zayas's novellas, which other critics have already characterized as precursors of "horror."[31]

In "La inocencia castigada" (Innocence Punished), Zayas's narrator lingers on a host of disgust triggers in this novella about the married and honourable Doña Inés, who is wooed and abused by the obsessive Don Diego. Inés rejects Diego repeatedly – she is a married and honourable woman – but he employs various perverse means to achieve sexual gratification, including contracting a Moorish necromancer to put Inés into a sleep-walking trance whereby she visits his house on multiple occasions to have sex with him. When the fact that she has been leaving her home at night is found out by others, despite her innocence, Inés is victimized further. Her husband, her brother, and her sister-in-law form a brutal triumvirate who torture her slowly, moving to a new town in order to achieve their sentence more efficaciously: "para hacer sin testigos la crueldad que ahora diré" (283) (so that they could accomplish without witnesses the cruelty I shall now describe) (192).[32] They entomb her alive in a wall and slowly starve her to death:

> En un aposento, el último de toda la casa, donde aunque hubiese gente de servicio ninguno tuviese modo ni ocasión de entrar en él, en el hueco de *una chimenea que allí había, o ellos la hicieron,* porque para este caso no hubo más oficiales que el hermano, marido y cuñada, habiendo traído yeso y cascotes, y lo demás que era menester, pusieron a la pobre y desdichada doña Inés, no dejándole más lugar que cuanto pudiese estar en pie, porque si se quería sentar, no podía, sino, como ordinariamente se dice, en cuclillas, y la tabicaron, dejando sólo una ventanilla como medio pliego de papel, por donde respirase y le pudiesen dar una miserable comida, por que no muriese tan presto [...]. (283; emphasis added)

> In a little room in the highest part of the house where not even servants would ever have occasion to go, *in the chimney space which was there or which they made* – no one knows, because the husband, brother, and sister-in-law were the only witnesses – they sealed in the poor unfortunate doña Inés, using plaster, rubble, and other materials they'd had brought up. They left her only enough space to stand upright, and if she tried to sit she couldn't, except maybe to crouch a little. They walled her in leaving only a tiny hole the size of half a sheet of paper through which she could breathe and they could pass her meager rations so she wouldn't die too quickly [...]. (192–3)

She is left for six years in this space that is not big enough for her to lie down in. The cruelty with which she is tortured in this way evokes disgust. The most disgusting images are those most vividly described and aligned with core disgust, taken from the narrator's description of Inés after her rescue once a neighbour hears the faint sound of her lamenting through the wall. Indeed, the image is disgusting, both in the presentation to us and then doubled through the experience of Inés's rescuers, who we are told feel pity:

> Sus hermosos cabellos, que cuando entró allí eran como hebras de oro, blancos como la misma nieve, enredados y llenos de animalejos, que de no peinarlos se crían en tanta cantidad, que por encima hervoreaban; el color, de la color de la muerte; tan flaca y consumida, que se le señalaban los huesos, como si el pellejo que estaba encima fuera un delgado cendal; desde los ojos hasta la barba, dos surcos cavados de las lágrimas, que se le escondía en ellos un bramante grueso; los vestidos, hechos ceniza, que se le veían las más partes de su cuerpo; descalza de pie y pierna, que de los excrementos de su cuerpo, como no tenía dónde echarlos, no sólo se habían consumido,

> mas la propia carne comida hasta los muslos de llagas y gusanos, de que estaba lleno el hediondo lugar. No hay más que decir, sino que causó a todos tanta lástima, que lloraban como si fuera hija de cada uno. (287)

> Her splendid hair which when she entered was like threads of spun gold was now white as snow and tangled and seething with lice. Since her hair was never combed they had multiplied in such number that her head effervesced with them. Her color was the color of death. Her body was so consumed and emaciated that you could count her bones as if the skin that covered them were a silken shroud. From her eyes down to her chin were two furrows worn deep by tears, as if a heavy cord had been impressed there. Her clothing had disintegrated so you could see most of her body through the tatters. Her feet and legs had no covering because her body wastes, which she couldn't dispose of, had consumed the flesh of her legs up to her thighs which were covered with sores and worms that swarmed in that gross place. What more can one say except that the sight filled everyone with pity. They wept as if she were their own daughter. (196)

The passage was already preceded by at least two of Rozin's eight disgust elicitors including Don Diego's sexual perversions (number 6, various ways of having sex with Inés, including raping her when she is in a trance) and the violations of the moral social code (number 8, the family knew what they were doing was wrong and sought to have no witnesses); now the passage contains all of the other elicitors (followed by renewed emphasis on the eighth): 1. contaminated foods; 2. bodily products; 3. related violations of hygiene codes; 4. vermin; 5. violations of the bodily envelope such as wounds or evisceration; and 7. signs of death and decay.

The story is told quite straightforwardly, in an unironic, unhumourous way, yet sharing techniques with Cervantes: for instance, just as Cervantes's narrator questions the kind of knife that was used to cut out Durandarte's heart (*daga o puñal*), Zayas's narrator wonders whether the tiny torture chamber was already in the house when they moved in or whether the tormenters themselves built it: "en el hueco de una chimenea que allí había, o ellos la hicieron" (283) (in the chimney space which was there or which they had made) (192). But, in contrast to Cervantes's treatment of this epistemological uncertainty in his novel, in Zayas's novella the distinction is not a pointless one used merely to create humour; instead, it points directly to the family's cruelty. We are not told by the narrator that the characters who come to Inés's aid at the end feel anything other than pity (both "lástima" and "piedad" are used). But surely both the characters and the reader are also supposed to experience disgust that should then be associated not just with the scene but with the plight of upper-class, good, and innocent women who are enslaved in patriarchy. Zayas uses disgust in what philosopher Arthur Danto calls "a disturbatory" manner, that is, in such as way that it is "intended [...] to modify, through experiencing it, the mentality of those who do experience it" (299; qtd in Korsmeyer 90). The incident is meant to disturb us, to make us feel disgust about society, and perhaps to rouse us to do something to change it. It is a kind of moral disgust, in Rozin's eighth category, which would align Zayas's treatment with the Deep Wisdom category. The disgust response in this moral situation is meant to be morally revelatory and is a visceral one, asking the reader first of all to feel how it is disturbing and only after that to reflect on the situation.

Similarly, in Zayas's novella "La fuerza del amor" (The Power of Love) another upper-class female character is made to endure a dangerous and horrifying visit to an *humilladero*, an altar outside the city of Naples that serves as a public execution dump for Naples. Doña Laura's visit is part of the magical solution that she has been promised will result in the return of her philandering husband despite his continued dalliances. Zayas's narrator has the reader linger on disgusting details by their sheer accumulation, though the word "disgust" is not used and the scene is described, rather, as dangerous and fearful:

> un humilladero de cincuenta pies de largo y otros tantos de ancho [...] estado y medio de alto, el suelo es una fosa de más de cuatro en hondura, que coge toda la dicha capilla; sólo queda alrededor un poyo de media vara de ancho, por el cual se anda todo el humilladero. A estado de hombre, y menos, hay puestos por las paredes garfios de hierro, en los cuales, después de haber ahorcado en la plaza los hombres que mueren por justicia, los llevan allá y cuelgan en aquellos garfios; y como los tales se van deshaciendo, caen los huesos en aquel hoyo que, como está sagrado, les sirve de sepultura. Pues a esta parte tan espantosa guió sus pasos la hermosa Laura, donde a la sazón había seis hombres que por salteadores habían ajusticiado pocos días había; la cual, llegando a él con ánimo increíble, que se lo daba amor, entró dentro, tan olvidada del peligro cuanto acordada de sus fortunas, pues no temía, cuando no la gente con quien iba a negociar, el caer dentro de aquella profundidad, donde si tal fuera, jamás se supieran nuevas de ella. (365–6)

> The chapel is about fifty feet long and the same across ... and the floor is a pit sunk about twenty feet deep. Surrounding this great pit there's just a ledge about eighteen inches wide along which you can walk around the chapel. At about the height of a man, and sometimes even lower, there are iron hooks in the wall. After criminals sentenced to death have been publicly hanged, their corpses are brought here and hung from these hooks. As the bodies decompose, their bones fall into the pit, which, being holy ground, serves as their tomb. A few days before, six highway bandits had been hanged. This is the dreadful place where Laura went. With the incredible courage her love inspired in her, she entered. Ignoring the great danger, she was mindful only of

> her terrible need. She felt less afraid of the people she was going to do business with than of falling into the abyss. If that happened, no one would ever know what had become of her. (176)

The description incorporates multiple disgust triggers, including rotting flesh, piles of corpses, and falling limbs and bones, in a description of death that is terrible and perhaps sublime in its evocation of the sheer magnitude of decaying bodies.[33] Yet it is described in a somewhat matter-of-fact manner in which the olfactory is strangely absent. The piles of dead bodies occupy a space of something the size of a very deep swimming pool (some fifty-by-fifty feet in area and twenty feet in depth). Yet, despite the visual disgust of the scene, Zayas limits the nausea by not including what would have been the overpowering stench of rotting flesh, the smell of which is never mentioned and which, it appears, Laura never detects. In many respects, Laura is not a mimetic correlate (wouldn't she smell the foul odour of rotting bodies?) and is still in something of a trance, steeling herself for the task at hand. The disgusting environment communicates more directly with the reader. In Zayas the reader is given access to the visually disgusting, and perhaps our blood pressure goes down as we are fascinated with the drawn-out, repulsive details, savouring them with loathing, since, as Korsmeyer says, the "profoundly repulsive may also fascinate" (37). This is the kind of fascination that Leontius experiences in Plato's *Republic* (Bk 9), where he was repulsed and yet simultaneously fascinated and could not avert his eyes from the spectacle of dead bodies that had been publically executed (qtd in Korsmeyer 41).[34]

In the novella "Tarde llega el desegaño" (Too Late Undeceived) disgust is strongly correlated with race and class. Once again something horrible is done by a man, Don Jaime, to a beautiful, innocent, high-born white woman, doña Elena. An upper-class male carries out the torture, but this time the horror is prompted by the guile of a nameless, black, female slave. When she is first presented to the reader and to the intradiegetic listeners (Don Martín and his friend), Doña Elena is beautiful, pale, dressed in rags, and dying of starvation, while holding in her hand a skull that the reader later learns is the skull of the decapitated head of her alleged lover and actual cousin, a receptacle from which she is forced to drink. While this beautiful white woman is forced to stay on the ground, another woman is invited to sit at the table with the white guests. Don Martín seems disgusted by her: "una negra, tan tinta, que el azabache era blanco en su comparación, y sobre esto, tan fiera, que juzgó don Martín que si no era el demonio, que debía ser retrato suyo, porque las narices eran tan romas, que imitaban los perros bracos que ahora están tran validos, y la boca, con tan grande hocico y bezos tan gruesos, que parecía boca de león y lo demás a esta proporción" (237) (black, so black that jet would pale in comparison. She was of such fierce aspect that don Martin thought if she wasn't the devil she was his very likeness. Her nose was as broad as the nose of the highly prized blood-hound. Her mouth, or snout, had thick protruding lips resembling the gaping maw of a lion and the rest of her was similarly repulsive) (146). Her physical appearance is described in animalizing terms and is incongruous to Don Martín, as he perceives a strong contrast between her face and what she is wearing: "Pudo muy bien don Martín notar su rostro y costosos aderezos en lo que tardó en llegar a la mesa" (237) (It took her so long to get to the table that don Martin was able to take careful note of her face and her costly dress) (146). What seems to be Martín's anger comes out in the narrator's choice of adjectives to describe her: "Traía la fiera y abominable negra vestida una saya entera con manga en punta" (237) (The fierce and abominable Negress was wearing a dress all of one piece made of scarlet brocade with long sleeves falling to a point) (146).

Martín's emotional response, while not explicitly labelled "disgust," seems somewhat akin to Vives's "offensa": it is not only the sight of Elena on all fours eating scraps fit for a dog that provokes the emotion – "la desdichada belleza estaba debajo de la mesa, los huesos y mendrugos, que aun para los perros no eran buenos, que como tan necesitada de sustento, los roía como si fuera uno de ellos" (237) (he gave crusts and bones not fit even for a dog to the ill-fated beauty beneath the table. Ravenously she gnawed at them as if she were a dog) (147) – but he feels indignation that a black slave is seated at the table, regaled by a white nobleman, when she is, according to his appraisal, better suited to the floor. From the perspective of Martín, who is meant to be a mimetic correlate, the scene involves several of Rozin's criteria for disgust elicitation: contaminated foods (1), related violations of hygiene codes (3), signs of death and decay (7); and violations of the moral social code (8); the situation is presented as if it were the opposite of how the two women ought to be treated based on their comparative levels of beauty and their distinctive races and social classes. Rozin's elicitor regarding "perverse sexual activities" (6) is also evoked when Don Jaime mentions that he has told Elena that the black woman shares his bed every night (if her sitting at the table offends Martín, then her lying in his bed having sex with Jaime is more shocking).[35]

Evocations of disgust can be used for subtle and complex aesthetic ends. While Zayas has strong moral reasons to be disgusted by aspects of her society, this type of pairing of the morally reprehensible with disgust elicitors typically is avoided by Cervantes, who favours a "Sceptical" rather than "Deep Wisdom" approach to the moral salience of the emotion of disgust. In contrast to the picaresque or Zayas, Cervantes arouses disgust but will generally do so only sparingly, catching the reader's attention and then transforming it with humour, not coupling strong physical disgust with moral disgust in the reader. Cervantes generates a very subtle use of disgust to aesthetic ends whereby the reader lingers on a description, experiences heightened curiosity, and is moved to laughter. In so doing

Cervantes engages more broadly in an aesthetics of allowing the reader to infer rather than telling the reader what to think or feel, an open aesthetics that invites free thinking and greater moral deliberation.[36] While Zayas's co-opting of disgust for moral reasons seems salutary from the point of view of twenty-first-century morality in the cases of Laura and Inés (where it is linked to the despair provoked by the philandering husband and to the cruel, inhumane torture brought about in the "logic" of patriarchy), the not-so-subtle racism of "Tarde llega el desegaño" in its evocation of an allegedly upside-down racialized world is illustrative of the moral problem of relying on a physiological disgust response for "Deep Wisdom." While Elena is innocent, Jaime is sadistically cruel and the black slave is guilty of having framed Elena, all of which point to a lack of justice in the patriarchal society; the narrative links the slave's physical description and especially her race to notions of disgust to help the implied reader feel the injustice. However, there is no wisdom in this view, which is something that should lead the current reader to consider the importance of a "Sceptical" view of the moral salience of this emotion. The problems that arise for today's reader vis-à-vis the evocation of disgust in these historical literary works shed light, in turn, on the philosophical question of "Scepticism" versus "Deep Wisdom" of the emotion.

NOTES

1 All translations are mine except where otherwise noted.

2 This passage is taken from the first edition of Lobera's book (Augsburg, 1530) which has "signe" instead of what would make more sense, "sigue." It is "sigue" in the second edition, which has a somewhat different title (Alcalá, 1542). As noted by López Piñero, this book on individual hygiene practices is part of a tradition that dates back to ancient times and the *Epistolé profylaktiké* of Diocles of Carystus in the fourth century BCE and to which medieval Arabic medicine contributed a great deal (19). According to Frank Collard and Evelyne Samama in their history of teeth and dentistry, emphasis on brushing teeth is not a commonplace in books on hygiene (243). However, the first recipe of the medieval Castilian *Manual de mugeres* provides a recipe for making the mouth look and smell better. Taken alongside Lobera's recommendation, this might suggest that teeth-brushing may have been a more common practice among aristocratic women and men in Castile than elsewhere in Europe: "Polvos para los dientes: Cinco onças de alabrastro, y quatro onças de porçelana, y seis onças de açúcar fino, y una onça de coral blanco, y otra de canela, y media de aljófar, y media de almizque. Todo hecho polvo. Limpiarse los dientes con estos polvos y enxaguarse la boca con vino blanco tibio" (Powders for the teeth: Five ounces of alabaster, and four ounces of porcelain, and six ounces of refined sugar, and

one ounce of white coral, and another of cinnamon, and half [an ounce] of pearl, and half of musk. All of it made into powder. Clean the teeth with these and rinse the mouth with tepid white wine) (Martínez Crespo 37).

3 Philosopher Amélie Rorty explains that the historical study of emotions is hindered by the enormous challenges of a common lexicon (4). In modern translations, "De offensione" has been translated as "disgust" but also "irritation." One modern Spanish translation uses "disgusto" (see Vives, *Tratado* 254). According to the *Diccionario de autoridades*, it referred to a physical bad taste and hence is related to modern disgust: "Dessazón, dessabrimiento al paladar o al gusto. Es compuesto de la preposición Dis, y el nombre Gusto. En lo antiguo se decía Desgusto."

4 That early moderns were aware of the disgust gape, well before Darwin's explicit description, is evidenced in select artworks. See, for instance, the doctor's expression as he examines the leper in Figure 5.1, an illustration from Hans von Gersdorff's *Feldtbüch der Wundtartzney* (Strassburg, 1517) and the variety of expressions of the onlookers in Figure 5.2, Boone's "Man Vomiting" (Flemish, 1651), one of which is clearly the disgust grimace. I thank Domenico Bertoloni Meli for drawing my attention to the Gersdorff illustration.

5 While the particular, specific triggers of what a "perversion" is are linked to specific historical cultures, pan-culturally most if not all cultures will have a category of perversion. For instance, in twenty-first-century United States many people would think that humans having sex with non-human animals or with human cadavers was disgusting.

6 Unique among emotions, material disgust requires sensory input, especially from smell and taste, but also from touch, sound, and sight. As Korsmeyer points out, the general property of disgust is "rottenness or foulness, for this emotion is vividly focused on the sensory qualities of things one might ingest or touch" (17). With disgust, as with any emotion, cognitive appraisals are made (thoughts and beliefs about intentional objects with associated feelings that occur over time), which inform the current and future episodes of the emotion. For a view of emotions as processes of multiple episodes over time see Goldie's *The Emotions*.

7 Core disgust is "revulsion at the prospect of (oral) incorporation of an offensive object" (32).

8 Kelly's theory on how disgust evolved is more complex; he calls it the "Entanglement and Co-Opting View." Entanglement entails disgust's being a "composite emotion whose two main components originally evolved to protect against poisons and parasites, respectively" (140). The poison mechanism evolved to avoid eating harmful foods; the parasite mechanism evolved to guard against parasites and hence looks for "signs of contamination or infection" (e.g., rotting corpses, vermin). The co-opting portion of this view is a further complexity: "once formed, disgust was co-opted to also play a number of roles in regulating the increasingly complex system of human social

interactions. In acquiring these new functions, however, disgust retained many of the features that allow it to effectively protect against poisons and parasites, rendering an imperfect fit between the emotion and the social issues on which it has been brought to bear." For Kelly, this explains why Rozin's eighth category seems to be a core disgust elicitor, but also, whenever the disgust is social, it has been co-opted (140–5).

9 Other philosophers who hold this skeptical view include Martha Nussbaum; on the other side, arguing that the emotion of disgust points to actual morality, is Leon Kass (Kelly 138).

10 Korsmeyer and Kelly published their respective books on disgust in the same year (2011), but make no references to each other's work.

11 Another useful way to think about triggers of disgust, beyond what I can treat in this essay, is boundary violation, key to anthropologist Mary Douglas's well-known analysis of purity and contamination, where impurity triggers disgust (dirt is not per se disgusting when it is on the ground, but if you put it on your plate, then it has violated a boundary), which was key for Kristeva's notion of the abject; see Korsmeyer (31n48). While these types of things are typical triggers, in the study of any emotion, be it disgust, jealousy, or any other, the emotion can be individuated with reference to the specific properties of its exemplary intentional objects (Korsmeyer 17).

12 See especially Goldie; Wagschal (*Literature*).

13 For instance, Seneca's on-stage displays of brutality and gore.

14 I cite from Murillo's edition of *El ingenioso hidalgo don Quijote de la Mancha*; English translations are from Raffel's edition of *Don Quixote*.

15 For an example, see Alonso Villegas, who writes about the body of Fray Pedro Nicolas Factor, "Al noueno dia estaba su cuerpo fresco, tratable, y sin mal olor, como se tomo por testimonio" (on the ninth day, his body was fresh, touchable, and without bad odour, as described by testimony) (80v); see also Ryan Giles's essay in this volume.

16 Raffel's translation preserves the idea in Cervantes that Maritorne's breath is awful, but achieves this by referencing "garlic and stale salad," when garlic is not specified in Cervantes's original; a literal translation of Cervantes's phrase would spell out that the salad in question is not a salad in today's sense but one of cured or seasoned meats that is eaten cold (fiambre).

17 In cognitive embodiment studies, the concept "stinky is bad" is the primary metaphor which is at the base of secondary metaphors such as "that person stinks" – which can mean that the person is bad at something or that he/she is a bad person, such as "he stank as a father." For a discussion of primary and secondary metaphors, see George Lakoff and Mark Johnson, *Philosophy in the Flesh*. See also my "Smellscape of *Don Quixote*."

18 In popular devotion to the five wounds of Christ, devotees clearly overcame any disgust aversion to the "sacred heart" and the "side wound," since these images in prayer books are often faded by having been repeatedly kissed.

19 For instance, see de Armas Wilson, "Dream Work in the Cave of Montesinos."

20 Ryan Schmitz analyses this passage as a parody of the "heart trope" in which a lover promises his heart to his beloved, in this case, literally and "with unflinchingly gruesome detail" (176).

21 Quotations are from Avalle-Arce's edition of *Los trabajos de Persiles y Sigismunda*; English translations are from Weller and Colahan's *The Trials of Persiles and Sigismunda.*

22 In yet another hypothetical cutting out of the heart, Don Quixote answers the Duchess's request for information on Dulcinea by saying that if he could show her his actual heart he would: "Si yo pudiera sacar mi corazón y ponerle ante los ojos de vuestra grandeza, aquí, sobre esta mesa y en un plato, quitara el trabajo a mi lengua de decir lo que apenas se puede pensar" (2.32:288) (Were I able to draw forth my heart and lay it in front of your highness' eyes, here on a plate, and on this table, it would spare my tongue the labor of trying to say what is almost unsayable) (520).

23 Such non-sensory perceptions remind one of Bishop Berkeley's famous musing about the tree in the woods. If a person's breath were bad, but no one smelled it, did it stink? More so than the sound of the tree in Berkeley's question, "stink" is an evaluative rather than purely physical denoting term. More important, the smell certainly did not disgust anyone if no one was there to be disgusted by it.

24 Javier Irigoyen notes that muleteers were often believed to be *moriscos* (11–12).

25 Quotations are from Sieber's edition of "La ilustre fregona" in the *Novelas ejemplares*; I cite from Michael and Jonathan Thacker's translation, "The Illustrious Kitchen-Maid."

26 Quotations from *El juez de los divorcios* and *El viejo celoso* are from Spadaccini's edition; I cite from Dawn L. Smith's translations of *The Divorce Court Judge* and *The Jealous Old Man*

27 The idea of stench travelling a specific distance is lost in Smith's translation; "a tres tiros de arcabuz" would be three times the distance of an arcabus shot (an arcabus is type of sixteenth-century rifle that can shoot approximately 50 metres away).

28 "Potroso" refers to the illness of "potra" (scrotal hernia), which Covarrubias calls "quasi putrida, es cierta enfermedad que se cria en los testiculos, y en la bolsa dellos." Meanwhile, the adjective "clueco" describes the broody hen, and according to Covarrubias derives from the clucking sound hens make (so attributing this behaviour to the old man is quite derogatory).

29 This initial vomiting is not a disgust response, but rather a simple sign that he has had food poisoning: "fue a tiempo que ya había obrado el bálsamo en el estómago de don Quijote" (224). I have treated this passage in some detail in "The Smellscape of *Don Quixote.*"

30 Quotations of "El coloquio de los perros" are from Sieber's edition; the English translation is that of John Jones and John Macklin entitled "The Dialogue of the Dogs."

31 See especially Castillo, who mentions various authors, including Quevedo, and treats Zayas closely, calling her descriptions "revolting and fascinating" (34).

32 For Zayas, I quote from Olivares's edition of "La fuerza de amor" (*Novelas amorosas y ejemplares*) and Yllera's edition of "La inocencia castigada" and "Tarde llega el desengaño" (*Desengaños amorosos*); I use Patsy Boyer's translations for all three.

33 For Kant the description would not be sublime because disgust is useless aesthetically, "obliterating all aesthetic liking" (Korsmeyer 45). But given the magnitude of this place of decaying bodies, it may conjure up an image of something beyond the understanding.

34 The spectacle of dead bodies is something that is also mentioned in a disgust-evoking way in Quevedo's *Buscón*, in the scene in which Pablos's uncle, the executioner, reminds Pablos that his own father's dead body had rotted along the side of the road. Quevedo increases the disgust there by implying that the flesh of the father has been incorporated into the meat pies that Pablos, the uncle and the latter's barbarous friends are eating, combining several disgust elicitors including rotting flesh and the ingestion of contaminated foods. Such profound disgust associated with the socially lowborn in Quevedo is absent from Zayas's "La fuerza del amor."

35 The effect of this elicitor is limited by Jaime, when he implies that the statement about sleeping with the slave was a falsehood merely meant to make Elena suffer " [...] a la negra [...] le di todas las joyas y galas de Elena, delante de ella misma, y le dije, por darla más dolor, que ella había de ser mi mujer, y como a tal se sirviese, y mandase el hacienda, criadas y criados, durmiendo en mi misma cama, aunque esto lo no ejecuto, que antes que Elena acabe, la he de quitar a ella también la vida" (249) (To hurt her more, I regaled the Negress with all of Elena's finery, clothing, and jewels. I announced that she would be my wife and would be served as such and she would enjoy full command over all my possessions, servants, and slaves, and sleep in my bed. This last I have not done, and I intend to put her to death before Elena's life ends) (158).

36 My argument that Cervantes avoids pairing an emotional disgust response with moral characteristics of a character shares some kinship with a broader view proposed by Howard Mancing, in which he has recently argued for Cervantes's continual technique in *Don Quixote* of allowing "a reader's inference of character thoughts [...] [a] sophisticated technique [...] that places greater cognitive demands on the reader [...] [and] affords the reader greater aesthetic satisfaction" (2–3). Mancing cites John Mullan, who refers to the modern narrator in this way: "The consummate omniscient narrator will often leave the reader to work out why characters act as they do" (*How Novels Work* 44).

PART THREE

Perception

6 Sight, Sound, Scent, and Sense: Reading the *Cancionero de Palacio*

E. MICHAEL GERLI

The manner in which human sense perception is organized, the medium in which it is accomplished, is determined not only by nature but by historical circumstances as well.

Walter Benjamin,
The Work of Art in the Age of Mechanical Reproduction

In his exploration of the materiality of texts and the performative nature of textuality Jerome McGann, author of an important book titled *The Textual Condition*, notes that "[texts] are produced and reproduced under specific social and institutional conditions, and hence [...] every text, including those that may appear to be purely private, is a social text. This view entails a corollary understanding that a 'text' is not a 'material thing' but a material event or set of events, a point in time (or a moment in space) where certain communicative interchanges are being practiced" (21). This observation leads me to explore some of the larger dimensions and processes involved in the materiality of medieval manuscripts, particularly those synergies of the medieval manuscript page that often have been ignored or, worse, erased by the discipline of philology and textual editing as they privileged the written message over all other manuscript elaboration and were scientifically codified, defined, and classified in the nineteenth century and practised without much reflection throughout the twentieth.

My point of reference for this exercise is the so-called *Cancionero de Palacio* (ms. 2653, Biblioteca Universitaria de Salamanca, or SA-7 in Brian Dutton's cataloguing scheme), which, as Keith Whinnom noted, is embellished with "dibujos de parejas desnudas, y de animales ocupados en el ayuntamiento carnal" (drawings of naked couples and animals engaged in carnal acts and copulation) (San Pedro 18), which frame courtly poems that were misleadingly described by Francisca Vendrell de Millás (87), the first modern editor of the work, and later by Alexander Parker in *The Philosophy of Love in Spanish Literature* (18, 20) as essentially Platonic in nature. To make matters worse, modern editors of the *Cancionero* such as Ana María Álvarez Pellitero have chosen to select and move around indiscriminately in their editions the drawings found in the manuscript, ignoring the images' relevance for the production of meaning in the text.

The manuscript pages of the *Cancionero* are replete with abundant, sensual, and, as we shall see, even fragrantly redolent figures that often serve as historiated capitals positioned at the beginning of verse stanzas (they are therefore deliberately placed and are not illustrations or extemporaneous marginalia created by itinerate readers), by means of which we are obligated to enter into the text's written message. In all of them there are close links established between the human form, the human faculties (touch, sight, smell, speech, etc.), and the natural world to produce anthropomorphic drolleries, puns, and narratives, whose meanings extend beyond the mere written words on the page. To be sure, some of the images are clear rebuses while others are anamorphic pictograms that allude to language and parts of words that trigger perceptions beyond the plain discursive statements inscribed on the page.

Sometimes a visual image employed may offer a distorted projection or perspective requiring viewers to concentrate or change their specific vantage point to decipher and recognize it. In some of the compositions and their accompanying illustrations links are established between the images and the human form, as in the anamorphic drollery at the centre of the folio in Figure 6.1 shows.[1]

The large, red, semicircular image with sprouting oak leaves (a symbol of gallantry and daring) is easily recognized as the initial capital E of the verse "El favlar bien me plazeria" (To speak would well please me) and forms an integral visual part of the text. Yet, while an essential piece of the composition, it literally projects from it, just as it requires that we cross it like a painted threshold to retrieve the textual message it initiates. The vibrant red E is placed at the very centre of the folio and visually stands out to serve as the capital of the second stanza in a four-stanza *canción* (song) by the poet Santa Fe. The entire composition addresses the poet's ardent desire but abiding reticence to address his lady, his longing to speak but his inability to do so for fear of her rejection. In the perusal of the text, as we proceed down the folio, the image functions almost like an enjambment, breaking the syntactical progression of the text and compelling the reader to stop, look, and ponder its colourful graphic make-up and consider its possible connections to the wording. As we do so, we realize that, far more than decorative, the image is an important visual extension and complement of the ideas of speech and reticence, the central themes of the poem. As we change perspective and

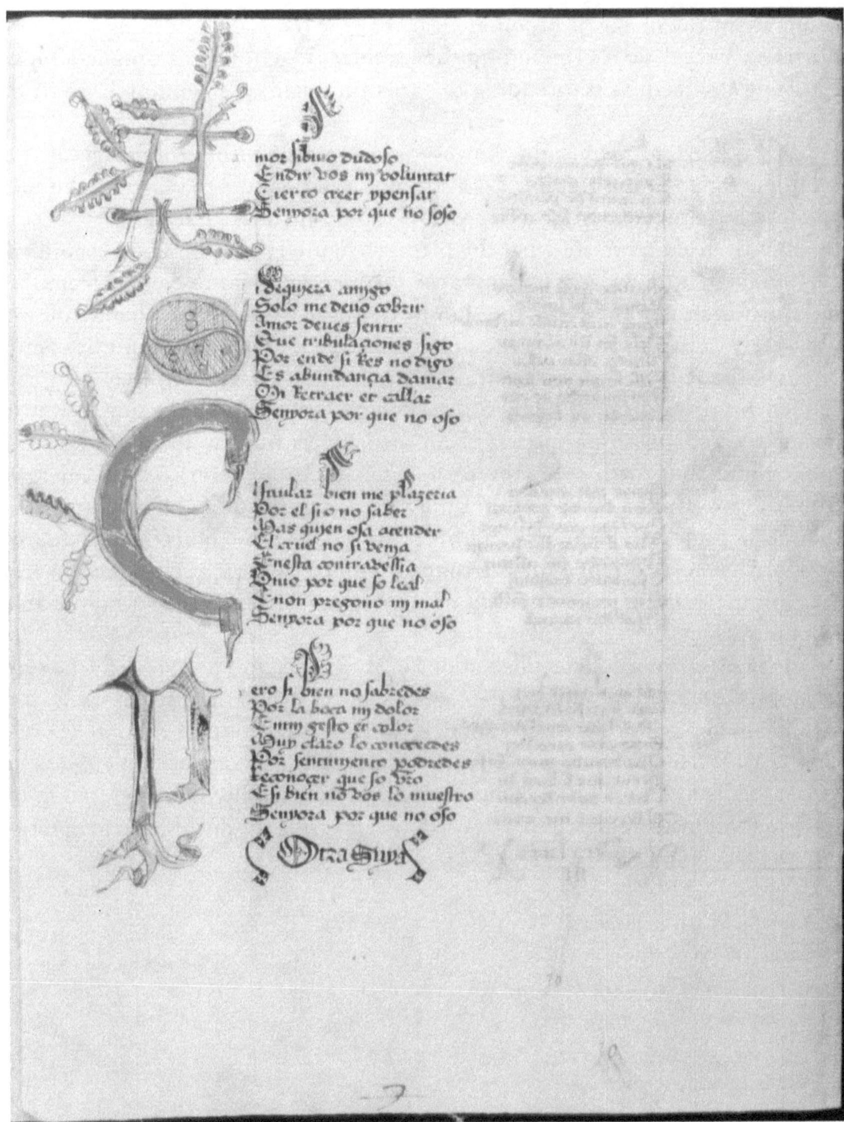

Figure 6.1. Illustrated manuscript initials. *Cancionero de Palacio* of Pedro de Santa Fe. Biblioteca Universitaria de Salamanca, ms. 2653, fol. 117v, detail.

think about the image, it becomes clear that the red E does nothing less than portray a buccal cavity (including the alveolar ridge!), with a tongue almost touching the teeth as if intending to speak but guardedly holding back from doing so.

Moving beyond mere sight, however, we see clearly that the image of the mouth descried in the graphic E is also employed not only to illustrate the text and lead into its reading but to represent graphically the actual auditory speech the mouth utters or recite what the pictured figure is saying. When examined closely, the written words that compose the message seem to emerge from the mouth, which almost spews them onto the page. Much like a banderole or phylactery in art history – or the much later speech balloons found in comic books – the text of the composition next to the stylized mouth conveys the spoken words as they are being articulated by the poet. We are not so much meant to read them, or process them visually, as to hear them as they are spoken and spill forth from the open, once-reticent, mouth. As it emerges from the mouth, the text serves not only to express the thoughts and words of the speaker but also his mood and his status vis-à-vis the object of his desire. In short, it seeks to represent the tone and tenor of the speech voiced in the text (on the graphic representation of audible speech see Wishart; Boone and Mignolo).

The manner in which the illustrations in the *Cancionero* complement the text to supplement word meaning as they seek to move beyond the visual is easily discernible in another of Pedro de Santa Fe's poems, the "Contrast d'amor" (Love's Contrast). When approached solely as a written text, the composition appears to be a rather conventional love complaint, whose only novelty is its application of seafaring and meteorological tropes, used for conveying the distress of a tempestuous love affair:

A qualquier parte que vaya
é todo viento contrario,
senyora, tan adversario
que non sé do me retraya.

Niebla et mal continente,
tu rostro siempre sañoso,
me fazen andar penoso,
manyas de triste poniente;
y, en tanto, me desmaya
este viento tan svario:

qu'a pesado adversario
no sé dónde me retraya.

Ergullo, brio, loçano
e gesto muy trihunfante,
condiçión es de levante,
me desmaya sotamano;
a viento qu'assí me'essaya
el caher es neçessario:
car sombrero adversario
no sé dónde me retraya.

Pobres respuestas et frías
que parten de trasmuntana,
me son la muerte mundana
de tu parte todos días;
aquí conviene que caya
a viento tan ordinario:
que a mortal adversario
no sé dónde me retraya.

La calor de mediodía,
de tus donayres partido,
ma'n la sangre convertido
por mucho caliente en frío;
non parte de mi la raya
d'este viento tan cossario:
car sombrero adversario
non sé dónde me retraya. (fols 131r–v)

Wherever I go / the wind's always contrary, / my lady, so adverse / that I know not where to retreat.

Clouded and unfamiliar havens, / your ever-wrathful countenance, cause me to wander in pain, / the custom of such a west wind; / and, so this fickle gale dismays me: / since from such a demanding adversary, I know not where to retreat.

Pride, impudence, self-assuredness, /triumphant expression, / the state of a tempest wind (levante), / feminine underhandedness which dismay me; / a wind that tries me that way/ought now just to abate: / to a protective shelter, / I cannot perceive where to retreat

> Poor and frigid answers / that arise from the cold north wind / are my daily death, / which comes every day from you; / here now such a dismal storm ought to be still: / from such a mortal adversary / I know not where to retreat.
>
> The mid-day heat, / that springs from your charms, has transformed my blood / from hot into cold as can be; / it fails to take from me the sting / of this corsair wind: / to a protective shelter / I cannot see where to retreat.

For readers schooled in *cancionero* verse, Santa Fe's "Contrast" seems to be an ordinary courtly complaint of unrequited love, save for its conspicuous maritime and meteorological imagery. Filled with allusions to the wind, the fog, the chill, inhospitable anchorages, and the blustery weather that evoke the perceptible tactile sensations of the body, it employs specialized navigational and nautical terms and imagery that compares the speaking voice's emotions to the perils of sailing on frigid, stormy seas. The appearance of terms such as *viento*, *niebla*, *levante*, *mal continente*, *trasmuntana*, *sotamano*, and *cossario* as metaphors that express the chilly, turbulent affair point to the poem's likely composition at the court of Naples, seat of the Aragonese seaborn empire at the time of Alfonso V, where we know Santa Fe exercised his poetic craft (Tato; Dutton 7: 436). The maritime lexemes acquire a symbolic value in the composition and are used to represent a "climate" of bleak, icy rejection in order to express the speaker's turbulent emotions and transmit his adversity and disappointment in love. The first sentiment expressed is that of the impossibility of finding a true direction – an exact course to take – since the lady in question is, like the wind, inconstant, variable, forceful, and ungraspable. Her countenance is an unfamiliar continent or land mass (mal continente), which refuses to offer safe harbour to the distressed mariner. Her gaze is the east wind (levante) that blows through Gibraltar, which at first offers the hope of clearing skies and the coming of the light, but in the end proffers only disappointment and the cold rush of a brutal, unrelenting gale (viento cossario). The unusual seafaring imagery thus points to a series of novel meteorological metaphors upon which the lyrical tension of the composition rests. However, when perused and looked at in its manuscript matrix, there is much more to Santa Fe's composition than its clever use of maritime and navigational imagery to articulate unrequited love. The "Contrast d'amor," like so many of the other compositions in the *Cancionero de Palacio*, is richly adorned with polychrome capitals and images like the one that visually evoked the affects and sensations of the reticent mouth about to speak.

The closing verses of Santa Fe's "Contrast" are transcribed in the manuscript in the following fashion:

Figure 6.2. Closing verses of "Contrast d'amor." *Cancionero de Palacio* of Pedro de Santa Fe. Biblioteca Universitaria de Salamanca, ms. 2653, fols 131v, detail.

The capital P of the stanza that reads "Pobres respuestas et frías" depicts a man under a black cloud struggling with a serpent just as it introduces the image of the *tramuntana*, the cold north wind that points not only to the frigid air from beyond the mountains, but also to the North Star (or literally the star "above the mountains," which in Catalan and French can denote "guide," as in the expression "perdre la tramontane," or to be "inopportunely disoriented," as used by Molière in *Le bourgeois gentilhomme*, "perdre la tramontane dans le pire moment" (4.6). The North Star, of course, is crucial to navigation and for finding one's way over the sea. The historiated capital P of the stanza is in the pictorial form of the stellar constellation Ophiuchus and cleverly advises us that the poetic voice of the "Contrast" is wandering in the dark, has lost its way, and is searching for direction.

But there is more. The figure of Ophiuchus, the Serpent Bearer, forms the constellation of the same name. It is centred on the equator and deemed crucial by navigators for quickly locating the North Star, since it stretches from the head of Hercules in the north to Scorpio in the south. Although the figure of Ophiuchus is a separate constellation, it is generally depicted as a man struggling with a serpent that attempts to twist and coil around his body (see Figure 6.3). The serpent, formed by the constellation Serpens, is usually joined to the figure of Ophiuchus to comprise a single, larger constellation that may serve to determine better the direction of east and west vis à vis the north-south coordinates represented by the head and the feet of the man (Kerigan and Moore 9).

All the signs of the zodiac have roots in mythology and relate to the legend of how the Olympian gods took animal shapes to flee the monster Typhon. In ancient mythology Ophiuchus is associated with unfaithful lovers and stems from when the suspicious Apollo set a crow to watch over his beloved Coronis. When the crow flew to Apollo to tell him that Coronis had been unfaithful, in his fury Apollo blamed the crow for not keeping Coronis's lover away from her and he transformed the crow into Ophiuchus, the Serpent Wrestler. The story of the Serpent Wrestler is also closely associated with Aesculapius in Ovid's *Metamorphoses* (Bk XV). At the same time, in judicial astrology persons born under the sign of Ophiuchus were considered to be flamboyant seekers who were sartorially self-conscious, favouring bright colours and the wearing of pleated clothing, not unlike the figure depicted in the *Cancionero de Palacio*. Finally, a person who is born under Ophiuchus is said to be extremely curious, passionate, and exceptionally jealous. Other traits may include an explosive temper, furtiveness, a thirst for knowledge, and sexual fascination (Berg).

Clearly, the illustrator who crafted the historiated P of "Pobres respuestas et frías" in the form of Ophiuchus appreciated the full connotations of the written stanza he was illustrating beyond its simple meteorological and navigational metaphors and coordinates, reading out and away from the stanza's more literal,

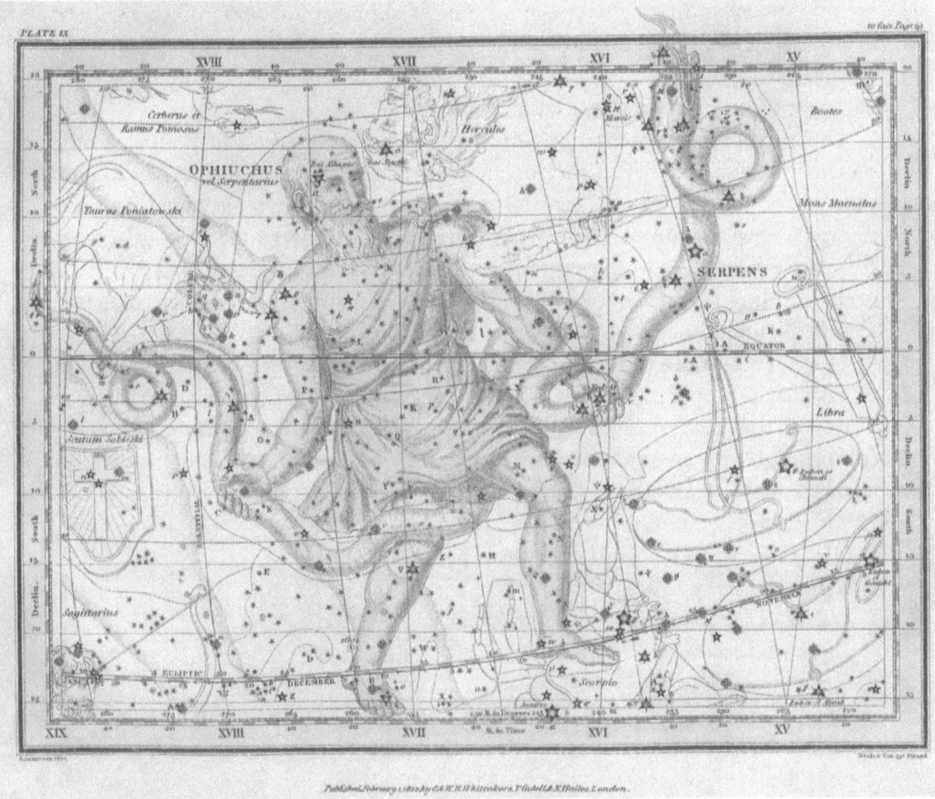

Figure 6.3. Ophiuchus or Serpentarius. Alexander Jamieson, *A Celestial Atlas* (London: G & W.B. Whittaker, 1822), public domain, commons.wikimedia.org.

word-bound sense. He embellished it with the portrait of Ophiuchus, which leads the knowledgeable reader beyond metaphors of mere navigation and dangerous weather to perceive and contemplate a love affair that, under a menacing cloud, has lost direction based on the suspicion of a rival lover and all the collateral meanings conjured in memory by the representation of the narrative of the Serpent Wrestler. At the same time, on a completely different level, the illustration leads the reader to ponder the moral struggle of the man and the serpent as an icon that invokes initial temptation and futile labours in the struggle against sin and passion. In this way the pictorial accompaniment to the text sets off additional cognitive processes of analogy and association that produce a supplement, a metalinguistic gloss that, more than a marginal note, optically opens up new referential possibilities for the poem's understanding. The image becomes a supratext, as opposed to a subtext, or a metalinguistic sign that propels us into another medium of perception which continues to flesh out imaginatively the inscribed and, by comparison, more transparent and undemanding textual meaning.

The pictorial ornamentations of the *Cancionero de Palacio* point to other semantic realms and set in motion new forms of reference, insight, and cognition, as their ocular input is transformed, elaborated, stored, recovered, and used to create new meanings. Their presence incites the viewer's memory to perceive correlative narratives to the written word that produce supplementary forms of understanding that generate a new now only partially verbal language that transcends the unadorned text.

There is still more to the illustrated "Contrast," however, as its accompanying visual images propel us towards other, non-visual, forms of cognition and perception – in this case to olfactory awareness. The concluding stanza of Santa Fe's composition as seen in the manuscript is also illustrated and begins with a line initial capital L presented in the form of a unicorn (see above). It reads as follows:

> L[in the form of a unicorn]a calor de mediodía,
> de tus donayres partido,
> m'an la sangre convertido,
> por mucho caliente et frío;
> non parte de mi la raya
> d'este viento cossario:
> car sobrero adversario
> no sé dónde me retraya.

> T[in the form of a unicorn]he mid-day heat, / which radiates from your charms, has transformed my blood / from hot into cold as can be; / it fails to take from me the mark / of this corsair wind: / to a protective shelter / I cannot see where to retreat.

As we might suspect, the image formed by the capital L does more than simply represent a unicorn. Doubtless inspired to put it there by the poet's reference to the effects of the warmth that, with the heat of noontime, radiates from his lady's charms (la calor de mediodía, / de tus donayres partido) and its influence on his humoral constitution (m'an la sangre convertido / por mucho caliente et frío), the illustrator prompts us to think about the unicorn as the picture conjures elements of the well-known legends regarding the beast that circulated both in oral lore and in scientific treatises (see O. Shepherd).[2]

The fable of the unicorn is associated with the allure of the feminine and basic sexual instinct. In the case of Santa Fe's "Contrast" the image of the beast on

Figure 6.4. The fable of the unicorn. British Library, Royal ms. 973.12, fol. 13r, detail.

the edge is used to exemplify seductive perils carried on the wind that can be far more dangerous than any storm at sea. The unicorn is said to be a ferocious beast that can be tamed only by its seeing and, most important, sensing the presence of a beautiful, unclothed virgin. It is drawn to the damsel not just by her visible, naked beauty but by the tug of the scent that emanates from her body. Pulled towards her first by her loveliness, the beast is subsequently lured to the lady by her aroma carried on the wind. Moved by its keen sense of smell, the heady scent of the damsel leads the creature to kneel before her and, finally, to fall in a faint under the influence of the intoxicating fragrance which issues from her lap. Full of erotic suggestion, the scene is admirably represented in ms. Harley 973.12 in the British Library, reproduced in figure 6.4. The position of the animal's snout in the damsel's lap and its rigidly stiff horn, so unyielding that it penetrates the frame of the picture, leave little doubt as to its phallic nature and comprise a clear message of the image's lubricious connotations.

In the second half of the thirteenth century Richard de Fournival in his *Bestiare d'Amour* (Bestiary of Love) forges a close link between the unicorn, feminine beauty, and basic sexual attraction. The *Bestiare* is nothing short of an attempt at seduction by means of poetic commentary on the images in the *Book of Beasts*. Mestre Richard, the name adopted by the speaking voice in the composition, seeks to engage his lady in conversation by illustrating the vagaries of human love through comparisons to the legendary animals of the *Bestiare*. The passions, he says, are not restricted to humankind but are reflected in the mirror of nature. They are characteristics of all of God's creatures.

When he speaks about the irresistible desire that draws him to his mistress, Mestre Richard appeals to the unicorn, attracted to the lady through its keen sense of smell. Comparing himself to the mythical beast, which possesses the finest olfactory perception in the animal kingdom, Mestre Richard confesses that he is captivated by the irresistible aromatic fragrance of his mistress' charms:

> Et par le flairier meïsme fui je pris, ausi com li unicornes ki s'endort au douc[h] flair de la virginité a la demoisele [...]. Si ke li sage veneor ki sa nature seivent metent une pucele en son trepas, et il s'endort en son geron. (*Il Bestiario d'amore* 56, ll. 13–14, 19–21)

> And just as the unicorn is attracted by the aroma of the young maid's virginity, was I seized [...] Like the wise hunter who subdues him by placing a virgin in his path, whence he kneels before her and falls asleep in her lap.

When the unicorn senses the lady, it is pulled to her as if by an irresistible force, led to its surrender and humbled before her, signalling its unconditional willingness to serve her. It is then that the hunter, like the one depicted in the image from ms. Harley, can capture and kill the creature, preserving its coveted horn to use in love philters, aphrodisiacs, and potions meant to intensify sexual arousal. It is only by means of the scent of a woman, and the promise of a physical encounter, that the unicorn may be restrained and captured. The driving source of power exercised by the lady over the unicorn is raw, sexual magnetism mediated by intense olfactory perception.

Under the rubric "de unicornu" Alain de Lisle in his *Quaestiones* (late twelfth century) provides the scientific reason for the unicorn's sensory inclinations. It is based on the theory of the corporeal humours (PL 210). The unicorn's *calidissima natura* (extremely hot constitution) Alain says, pulls the beast towards its opposite constitutional element, the *femina frigida et humida* (cool and humid woman). The excess of warm humours dilates the unicorn's heart, inflaming its nasal passages. When the beast senses the cool, moist aura that emanates from between the lady's thighs, however, it is drawn to her and puts its head upon her lap in absolute surrender. Alain notes that the damsel's role in the affair is also far from passive, often complementing the aromas that radiate from her body with seductive, beckoning gestures aimed at tempting the animal into total submission. In short, the unicorn was clearly understood to be something other than just a complement to feminine beauty. The image of the unicorn in the margins of Santa Fe's poem thus elicits what Alain's French contemporaries might have called *l'odeur de femme*, and modern science refers to as pheromones. More than the stormy passion invoked in the words of Santa Fe's composition, the illustration calls to mind the material emanations of the female body, whose provocative, fragrant sway aggravates the winds of love and physical attraction that continue to beleaguer the speaking subject in the composition.

For the person knowledgeable in the lore of the unicorn it is evident that there is an entirely different sexual and olfactory dimension meant to be drawn out in the reader/looker of the *Cancionero de Palacio*. When the written verses are combined with the image of the beast, an instinctive, olfactory understanding of the text immediately occurs. It is also clear that the unicorn signifies by visual analogy, as in semiotics, and points to a larger meaning or narrative that is greater either than the illustration or the text if each were to be taken alone. The combination of image and text elicit the olfactory cognition commonly attributed to the unicorn, which generates a larger figurative sense beyond the text when the words and the colourful image of the animal are combined. If approached consonantly, text and image at the level of the manuscript page produce a kind of sensorial supplementarity as messages and meanings that are neither exclusively textual nor exclusively visual arise from the experience of both reading and looking in the *Cancionero de Palacio*.

Although Santa Fe's "Contrast" ends with the stanza where we see the L in the form of a unicorn, the visual, olfactory, and sexual provocation produced by the image doubtless continued to arouse the illustrator's imagination. In Santa Fe's "Copla esparça" (an *esparça* is a kind of witty composition meant to entertain and amuse), which follows the "Contrast," the illuminator, still in olfactory unicorn mode, makes a series of explicit sexual puns and jokes from the margins about the new text that is being embellished (see figure 6.5). By means of the following image, the wording of Santa Fe's rather innocent, even abstract, composition (as worded text it works off references to medieval faculty psychology; on faculty psychology and desire in medieval and early modern Spain see Folger), becomes daringly risqué. In it the poet broods over the wisdom of terminating his affair and concludes that it is impossible to do so, considering the rare nature of its origin and the impossibility of erasing the lady's image from his mind. The initial word of the composition, *Con*, meaning *with* in Castilian, inscribed in the manuscript on the heels of the unicorn image above it, produces the cross-linguistic pun in Catalan – *con* or *cunt* – which in turn compels the mischievous illustrator to portray

Figure 6.5. Opening verses of "Copla esparça." *Cancionero de Palacio* of Pedro de Santa Fe. Biblioteca Universitaria de Salamanca, ms. 2653, fol. 131v, detail.

in the left margin a woman (presumably the poetic speaking voice's alluring lady) with her legs spread wide. In addition, there is a split caption to the image that reads *miami-* (myfri-) just above the woman's head, and *-co* (-end) just below her genitals, which obliges the reader to scan the image both visually and textually from head to bottom, as it were, in order to capture fully its lewd implications.

Briefly, then, the poetic voice of the *esparça* complains of the desire to end the affair but also the impossibility of doing so. Santa Fe cannot drive out the picture (literally the imprint) of the lady from his mind – "¿cómo quitar poría / la prenta de su semblança?" (fol. 131v) (how can I purge the imprint of your likeness?) – since he is conquered by her semblance, which remains the sublime cause of his passion. Given the thought's origin in her likeness and defeated by the prospect of being able to end the relationship, Santa Fe concludes that it is only natural to forgo censure and stop resisting: "Non basta seso nin arte / tal desgrado abandone, / mas pensando donde parte es forçado que perdone" (fol. 131v) (There is no thought or art that can dispel my displeasure; yet, on seeing from whence it arises, it's unavoidable that I pardon it). The illustrator's eye, with the image of the unicorn directly above, subverts whatever uplifting thought a reader might have brought to the text of the *esparça* by graphically portraying the image of what, from the margins, signals the actual vision of the lady impressed on the poet's mind and the cause of his irresistible attraction.

In this way the images of the *Cancionero de Palacio* function in an iconic fashion and invite the reader-viewer to think through both the written word and the figure depicted next to, and even above, it on the page. Almost as they do in an ekphrasis, the images cast ancillary meanings over the text next to which they appear. The vivid pictures invite attention and are designed to make reader-viewers "perceive" the person or thing depicted in the book in ways that go beyond the uniquely verbal or strictly pictorial representation of it. The illustrations provide additional means for further understanding the words and thinking both about them and beyond them. They are testimonials to the importance of the full materiality of the page in medieval reading and to the complex, cognitively multidimensional nature of it.

In general, as we leaf through the *Cancionero de Palacio*, we see that the images constitute a summons to change, revise, and extend the meaning of the worded text – indeed, to gloss, rewrite, and reimagine it, often in unsuspected ways. The *Cancionero* becomes a self-consciously "open text," or one that invites the reader-viewer's collaboration in the production of the meanings that can be found in it (Eco 7), launching a myriad of frequently hidden possibilities in its sense, form, cognition, and significance. At every step there are accompanying narratives that arise from the pictures in the margins, storylines that may lead to different cognitive ways of approaching the text and to additional, enriched ways of understanding that uncover the fuller possibilities of meaning in the poetry copied in the *Cancionero*.

The *Cancionero de Palacio* places the historiated initials of the text specifically at the beginning of each stanza to produce an effect that at first appears to be not unlike the *motes*, *empreças*, and *invenciones* that formed such an important part of fifteenth-century Castilian courtly culture (see Macpherson; Rico; Casas Rigall). By doing so, the drawings were meant to provoke reflection and encourage the beholder to search for a whole new range of significations and nuances embedded in them and in the poem that they illustrate. Moreover, the illuminated capitals on the page were calculated to function as integral parts of the manuscript at the time of its creation and, therefore, as deliberate, essential elements of any message that might be conveyed by reading or contemplating each of its folios. Although the scribes of texts and their illustrators could often be one and the same person, illuminators were usually different from scribes and followed them in the crafting of a manuscript. Regardless of whether the texts and the images in the *Cancionero* are the work of one or two hands, however, the images are not like random glosses or bits of marginalia placed there by itinerant readers. They and the verses they illustrate are clearly intended to be one of a piece, components of a larger meaning.

NOTES

1 I am grateful to the Biblioteca Universitaria de Salamanca, where the *Cancionero de Palacio* is kept, for permission to reproduce the images used here. Translations are my own.

2 Although bestiaries, per se, are relatively scarce among surviving manuscripts in medieval Iberia, evidence of their knowledge and circulation does abound in direct and indirect allusions to them in both the plastic arts and literature. The legend of the unicorn circulated widely in the courtly milieu that produced the *Cancionero de Palacio.* It was an amply disseminated narrative that could be found in love poetry and sentimental prose in the fifteenth century. As shown by Deyermond ("Sirens"). This is the case with the Marqués de Santillana's "Sonnet XXIII," the *Coronacion de la Señora Gracisla* by Juan de Flores, *Lo libre de les dones* by Eiximenis, *El libro de las bienandanzas e fortunas de Lope García Salazar,* and *Celestina,* in addition to various compositions by other *cancionero* poets such as Costana and Alvar Gómez de Ciudad Real.

In examining striking images in other medieval manuscripts similar to the ones just reviewed, Michael Camille observes how they are "exactly the opposite of spontaneous unconscious associations" and how "medieval artists created marginal images from a 'reading,' or rather an intentional misreading, of the text" (41) not specifically to illustrate it but to interpret it and comment upon it. In this way, "marginal images are *conscious* usurpations, perhaps even political statements about diffusing the power of the text through its unraveling [...] rather than repressed meanings that suddenly flash back onto the surface of things" (42).

Doubtless aware of the potential for humour, ironic contradiction, and subversion in the possibilities of the written word, the illustrator of the *Cancionero de Palacio* was prepared to pursue these possibilities and create unsettling emblems placed at crucial points in the verse transcriptions to form visual glosses based on extra-textual lore and narrative. The conflicting messages posed by the anonymous illustrator's initials in the *Cancionero de Palacio* are, then, sophisticated literary inflections, highly developed acts of interpretation that arise from the borders of the manuscript. Through their intentional, doubtless comical, modulation the illustrator sought to extend the thematic and epistemological frames of each poem so as often to include the presence of opposite or concealed messages. By adopting certain discrete images, the artist inscribed his own complex, resistant reading of each poem to reveal the ever present allure of ironic commentary.

The illuminations of the *Cancionero* allow us to see what could be conjured by the late medieval imagination when confronted with a carefully crafted text intended to evoke love's suffering. When Santa Fe's words are experienced in the context of the manuscript and its framing illuminations, a new cognitive dynamic emerges that takes on ingenious forms and generates ambiguous, repeatedly carnivalesque discourses that reflect the medieval mind's attempt to separate out the spirit from the flesh. In the *Contrast* the illustrator ironically grafts explicit sexual energy on to courtly love, evoking scent to cast the emblem of physical desire over it and give the lie to its innocence. By means of these illustrative images, spiritual refinement and sensory animal eroticism are revealed to coexist simultaneously, one as determiner and boundary of the other in a constantly shifting pattern. In blending the libidinal images of love with the solemn language of courtly devotion, the illustrator inverts the well-mannered message contained in the words of the poem, challenges it from the edge of the page, and reveals the ambivalence and sublimations of courtly passion, which in the medieval mind is never able to free itself from physical desire. The outcome is a highly nuanced idiom nurtured by both text and image that generates an interrogation of the actual nature of Santa Fe's declaration of suffering; an ingenious amplification of his words that exposes the abiding presence and attraction of the animal and natural world and, as a result, probes the endurance of courtly discipline, restraint, and authenticity. The texts of the *Cancionero de Palacio* can be fully understood only within the larger sphere of their illustrations, which, like a siren's song, call forth raw sexual meaning and discernment at the height of ostensible courtly sincerity.

One thing remains sure: the *Cancionero*'s pictorial embellishments served as a medium for the perception and expression of ideas and sensations that went considerably beyond, if not entirely against, the sense of the written words deployed in it. Through the visual images and their evocations the surface implications of texts and language are destabilized and the reader-viewer is led to uncover deeper tensions that structure and define meaning in the manuscript. The illustrator of *Palacio* read the poems not as a series of mere texts evocative of emotional states, but as a catalogue of emblems or as a storehouse for the evocation of themes, ideas, sensations, and feelings that bring forth contradiction and serve as a touchstone for a specific style of dialogical reading and interpretation. By conjoining the images with Santa Fes's evocation of love's torments, the illustrator pointed to the clashing forces that define the medieval understanding of eros.

From this it remains clear that the *Cancionero de Palacio* comprises more than a mere written text in the late medieval Castilian poetic repertoire. As it was read and, most important, seen, it was also envisioned as something more than its individual parts. The convergence of text and image in the *Cancionero* extends itself well beyond the strictly ideational and virtual world of words, thought, and memory to manifest itself in the realm of the senses. Shunning a strictly verbal constitution, it takes on pictorial, sonic, and even olfactory dimensions that become interdependent with the written word. A dynamic and truly protean text, it thus produces forms of multidimensional cognitive insight. Simultaneously reading and looking at the *Cancionero* allows us to explore some of the larger dimensions and processes involved in the materiality of medieval manuscripts, and appreciate how, by means of the human faculties that exceed plain reason, its illuminated folios often engage different levels of knowledge, intuition, and perception.

The sensory calques and puns generated by the *Cancionero*'s illustrations raise important theoretical questions about the nature of medieval reading and the manuscript page and demonstrate that the latter constitutes much more than a seamless, homogenuous medium of communication. In fact, it is clear that the illustrated manuscript page constitutes itself as a field of competing discourses, media, and presences: the poet, the scribe, the illuminator, and the rubricator all could seek to rival and displace, as well as complement, each other on it through their use of different forms of representation. Each was independent of the other and, at the same time, called attention to or substituted the other in the exercise of his craft. In the examples just examined the purely graphic elements of the page fail to explain or describe – that is, to illustrate – the accompanying text. They cannot be taken as mimetic renderings of the verbal into the visual, but rather must be seen as visual subversions of the verbal. In short, the illustrated folio page is never the expression of a single isolated individual with a univocal message. Its realization required the participation of a number of hands and imaginations and its perusal produces an epistemological effect that can never be captured through ordinary textual editing. The *medieval* manuscript page calls for interactive reading, for careful attention to a greater heteroglossic and sensory effect, in order to capture its full, often contradictory, symbolic unity.

Beyond this, the appreciation of the interactive nature of the reading process in illuminated manuscripts should lead us to question the traditional hierarchies that govern our own modern textual economies, which unfailingly privilege the text over the image and place visual representations in ancillary roles, sometimes even dispensing entirely with them, or in the case of the edited *Palacio* manscript, moved about haphazardly within the body of an edition, rendering them as mere decorations. In conclusion, what would happen if the reverse were true? Or if the medieval imagination approached both the visual, the verbal, and the sensorial as signs that carried equal authority?

7 Treating Sensory Ailments in Early Modern Domestic Literature

CAROLYN A. NADEAU

For humanists in early modern Spain and other parts of Europe physical functions and psychological states were interdependent.[1] Drawing on the Aristotelian doctrine of sense perception outlined in *De anima*, which states that what is understood on an intellectual level is first known through the senses, Humanists privileged sight and sound as "higher" senses but also acknowledged, via the convivial feast, that the "lower" senses of taste, touch, and smell are also key to the pursuit of knowledge. But what happens when one or more of the physical senses ceases to function as it should? If any of the senses were damaged, how would the loss be dealt with in order to restore harmony between the physiological and the psychological? In what ways did the leading medical doctors of sixteenth-century Spain address issues of both injury to the senses and maintaining their proper functioning? Moreover, how did their assertions affect the general public?

To answers these questions, this essay explores the means by which healthcare providers treated the senses. At leading universities in Spain doctors published translations and critical editions of established classical medical texts as well as their own original works, which described ingredients for remedies that improved ailments of touch, for eye and ear infections, gum and tooth disease, and plague symptoms. Compared with the other organs, the nose was rarely dealt with as an illness; rather, as part of the olfactory sense, the nose became an effective vehicle for treating infection and disease through inhaling perfumed waters, scented pouches, and other fragrances. Doctors were involved in ongoing debates of the future of medicine and whether the study of medicine should continue through the accepted approach of traditional Galenism or should consider ideas that encompassed a pro-innovative Galenism, which relied on observational analysis.[2]

Although the academic publications of reputable physicians such as Andrés Laguna (1494–1560), Francisco Vallés (1524–92) (both of whom promoted an innovative approach), and Luis Mercado (1525–1611?) (who supported a traditional one) held sway over institutions of higher learning, I am more drawn to the manifestations of healthcare delivery as seen through the lens of matrons and the handwritten, prescriptive, domestic manuals that form part of a compendium of household recipes for food, health, hygiene, and beauty. These anonymous manuscripts, which range from the late fifteenth century to the early seventeenth century, were written in several different hands and, most likely, over several generations.

This essay seeks to strengthen our understanding of how women approached the physical senses and how they cared for members of their domestic communities in sickness and in health. Authorship, intended audience, and structure radically differed between domestic and academic texts, but the theory behind treating failed senses is strikingly similar. Using four anonymous domestic manuals and the writing of three leading Spanish academics of the day, the essay examines ingredients and remedies for eye and ear infections, for gum and tooth disease, and for plague symptoms associated with touch. An examination of the medical treatment of the senses recorded in domestic and academic literature will strengthen our understanding of how women who managed households and men who attended to kings and lectured and published within the academy approached the physical senses in sickness and in health.

Women and Medicine

While the professionalization of medicine left little room for women practitioners to study at universities, publish theories, or practise medicine legally, in early modern Spain women were still the main source of primary care for their families.[3] According to Luis García Ballester, in Valencia in the first third of the sixteenth century there were "between five and seven doctors per ten thousand inhabitants," leaving plenty of room for informal medical practices for both men and women (*Medicine* 247). Indeed, from the Middle Ages into the early modern period women were primary caregivers in all-female religious institutions, served as medical attendants in both hospitals and private homes, engaged in family practices when the spouse was a medical practitioner, and continued their role as midwives. At home women practitioners across the country birthed children, prepared remedies for the ill, cared for all family members, produced beauty aids for both men and women, in addition to being responsible for the preparation of the daily meals. Most of this knowledge was transmitted orally, but there are several manuscripts still available today that have preserved common household remedies.

Domestic manuals complement medical texts, as they provide evidence of health-related practices performed in the home. As Elaine Leong has signalled, "they concentrate on the practicalities of doing and making rather than presenting theoretical frameworks, they give a sense not only of householders' areas of interest in natural knowledge but also of the types of activities carried out within early modern homes" (83). Although Leong is referencing traditions in England, this tendency also holds true in Spain.[4] For the most part authorship remains anonymous, yet several critics contend that these manuals were written by and for women (Pérez Samper; Martínez Crespo), while others have identified names of authors based on comments and clues provided within the manuscript itself (Oliván Santaliestra and Pilo).

The only one available today in edited form is *Manual de mugeres en el qual se contienen muchas y diversas reçeutas muy buenas* ("A manual for women in which is contained many, very good and diverse recipes") (1475–1525). It contains 145 recipes and is organized into the following seven categories: medical remedies (22+1), fragrances (24), facial cosmetics (31), waters and other recipes for the hands (10+1), washes and other remedies for the mouth (13), food recipes (29), and treatments for the hair (13+1) (30).[5] However, in the manuscript they do not follow said order: recipes from each section are scattered throughout. Thus, recipes for making sausage and preserving peaches share pages with remedies for earaches and ointments for rashes as well as instructions for making shampoo and tooth powder.

In addition, three unedited manuscripts are housed in the National Library of Spain (BNE).[6] *Livro de receptas de pivetes, pastilhas e vvas perfumadas y conserbas* (A book of recipes for incense, tablets and perfumes and preserves) (BNE mss 1462, sixteenth century) begins in Portuguese but after the first 15 of 65 folios, the language switches to Castilian. It contains 108 household recipes, several of which deal with eye infections, two that treat oral hygiene, and two that deal with eruptions of the skin related to the plague and to breast cancer. *Recetas y memorias para guisados, confituras, olores, aguas, afeites, adobos de guantes, ungüentos y medicinas para muchas enfermedades* (Recipes and other records for stews, preserves, fragrances, waters, cosmetics, skin softeners, ointments and medicine for many illnesses) (BNE mss 6058, sixteenth–seventeenth centuries), is actually compiled of three different books with a total of 207 recipes of which 150 pertain to food. The first two books treat only edible recipes, while the third and final book, *Libro en que se hallaran diversas memorias ansí para adobar guantes como para azer muchas y diferentes ollores. Agua almizcada y otras aguas y cosas de buena ollor* (A book in which is found diverse records such as for softening gloves or for making many and different fragrances, musk-scented water and other waters and things of good aromas) contains a series of recipes for perfumes, scented oils and waters, incense, and softeners. In this manuscript only three recipes treat disease related to the senses and all three are exclusively related to oral hygiene. The third work, *Receptas experimentadas para diversas cosas* (Tested recipes for many things) (BNE mss 2019, sixteenth–seventeenth centuries), is enormous, containing over 700 recipes that, like the other manuals, deal with food preparation, hygiene, health, and beauty.

In all of these manuscripts the anonymous authors approach the senses in different ways. For sight and hearing, remedies are curative and treat the individual only after a problem has occurred, for example, eye and ear infections and seeing and hearing loss. For the senses of taste and touch, at times recipes are curative – gum disease or sores from the plague; at other times they are geared towards maintaining proper hygiene and

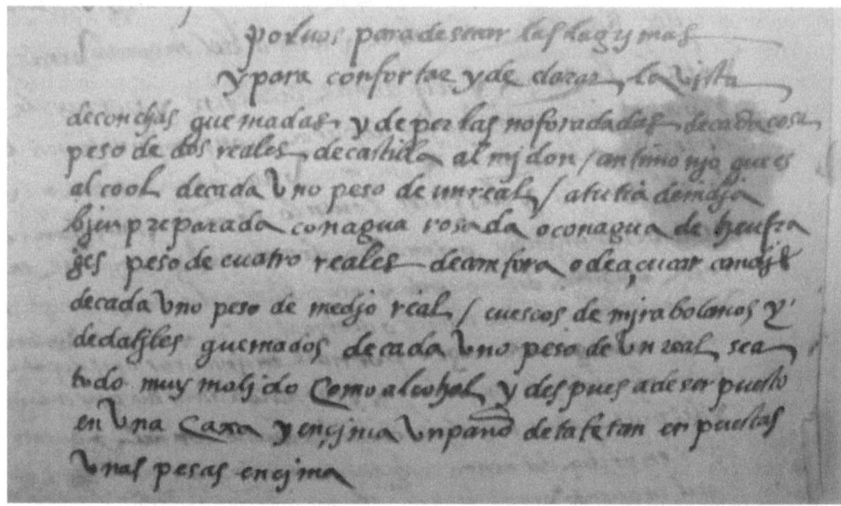

Figure 7.1. Recipe 1: "Polvos para de secar las lágrymas y para confortar y de clarar la vista." National Library of Spain, ms. 2019, 169v, detail.

even beauty, brightening teeth or hand softeners. In fact, the majority of recipes in all four works that relate to the skin and sense of touch focus on beauty much more than on health. Finally, regarding the sense of smell, I have found no recipes in any of these manuals that treat ailments of the olfactory glands or nasal cavity, but recipes involving the sense of smell and inhaling through the nose in an effort to cure other ailments are abundant in all four manuscripts. Perfumed waters, incense sticks, and fragrant pastes, when inhaled, were effective remedies against "bad air" diseases like the plague.

Sight

Recipes that deal with eye infections include topical powders directly applied to the eye and rinses used to flush the eye. Titles usually reveal what kind of eye infections the remedy addresses but many, such as "polvos para los ojos" (powders for the eyes), "recepta para los ojos muy provada" (a well proven recipe for the eyes), or "memoria de aguas para sanar los ojos" (record of waters for healing eyes) offer remedies only for unspecified ocular problems. Others, such as "para los ojos mando están ynchados y encarnicados" (For eyes that are swollen and bloodshot I prescribe) or "polvos para de secar las lágrimas y para confortar y de clarar la vista" (powders for drying up teary eye, for comfort and improving vision), give a stronger indication of the specific problem (see Figure 7.1).[7] In the latter recipe, the author includes a series of animal, vegetable, and mineral ingredients that are ground into a fine powder:[8]

> De conchas quemadas y de perlas no foradadas de cada cosa peso de dos reales de Castilla. Almidón, antimonio que es alcool de cada, no peso de un real. Atutia de media bien preparada con agua rosada o con agua de heufrages, peso de cuatro reales. De comfora o de açucar candi de cada uno peso de medio real. Cuescos de mirabolancas y de dátiles quemados de cada uno peso de un real. Sea todo muy molido como alcohol y despues a de ser puesto en una caxa y ençima un paño de tafetán enpuestas unas pesas encima. (ms. 2019, 169v)

> From scorched shells and pearls not yet perforated, from each the weight of two Castilian reals. Starch, antimony, which is alcohol, of each less than the weight of one real. Half-strength tutty well prepared in rose water or with Euphrates water, the weight of four reals. Camphor or rock candy each one the weight of a half of real. Scorched myraballum seed and date pit, each one the weight of one real. Grind everything well together like alcohol. After it should be stored in a box covered with a taffeta cloth and weights placed on top.[9]

To get a better understanding of these ingredients, we must turn to the academic literature and the medical culture that permeated sixteenth-century Spain. In particular, the translation and annotations of Andrés Laguna of Dioscorides's *De materia medica* (On medicinal substances) are instrumental in understanding the site of domestic natural inquiry and production.

Pedacio Dioscorides Anazarbeo (Pedanius Dioscorides of Anazarbus) (1555), Laguna's publication on Dioscorides's *De material medica*, was reprinted more than twenty times. In this work we find descriptions of the natural world, animals, plants, and minerals, as they relate to maintaining good health and treating disease. With each entry Laguna presents the known names of the product, provides a translation of Dioscorides's original text, and follows with his own annotation on the entry.[10] He refuted commentaries made by earlier translators and pointed out their inconsistencies and errors. Analysing the nuances of a translated word's meaning also brought into question the validity of the original texts and instigated a new direction in Galenism. Throughout his life Laguna supported the theory of the four humours that Hippocrates had developed and later Galen refined, which became the basis for Galenism, but he became increasingly aware of the importance of empirical evidence. This type of scepticism, coupled with the scepticism of the value of a given translation, opened the door to re-evaluating humorism and Galenism.[11]

In the introduction to *Pedacio Dioscorides Anazarbeo* Laguna begins by emphasizing both the validity of Galen's findings and the importance of empirical

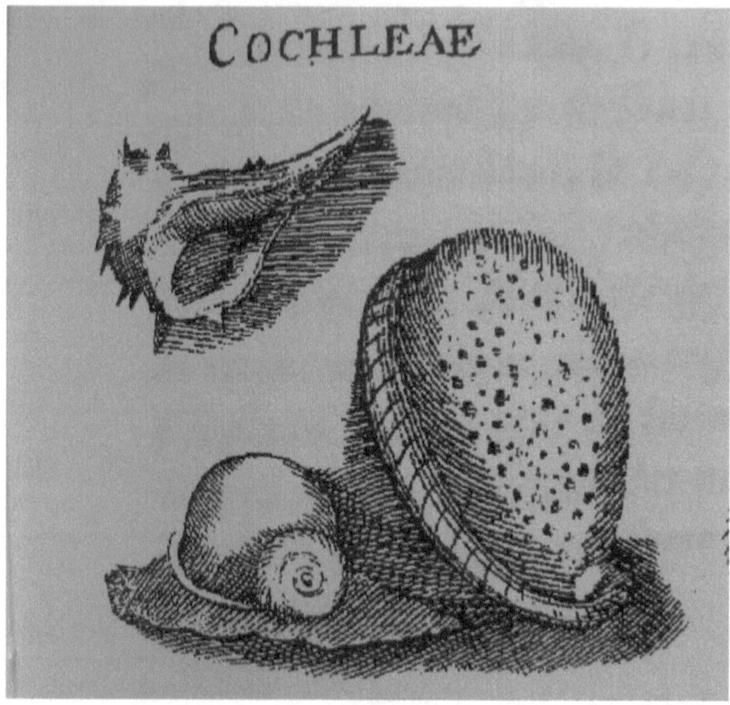

Figure 7.2. "Cochleae" Francisco Suárez de Ribera, *Pedacio Dioscorides Anazarbeo* (bk II, 20). With permission of the New York Academy of Medicine.

analysis: "Ser del todo imposible, que puedan conocer la facultad de las medicinas compuestas, ni componerlas, ni seguramente usar della los que ignoran la natura, y virtud de las simples, demuéstralo en muchos lugares Galeno, y *también la viva razón lo amonesta*" (It is entirely impossible to know the ability of compound medicine, mix them, or use them with confidence, for those ignorant of the nature and virtue of simple medicine. Galen proves this in many places and *sharp reasoning admonishes it*) (2; my emphasis). By stressing the use of *sharp reasoning*, Laguna highlights the importance of clinical observation and a move away from sole reliance on the classical texts.

Dealing with the sense of sight, Laguna includes explanations for almost all of the products cited in the anonymous manuscripts. Returning to "Polvos para de secar las lágrymas y para confortar y de clarar la vista," we note that Laguna's explanations of shells, starch, eyebright water, camphor, tutty, and antimony consistently highlight their effectiveness for eye infections. Scorched shells are cited for improving several eye disorders: "la ceniza de los caracoles con su carne quemados, mezclada con miel, y aplicada, deshace los cicatrizes, que deforman los ojos, resuelve las nubes, [y] fortifica la vista" (the ash from scorched snail shell and flesh, mixed with honey and applied, gets rid of scars that deform eyes, clears up cloudiness [and] strengthens eyesight) (bk II, chap. IX). Similar explanations are provided for starch, eyebright and camphor.[12]

The ingredient that most consistently appears in recipes for treating the eyes is tutty, or zinc oxide. In fact, of the thirteen recipes that focus on the eyes, ten include tutty. In his chapter on *calmia*, Dioscorides explains that it is the same as *Tuthia vulgar* (bk V, 36). He continues by explaining that a certain type of cadmia called *botryitis* or *onychitis*, "sirve mucho para las medicinas que suelen administrarse a los ojos" (is very useful for medicines that are usually administered for the eyes) (bk V, 36). Laguna also concurs that *botryite* is what pharmacists call *Tuthia*: "La Botryite no es otra cosa, sino aquella parte de ollín, que por ser más ligera, suele apegarse a la cumbre de la hornaza, y colgar de ella como un razimo, de donde le vio el nombre" (Botryite is nothing more than that part of soot that, because it is lighter, sticks to the top part of the kiln and hangs down from there like a bunch of grapes, which is where it gets its name) (bk V, 39).[13]

In his introduction to *stibio*, Dioscorides explains that it is called *alcohol* in Castilian and *antimonio* or *antimony* in Italian. He notes that antimony dilates the pupil and cleanses "la suciedad de los ojos" (the sleep from the eye). However, in his annotation to Dioscorides's entry, Laguna has much more to say on this topic and takes the opportunity to criticize how antimony has evolved into a more vulgar use: "las mujeres suelen teñirse las cejas, y alcoholarse los ojos. Porque yá por nuestros pecados la gran corrupcion, y adulterio de toda buena costumbre, convirtió en disfraz, y afeyte, lo que fue producto, y hallado para salud, y beneficio del cuerpo humano" (women often colour their eyebrows and darken their eyelashes and edges of their eyelids. Because today, on account of our sins, the great corruption and adultery of all good habits have turned into pretense and cosmetics what was a product developed for our health and benefit to the human body) (bk V, chap. LVIII).

Many male authors of the day criticized women who used cosmetics. They saw the application of *afeites* and *colores* as artificial and deceptive, often associated with public women. These attacks against women's use of make-up come in direct conflict with one of the main purposes of the prescriptive domestic manuals. In addition to the health remedies, an even more substantial contribution to these texts are recipes for beauty products, including facial cosmetics, hair treatments, and skin softeners. However, from a theological perspective beauty reflected internal virtue and wearing make-up was an affront to God's gifts. Fray

Luis de León (1968) writes that wearing make-up is an outward manifestation of internal moral filth:

> ¿Qué pensáys las mujeres que es pintaros? Traer pintado en el rostro vuestro deseo feo. Mas, no todas las que os pintáis deseáis mal. Cortesía es creerlo. Pero, si con la tez del afeite no descubrís vuestro mal deseo, a lo menos despertáis el ajeno. De manera que, con esas pinturas sucias, o publicáis vuestra susia anima, o ensuciáis las de aquellos que os miran. Y todo es ofensa a Dios. (124)

> What do you women think wearing make-up is? You wear your ugly desires painted on your face. But, not all who wear make-up yearn for wrongfulness. It is only right to believe that. But if you do not see your own evil desire in your painted face, at least you awaken some foreign desire. In this way with those dirty positions you divulge your dirty spirit or you tarnish that of those who look at you. And all of this is an affront to God.

Fray Luis makes it clear that there was little room to pursue a morally correct lifestyle if a woman painted her face. Poets also repeatedly attacked women who wore make-up. Quevedo is, perhaps, the most notorious:

> Tu mayo es bote, ingüentes chorreando;
> y en esa tez, que brota primaveras,
> al sol estás y al cielo estercolando. (vv. 12–14)

> Your May is a jar, ointments dripping; / And on that skin that oozes out spring, / You face the sun and to the sky you shoot manure.

Here, Quevedo likens a woman's painted face to excrement, an ingredient actually used in recipes to enhance beauty and for medicinal purposes. In "polvo para los ojos" (powder for the eyes), for example, the author maintains that zinc oxide be finely ground with lizard dung and applied twice daily to the eyes for improving vision (*Manual de mugeres* 51).

Regarding the eyes, two recipes stand out for their overlap of health and beauty. Like the recipe for drying up a teary eye that appears in both *Receptas experimentadas* and *Manual de mugeres,* two other almost identical recipes titled, "para alcoholar los hojos" (for cleansing/applying makeup to the eyes) (ms. 2019, 149r) and "polvos para alcoholar los ojos" (powder for cleansing/applying makeup to the eyes) (*Manual de mugeres* 75) also appear in both manuscripts.[14] In *Tesoro de la lengua castellana* Covarrubias provides the following definition for *alcohol:* "es cierto género de polvos, que con un palito de hinojo teñido en ellos le passan por

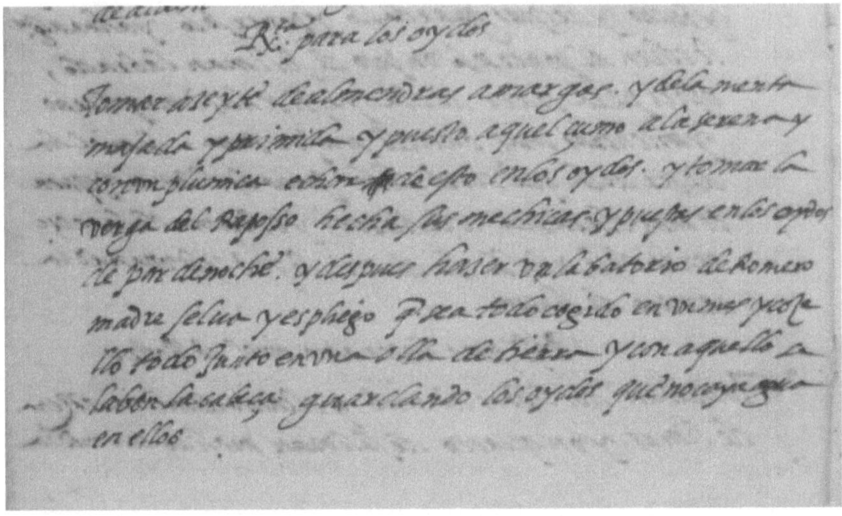

Figure 7.3. Recipe 2: "Receta para los oydos." National Library of Spain, ms. 2019, 21v, detail.

los ojos para aclarar la vista y poner negras las pestañas y para hermosearlos" (it is a certain type of powder that, with a small fennel stick dipped in it, is applied to the eyes to improve vision or blacken eyelashes and embellish them) (76). The only real difference between the two is the option of using eyebright water in the former, but what is intriguing about both is the very ambiguity of their purpose. Are these recipes included for improving vision or enhancing the beauty of an individual's eyes? Most likely, the answer is both.

Hearing

Recipes for hearing loss and earaches are not as frequent as those dealing with damaged eyes. In fact, of the some 1,200 recipes that make up these four manuscripts, only four deal with ailments related to the sense of sound. However, unlike the sight recipes that share many of the same ingredients, all four hearing recipes are unique in their configurations. One recipe, "receta para los oydos" (recipe for the ear) generically treats ailments of the ear using almond oil and crushed mint (*Receptas experimentadas* 21v) (Figure 7.3).[15]

Another, "remedio para dolor de oídos" (remedy for earaches), uses ivy as its main ingredient, and a third that deals specifically with ringing in the ear, "receta para los oydos para quien tiene ruido en la cabeça" (recipe for the ears when one has ringing in the head), uses the warm liquid collected from burning young ash wood as a remedy.[16]

Perhaps the most noteworthy recipe, and the most controversial by today's standards and, according to Laguna, by the standards he sets, is also the recipe for the most serious of the four ear diseases, "remedio para la sordedad" (remedy for deafness). This recipe is striking to today's readers because its main ingredient is urine:

> Tomaréis la orina en una escudilla de barro que no sea vidriada. Y batidla mucho con una cuchara por espacio de una hora. Y después de batida, haced unas mechas de estopa o algodón tan grandes que tapen el oído, y no más largas de cuanto lleguen a lo vacío. Mojaréis una de aquestas mechas en aquella orina y ponedla en el oído donde estuviere la sordedad. Y tenedla por espaçio de un credo, y sacadla, y tornadla a mojar, y tornadla a poner. Y poned encima un cabezalejo como de sangría, y tocaos la cabeza con un paño de manera que tapéis el oído; y echaos sobre el uno salgáis al aire. Y haced esto cuatro o cinco veces al día, entre día y noche, y hazedlo treinta días. Y la orina la tomaréis de tres a tres días. Y si oliere muy mal, la tomaréis de dos a dos días. (*Manual de mujeres* 50)

> Place urine in an earthenware bowl; it should not be a glass one. And whip it with a spoon for the space of an hour. And after it is whipped, make small pieces of burlap or cotton big enough to cover the ear but not so large that they spill out over the ear. Soak one of these pieces in the urine and place it in the deaf ear. Leave it there for [as long as it takes to recite] a Creed, remove it, resoak it and put it back again. And put on a cover cloth, the type you would use for bloodletting, put a cloth around the head so that the ear is entirely covered; lie ear-side up to get air. And do this four or five times a day, both day and night, and do it for thirty days. Change the urine every three days. And if it smells really bad, change it every two days.

In the section on urine Dioscorides explains that it has a wide range of curative properties, including therapy for poisoning by venomous bites, skin conditions, edema, eye infections, acid reflux, and, not surprisingly, bladder and kidney infections. He cites remedies that include drinking one's own urine, dog urine, and that of other animals (bk II, chap. LXXIII). With regard to its healing properties for ear infections he includes several examples: "Hervida en una cascara de granada, y assi caliente instilada en los oídos, enjuga la material que mana dellos, y mata los gusanos que allí se engendran [...]. La orina del toro instilada con myrra modera los dolores de los oídos. La del puerco montés tiene la misma fuerza [...]. Instilada en los oídos les quita el dolor" (boiled in pomegranate rind, and thus warm it is instilled into the ear, it dries out the substance that drains from it, and kills worms that are breeding there [...]. Urine from a bull instilled with myrrh subdues earaches. Boar urine has the same strength [...] instilled in the ear, it alleviates the pain) (bk II, chap. LXXIII).

In his annotation on this entry, Laguna does reiterate the curative properties of animal urine from different sources, but he also returns to Galen to caution other healthcare providers of the overuse of urine, and other animal waste products, as remedies for the sick. "Reprehende Galeno, y con mucha razon, los Medicos, que teniendo a cada passo una infinidad de saludables medicinas, y muy gratas al pueblo humano para todas enfermedades, le inficionan con orina, y estiercol, cosas ya una vez desechadas de la naturaleza, como abominables, e inútiles" (Galen reprimands other doctors, and very rightly so, that although they have an infinite amount of healthy medicine at every turn that is agreeable to all people for all illnesses, they infect them with urine, and dung, things already discarded by nature as detestable and useless) (bk II, chap. LXXIII). The fact that the domestic manuals rarely recommend urine to restore health to failing senses or for other ailments aligns them with Laguna's "modern" Galenic theory that urine is not always the best restorative.

Taste

While recipes that treat the eyes and ears are curative in nature and directly address the "higher" senses of sight and hearing, instructions for maintaining a healthy mouth and curing tooth and gum decay are only indirectly tied to taste. They also extend beyond a curative capacity to include preventative remedies. A third difference between the types of recipes is simply quantity. The number of recipes that focus on oral hygiene more than doubles those that treat issues of sight and hearing combined and implies that it demanded a lot of attention. All four manuals contain recipes for ensuring oral hygiene and though not technically a curative for problems related to the gustatory system, there does exist a correlation between healthy gums and teeth and one's sense of taste.

In *Recetas y memorias*, the author includes three simple fruit juice mouthwashes that involve boiled pomegranate peel and grape juice; pomegranate or its rind, rosemary shoots, and myrrh boiled in red wine; and quince juice (164r) (Figure 7.4).[17] In other recipes vinegar and white wine act as antiseptics in mouthwash recipes and in recipes to prevent teeth decay. Often herbs and spices, such as cinnamon,

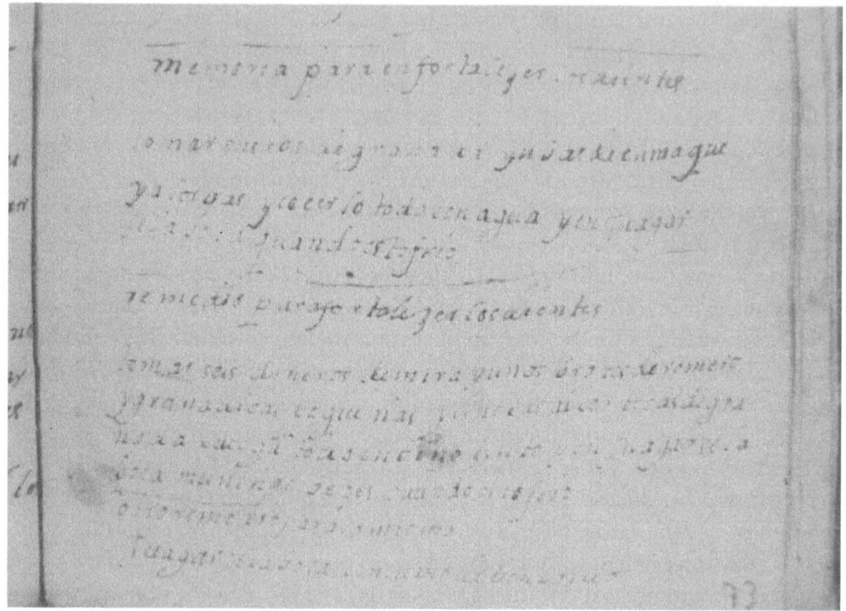

Figure 7.4. Recipe 3: Three mouthwash recipes. National Library of Spain, ms. 6058, 164r, detail.

rosemary, sage, nutmeg, ginger, and cloves are added to eliminate, or at least mitigate, halitosis. Other rinses are more curative in nature. For example, in "Para dolor de muelas" (For tooth aches) white vinegar with myrrh, aromatic resin, and pennyroyal are combined (*Livro de receptas* 45v).[18]

Powders and pastes also are suggested for treating the mouth. In one curious recipe, "polvos para limpiar y encarnar los dientes" (powders to clean and heal the teeth), seashells are ground up, and a warm, wine-soaked cloth smeared with the shell powder is applied on the teeth and left without rinsing (*Manual de mujeres* 73). In another recipe alabaster, porcelain, white coral, pearl, cinnamon, musk, and fine sugar are ground into a fine powder and then applied to the teeth before rinsing with wine (*Manual de mugeres* 37).

In addition to mouthwashes and tooth pastes and powders, instructions for making incense fill the pages of the manuscripts. One recipe, "pebetes para los dientes" (incense for the teeth), contains no less than nineteen ingredients:

> Media onza de encienso, media de almáciga, media de sangre de drago,[19] media de raíz de noguera, media de salvia, media de mata, media de alumbre quemada,

media de consuelda de roca, media de coral blanco, media de coral rojo, un cuarto de onza de cagibia,[20] otro cuarto de galigal,[21] otro de canela, otro de clavos, media onza de cuescos de dátiles quemados, media onza de rosas balasticas, media de piedra pomez blanca y media onza de polvo de grana. Amasado todo, muy polvorizado con alquitira almizclada. Y hechos los pebetes, secadlos al sol o a la sombra. (*Manual de mugeres* 45)

A half ounce of aromatic resin, half of mastic, half of dragon blood, half of walnut tree root, half of sage, half of mastic, half of burnt alum, half of rock comfrey, half of white coral, half of red coral, a quarter of an ounce of *cagibia*, another quarter of galangal, another of cinnamon, another of cloves, a half-ounce of scorched date pits, a half-ounce of *balastic* roses, a half of white pumice stone, and a half-ounce of powdered grains of paradise. Pulverize it well all together with musk-scented gum. And once the sticks are made, dry them in the sun or in the shade.

If ingredients were too difficult to gather or too expensive to incur, other simpler alternatives were also available. "Para el dolor de dientes o de muelas" (for tooth ache or molar ache) offered a quick fix to serious dental decay: "tomaréis la simiente de hierbabuena y la pondréis sobre las brasas. Y recibid el humo de ella en la boca. Os quitará el dolor y os matará los gusanos" (take the seed of spearmint and put it on live coals. And inhale its smoke into your mouth. It will stop the pain and kill the worms) (*Manual de mugeres* 46).[22] In addition to the visual image of worm decay in the mouth, these incense recipes impress upon the reader an acknowledgment of women's extensive knowledge of the flora and fauna that improve health and the economics behind it. Preparing remedies for the family required the luxury of time and money, and often substitutes or adulterations were necessary.

To ensure against illicit activity in the selling of these pharmaceuticals, Francisco Vallés, who served as chief apothecary at El Escorial and chief medical doctor to Philip II, published the work, *Tratado de las aguas destiladas, pesos, y medidas de que los boticarios deuen usar* (Treatise on distilled waters, weights, and measures that a pharmacist should use) (1592). He opens the treatise with a resolution on the types of stills that can and cannot be used in the proper fabrication of waters.

Mandose a todos los boticarios destos Reynos, que de aquí adelante ninguno tenga ni venda agua destilada para tomar por la boca, que no sea hecha en Alambique de vidrio, y en baño: de manera que ninguna de las tales sea hecha en Alquitara de cobre, ni plomo, ni estaño, ni de otra ninguna material en fuego seco, sino en vidrio, y en baño de agua o vapor. (2r–v)

> Be it so ordered that all pharmacists of these kingdoms, that from here on out, no one sell distilled water taken orally, which is not made from a glass still, and a bath: in this way none of them should be produced in a copper, lead, or tin still or from any material over direct heat but rather in glass with a water or steam bath.

In the domestic manuals, when material is prepared in a still, it is identified only as a glass still; there are no references to stills made from metals.

In addition to regulating pharmaceutical guidelines, Vallés, together with the Belgian Andreas Vesalius, was at the forefront of the Galenic debates on the future direction of natural philosophy.[23] In his ten-volume compendium, *Controversiarum medicarum et philosophicarum libri decem* (Medical and philosophical controversies in ten books) Vallés incorporates the term *physiology* into his work to distinguish that part of natural philosophy that treats human nature. In his introduction he explains, "he pensado distribuir toda la obra en diez libros, de los que los dos primeros contendrán las controversias comunes a filósofos y médicos [...]. Por consiguiente, trataré en primer lugar lo referente a la parte fisiológica, pues ésta es a la vez el final de la filosofía y el principio de la medicina" (I have decided to publish the entire work in ten volumes, of which the first two contain the most common controversies for philosophers and doctors [...]. As such, I will first deal with what pertains to the physiological part, since it is both the end of philosophy and the beginning of medicine) (cited in López Piñero and Calero 81). This conscious decision to debate the limitations of Galen's natural philosophy is a central tenet of the severe division within Europe on how medical science should be taught at universities and practised.

Understanding how the senses worked, whether the origin of the sense was at the point of contact with the sense itself or in the brain, was another aspect of the controversy. Vallés raises the issue, acknowledging both sides of the debate.

> Hay que sopesar ahora si es verdad lo que hemos dicho, esto es que la visión se realiza en los ojos, la olfacción en la nariz y la audición en los oídos: o si todas las sensaciones se realizan en el propio cerebro, y sube las especies de los colores a través de los ojos, las de los sonidos a través de los oídos, las de los olores por la nariz, las de los sabores por la lengua, las de las cualidades táctiles por toda la piel, como opinaron algunos filósofos. (Cited in López Piñero and Calero 196)

> One must now consider if what we have said is true, that is, if sight is realized in the eyes, smell in the nose, and hearing in the ears, or if all these sensations are realized in one's own brain and all sorts of colours are carried up through the eyes, all sorts

of sounds through the ears, all sorts of smells through the nose, all sorts of tastes through the tongue, all sort of tactile qualities through the skin, as some philosophers have opined.

This type of theorizing on the sensory functions is completely absent in the domestic manuals, which almost exclusively focus on the practical treatments for the senses.

Touch

In terms of remedies for ailments related to touch, it could be argued that all remedies are connected to this sense, as nothing is applied to the body without touch. Touch, like the previous "lower" sense, taste, is developed in terms of not only the curative but also the preventative. In fact, in all of these manuals, most "touch" recipes deal with maintaining good skin or beautifying it, while only four address skin diseases. Here, I will limit my discussion to those curative remedies that focus on healing lesions, ulcers, and abscesses related to the plague or cancer.

In the domestic manuals there are three recipes for ointment to alleviate sores related to the plague and to breast cancer (*Livro de recetas* 29v–30v, 52v; *Manual de mujeres* 41).[24] The first, "Recepta para hazer ungüento de secas para qualquier genero dellas y para pestilencia y pechos de mujeres el qual solía hazer el Maestro Rincón en Valladolid, dize el titulo del Pro Regibus et principibus et magnis amicijs" (Recipe for making ointment for tumours of any type and for pestilence and women's breasts that Master Rincón of Valladolid used to make, its title reads for kings, important citizens, and great friends), is one of the more extensive recipes and begins by gathering fresh lilies, cattails, calendula, and chamomile in the spring; preserving the petals in oil; and boiling some of their roots and bulbs together with elkhorn fern. Once made, this base can be used throughout the year to make an ointment that is then applied topically. The author continues by reassuring readers that "Es ungüento muy provado y que haze grandes effectos y nunca daña y puedense untar con el las vezes que paresciese asta que se les quite el dolor" (it is a well-proven ointment and has very positive effects and is never harmful and can be applied as often as necessary until the pain goes away) (see Figure 7.5).[25]

Another remedy specifically targeted at those suffering from the plague blends grated cow horn, honey, and poppy water to form a liquid that is administered to the patient. A second option includes syrup made from lemons and the madroño tree. The author explains that this recipe should be used only after

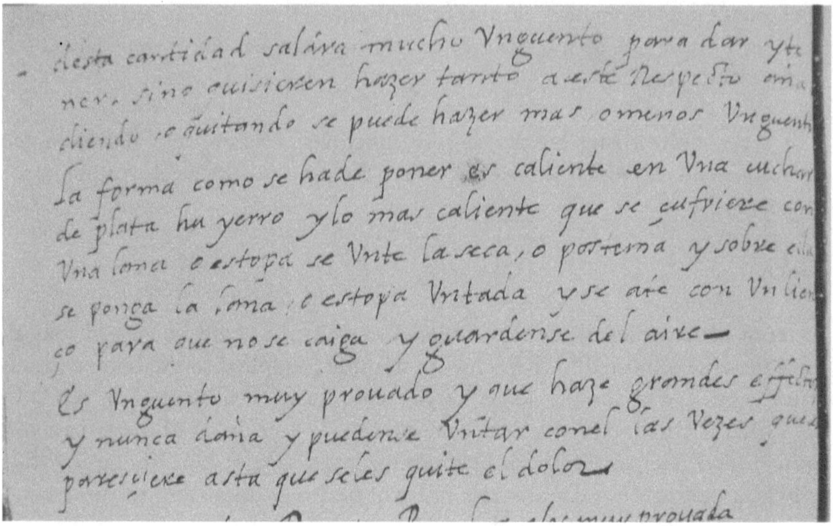
desta cantidad saldra mucho Vnguento para dar y te-
ner, sino quisieren hazer tanto a este Respecto min-
diendo o quitando se puede hazer mas o menos Vnguento
La forma como se hade poner es caliente en Vna cuchar
de plata o yerro y lo mas caliente que se sufriere con
Vna lona o estopa se Vnte la seca, o postema y sobre ella
se ponga la lona o estopa Vntada y se ate con Vn lien-
co para que no se caiga y guardense del aire—
Es Vnguento muy prouado y que haze grandes efectos
y nunca daña y puedense Vntar con el las Vezes que
pareciere asta que se les quite el dolor

Figure 7.5. Recipe 4: "Recepta para hazer ungüento […]." National Library of Spain, ms. 1462, 30v, detail.

bloodletting, cupping, and poultices have been attempted: "Y quanto hiziéredes esto ha de ser aviendo usado primero de las otras mediçinas de sangrias, y bentosas y emplastos. Será la sangria del mismo lado a do estubiere la seca de la vena más çercana a ella" (And when you do this, it should be having first tried other medicine like bloodletting and cupping and poultices. The bloodletting should be on the same side where the tumour was, from the vein closest to it) (*Manual de mugeres* 55).

The reference not only to bloodletting, but specifically to where it should occur, echoes the ideas put forth by Luis Mercado (1525–1611?), who replaced Vallés as physician of the king's chamber and continued serving in this position through the reign of Felipe III until his own death (see Figure 7.6). Mercado was particularly fervent regarding Galen's theories of pathology, but he laid down innovative ideas regarding surgery, gynecology, and pediatrics. The biographer Juan de Riera states that "la obra de Mercado es un excepcional exponente de lo que fue el saber médico renacentista, tradicional en sus fundamentos doctrinales y moderno en bastantes capítulos clínicos" (the work of Mercado is an exceptional model of Renaissance medical knowledge, traditional in its doctrinal foundation and modern in many of its clinical chapters) (22).

Figure 7.6. Portrait of Luis Mercado. *Libro de la peste.* New York Academy of Medicine, detail.

Mercado is best known for his four-volume *Opera omnia* (Complete works), which was published in Spain between 1594 and 1613, republished in both Frankfurt and Venice in the first two decades of the seventeenth century, and published as separate parts many times over (Riera 103–5). In addition to this grand collection, Mercado also authored an important book on the plague, which had entered

Spain in 1596 in Santander and in the following year surfaced in Toledo, San Sebastian, Laredo, and Valladolid. In a royal document directed to Mercado the king commanded Mercado to publish a definitive work on the subject.

> Por la necesidad precisa que se entiende hay en los míos Reinos de Castilla de ocurrir a esta manera de peste tan general y perniciosa, pareció ser cosa necesaria se hiciese de ello un Tratado, para que en todas las provincias, ciudades, villas [...] se sepa y entienda con certidumbre qué enfermedad y qué orden se debe tener en la guarda y providencia de los lugares sanos [...] os lo he querido cometer y encargar, como por la presente lo hago, para que de hecho se imprima, como le he mandado, y distribuya luego por los procuradores de Cortes de los dichos mis Reinos, sin que haya dilación ni sea necesaria otra diligencia. (Cited in Riera 55)

> On account of the precise need that is understood to be happening in my kingdoms of Castile in such a widespread and pernicious way, it seemed to be necessary that a treatise be written about it, so that all provinces, cities and villages [...] know and understand with certainty what illness and what order one should follow in the security of and measures for healthy areas [...] I have wanted you to commit and take charge of, for this reason I am doing it, so that in fact it gets printed, as I have ordered, and distributed afterward by the consuls of the Court of each of my said kingdoms, without any delay or without any need for any other report.

Mercado first published his work in Latin in 1598 and a year later in Spanish: *Libro en que se trata con claridad la naturaleza, causas, providencia, y verdadera orden y modo de curar la enfermedad vulgar, y peste que en estos años se ha divulgado por toda España* [...] (Book in which are treated with clarity the nature, causes, steps, and true order and way to cure the vulgar disease and plague that has recently spread throughout all of Spain). In this treatise he lays down the rules for bloodletting: "y si se ha de hacer, se advierta que sea de la parte y vena más propincua a la hinchada, porque sin llevar humores venenados por otras partes, más fácilmente naturaleza se incline a la parte próxima adonde la empezado" (and if it need be done, be advised that it be done on the part and vein closest to the swelling, so that without the infected humours being transported to other parts, it be naturally more easy to favour the part closest to where it began) (282–3). Once again, by comparing instructions in the domestic manuals to those outlined by leading medical doctors, we see that the same practices for treating pestilence outlined by the top expert in the field are being outlined in the women's manuals.

In early modern Spain women managing a household approached diseases related to touch as well as taste, hearing, and vision with a theoretical base that finds its roots in academic medical texts. In the prescriptive domestic manuals we find instructions that conform to the rules put forth by Mercado, Vallés, and Laguna. But the domestic manuals differ, as they put into practice the leading precepts of natural philosophy and focus on the very production of cures. The multiple compilers of each manual wrote functional guides for women to care for families. Monica Green has called these recipe books the first genre of women's medical writing (*Making* 308), but Leong considers these manuals collaborative projects not only authored by mothers and daughters but also containing contributions from fathers, husbands, brothers, and sons (84). In the case of Spain, Pérez Samper has argued that at times the authorship is exclusively female and other times it is a mixture of both male and female (135–9). Whatever the case of authorship, this essay brings to light how authors of domestic manuals drew from the writings of established academic medical doctors. Where they radically differed was in their approach to beauty. In all of the domestic manuals recipes support women's choice to enhance their beauty through make-up. As we have seen in Laguna's attack on cosmetics, this is certainly not the case in academic texts. Finally, based on the extensive recipes for vision, hearing, taste, and touch, and for the ways in which the olfactory sense was used to cure other sensorial diseases that are found in these four anonymous manuals, there remains little doubt that domestic spaces were a site of cultural production and, more specifically, a site for primary health care and, in case of illnesses and disease, medical intervention.

Appendix 1 Domestic manuals and recipes related to sensory ailments

Manual de mugeres			
Eyes (3/13)	Ears (2/4)	Mouth (14/31)	Skin (2/4)
Polvos para los ojos (51)	Remedio para la sordedad (50)	Polvos para los dientes (37)	Ungüento para postemas (41)
Polvos para alcoholar los ojos (75)	Remedio para dolor de oidos (46)	Pebetes para los dientes (45)	Remedio contra la pestilencia (55)
Polvos para secar las lágrimas y aclarar la vista (39)		Remedio para las muelas (46)	
		Remedio para los dientes (46)	
		Remedio para dolor de oídos (46)	
		Para el dolor de dientes o de muelas (46)	
		Remedio para los dientes (46)	
		Remedio para las muelas (46)	
		Remedio para el neguijón (49)	
		Polvos para limpiar los dientes (50)	
		Agua para las encías (56)	

Manual de mugeres			
Eyes (3/13)	Ears (2/4)	Mouth (14/31)	Skin (2/4)
		Conserva para encarnar los dientes (72)	
		Polvos para limpiar y encarnar los dientes (73)	
		Lavatorio para las encías (73–4)	

Livro de receptas (ms. 1462)			
Eyes (4/13)	Ears (0/4)	Mouth (2/31)	Skin (2/4)
Recepta para los ojos muy provada (30v)		Para dolor de muelas (45v)	Recepta para hazer ungüento de secas para qualquier genero dellas y para pestilencia y […] (29v–30v)
Memoria de aguas para sanar los ojos (35v)		Memoria para hacer polvos para los dientes (50v)	Memoria de curar çaratanes (52v)
Otra agua (35v–36r)			
Para los ojos mando están ynchados y encarmicados (52v)			

Receptas experimentadas (ms. 2019)			
Eyes (6/13)	Ears (2/4)	Mouth (12/31)	Skin (0/4)
Recepta para los ojos (136 v)	Receta para los oydos (21v)	Reçepta para hazer agua para los dientes (17v)	
Recepta para alcohol para quitar las lagrimas de los ojos. (124v–125r)	Receta para los oydos para quien tiene ruido en la cabeça (23v)	Recepta para los dientes (21v)	
Recepta de un agua excelentísima que dio el cardenal pogio para los ojos (232r)		Aguapara los dientes (28r)	
Para alcoholar los hojos (149r)		Recepta para quitar mal de muelas (34v)	

Receptas experimentadas (ms. 2019)			
Eyes (6/13)	Ears (2/4)	Mouth (12/31)	Skin (0/4)
Para los ojos (169v)		Recepta para afirmar los dientes y para ponerlos blancos de la señora condesa de Lerín (34v–35r)	
Polvos para de secar las lagrymas y para confortar y de clarar la vista. (169v)		Agua para los dientes (40r)	
		Recepta para polvora par los dientes (62r)	
		Recepta para los dientes (62v)	
		Memoria de polvos de dientes (210r)	
		Memoria de polvos de dientes para encarnar (210r–v)	
		Para apretar los dientes (239v)	
		Para hacer los dientes blancos (241v)	

Recetas y memorias (ms. 6058)			
Eyes (0/13)	Ears (0/4)	Mouth (3/31)	Skin (0/4)
		Memoria para enfortalezer los dientes (164r)	
		Remedio parar fortalecer los dientes (164r)	
		Otro remedio para lo mismo(164r)	

NOTES

1 I would like to gratefully acknowledge the assistance of Arlene Sheener in the Coller Rare Book Reading Room of the New York Academy of Medicine, who provided excellent support for researching the work of Laguna, Vallés and Mercado. I would also like to acknowledge the support of two Illinois Wesleyan grants: a Mellon

Foundation *Recentering the Humanities* Mellon Fellow Series grant and an Artistic and Scholarly Development grant.

2 For more on the transmission of Galen's work in European universities, see García Ballester (*Historia social* 77–97), González Manjarrés (25–35), and Temkin.

3 For a history of the professionalization of medicine and the simultaneous exclusion of women, see Benton; M. Green (*Making*).

4 With respect to early modern Spain, Jean Dangler presents an overview of women healers and the professionalization of medicine. See also Pérez Samper. For more on the production of domestic manuals in early modern England see Field. And, in terms of readership, Monica Green has researched the medical literacy of lay women in the Middle Ages. She reports from the twelfth to the sixteenth century only intermittent accounts of medical texts that were owned by women ("Possibilities").

5 The numbers in parentheses indicate how many recipes are found in each category. The +1 sign indicates an exception. In the case of medical remedies, an additional recipe is included entitled "Betum para soldar bidrio" (Bitumen for soldering glass). Martínez Crespo speculates that the bitumen "cures" a problem or that the verb *soldar,* related to *cicatrizar* (to scar), might explain why it appears here (40n38). In the case of the other two, the additional recipes are listed in the index under "Tabla de lavatorios, polvos y otras cosas para los dientes y ençias contenidas en este libro" (Index of washes, powders and other remedies for the teeth and gums found in this book) instead of under the headings for their respective categories.

6 For additional information regarding ownership of the manuals and historic figures whose names are attributed to specific recipes, see Pérez Samper.

7 All titles and their corresponding manuscripts, organized by the sensory body parts, eyes, ears, mouth, and skin, are listed in Appendix 1. I have excluded the nose, as recipes dealing with the sense of smell are written to cure other ailments and do not address the nose itself.

8 *Manual de mujeres* has a recipe almost identical to this one, "Polvos para secar las lágrimas y aclarar la vista" (Powder for drying up teary eye and improving vision) (39).

9 All translations in this article are my own.

10 In the 1733 copy at the New York Academy of Medicine entries also include a narrative and an illustration provided by Francisco Suárez de Ribera, chief medical doctor for Philip V.

11 Concepción Baranda has examined the narrative strategies Laguna uses to convince his readers of his interpretation. For more on Laguna's impact on Renaissance medical humanism see González Manjarrés and Calero, and for Laguna's influence on Cervantes's writing see López-Muñoz.

12 Regarding the use of starch, Dioscorides explains: "es útil el Almidón contra los humores que a los ojos distilan" (starch is useful against humors that discharge from eyes)

(II.XCIL). In describing *tragio*, a plant native only to Crete, Dioscorides treats a subgroup, *tragonceros.* In his annotation, Laguna explains that as an elixir it combats diseases for the eye: "El agua destilada de toda la yerva, y echada en los ojos, clarifica potentemente la vista" (Water from distilling the entire plant and applied to the eyes, has a powerful effect on eyesight) (IV.LI). Later, he notes that *tragio* is remarkably similar to *euphrasia*, or *eyebright*: "assí comida, como aplicada [...] esclarece mas que ninguna otra cosa la vista" (either eaten or applied [topically] [...] it clears one's vision more than anything else) (IV.LI). Laguna describes camphor as a "soberano remedio contra qualquier mal caliente de ojos" (excellent remedy for any excessive heat of the eye) (I.LXXII).

13 In the *Oxford Latin Dictionary* the definition of *botryitis* is "cadmia ~is, Cluster-shaped oxide of zinc" (240).

14 The complete recipes are as follows:

"Para alcoholar los hojos" (For cleansing/applying makeup to the eyes): "Atutía quemada en un crisol. Y apagada nueve vezes en agua rosada o en agua de eufragia. Y después curada al ayre y después de muy molida ha de ser pasado por un cedaço muy cerado" (Scorched zinc oxide in a crucible. And doused nine times in rose water or eyebright water. And after [being] air cured and finely ground, it should be passed through a fine mesh sieve) (ms. 2019 149r).

"Polvos para alcoholar los ojos" (Powder for cleansing/applying makeup to the eyes): "Atutía quemada en un crisol nueve veces, y muerta en agua rosada y curada al aire. Y después molida y pasada por un cedazo muy espeso. Alcoholarse los ojos con estos polvos" (Scorched zinc oxide in a crucible nine times and doused in rose water and air cured. And after finely ground and passed through a heavy straining cloth. Cleanse the eyes/apply makeup to the eyes with this powder) (*Manual de mugeres* 75).

15 The complete recipe is as follows:

"Tomar azeyte de almendras amargas y de la menta majada y primida y puesto aquel çumo a la serena y con un plumica echar de esto en los oydos y tomar la verga del reposso hecha sus mechicas y puestas en los oydos de por de noche. Y después hazer un labatorio de romero, madre selva y espliego que sea todo cogido y con aquello se laban la cabeça, guardando los oydos que no caya agua en ellos" (Take bitter almond oil and oil from mint that has been crushed and squeezed and set that juice aside to rest overnight. And with a small feather, add drops into the ear and take shreds of a small stick soaked in the oil and place them in the ear overnight. Then make a wash of rosemary, honeysuckle, and lavender all mixed together and with this wash the head, being careful not to let water get into the ear) (ms. 2019 21v).

16 The complete recipe is as follows:

"Tomen el fresno tieso quatro maderos gruesos y ponganlos sobre unos morillos al fuego y aquella agua que saliere pongan una escudilla de plata debaxo y tomen ell agua que cayere caliente lo mas que lo pudiesen çufrir y echensela en los oydos y si es en mayo es mejor" (Take four thick logs of young ash and place them on andirons over an open flame and place a silver bowl under it for whatever water is released and take that water, as hot as is tolerable, and drop it in the ears and if it is May it is better) (ms. 2019 23v).

17 The complete recipes are as follows:

"Memoria para enfortalezer los dientes" (Record for strengthening teeth): "Tomar cascos de granada y ubas de cuma que ya los has y cocerlo todo con agua y enjuagarse la boca quando este frío" (Take pomegranate peel and grape juice that you already have and boil it all in water and rinse your mouth when it is cool) (ms. 6058 164r).

"Remedio para fortalecer los dientes" (Remedy for strengthening teeth): "Tomar seis dineros de mira y unos brotes de romero y granadicas pequeñas y si no las ai cortezas de granada cueçgan todo en vino tinto y enjuagarse la boca muchas bezes cuando esta frío" (Take six coins of myrrh and some rosemary shoots and small pomegranates and if you don't have them, pomegranate peel, boil everything in red wine and rinse your mouth many times when it is cool) (ms. 6058 164r). "Otro remedio para lo mismo" (Another remedy for the same): "Juagarse la boca con cumo de benbrillos" (Rinse your mouth with quince juice) (ms. 6058 164r).

18 The complete recipe is as follows:

"Vinagre blanco y cuartydo, cuatro maravedís de myrra y cuatro de incienso y un puñado de poleo y mollelo de culebra todo cozido con el vinagre ya tapallo que no se salga el vajo enjaguarse con ello algo caliente" (A quarter of white vinegar, four maravedis of myrrh, four of aromatic resin, and a handful of pennyroyal and mix it back and forth. Everything boiled with the vinegar then cover it so the vapour does not get out. Rinse with it still warm) (ms. 1462 45v).

19 *Sangre de dragón* or *dragon blood* carries the name of the legendary creature but in reality is the deep red resin derived from the fruit or trunk of the *calamus draco* palm tree.

20 Although I have not been able to identify *cagibia*, I surmise it might have some relation to nutmeg or another similar spice, as spices in this family are often grouped with ginger, cinnamon, and clove.

21 *Galangal* is the rhizome of plants in the ginger family with medical and culinary properties similar to those of ginger.

22 Since antiquity, people had believed that tooth decay was caused by a worm that burrowed into the teeth, similar to worm-infested wood.

23 Andreas Vesalius (1514–64), who taught at the University of Padua and was imperial physician to Carlos V and later to his son Philip II, is well known as the founder of modern human anatomy.

24 Unfortunately, the recipe, "memoria de curar çaratanes" (record of curing breast cancer), is incomplete.

25 The other two ointment recipes dedicated to curing plague and cancer sores are animal based. "Ungüento para postemas" (Ointment for abscesses) contains poultry fat and eggs among its ingredients (*Manual de mugeres* 41), while "memoria de curar çaratanes" (record of curing breast cancer) contains octopus (*Libro de receptas* 52v).

8 Cervantes's Exemplary Sensorium, or the Skinny on *La española inglesa*

CHARLES VICTOR GANELIN

Any consideration of Miguel de Cervantes's 1613 *Novelas ejemplares* (*Exemplary Novels*), whether with a focus on the whole or on individual novellas, leads the reader on a winding, even "Byzantine," path (as in *La española inglesa* [The English Spanish Girl] or *El amante liberal* [The Generous Lover]) through explorations of the human condition, literary dialogue, theoretical excursus, and taste and cultural shifts representative of the tumultuous times of Cervantes's life. The bibliography, with many superb exemplars, listing the so-called realist and therefore more "quintessentially Cervantine" short narratives, historically has been much more extensive than that dedicated to the "idealist" novellas, as Gaylord calls them; she argues that the breathtaking thematic and structural range of the collection, especially of "the grid-resistant diversity of the motley 'hybrids,'" opens them to expansive approaches ("Cervantes's Other" 112). This essay on *La española inglesa* seeks to contribute to that tradition by focusing on literal and figurative skin and its relation to the sense of touch, as it allows an entry into Cervantes's highly sensorial, corporal literary creations.[1]

Cervantine imagery takes many forms, and one of the common denominators in *La española inglesa* as well as in other examples of the collection is a focus on the human body and the constellation of possibilities in its representation. Elsewhere I have written on Cervantes's employment of the fives senses as an organizing principle, particularly with regard to the sense of touch. Closely related to this polemic sense (polemic because of its placement at the bottom of the traditional hierarchy, although its centrality and widespread loci enhance its importance) is the point of contact, skin, whose power to sense, to cover, to protect, to identify, and to signify has fascinated and preoccupied human beings throughout history. Skin as object of intellectual pursuit has taken on apparent urgency during recent decades with a developing interest in matters cultural, literary, or historical, as the lengthy bibliography on the subject attests.[2] Clothing, too, with its long and detailed functions as class, gender, and nationality markers, shares importance with our skin,[3] and Kafka, as an observer of metamorphosed external forms, draws a connection between the body surface and a second skin of clothes, which he calls "'natural fancy dress'" (qtd in Benthien 111). We can extrapolate from Kafka's insight any number of observations about "skin," whether the literal physical covering of the body or its metaphorical portrayals. The many forms of covering may be a molecular mass of solid protection (an image itself with a lengthy resumé, ranging from medieval castle fortifications to science fiction creatures) or something porous and pervious, such as Don Quixote's armour. Skin in its widest functions is a negotiator between boundaries: between the external world and the body's interior as well as between outward constructions of self and an inner "essence" of who the individual believes her/himself to be. Skin, or hide – in order to generalize to any kind of surface covering – may be exposed, displayed, and even changed, and with this evolution the individual reflects the new circumstance.

Cervantes's diverse characters fully engage their worlds with all their sensory receptors; he creates numerous metaphors for skin as a way to enhance its importance in how it both envelops and reveals. Skin is the extended locus for the sense of touch and is a powerful literal edge vis-à-vis the body, which is central to contact with the world external to ourselves. Skin, as Jablonski has written, "is a potentially ever-changing tapestry that tells the world about who we are or who we want to be" (3). The alterations to skin and its protective coverings play a significant role in *La española inglesa* precisely because its literal loss creates fundamental challenges to the tale's protagonists, the Spanish Isabela and the Englishman Ricaredo; it addresses the relationship among images of skin, spoils of war, and the sense of touch. A brief plot summary may be helpful. The English nobleman Clotaldo, as part of the English defeat of the Spanish at Cádiz, takes home to his wife the beautiful seven-year-old Isabela; the girl is raised a Catholic (Clotaldo and family secretly practise the faith) and draws the interest of Clotaldo's son Ricaredo. Years later Isabela is presented at court to Elizabeth I, who both accepts her Catholicism and promises her to Ricaredo, but first demands that he prove his valour beyond reliance on his family name by engaging in military combat at sea. Upon his return to court the queen confirms the betrothal, but Isabela is soon poisoned and disfigured by an envious lady-in-waiting. Ricaredo cares for her at the family home, and Isabela recovers her beauty as well as her health. Ricaredo undertakes a kind of pilgrimage to Rome, but is captured by Turks as he sails anew for England and imprisoned for two years, during which time Isabela has returned to her home country of Spain (but now to Sevilla) and, believing Ricaredo dead, opts to profess in a convent. As she is about to enter, Ricaredo appears and they reunite and wed.

The above synopsis points to dual religions (one outward, another inward), bodily disfigurement, captivity, recuperated national identity, and potential seclusion in a nunnery; each of these "events" is associated with external markers, real or metaphorical, on the body. One of the problems a reader confronts when investigating skin as both body part and metaphor is the difficulty of transmission and reception of the implied sense of touch that skin carries with it and how to make it felt through reading; of all the senses only touch offers that "vital dimension" of immediacy (Connor 34). An equally vexing issue is the language employed to convey a sense of the senses, a conundrum at the heart of metaphorical representation. Asifa Majid and Stephen Levinson indicate that the language to express individual moments of conscious experience (qualia), as in the sensing of an object, can use only an example of it to define what is actually sensed (ostension). The authors note that this situation holds true "even if the corresponding qualia are subjective and ineffable" (6). The reader is at one further remove from skin and touch than, for example, the viewer of a painting. In reading about any of the senses we "see" or "smell" only through images of examples created in language; therefore success in bringing the reader closer to "sensing the sense" depends on the force and forcefulness of metaphor because, ultimately, skin – real and metaphorical – must be made to be felt. Cervantes excels at communicating a sense of the senses and exhibits many telling images of this nature in addition to *La española inglesa*, revealing "skins," for example, as clothing that reflects class (*Rinconete y Cortadillo*) or hides true social status (*La gitanilla* [The Little Gypsy Girl], *La ilustre fregona* [The Illustrious Kitchen Maid]); as objects that signal or are reflective of a mental state (the house in *El celoso extremeño* [The Jealous Old Man from Extremadura]; "glass" in *El licenciado Vidriera* [The Glass Graduate]); and, of course, as skin itself (*El casamiento engañoso* [The Deceitful Marriage] and *El coloquio de los perros* [The Dialogue of the Dogs], particularly with regard to Da. Estefanía, Campuzano, and Cañizares).

The initial lines of *La española inglesa* – its covering, in a manner of speaking, or its outer skin – contain a key word: *despojos* (spoils [prizes]).[4] The placement of the word as the first noun in the story calls attention to itself because one significant object of the preposition "entre" (among) is the young Isabela, an item carried away by the nobleman Clotaldo following England's decisive and brutal 1596 victory over Spain at Cádiz:[5]

> Entre los despojos que los ingleses llevaron de la ciudad de Cádiz, Clotaldo, un caballero inglés, capitán de una escuadra de navíos, llevó a Londres una niña de edad de siete años [...] Clotaldo [...] llegó a Londres y entregó por riquísimo despojo a su mujer a la hermosa niña. (243–4)

> Among the prizes which the English raiders took away from the city of Cádiz was a little girl of about seven, whom Clotaldo, an English gentleman and the commander

> of a squadron of ships, took to London [...] Clotaldo [...] arrived in London, and handed the beautiful child over to his wife, as a rich piece of booty. (5)

The opening two paragraphs of the *La española inglesa* set in motion a variety of motifs – separation, changing economic systems, the clash of countries and religions – which have elicited diverse critical responses. Readers have focused on *Española*'s symmetrical structure (Aylward, who also summarizes earlier writings on the structure, 124–5; Torres), its blending of fiction and history (Ricapito; Johnson "Practice"), Spanish-English relations (Cruz "Vindicating"),[6] and development of a more modern economic system and the growth of bourgeois classes (Johnson "Practice"). It has also been viewed as Christian romance, particularly by El Saffar, Forcione, and Collins; Collins sees Cervantes's genius in his production of an almost Erasmian, utopian "community of Christian brotherhood" (70) by extending the romance genre to near breaking through inclusion of historical events that threaten the illusion of a spiritual transfiguration (71). These important readings can serve as background to my particular study of this narrative.

In a discussion of a possible date of composition of 1604–5 for *La española inglesa* Johnson holds that improved relationships between Spain and England were due in part to the possibilities of a dynastic marriage, a 1604 negotiated peace, and the visit of English officials to Valladolid in 1605 ("Practice" 388–9). While the specific compositional timeframe does not bear directly upon this essay, other events of these years, detailed by Anne Cruz in "Vindicating," are germane. The circulation of religious images that were integral to the education imparted to Catholic English boys in Sevilla and Valladolid in their preparation for the priesthood became related to the 1596 attack, as churches were burned and idols destroyed (43–5, 48). Much of the furore arising out of the pillaging (a forceful claiming of spoils) concerns the basic division between Catholics and Protestants over the post-Tridentine reinforcement of Catholic belief in supposed idols; both sides, of course, held that God was on their side (45). In 1600 one damaged icon in particular, the *Santa María Vulnerata*, was sent to Madrid and then to Valladolid, and the statue's mutilation – limbs cut off, the virgin separated from her child – came to represent the martyrdom suffered by English Catholics through their mutilation at the hands of the English Protestant rulers (49).

The importance of religious iconography in the Catholic Church during the early modern period hardly needs to be reviewed, yet tantalizing is the possibility that Cervantes suggests a link, even in the popular imagination, between the *Vulnerata* and the kidnapped Isabela of the novella. Cervantes was most likely in Sevilla during the naval skirmish (Johnson, "Practice" 385–6) and, as the Spanish court resided in Valladolid from 1601 to1606, would have found himself there as well as in Madrid. To the extent that *La española inglesa* is informed by the structure of Christian romance, the recuperation, repair, and moving of icons could become symbolized in Isabela's kidnapping, illness, recuperation, and eventual return to Spain. While below I will detail Isabela's physical suffering and the destruction of her skin, I find her representation as a stalwart Catholic enveloped in Marian imagery, broken and made whole like the statue, an outward manifestation of inner fortitude. This religious facet maintains a curious balance with the economic one, again stemming from the use of the word *despojo*. Isabela, Johnson indicates, "has a use value, not an exchange value" and she indeed becomes "useful" for Clotaldo and, later, his son Ricaredo (400). "Despojo" elicits an impertinent curiosity: according to Corominas, it derives from *despoliare*, "despojar, saquear" (to despoil, to sack) and *spoliare*, which in turn follows from *spolium*, "pellejo de los animales" (animal hides), "botín" (booty; animal hides were indeed rich booty from a violent encounter). "Despojo" itself is defined in the *Diccionario de autoridades* as "lo que se halla abandonado por la pérdida de un exército, o por la muerte o desgracia de alguno" (recuperated objects abandonded by a losing army, or by one's death or misfortune); "la ruina violenta de que padece alguno, o alguna cosa" (the sudden mishap that befalls someone or something; the plural despojos may refer to "las sobras o relieves de una cosa" (residue of an object). "Despojar," whence "despojo," opens numerous possibilities for the narrative: the verb can mean, according to *Autoridades*, "quitar y privar a alguno de lo que goza y tiene" (to remove and deprive someone of something enjoyed or owned) or, equally apropos, "En lo forense vale quitar jurídicamente la possesión de los bienes o habitación que no tenía para dársela a su legítimo dueño [...]" (In legal terminology it means to legally remove goods or living quarters from one who took them, in order to return them to their rightful owner). Spoils, then, in Spanish and in its relationship to *pellejo* or hide, are symbols that may have porousness as a condition, especially in this partially metaphorical use of the term that Cervantes employs. Porousness allows for movement from an inside to an outside, revealing the body to be "a dynamic and porous edifice continually producing 'superfluous excrements' which must be removed [...]" (Schoenfeldt 13). In the case of "spoils" gained, for instance, in bellicose activity, objects – whether money, material objects, or religious icons – are moved in and out of societies and, in the case of the ransacked Cádiz, removed from a despoiled city. Isabela is displaced from her rightful "owners" at the outset, but in the conceptual polyvalency of "spoils" by the end of *La española inglesa*, we shall see that, despite a return to Spain, she remains an economic "despojo."[7]

The state of being a spoil sheaths Isabela throughout her quasi-peripatetic life. *La española inglesa* is a story about skin and its implications, and so it is helpful at this juncture to elucidate the role of skin, "the symbolic surface between the self and the world," a part that symbolizes the whole of the human body, an other of the self whether enclosing or masking (Benthien 1, 13). We "display" ourselves to the world and come into physical contact by means of our skin because it represents who we are or perhaps need to be. Michel Serre speaks of a "skin dress," an individual's "memoire extériorisée," the malleability of skin (36; also see Benthien 220):

> La peau, cire dure et douce, reçoit ces pesanteurs variables selon la force des choses et la tendresse de la région, d'où ces [...] traces et marques, notre mémoire et notre histoire, parchemin de nos expériences. Notre robe cutanée porte et expose nos souvenirs, non pas ceux de l'espèce [...] mais ceux de la personne, à chacun son masque, sa mémoire extériorisée. (35–56)

> Skin, hard and gentle wax, receives these changing impressions according to the objects' force and the tenderness of the area, from where [...] traces and marks, our memory and our history, the parchment of our experiences [emerge]. Our cutaneous clothing bears and exposes our memories, not those of the species
> [...] but those of humanity, each with their own mask, their externalized memory. (Translation mine)

Serre's use of wax (cire) and parchment (parchemin), with their possibilities for marking and inscription, permits an association with real and metaphorical skin. In this way even the religion that one practises outwardly is akin to a thick hide (pellejo) or the hard wax of skin one dons in order to match the required outward appearances of one's society, literally to have it impressed upon a body. Clotaldo and family's secret practice of Catholicism within Protestant England is yet another layer worn behind closed doors. The "true" religion must be revealed only inwardly, underneath, lest its uncovering lead, often in reality, to a practitioner's losing his hide (flaying) in public punishment for apostasy. So a secretly kidnapped child is brought to a family who surreptitiously adheres to religious beliefs held suspect by the crown (though, in the world of the novella, Queen Elizabeth praises the child for maintaining her faith) and where the son harbours a clandestine, and seemingly brotherly, love for Isabela; every aspect of the family's existence finds itself under literal and metaphorical wraps, skin over skin. Isabela is similarly covered in the veil of a new language, keeping her original tongue for private use on the occasions that Clotaldo invites to his home other privately Catholic Spaniards residing in England. Always in the background, then, is the "trace" or living reminder of an originary covering.

Skin is also the primary conduit of the ubiquitous, nearly uncontainable sense of touch, and both lend themselves to metaphorical constructions of covering. Touch comprehends an extended and extensive site of mixed reception; as a writer of sensorial projection, Cervantes on more than one occasion ensures that we know that his characters consciously employ the sense of touch as part of "todos los cinco sentidos" (all five senses), a phrase that we find more than once in the *Quixote* as well as in the *Exemplary Novels*. Sancho Panza intends to put his senses to work as protection in order to avoid ingesting anew the bálsamo de Fierabrás: "pienso guardarme con todos mis cinco sentidos de ser ferido ni de ferir a nadie" (I plan to use all my five senses to keep from being wounded or wounding anybody else) (1.21:296).[8] Ingestion is a form of touch, as Aristotle explains that "all objects that we perceive by immediate contact with [sense-organs] are perceptible by touch," and "touch takes place by direct contact with its objects" (*De anima* III.I 424b27–8; III.13 435a17–18); in *De sensu* Aristotle states, "the faculty of taste is a particular form of touch" (2 438b29–30).[9] The humorally hot and moist Campuzano in *Casamiento/Coloquio* claims to be in control of his "God-given" (his term) five senses as a way of assuring Peralta of his shaggy-dog tale's veracity, yet *his* skin and sense of touch had been infected by that of the infectious (and communicable) Doña Estefanía. For her part, the witch Cañizares expresses the need to dampen the senses prior to engaging in an orgiastic witch's sabbath. She had covered the skin of her naked body with an unguent to deaden particularly her sense of touch; the verb used is "amortiguar," "castigar alguna parte del cuerpo de suerte que sienta poco" (to deaden sensation of a body part so that it feels little) (*Dicc. aut.*).

Cervantes delves throughout his prose works into the "tension between the quotidian immediacy of cutaneous contact and the philosophical profundity of touch, between 'immediate' and 'deep' metaphorical touching," as Mark Paterson eloquently states (2). In probing that charged in-between space of tactility, Cervantes trades on a discourse prevalent within the wider cultural context of early modern Spain. Fernández de Ribera's 1623 satire *Los anteojos de mejor vista* offers this observation on touch: "Todo este sentido, y aún los demás, están reducidos al tacto: hoy se juzga a ciegas, se cura a ciegas (aunque sanan pocos) y se vive a ciegas" (This sense, much like the other ones, is completely reduced to touch: nowadays people judge blindly, cure blindly [hence so very few are healed] and live blindly) (qtd in García Santo-Tomás, "Occhiali" 66; trans. García Santo-Tomás). Similarly, the moralists of the early modern period warn against touch particularly with reference to the pleasures of the flesh (whence touch's relegation to the lower stratum of the sense hierarchy), while they speak to the *interior* senses in order to foster spiritual growth. Fray Domingo Lopéz's 1717 *Talentos del Superior. Symbolos en los cincos sentidos corporales* lays out the following: "Aviendo el Superior rezibido en su corazón, como dócil [...] los toques de Dios, y de su Divina Palabra, el modo conque ha de proceder en las materias de su govierno, es tocándolas [...]" (Once the Superior has received docilely in his heart the touch of Good, of his Divine

Word, he will now proceed in his own duties by touching them) (fol. 134). In this case the reference is to the Word made Flesh, a literalization or concretization of biblical metaphor. López continues: "Y como engaña con los semblantes los ojos, y con las vozes los oídos; toque el Superior las verdades, que tanto tendrá de aciertos, quanto quitare de engaños" (And as eyes deceive with false appearances, and the ears with untrue voices, let the Superior touch the truth as he will touch correctly just as he will remove deception) (fol. 135).[10] From touching upon truth, López moves to the equally metaphorical, perfecting internal touch, again expressed through reference to the corporeal sense: "sin que lo sensato se toque, no se perficiona el sentido. Y assí ni se oyrá con perfección, ni se verá sin engaño, ni se gustará con bondad [...] que materias no tocadas, no dan satisfacciones cumplidas" (without touching the senses, the sense itself cannot be perfected. Therefore nor will you hear perfectly, nor see without deceit, nor love with goodness, for matters that are not touched do not yield complete satisfaction) (fol. 135). Alonso de Silva y Arteaga, in his 1701 *Tardes de Cuaresma*, also lays out the function of touch in both the physical and the spiritual realms. He first cites St Ambrose for evidence that touch distracts from a more noble reception that other senses might yield: "el tacto respecto de los demás sentidos, era como capitán de vandoleros, porque goza de lo que los otros roban, y los trae, como a jornal, para que le sirvan en sus deleytes" (touch with respect to the others senses is like the leader of thieves, because he enjoys what others rob, and he appropriates them as his payment so that they serve him in his pleasure) (fol. 281). Silva y Arteaga recognizes that touch is also essential to completeness as part of the five senses and brings to bear Saint Augustine to lend authority to his argument: "comparando los sentidos con los elementos, aplico el tacto a la tierra con grande propiedad: porque con el servicio de los demás medra; y siendo vno los comprehende a todos" (comparing the senses to the elements, I apply touch to land quite appropriately, because it becomes all the more important in the service of the other senses, and being one, it takes in all of them) (fol. 281).[11]

The tensions between moralist writings and humanist Cervantine prose, between internal and external senses, and between the interior and exterior of bodies reflect bonds of love as well as the coarser nature of human foibles. Let us keep in mind Fray Domingo López: "materias no tocadas, no dan satisfacciones cumplidas" (matters that are not touched do not yield complete satisfaction). Cervantes's narrative touch in *La española inglesa* as well as in other *novelas ejemplares* trades on the important image laid out in the prologue to the collection: "Mi intento ha sido poner en la plaza de nuestra república una mesa de trucos, donde cada uno pueda llegar a entretenerse, sin daño de barras; digo sin daño del alma ni del cuerpo" (My intention has been to place in the main square of our Republic a billiard table, where everyone can come for pleasure without harm to the soul) (52; translation mine). Cervantes draws an awareness to sensory perception and reception, to the touch that guides in a way suggested by the "mesa de trucos," or billiard table, played with a wooden cue stick, "de cinco palmos, alisada, y pulida" (five hands in length, smoothed and polished) (*Dicc. aut.*, s.v. "taco"). That same controlling, gaming image suggests the scattered movement that results when one ball strikes another: Cervantes extends his touch not only towards the sensory realm of contact with the world, but also to the shifting grounds of generic forms, each one a ball from the table knocked about into new orders. The fluid, outward arrangement of the balls on the table necessarily changes with each player's turn, and each new spatial relationship affects the next player's strategy. Gaylord elaborates on the tricks implicit in the game's name with regard to narrative conventions that have lost their effectiveness and to the exemplarity that no longer points to the moral standards of another time (117).[12] My essay's focus on skin and touch, then, is concerned with the arrangement of the characters, their changing appearances, and their shifting relationships. Their coverings, whether clothing or skin that hide or reveal, become surfaces that must be erased and replaced in some way to find a truer being underneath. We find ourselves in Merleau-Ponty's phenomenological "thickness of the world" (qtd in M. Paterson 21), where the body and its coverings keep the "visible spectacle [...] constantly alive" just as the "lances, y golpes" of the gaming table keep everything in motion."[13]

Movement in *La española inglesa* takes distinct forms. Geographical displacement is its primary characteristic, and equally important are the changing bodily, sensorial spectacles evinced through different types of skin: the physical bodily covering or the clothing that becomes a second skin and that can be in accordance with or in opposition to the "true" person wearing it. Apparel as a system of codified images also permitted an observer to distinguish among social and professional levels (Donahue 105). The *Novelas ejemplares* are replete with shifting wardrobes: Leonora (*El celoso extremeño*) wears new attire in her marriage to the wealthy Carrizales (Donahue 110); Estefanía and Campuzano (*El casamiento engañoso*) display fake "riches" of pseudo-gold and brocade; Preciosa (*La gitanilla*) is dressed in her gypsy wardrobe; and Leocadia (*La fuerza de la sangre*) dazzles with her luxurious wardrobe as her mother-in-law to be sees to the wedding with her son (Donahue 111). These contextual markers appear as well in *La española inglesa*. For Isabela's first appearance at court, her "parents" preferred her to dress the part of Ricaredo's intended spouse, not, as she literally is, a "prisionera" (prisoner) (248; 11). The precise description of her garb is telling:

> Otro día vistieron a Isabela a la española, con una saya entera de raso verde acuchillada y forrada en rica tela de oro, tomadas las cuchilladas con unas eses de perlas y toda ella

> bordada de riquísimas perlas; collar y cintura de diamantes, y con abanico a modo de las señoras damas españolas [...]. (248)

> On the following day they dressed Isabella in the Spanish style, with a long dress of slashed green satin, lined with cloth of gold, the slashes pinned by "esses" of pearls, and the whole edged with rich pearls, a necklace and waistband of diamonds, with a fan in the style of Spanish ladies [...]. (11)

But the paragraph closes with a reiteration of Isabela's actual state: "toda esta honra quiso hacer Clotaldo a su prisionera por obligar a la reina la tratase como a esposa de su hijo" (248) (Such was the honour Clotaldo did to his prisoner, so that the queen should treat her as the wife of his son) (11). The implicit tension between how Isabela is arrayed and who she is (cutaneous contact vs. profundity of touch; her surface Englishness vs. her deep-rooted Spanish identity) marks the difference between the two skins, regardless of the impeccable demonstration of grace she displays in conversation with Queen Elizabeth. The word "prisionera" frames the paragraph and the description as well; the reiteration of one charged, truthful word counterbalances the delightfully elegant portrait of the young Spanish woman and underscores how much a spoil she is, particularly in her exchange value for the role of beautiful wife. The insistence on "prisionera," too, turns it into a trope that plays out further with the queen who insists Isabela remain at court with her under her protection. The desire to ennoble Isabela reinforces her position as "spoil"; the language employed by the queen leaves no doubt about objectification: "Clotaldo, agravio me habéis hecho en tenerme este tesoro tantos años ha encubierto; mas él es tal que os haya movido a codicia: obligado estáis a restituírmele, porque de derecho es mío" (249) (Clotaldo, you have done me wrong in keeping this treasure hidden for so long; she is a treasure which has moved you to avarice; you must return it to me, since it is mine by right) (13). "Tesoro" (treasure) as a description of a woman cuts two ways: it acts as a modifier to reinforce great beauty, but it also continues to lock Isabela within a prisoner's "skin," within her splendorous gown, within the court, within a country not hers.

The combination of Isabela's raiment, betrothal to Ricaredo, and privileged situation at court, elements that signal a superficially strong place, ironically renders her overall position unstable. First, during the young woman's appearance before the queen an anonymous attendee comments enviously, "Buena es la española: pero no me contenta el traje" – a probable reference to her garments "à la española" (in the Spanish style) (249) (A fine Spanish girl indeed, but I do not like her dress) (13).[14] Second, one of the queen's ladies, angry that her own son's desire to marry the young Spanish woman has been impeded, poisons Isabela with tainted sweets ("conservas"). Once Isabela ingests the defiled food – a poison that both covers and seeps through food's surface skin to destroy its essence – her physical reaction reveals how deeply infected she has become:

> se le comenzó a hinchar la lengua y la garganta, y a ponérsele denegridos los labios, y a enronquecérsele la voz, turbársele los ojos y apretársele el pecho [...]. Finalmente, Isabela no perdió la vida, que el quedar con ella la naturaleza la co[n]mutó en dejarla sin cejas, pestañas y sin cabello, el rostro hinchado, la tez perdida, los cueros levantados y los ojos lagrimosos. (268–9)[15]

> Isabella's tongue and throat began to swell, her lips went black and her voice hoarse; only the whites of her eyes could be seen and she had pains in the chest [...]. In the end, Isabella did not die, although Nature commuted the sentence only so far as to leave her without eyebrows, eyelashes and hair; her face was swollen, her complexion ruined, her skin leathery, and her eyes watery. (39)

The disfiguring poison erases the young woman's beauty as the foreign substance flays the surface of her physical self, her literal skin, as well as the contours of her non-Spanish upbringing: the queen accedes to Ricaredo's request to care for Isabela at his parents' home, a comforting nest of Catholicism where she can begin to recuperate her health, physical attractiveness, and singular dedication to her native religion. On the one hand, the loss of skin purges Isabela of any "contamination" accrued in her life not only in a Protestant country but also within the ahistorically tolerant court of Elizabeth I; on the other, as a plot device the poisoned sweets act as pharmakon: they kill off her "old" self, the half-Spanish, half-English girl; it permits Ricaredo's further maturation as he sees beyond the superficial and accepts Isabela's inner beauty (what Francisco Sánchez, in a related context within the story, calls her "belleza católica" [77]) (Catholic beauty); it gives life to a regenerated skin and renewed, deep beauty that reaches its plenitude once she has returned to Spain.[16] The meaning of the old skin slips away as a new definition grows. Skin is indeed language.

The dermis in *La española inglesa* also points to a different sort of skin, the physical home itself. A home and a country are intended to be safeguards, yet Isabela's parents, Cádiz, and the Spanish navy could do nothing to protect a little girl abducted as spoils in an ignoble gesture by an English nobleman. Her final journey, in stages from court to Clotaldo's home to Sevilla, leads her to establish her own fruitful place in its economic prosperity. These "homes" where Isabela has lived, these second skins, are protective and are part and parcel of our general sensing of the world: "La maison construit autour de nous un sensorium orthopédique, inversement le sensorium bâtit notre petite maison portative, notre vaisseau frêle, membrane molle prête a crever à la moindre épine agressive" (The house constructed an orthopedic sensorium around us, inversely the sensorium builds our small portable house, our frail vessel, soft membrane ready to burst at the slightest prick of a thorn) (Serre 157; my trans.).[17] Interestingly, Serre also suggests that we build our houses for fundamental biological reasons: "comme une variété de mammifères ou de primates mous qui, après avoir perdu la toison, inventa la maison et la remplit incontinent de boîtes gigognes" (like a kind of mammal or weak primate who, after having lost its fur, built the house and filled it at once with nested boxes) (157). Isabela has followed this model precisely, losing her skin along with its representations and connotations of beauty, and her home, with its hoped-for promise of security. Not until her return to Sevilla, with her second skin and her beauty restored, is she freed from the necessity of imposed second skins.[18] The final scene of the novella importantly takes place outside the convent where Isabela was about to profess (she believed Ricaredo dead during what had become a voyage of pilgrimage, capture, and rescue) until Ricaredo appears as a device of deus ex machina, to fulfil his promise of matrimony.

Ricaredo himself has undergone an essential transformation as well from vainglorious military commander in the service of Queen Elizabeth to rescued and humbled nobleman. He, like Isabela, finds change in both his "natural fancy dress" and his literal skin throughout travels as well as travails, a passage from pomp to purification. After a successful naval campaign carried out at the queen's command – recall her insistence that he merit Isabela's hand of his own accord – his appearance at court earns him and his marriage plans royal approbation. Just as Isabela's costume takes centre stage when she is presented to the queen, so Ricaredo's outfit calls attention to itself:

> Venía armado de peto, espaldar, gola y brazaletes y escarcelas, con unas armas milanesas de once vistas, grabadas y doradas, parecía en extremo bien a cuantos le miraban; no le cubría la cabeza morrión alguno, sino un sombrero de gran falda, de color leonado, con mucha diversidad de plumas terciadas a la valona; la espada, ancha; los tiros, ricos; las calzas, a la esguízara. (259)

> As he was approaching wearing breast-plate, backplate, gorget and pouches, the full Milanese armour of eleven pieces, all decorated and gilded, everyone who saw him admired his appearance. He was not wearing a helmet, but a hat with a broad brim, tawny in colour, with a variety of feathers, at a rakish angle; he had a broadsword with rich scabbard, and wore Swiss breeches. (25)

Though Queen Elizabeth recognizes Ricaredo's valour and, in economic-laden language, fulfils her promise to grant him his marriage, his appearance remains at odds with his deeds. McKim-Smith and Welles summarize the *au courant* style Ricaredo wears, his short armour permitting observers to note his clothes underneath, his hat powerfully flamboyant (87). He dresses, it seems, to call attention to himself through sartorial braggadocio that almost comes across as satire.[19] Indeed, in this scene at the English court, once the queen departs, a little girl looks underneath his *escarcelas* – "la armadura que cae desde la cintura al muslo" (armour that covers from the waist to the thigh) (*Dicc. aut.*) – with her gaze directed towards the "loin and groin area" (McKim-Smith and Welles 87–8); the vignette calls out Ricaredo's vanity, immaturity, and perhaps lack of discretion in having covered himself in such ostentatious, suggestive, and revealing attire. Only towards the novel's close, after his final journey, from which he returns wearing the simple Trinitarian robe of those who ransomed him (and Cervantes from his five-year captivity), does he become firmly grounded as a more mature, less effeminate male. His presentation at the convent door is described as distinctly at odds with the sumptuous court clothing representative of military glory and speaks to a truer skin worn publicly, a delicate redemptive covering, regardless of the cloth's coarseness. The moment of Ricaredo's appearance is illustrated with skin-related markers:

> hendiendo por toda la gente hacia ellos venía aquel cautivo, que habiéndosele caído un bonete azul redondo que en la cabeza traía descubrió una confusa madeja de cabellos de oro ensortijados y un rostro como el carmín y como la nieve, colorado y blanco, señales que luego le hicieron conocer y juzgar por extranjero de todos. (277)[20]

> forcing his way through the crowd towards them, the prisoner, who, when a round blue cap he was wearing fell off his head, revealed that he had a mass of curly yellow hair and a fair pink and white complexion, which immediately made him recognizable as a foreigner. (49)

Cervantes makes it clear in a more forthright way than he had done with Isabela that Ricaredo is now the foreigner; though still and always the ruddy-faced Englishman, he had to survive an annealing test, like Isabela's poisoning, that reduced him almost to the skin of his teeth: when captured by a Turkish galleon and forced on board, "nos desnudaron hasta dejarnos en cueros" (281) (they stripped us naked) (55). Ricaredo's continuing description of the skirmish brings the two protagonists full circle: the Turks, he recounts, "Despojaron las falugas de cuanto llevaban" (281) (they looted the launches of everything within them) (55). With the renewed emphasis on spoils, "despojos," Ricaredo and Isabela now share a fundamental experience: both have been spoils of battle, both have been reduced to the rawness of exposed, mistreated skin, and both have been forced to reassess their corporeal and sensorial relationship to the world.

Ricaredo and Isabela evolve from narrowly defined objects to fuller expressions representative of changing positions in an unstable world. McKim-Smith and Welles note that ruptures in Old World constructs give way to new world orders and often appear in the sartorial system (98), the medium through which the new order attempts to *contact*, to touch in its metaphorical profundity as well as quotidian immediacy, the changing contours of an evolving social contract. The visual experience afforded by outward skin testifies both to what is fading away and to what is fast approaching; style reflective of changing empires is holding on to the known while seeking a way to accommodate the "commingling" of nations and religions to which McKim-Smith and Welles allude (98). Francisco Sánchez has noted that the English court had received Isabela with great praise, described as she is in astrological terms: "se adelantó Isabela; y como quedó sola, pareció lo mismo que parece la estrella o exalación que por la región del fuego en serena y sosegada noche suele verse, o bien ansí como rayo del sol que al salir del día por entre dos montañas se descubre" (249) (Isabella went on alone; as she moved away from them she seemed like a star which moves on a serene evening across the sky, or like the rays of the sun as it shows itself between two mountain peaks at dawn) (11). Ensuing references to a "cometa" (comet) and "incendio" (fire) call up the hearts all aflame among male court observers and even prefigure the suffering endured by Isabela, who had shone too brightly.[21] A comet, after all, enjoys but an ephemeral existence from the perspective of the human eye. But her grand triumph – recuperation and reunion with Ricaredo – finds her not standing alone, exposed, a "tesoro" (250) on display, as she had been in England, but among a crowd of observers, well-wishers, as well as members of the Church hierarchy: "hicieron a Isabela uno de los más honrados acompañamientos que en semejantes actos se había visto en Sevilla [...] tal era el deseo que en todos había de ver el sol de la hermosura de Isabela, que tantos meses se les había eclipsado" (276–7) (they provided Isabella with one of the most noble escorts that had ever been seen in the city of Seville [...] such was the desire everyone had to see the sun of Isabella's beauty after its eclipse of so many months) (49). She has changed from comet to sun, a more permanent fixture in the heavens as well as in heaven on earth, feeling comfortable in her own skin. The crowd around her, the rich fabrics she had worn earlier that now grace her body one more time, the hard-earned recovered beauty are integral to her being in the sense that they serve to reintegrate her into a society where she belongs; all are new skins, delicate yet sturdier than before, protecting her from the edges inward.[22]

Cervantes ties astute observation of economics and history to a framework of a hybrid literary genre and holds it together with the skin of his narrative, itself exemplified in skin imagery focused on Isabela and Ricaredo.[23] Steven Connor has stated with consummate focus that "skin insists" (10), and in Cervantes it not only insists but controls as the connective tissue to the spoils of war that define the primary characters. Skin is the outer edge with the power to make itself central. Force and power are vested in edges and fringes, whether in clothing or in skin itself, given that skin is located at the very edge of our being yet holds us together and projects our self out to the world. The aegis or protective shield worn by Athena, Connor argues, is edged with snakes to protect her and to remind potential attackers of the defeated Gorgon's hair; likewise Jesus's healing power is contained in the hem of his robe (265). Such are the "liminal potentialities" Cervantes incorporates within his novella (Torres 115). Isabela as well as Ricaredo have paid their pound of flesh and become bound to one another in an act of inversion and complementarity, the *española inglesa* and the "inglés español" (Spanish Englishman). These transformations, through loss and regeneration of skin, effect apparently unifying changes to character and plot. Ricaredo casts off his pomp and wears a cloth that permits a public declaration of a Catholic in a Catholic land. Isabela, a spoil bandied about as a treasure may gain a true and tested man as husband, but her final conversion is to a prize, a "renewed" object of exchange that now permits her parents to regain the fortune lost in the sack of Cádiz.

Just as Cervantes leaves his beloved (and careful) readers with frequently ambiguous endings, so I conclude this brief essay on skin, touch, and spoils with an opening to further discoveries. The billiard table image of the prologue to the *Exemplary Novels* implies a need for dexterous manipulation of the metaphorical cue, the putting into play of concepts that often signal shifting values and promulgate new ways of reading the world. The final paragraph of *La española inglesa* contains the example or "moral" Cervantes offers to his tale, but, to trade on the conversions experienced by the novella's two protagonists, he exemplifies how and why the reader must take care in seeking its wider meaning: "Esta novela nos podría enseñar cuánto puede la virtud y cuánto la hermosura, pues son bastante juntas y cada una por sí a enamorar aun hasta los mismos enemigos" (283) (This novel [could] teach us the power of virtue and of beauty, since separately and together they are sufficient to make even enemies love each other) (57). The conditional form "podría" indicates the possibilities of harmonious unions growing out of virtue and beauty but as a *possibility*, a "what if" in the search of a greater perfection.[24] Torres notes that this statement, directed to the reader, creates an "ironic, critical distance" to warn the reader of a too literal understanding in order to accept that a change of skin and its sensorial implications brings us in touch with ideals themselves through wider social, economic, and political transformations (132; also see Avalle-Arce 100n127). "Materias no tocadas, no dan satisfaciones cumplidas": sense perception "changes with humanity's entire mode of existence," as Walter Benjamin once wrote (qtd in Halliday 216). Cervantes strives to effect these changes whether by portraying realistic worlds in selected novellas or "imagined communities" as in *La española inglesa*, where images are almost literally touched, like those round objects of the *mesa*, and moved into potentially infinite constellations as recognition of their capacity for offering evolving truths in Cervantes's exemplary sensorium.[25]

NOTES

1 I would like to thank Catherine Larson and Carolyn Nadeau for their insightful comments and suggestions on an earlier draft of this essay.
2 No listing can be complete, but I would begin with Serre, Connor, and Jablonski. Connor, particularly, summarizes contemporary philosophical writing on skin, and Jablonski provides a sociobiological perspective.
3 With regard to Cervantes a good starting point is the special issue of *Cervantes* (24.1 [2004]), edited by Elaine Bunn. The six essays included therein and their accompanying lists of works cited will yield fruitful information for interested readers. The development of cognitive approaches to early modern Spanish literature led Julien Simon to guest edit a special number of *Cervantes* (32.1 [2012]).
4 Translations from the *Exemplary Novels* are from Price (see Ife ed.). While Price translates "despojos" as "prizes" – here indicated in brackets – I believe "spoils" more accurately reflects the context. Johnson, among many other critics, refers to "spoils" or "spoil" in that sense.
5 Johnson ("*La española inglesa*" 400) had elaborated on the immediately "dehumanized," "spoil of war," Isabela.
6 The complicated relationship between Spain and England presents a complex tapestry. Cruz's *Material* brings together essays that address the fundamental strands. While only one study focuses directly on *La española inglesa* (de Armas), others contribute to clarifying the wider politico-religious picture.
7 We find similar constructs in Tudor England, as Pollard and Cahill, among others, inform us.
8 Grossman's translation (155).
9 The Aristotelian treatises on the senses are widely commented on, and a recent explanation of the difficulties found in Aristotle's descriptions of the senses and sense organs can be found in Johansen.
10 Here and below, in citing from the early modern treatises, I regularize accents but not spelling. The translations are my own.
11 The association of touch with earth (as one of the four elements) follows Aristotelian doctrine.
12 My reading of the prologue is influenced as well by Boyd and Lorenzo: Boyd writes that "The text of a *novela*, like any other piece of writing, is fixed; the possible

configurations of the balls on a billiard table, once the game starts, are infinite, and different in every game; there are no rules for reading a story in the sense that there are rules governing the play at the *Mesa de trucos*" (54).

13 The phrase "lances, y golpes" is from the *Diccionario de autoridades* definition of "trucos": "Juego de destreza, y habilidad, que se executa en una mesa dispuesta à este fin con tablillas, troneras, barra, y bolillo, en el qual regularmente juegan dos, cada uno con su taco de madera, y bolas de marfil de proporcionado tamaño, siendo el fin principal dar con la bola propria à la del contrario, hacer barras, bolillos, tablillas, echar trucos altos, y baxos, respectivamente en las varias especies de este juego, con otros lances, y golpes, con que se ganan las rayas hasta acabar el juego, cuyo término puede ser voluntario, aunque regularmente suele ser de quatro, ocho, ù doce piedras, ò rayas." I find it curious and a felicitous coincidence that a game is often won once a player has earned up to "doce piedras, o rayas," a quantity that corresponds to the number of *novelas* in Cervantes's collection.

14 Johnson (*Material* 173–7) had written that dressing "a la inglesa" and "a la española" was a sign of mutuality, a point noted as well by McKim-Smith and Welles (84). My take on Isabela's clothing – she *was dressed*, after all, and did not *dress herself* – is that it sows divisiveness, a further result of the originary rash action by Clotaldo, he who had kidnapped Isabela in the first place.

15 Curiously, the narrator describes the poison's effect only on Isabela's face and offers not a word about physical changes to other parts of her body. Cervantes seems to present a portrait of near-martyrdom, creating a magic venom with the curative result of eliciting Ricaredo's compassion as proof of his profound love for Isabela.

16 Though my focus in this essay is not on the romance structure of the novella, I do concur with Marsha Collins's view of Isabela's poisoning as "the peripetal point signaling the narrative's ascending evocation" (59). The clever employment of "peripetal" reinforces the multifaceted movements throughout Cervantes's text.

17 Benthien (29) also picks up on this extended imagery employed by Serre in a chapter she entitled "Boîtes" (Boxes).

18 Sawday talks about the early modern culture of dissection and its representation, where images of the dissected individuals take part in the process, often holding up their own skin to reveal their viscera (110). Benthien also notes this practice (68) and later addresses a woman who has had skin removed: a flayed woman is "no longer a woman. Femaleness lies only in the dark and muddy breeding ground in the depths of the body [...] But woman is not surface *or* container [...] woman as hollow space with an enveloping, smooth external skin. If that skin is removed, her body also ceases to be a 'container'" (89). Later in his study Sawday discusses Marsyas, who was punished with flaying for having challenged and lost to Apollo in a musical contest (185–6). Skin, metaphorical and real, plays a much larger role in *La española inglesa*

as well as in the larger arena of early modern texts than can be explored in the space allotted for this essay.

19 The scene raises the issue of Ricaredo's masculinity, as the narrator's description evokes Mars as well as Venus (259). McKim-Smith and Welles relate this evocation to paintings of both mythic figures (87–90), and Martínez-Góngora discusses at length the suggestions of masculine anxiety that appear throughout this *novela ejemplar*.

20 Martínez-Góngora notes that this description contains "rasgos aplicados comunmente [...] [a] la belleza femenina" (38). Ricaredo lives within a many-layered skin, each level characterized by an unusual combination of hard (armour, jewels) and soft (doublet, an unruly skein of blonde hair). The dyad Mars/Venus fits within these parameters as well, and de Armas indicates that the union of those two produces Harmonia, reflecting both the vision of an accepting England as well as the stability forthcoming from the marriage of Isabela and Ricaredo (96).

21 For a full treatment of the astrological implications of these fiery descriptors, allusion to a 1604 *nova*, and the "what if" scenario Cervantes portrays through ahistorical plotting, see de Armas ("Heretical"), particularly 92–7.

22 Once Ricaredo tells the story of his most recent travails, of the letters of credit involving a Florentine merchant and other middlemen, and of his freedom, two Church representatives urge Isabela "que pusiese toda aquella historia por escrito para que la leyese su señor el arzobispo" (to put tell her story in writing for his Lord Archbishop) (282). The rewriting of the tale (Cervantes's novella itself is the first writing) allows Cervantes an additional wink at questions of genre. Does Isabela write down this story for the archbishop's edification? his entertainment? Cervantes introduces a new narratee, a "vuestra merced" (Your Grace), which has the effect of reducing or at least taming the romance in order to heighten its peripatetic nature as a class of picaresque, Isabela and Ricaredo having rowed to a safe port (the metaphor is apt in this case) and finding themselves "en [su] prosperidad y en la cumbre de toda buena fortuna" (enjoying great prosperity and at the peak of all good fortune) (*Lazarillo* 205).

23 Recent studies of *La española inglesa*, particularly by Stoops and Olid Guerrero, both of whom focus on Queen Elizabeth as portrayed by Cervantes, lend themselves to an even more extensive meditation on skin than can be taken up here. The pictorial representation of Elizabeth brought to bear by Stoops (181–2ff) in her discussion of alchemy is also fertile ground for images of skin and how Elizabeth was seen in portraiture and in the public imagination and how she fashioned herself. For Elizabeth as seen by the seventeenth-century writer Antonio Coello see Quintero.

24 Avalle-Arce's edition has the verb as "podrá," which would change the meaning and interpretation significantly, but this form appears to be a typographical error (100). The notes Avalle-Arce places throughout his edition place in italics the words or

phrase to which the note refers, and at 100n127 he has "*Nos podría enseñar*," with no further indication concerning "podrá" or "podría." Price based his translation – a parallel edition – on the 1613 *princeps*, Schevill and Bonilla, Avalle-Arce and Sieber (xvi), yet he maintains the future tense of "podrá," as does the García López edition (263). The *princeps* that serves as the basis for Florencio Sevilla Arroyo and published online (*princeps* and edition) in the Biblioteca Virtual Miguel de Cervantes likewise indicates "podría" (fol. 111r).

25 "Imagined communities" is Benedict Anderson's now widely disseminated concept of communities constructed by those who feel themselves a part of one regardless of national boundaries. Cervantes imagined many fictive constellations where borders were unrelated to their physical placement on a map. Anderson's notion has been widely applied to authors' literary worlds, as even a cursory perusal of the MLA's *International Bibliography* makes clear.

PART FOUR

Sensing Empire

9 The Senses of Empire and the Scents of Babylon in the *Libro de Alexandre*

EMILY C. FRANCOMANO

"Quïérovos un poco todo lo al dexar, / del pleit de Babilonia vos quïero contar, / cómo yaz' assentada en tan noble lugar, / cómo es abondada de ríos e de mar" (For a while I want to cease talk of all else; / I wish to give you an account of Babylon, / how it lies set in land of such splendour, / and how it is favoured by rivers and sea) (st. 1460).[1] The *Alexandre* poet's detailed illustration of Babylon has long been read as more than a mere digression inserted to bring "relief for the reader after the long narrative of [Alexander's] second battle" (Michael 262).[2] This placement of the depiction of Babylon at the midpoint of the *Libro de Alexandre* is clearly not coincidental; Babylon, the *axis mundi*, is also the axis upon which the *Alexandre*, along with Alexander's ambitions, conquest, and eventual downfall, turns. Alexander desires and is destined to have Babylon, but also to die there, poisoned by a traitor.

The *Alexandre* poet made the most of the rich allegorical possibilities of Babylon, a multivalent biblical *figura*, a type and image that "flourished within a discourse that built fantasy upon fantasy" (Van De Mieroop 257). Moreover, in a work in which the poet continually appeals to the senses, the description of Babylon is the most sensual and rhetorically synaesthetic episode of the *Alexandre*. The poet's audience is invited not just to *see* its majestic architecture, healthy and well-dressed inhabitants, and the abundant gems and other worldly goods produced and traded there, but also to listen to its birdsong and minstrels, to smell the plethora of spices ground in its mills, and to taste and feel the salubrious water streaming from its fountains. Gordon Rudy defines rhetorical synaesthesia as a "strategy or technique of mixing or 'breaking' sensory tropes or metaphors. What is mixed or 'broken' are the distinctions between the five senses" (14). Although Rudy is concerned with how rhetorical synaesthesia is used in medieval mystical writing, it is a useful term for thinking about how vernacular poets appeal to the senses of their audiences, who are invited to listen, see, smell, touch, and taste the scenes they vividly describe. In this way the concepts of rhetorical synaesthesia and ekphrasis (vivid description) are closely related and at times intersecting poetic devices. Moreover, the synaesthetic ekphrasis of Babylon extends beyond the five corporeal senses to appeal to the inner, rational senses of the *Alexandre's* audience.

In his ekphrasis of Babylon, the poet offers "exuberant cascades of sensual gratification" (Gumbrecht 2), inviting us to consider the roles that the senses and sense perception play in the *Alexandre* and how they are related to allegorical sense in the poem's meditation upon the rise and fall of Alexander the Great. The poet's rhetorical synaesthesia is also an invitation for us, as twenty-first century readers of the *Alexandre*, whose primary point of contact with the poem is textual, to recall the "somaesthetic" dimensions of medieval poetry, which was performed, brought forth from a speaking or singing body, to be enjoyed through the eyes and the ears of the audience.[3]

The poet's first direct appeal to the senses occurs in stanza three, where he asks the audience to lend their ears to his story:

Qui oir lo quisiere, a todo mi creer,
avrá de mí solaz, en cabo grant plazer,
aprendrá buenas gestas que sepa retraer,
averlo an por ello muchos a connoçer. (st. 3)

Whoever wants to listen, I believe with all my heart,
will gain from me delight and finally great contentment.
He will learn of fine deeds of which he may tell
and through it he will come to be known by many.

In the context of the *captatio benevolentiae* it is not surprising that the poet links listening to entertainment, instruction, memory, and fame.[4] However, it is notable that he links pleasure and the acquisition of knowledge to the sense of hearing. The poet places the audience in a position analogous to Alexander's listening to his tutors, just as the relationship between storyteller and audience, sage and disciple, will be mirrored by Alexander's telling his troops of their exemplary ancestral heritage in his recounting of the Trojan War.

Introducing his audience to the preternatural intellect of his hero, the poet remarks:

Nada non olvidava de cuanto que oyé,
non le cayé de mano quanto que veÿé;
si más le enseñassen, él más aprenderié;
sabet que en las pajas el cuer non tenïé. (st. 18)

He forgot nothing of all that he heard.
He let slip nothing of all that he saw.
The more he was taught, the more he would learn.
His head, I assure you, was not in the clouds.

Alexander's faculties, the poet reports, work just as they should: all he sees and hears is committed to memory. The account signals the two senses that were thought to be the "highest" of the human corporeal senses in the Middle Ages, sight and hearing.[5]

The *Alexandre* was composed at some point in the early decades of the thirteenth century, just before Aristotle's work on the senses began to circulate widely in academic and intellectual circles (Dod 43).[6] The Aristotle we see in the *Libro de Alexandre* is the vernacular Aristotle of wisdom literature, the famed teacher who also appears in works such as *Bocados de oro* teaching essential life lessons to his male disciples. Nevertheless, earlier influential work on the senses acknowledged the necessity of the corporeal senses for the acquisition of knowledge while also condemning the senses as the conduits of temptation and as continual reminders of original sin. Augustine's reflections in Book XI of *The Trinity* provide a useful example of the connections between the inner and outer senses and the power of bodily sensations:

> No one will doubt that just as the inner man is endowed with understanding, so is the outer man with sensation [...]. And by the very logic of our condition, according to which we have become moral and carnal, it is easier and almost more familiar to deal with visible than with intelligible things, even though the former are outside and the latter inside us, the former senses with senses of the body and the latter understood with the mind [...]. And yet, as I have said, we have grown so used to bodies, and our interest slips back and throws itself out into them in such a strangely persistent manner, that when it is withdrawn from the uncertainties of bodies to be fixed with a much more assured and stable knowledge on things of the spirit, it runs away again to those things and seeks to take its ease in the place where it caught the disease. (303)[7]

Sight, in particular, was considered the outer, material sense closest to the inner, spiritual senses, and to what Augustine called "mental vision."[8] For Augustine, the corporeal senses could grasp only objects of this world, "limited by time and space," while inner senses were capable of perceiving immortal, spiritual objects (Rudy 36). Medieval thinkers and writers rehearsed their predecessors' ideas of the close relationships between cognition and sensory perception (see Vogt-Spira). Isidore of Seville, whose writings were probably known to the *Alexandre* poet, also privileges sight among the senses: "It is called vision (*visus*) because it is more vivid (*vivacior*) than the rest of the senses, and also more important and faster, and endowed with greater liveliness (*vigere*), like memory among the rest of the faculties of the mind. Moreover it is closer to the brain, from which everything emanates" (XI.i.18, 232). Isidore, so interested in the meanings of words, explains how prophetic "vision" differs from yet resembles the senses:

> [There is] a third kind of vision which is neither by bodily senses nor by that part of the soul where images of corporeal things are grasped, but by insight (*intuitus*) of the mind where intellectual truth is contemplated, as the gifted Daniel saw with his mind what Belshazzar had seen with his body. Without this kind of vision the other two are either fruitless or positively lead into error. Still, the Holy Spirit governs all these kinds of vision. (VII.xiii.40, 168)

Isidore's description of the five senses, however, speaks to the nature of ekphrasis itself:

> The body has five senses: vision, hearing, smell, taste, and touch. Among these, two become active or inactive, while another two are always receptive. They are called senses (*sensus*), because with their help the soul activates the entire body in a most subtle way with the power of sensation (*sentire*). Hence one speaks of things that are present (*praesentia*), because they are "before the senses" (*prae sensibus*), just as we call things that are present to our eyes "before our eyes" (*prae oculis*). (XI.i.18, 232)

Moreover, as Isidore explains in his discussion of memory and will, the senses are directly related to sense: "Will is said to be sense (*sensus*) with regard to what it senses (*sentire*) – whence also the word 'idea' (*sententia*) derives its name" (XI.i.11, 231–2).

In the episodes leading to the epicentre of the poem, the *Alexandre* poet carefully prepares the way towards his extended and synaesthetic ekphrasis of Babylon. Early on in the poem Babylon heads the list of Alexander's ambitions:

> Ya contava por suya torre de Babilón
> India e Egipto, la tierra de Sión,
> África e Marruecos, quantos regnos y son,
> quanto que Carlos ovo bien do el sol se pon. (st. 88)[9]
>
> He already counted as his the Tower of Babylon,
> India and Egypt and the land of Sion,
> Africa and Morocco and all the kingdoms they contain,
> all that belonged to Charles as far as the setting sun.

Babylon is again imagined under Alexander's grasp in the decoration of his shield:

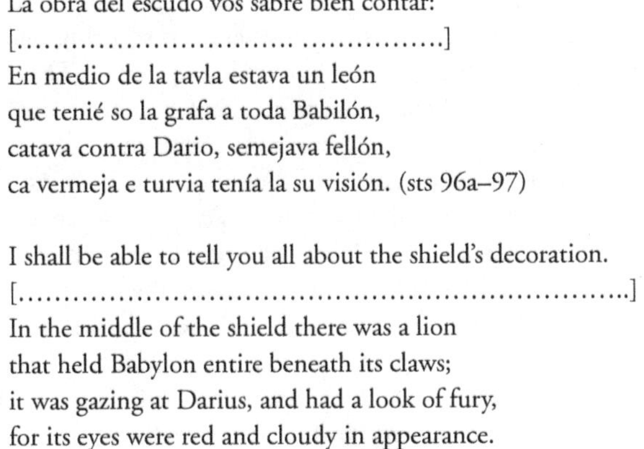

> La obra del escudo vos sabré bien contar:
> [.............................. ....]
> En medio de la tavla estava un león
> que tenié so la grafa a toda Babilón,
> catava contra Dario, semejava fellón,
> ca vermeja e turvia tenía la su visión. (sts 96a–97)
>
> I shall be able to tell you all about the shield's decoration.
> [..]
> In the middle of the shield there was a lion
> that held Babylon entire beneath its claws;
> it was gazing at Darius, and had a look of fury,
> for its eyes were red and cloudy in appearance.

Alexander's vision of his future as the conqueror of the known world is neatly linked to the poet's shield ekphrasis, the first of many virtuosic vivid descriptions in the *Alexandre.*

Several scholars have studied the visual elements in the *Libro Alexandre*, most recently Clara Pascual-Argente, whose work on the tomb ekphrases shows that the Spanish poet wished not to exploit the tensions between word and image, but rather to deploy the coexistence of visual and verbal as "mnemonic rather than mimetic" forms of representation in the interests of the "creation and transmission of a cultural memory of the classical past" (74, 92).[10] The retelling of the narrative of Troy and the viewing of images on the tombs and shields are two of the many ways in which the past is made present for both the protagonists and the audience of the *Alexandre.* Pascual-Argente's convincing analysis of the function of the tomb ekphrases in the *Alexandre* concurs with Claire Barbetti's more general conclusions regarding the workings of ekphrasis in medieval literature: "word and image cannot help but work together [...] medieval ekphrasis tends toward contemplation, instruction, a processing of the cultural image trove and, often, a revision of it" (6, 8).[11]

In the *Alexandre*, ekphrasis is not only a device that stresses moral and typological value above and beyond verisimilitude. By bringing images vividly before the senses of the audience, as the description of Babylon demonstrates, ekphrasis is synaesthetic. Indeed, the poet's vibrant descriptions rely upon the "underlying idea" in rhetoric that "literature can arouse something analogous to sensual perceptions, the ideal result [...] being that the induction by means of texts becomes undistinguishable from that which is brought about by means of the perception of the external world" (Vogt-Spira 55). Ancient rhetors, in fact, understood ekphrasis as a device that appealed to more than just the mind's eye. A precedent for extending the notion of ekphrasis beyond "seeing," can be found in the *Imagines* of Philostratus the Elder and Philostratus the Younger, who refer frequently to how paintings evoke aromas, flavours, and melodies, which they in turn bring before the eyes and the other sensory organs through their verbal descriptions.[12] The link between the vivid recreation of images before the mind's senses and memory is synaesthetic in multiple ways. Not only do the descriptions create an "intersensorial transfer of adjectives from concrete to abstract," but they also imagine the transfer of stimulus from one sensory organ to another (Tiez 3). Moreover, in addition to the comingling of the senses as audiences or readers imagine and, in a sense, experience the stimulation of multiple corporeal senses, the inner, "common sense" or rational faculty of the mind is stimulated and memory activated.[13]

As Marina Brownlee has observed, the poet presents the prophecy of Daniel foretelling Alexander's vanquishing Darius at the mathematical centre of the poem, a "structurally significant" point where hidden truths are often are often revealed in medieval romance (265). "Danïel el profeta niño de Dios amado, / dentro en Babilonia l'ovo profetizado: / que vernié en la sierra un cabrón mal domado, / quebrantarié los cuernos al carnero doblado" (Daniel the prophet, the beloved child of God, / had made the prophecy in the land of Babylonia, / that an untamed goat would come to the mountains / which would shatter the twin horns of the ram) (st. 1339). The prophecy is pleasing to Alexander, but it is clear to the poet and his audience that Alexander can appreciate only half of its meaning because, despite his famed wisdom, Alexander's knowledge is limited. Alexander is capable of typological interpretation. He knows that he is the "carbon mal domado" of the prophecy, just as he understands and teaches his troops that they must understand the history of Troy as an exemplum. Nevertheless, as Brownlee concludes, Alexander's reading of the prophecy is representative of how, throughout the poem, "there is a consistent program of what amounts to a correct interpretation in pagan which simultaneously constitutes a misinterpretation in Christian terms" (266). With regard to the retelling of the Trojan war, María Rosa Lida de Malkiel similarly remarks, "Alejandro concluye por sostener no muy ortodoxamente, el valor supremo de la gloria mundana" (181–2). As Weiss concludes, "running throughout the narrative is the motif of a hidden truth which the main characters may dimly perceive or which they actively try to suppress or ignore" (118). This contrast of interpretive perspectives is important for the poet's construction of the episodes that take place in Babylon and the way in which he appeals to both inner and outer senses in the synaesthetic ekphrasis of the city.

Alexander's single-minded powers of interpretation are showcased when, having completed his studies and received instruction through his eyes and ears, he is ready to taste conquest. His first taste is at once metaphorical and corporeally sensual.

Before engaging in battle, Darius and Alexander exchange letters and symbolic gifts. Darius first sends Alexander tokens that are intended to symbolize the upstart's youth and inexperience: "correuela que çiñas, pello con que trebejes, / bolsa en que los tus dineros los condenses" (a belt for you to wear, a ball with which to play, / a bag in which you can keep your money) (st. 783bc), and then sends him a sack of common melon seeds intended to symbolize the immeasurable quality of his power "tanto podrié nul omne el mi poder asmar / quanto esta simiente podriedes vos contar" (No man could reckon the extent of my power / any more than you could count the number of these seeds) (st. 811cd).[14] Alexander, with his characteristic blend of learning and muscle, replies with alternate interpretations, transforming both the material and the meaning of the gifts, effectively schooling Darius:

Los donos que me diste te quiero esponer,
– maguer loco me fazes, sé los bien entender – :
la bolsa sinifica todo el tu aver,
que todo en mi mano es aún a caer.

La pella que es redonda tod' el mundo figura:
sepas que será mío, est'es cosa segura;
faré de la correa una açota dura
con que prendré derecho de toda tu natura. (sts 800–1)

I wish to explain for you the meaning of your gifts
– although you call me foolish, I understand them well –:
the bag is a sign of all the wealth that you possess,
which will all one day fall into my hands.

The ball, which is round, represents the whole world:
you should know it will be mine, there can be no doubt.
From the belt I shall fashion a cruel whip
and with it take my vengeance over all your line.

Alexander's second response signals his desire to consume the world, as he scoffs at Darius's presumed power: taking the seeds from the bag, he chews them up, declaring that they are just as sweet, soft, and easy to eat as all Persia will be. The scene foreshadows future references to Alexander's pathological appetite for conquest, likened to the "idrópico que muere por bever" (the man with dropsy who is dying to drink) (st. 1924c). Alexander fills the sack with pepper and writes:

Un grano de pimiento tiene más amargura
que non toda la quilma d'aquella tu orrura;

assí fazen los griegos que son gent fuert' e dura,
que más val de nos uno que mill de tu natura. (st. 818)

One grain of pepper has more sharpness in it
than the whole bag of rubbish of yours;
the Greeks are like that too: a people strong and tough,
one of us worth more than a thousand of your kind.

Alexander's threats equate eating with both conquest and defeat, while also recalling the familiar medieval equations of rumination and digestion to reading and interpretation (Carruthers, "The Book" 165–7). Pepper, which will be important in the description of the conquered city of Babylon, not only is sharper, more pungent and bitter than melon seeds, but also carried other connotations. In addition to being a costly exotic spice, pepper was aligned with traditionally masculine humours, thought to aid in the production of semen due to its dry heat and thus contrasted starkly with the melon, classed as wet and cold and consequently female (Dalby 88–94). Alexander's bitter gift attacks on multiple and mutually reinforcing levels.[15]

The conquest of Babylon provides an opportunity for the poet to describe the marvels of the city, to bring them vividly before the senses of the audience, and thus, just as Alexander chewed and consumed the sweet and soft melon seeds, to ingest the images of Babylon.[16] For the medieval poet and his audience Babylon represented many and divers things. It was the sinful city of Revelation, the "demonic parody" of the heavenly city of Jerusalem in Northrop Frye's words (158), and also could represent the corruption of the Church.[17] Babylon was also a type for Eden before and after the Fall, the place of creation and plenty, on the one hand, and a place of loss and damnation on the other. Following a commonplace in patristic exegesis, the *Alexandre* also sees Babylon as the place where the tower of Babel was built and destroyed, where linguistic unity and understanding were lost to an inheritance of confusion, misunderstanding, and translation. Thus, as Brownlee observes, the poet and his audience would have understood Babylon as "one of the most highly charged emblems of failure in the Christian faith" (267). Situated on the Euphrates River, in the middle of the Fertile Crescent, Babylon had a long history as a great trading city, and ancient lore considered it to be the very centre of the world, a place where heaven and earth met (Van De Mieroop 274). In the *Alexandre* Babylon's terrestrial centrality is heightened by the geographical inaccuracy of the description, which states that both the Tigris and the Euphrates run through the city (st. 1465).

Throughout the extensive and synaesthetic ekphrasis, the *Alexandre* poet made the most of Babylon's multivalent typological connotations. The first part is above all aromatic:

Yaze en lugar sano, comarca muy temprada,
nin la cueita verano nil faz la invernada;
de todas las viandas es sobra abondada,
de los bienes del siglo allí non mengua nada.

Los que en ella moran dolor non los retienta,
passan los mançebillos en dulçor su juventa,
el viejo la cabeça non l'ave tremolienta,
en ella son los árboles que llevan la pimienta.

Allí son las especias: el puro galingal,
canela e gengibre, clavos e çetoal,
ençens' e ananomo, bálsamo que más val,
girofe, nuez moscada e nardo natural.

De sí mismos los árboles tanto han buen olor,
non avrié ante ellos fuerça ningunt dolor,
por esso son los ombres de muy buena color,
bien a una jornada sienten el buen odor.

Los quarto ríos santos todos los ha vezinos,
dizen que los dos fazen por ella sus caminos;
muelen solas especias más de quatro molinos,
más quatro muelen pebre, otros quarto cominos. (sts 1461–5)

It lies in a healthy place, a temperate region:
neither summer nor winter brings it trouble;
it has a rich abundance of all kinds of food,
lacking nothing of the riches of the world.

Those who dwell there are assailed by no pain,
and children pass their youth in sweet enjoyment;
the old man never has a head that quivers,
and in this city are the trees that bear pepper.

Spices, too, are found there: pure galanga,
cinnamon, ginger, cloves and zedoary,

incense and cassia, balsam of greater cost,
syzygium, nutmeg and spikenard.

The trees in themselves have a scent so fine
that no pain, in their presence, could have an effect,
wherefore the men have such a healthy complexion,
and the scent is perceived while a good day away.

All four sacred rivers it has as its neighbours:
two of them are said to trace their paths through the city;
there are more than four mills there to grind only spices,
four more grind pepper and another four cumin.

Babylon, like Berceo's *prado* in the *Milagros de Nuestra Señora*, is a *locus amoenus,* where nature provides for all bodily needs and comforts, "a place of pleasure, a place where time is suspended and the senses, saturated" (Zink 23). The abundance and marvel of the place inspires the poet to exclaim, "¡assí aya en paraiso posada!" (May I have such a resting place in Heaven!) (st. 1494c), and several studies have noted the Edenic qualities of the Babylon described in the *Alexandre.*[18]

In the first stanzas of the description Babylon exudes the "odour of Paradise": pepper, galingale, cinnamon, cloves, zedoary (white turmeric), incense, amomum, balsam, nutmeg, spikenard, and cumin are grown, milled, and traded in the city, and, as the poet tells us in stanza 1465, the odour is both healthful and medicinal.[19] As Paul Freedman notes, the medieval geographical imagination associated spices with Eden, because of their origins in the far-off East: "the odor of paradise and the image of purity and eternity were not just abstract metaphors but vivid concepts that permeated the geographical lore related to a tantalizing and ultimately practical question: where did spices come from?" (89). One of the functions of medieval stories about Alexander the Great was precisely to reveal such mysteries of the east. Similarly, Michael Krondl remarks, "Eden didn't just have a location [...] it had a taste and an aroma. Paradise smelled like spices, for it was there these precious commodities grew. The connection was made explicit when melegueta pepper was called 'grains of paradise,' despite its African origin" (12–13).[20] Many of the spices listed are described by Isidore of Seville in the *Etymologies* in his sections on scents and ointments (*De odoribus et unguentis*), aromatic trees (*de aromaticis arboribus*), aromatic or common plants (*De herbis aromaticis sive comunnibus*), and Asia (*De Asia*). "Scent (*odor*)," Isidore explains, "is named after 'air' (*aer*). It is called incense (*thymiama*) in the Greek language, because it is scented, for a flower that bears a scent is called thyme (*thymum*) [...]. Incense (*incensum*) is so called because it is 'consumed by fire' (*igne consumere*) when it is offered." Spices, according to Isidore, "are whatever India or Arabia or other regions produce that have a fragrant scent. They seem to have gotten the name 'spice' (*aroma*) either because they are proper for putting on altars (*ara*) for invocations to the gods, or because they are known to blend and mingle themselves with air (*aer*). Indeed, what is scent if not air that has been tinctured by something?" (XVII.viii, 348; XI.xii, 113).[21]

The poet's enumeration of spices is also reminiscent of the Song of Songs and of later poetic descriptions of paradisiacal gardens.[22] The lover's garden in the *Roman de la Rose,* for example, is filled with aromatic trees and spices:

> De noiers i ot grant foison
> qui charjoient en la soison
> itel fruit com sonts noiz muguetes,
> que ne sont ameres ne fadetes.
> [. . . . .].
> Si trovast, qui en eüst mestier,
> clos de girofle et requalice,
> ou vergier, mainte bone espice
> graine de paradis novele,
> citonaut, anis et canele
> et mainte espice delitable
> que non mangier fait après table. (Guillaume de Lorris vv. 1330–43)[23]

> There was a great abundance of nut trees that in their season bore such fruit as nutmegs, which are neither bitter nor insipid [...]. He who needed to could find many a good spice there, cloves, licorice, fresh grains of paradise, zedoary, anise, cinnamon, and many a delightful spice hood to eat after meals. (Guillaume de Lorris, *Romance of the Rose* 48)

The Song of Songs, portraying the sister-bride as a walled garden, contains a similar inventory of spices:

> While the king was at his repose, my spikenard sent forth the odour thereof.
> A bundle of myrrh is my beloved to me, he shall abide between my breasts.
> A cluster of cypress my love is to me, in the vineyards of Engaddi.
> [. . . . .]
> How beautiful are thy breasts, my sister, my spouse! Thy breasts are more beautiful than wine, and the sweet smell of thy ointments above all aromatical spices.
> [. . . . .]
> Thy plants are a paradise of pomegranates with the fruits of the orchard. Cypress with spikenard.

> Spikenard and saffron, sweet cane and cinnamon, with all the trees of Libanus, myrrh and aloes with all the chief perfumes. (Song of Solomon 1.11–13 and 4.10, 13–14, Douay Version)

Patristic and medieval commentators on the Song of Songs associated the fragrances with divine presence, something that could be sensed but remained unseen. Bernard of Clairvaux, whose commentaries on the Song of Songs resound with intersensorial references, speaks of sensing "the fragrance of every psalm" and of how the Gospels spread "the sweet savor of Christ." Bernard continues that although Paul "does not allow me to hear the ineffable words" of divinity in his epistles, "yet truly he bids me to desire them, and I may freely catch the fragrance of what I may not hear" (10–11).

Commentators who wrote about the sense of smell tended to consider it an intermediate sense, not ranked as high as sight and hearing, but not as low as taste and touch because, like sight and hearing, it was thought to be mediated through the air and did not require direct contact with the body (Rudy 8).[24] Even though Isidore sees vision as the superior sense, his remarks on smell reveal the connection between odours and knowledge:

> Nostrils (*naris*; ablative *nare*) are so called, because through them odour and breath ceaselessly "swim" (*nare*), or because they warn us with odor, so that we "know" (*noscere*, with forms in *nor-*) and understand something. Hence the opposite: those who do not know anything and who are unrefined are called ignorant (*ignarus*). Our forefathers used the word for "smelling something" (*olfacere*) to mean knowing (*scire*). (XI.i.47, 234)

By beginning his extensive and synaesthetic ekphrasis of Babylon with fragrance, the poet invites his audience to reflect upon what is felt, but not seen, and to connect the outer senses with the inner, perhaps in order to be ready to understand the deeper meanings of the narrative he inserts at the crux of his description of the umbilicus of the world, the destruction of the tower Babel.

Like the senses themselves, fragrances held ambivalent meanings for medieval audiences. While evoking the mystical and divine valences of fragrant spices, the aroma would also have connoted the more worldly activities of trade and the accumulation of wealth as well as the temptations of greed and bodily appetites. Spices – medicinal, exotic, sensorially rich – typify how food was at once "a physical necessity" and "a moral and spiritual danger of considerable importance to the soul" (Grieco 143). Twenty-four stanzas enumerating the precious gems found in Babylon's "sanctas aguas" (holy waters) and their virtues follow the aromatic introductory stanzas of the description. After the lengthy lapidary passage the audience is called to admire the waters, crops, livestock, and people of Babylon. In this extended ekphrasis, which paints the centre of the world as a centre of high commerce, wealth and sensuality are paired as wonders for the senses.

Nevertheless, medieval audiences also would have appreciated the dangers of temptation in the sweet-smelling and sensually gratifying city. The poet alludes to these dangers and to the importance of interpreting the description and history of Babylon when he explicitly connects Babylon's vibrant trade with Alexander's death by treachery:

> Pero y fincan cosas que non son de dexar:
> cómo le vienen grandes ganançias por la mar;
> las más naves del mundo y suelen arribar,
> solamente con esso devrié rica estar.
>
> Embían pora África e también por Europa
> las naves muy cargadas d'espeçias e de ropa;
> por y traxo Antípater en mal punto la copa
> ond priso Alexandre en mal punto la sopa. (sts 1502–3)
>
> But matters there remain that are not to be left:
> how great gain comes to the city by sea;
> most of the world's ships are wont to arrive there
> and with that alone it should be rich indeed.
>
> They send out to Africa and also to Europe
> ships heavily laden with spices and clothes;
> thence did Antipater, in ill moment, bring the cup
> from which Alexander, in ill moment, did sup.

This foreshadowing of Alexander's death provides the poet with the perfect segue into his retelling of the fall of the tower of Babel, a fall provoked by the desire of the ancient, giant inhabitants of Babylon to reach heaven and be like God. The insertion of this biblical story of a fall precipitated by overweening ambition into the topographic sketch of Babylon, the "brightest jewel in Alexander's crown" (Michael 262), clearly invites the *Alexandre*'s audience to read typologically.[25] The move from the outer senses stimulated by ekphrasis to the inner senses of allegory is not coincidental.

The poet announces his desire to describe the magnificent walls, towers, and gates of the city (st. 1504), but he is diverted by the memory of the Tower of

Babel and the punishment meted out by God for the "grant locura" of the giant inhabitants of the city:

> Metió Dios entre ellos tamaña confusión
> que olvidaron todos el natural sermón;
> fablavan sendas lenguas cad'una en su son.
> non sabié un del otro quell dizié o que non.
> [.................................]
>
> Assí está oy día la torre empeçada,
> pero de fiera guisa sobra mucho alçada,
> por la confusïón que fue en ellos dada,
> es toda essa tierra Babilonia llamada. (sts 1508, 1511)
>
> God set among those men such great confusion
> that they all forgot their natural form of speech;
> they spoke separate languages, each with its own ring,
> and could not tell what each other was saying or not.
> [...]
>
> So it is today, the tower has been started
> but in a bad way, and built too high.
> Through the confusion which was inflicted on them,
> all the land bears the name of Babylonia.

The medieval poet, and at least some of the members of his audience, attuned to typological interpretation, would have seen in the story of the destruction of the Tower of Babel not only a recapitulation of Adam and Eve's expulsion from Eden, but a prefiguration of Alexander's pride. The retelling of the Babel story is a deliberate excursus within the ekphrasis of Babylon, inserted between the descriptions of its material wealth (sts 1460–1500) and architectural design (sts 1519–31). The effect of this structure is a shifting from the appeal to the corporeal senses through vivid description, to an appeal to interpret typologically, and then to a return to the corporeal senses and ekphrasis. Thus, mental and physical vision are joined and the ethical dimensions of the poet's synaesthetic ekphrasis underlined. The poet concludes by worrying he will not be believed (sts 1532–3), but the completeness of the description is designed to impress the full, multisensory and typological experience upon the memory. Babylon, a sensually and allegorically overpowering figure capable of evoking both the prelapsarian world of abundance and completeness as well as the Fall and its consequences, is emblematic of what Gabrielle Spiegel characterizes as the "paradoxes generated within medieval considerations of the place of the senses in an epistemological understanding of man as reliant upon the senses for knowledge, but whose proper goal was to overcome the implications that this fundamental belief had for the deeper search for a truth that lay beyond sense perception" (186). The scents of Babylon reveal the allegorical sense of the city.

The poet stresses Alexander's corporeal senses in his conquest of the realms that lie beyond human reach and knowledge. Despite the fact that he has become, as his men remind him "señor [...] del mundo" (lord of the world) (st. 2274b), Alexander desires to know more, to go where "nunca pudo omne" (none had ever managed) (st. 2269b) and "descobrir las cosas que yazen sofondidas" (to discover the things that lie buried) (st. 2291b), to see both known and unknown realms, to physically penetrate the heavens and the depths of the sea. His men warn him against pushing against the limits of what is possible: "Señor, mal nos semeja buscar cosas atales, / las que nunca pudieron fallar omnes carnales" (It seems to us wrong, lord, to search for such things, / as no men of flesh ever managed to find) (st. 2272cd).

During Alexander's deep-sea sojourn the poet stresses how much Alexander has seen, repeating forms of the verb *ver* four times (sts 2311–16) and leading the hero to reflect upon the nature of *soberbia*. Nevertheless, and despite the fact that Alexander can translate what he sees under the sea into all aphorisms – "Las aves y las bestias, los omnes, los pescados, / todos son entre sí a vandos derramados; / de viçio e de superbia son todos entecados, / los flacos de los fuertes andan desafïados" (The birds and the beasts, the men, the fish, / are all divided into bands among themselves. / They are all afflicted with vice and with pride / and the weak are oppressed by the strong) (st. 2320) – he cannot read deeply enough to understand the meaning of what he has seen. *Ver* does not translate into *asmar* and *judgar*, that is, into true knowledge: "Si como lo sabié el rëy bien asmar / quissiesse a sí mismo a derechas judgar" (If, just as the King was well able to see this, / he were willing to pass judgment rightly on himself) (st. 2321ab). The episode provides the poet with an opportunity to discourse further on Alexander's ambition and pride and also to sermonize on the seven deadly sins.

The emphasis on Alexander's corporeal senses is intensified in the recounting of his flight:

Tanto pudo el rey a las nuves pujar,
veyé montes e valles de yus de sí estar,
veyé entrar los ríos todos en alta mar,
mas cóm yazié o non, nunca lo pud' asmar.

Veyé en quáles puertos son angosotos los mares,
veyé grandes peligros en muchos de lugares,

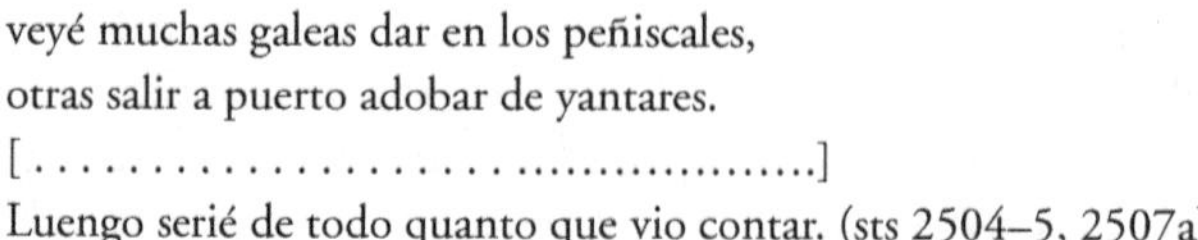

veyé muchas galeas dar en los peñiscales,
otras salir a puerto adobar de yantares.
[.......................................]
Luengo serié de todo quanto que vio contar. (sts 2504–5, 2507a)

The King was able to soar so high into the clouds
that he saw mountains and valleys lie below him;
he saw the rivers all flow out into the high seas,
but their extent he could never imagine.

He saw in which harbours were the sea's waters narrow;
he saw great dangers which lay in many places;
he saw many galleys be wrecked on the rocks
and others come to port and make ready for the feast.
[.......................................]
It would be a long tale to tell all that he saw.

Throughout, Alexander's access to the world and its mysteries is through the corporeal senses; his reliance upon them is, I would argue, part of the poet's expression of his thirst for fame, conquest, and knowledge as one rooted in the pre-Christian understanding of the world.

As mentioned above, Alexander, despite all his mental faculties, is unable to fully interpret Daniel's prophecy, which foretold not only the conquest of Babylon, but also the destruction of the conqueror. Alexander sees what is hidden to the eyes of ordinary men, but he still sees with the physical and mental vision of a pagan. The *Alexandre* poet presents Babylon as a *figura* that reaches backward and forward in time, not only to the construction and destruction of the tower, but also to the redemption of Babel by the Pentecostal gift of tongues and to the eventual reconciling of Jerusalem with its demonic parody. Alexander's vision is bound by his mortality. The poet and audience view the story from a perspective that is at once postlapsarian and postredemptive; Alexander's reading of prophecy and consequent understanding of the world he sees is postlapsarian and pre-redemptive.

The exchange of threats and aromatic gifts and the long description of Babylon are interrelated ekphrastic moments in the work where the poet appeals to senses other than sight and hearing, namely, taste and smell – lower senses – which nevertheless have had a long history in mystical and theological writings. Significantly, they are connected to key moments in which Alexander's ambitions are expressed and his downfall foreshadowed.

The poet's final extended ekphrasis – the description of Alexander's richly decorated tent in Babylon (sts 2539–95) – also clearly connects the use of the senses with mental vision, the rational faculties and interpretation. The cupola of the tent depicts three scenes of fallen pride: Lucifer's descent, the Fall of Adam and Eve, and the destruction of the tower of Babel (sts 2550–2), as well as a scene of Noah and the flood, representing both divine retribution for iniquity and salvation (st. 2553). The tent also depicts a recapitulation of the Trojan War (sts 2567–74). The biblical scenes in the tent represent, as Cacho Blecua notes, "la crónica anunciada del castigo y caída de Alejandro" (123). Yet Alexander, as before, can appreciate only part of the significance of the stories: "Quand' el rey Alexandre estas gestas veyé, / creçiél' el coraçón, grant esfuerço cogié" (When King Alexander saw these exploits, / his heart swelled up and he took great courage) (st. 2575ab). Other portions of the tent contain painted upon them a *mapamundi*, where the conqueror "podié perçebir / quánto avié conquisto, quant podié conquerir" (Alexander could have sight of it all: / all that he had conquered and all he might still) (st. 2587ab), and a visual retelling of Alexander's own story. The tent thus creates a sense of *mise en abyme* as it brings before Alexander's and the audience's eyes an ekphrastic encapsulation of the entire work. Importantly, as Simone Pinet argues ("Será todo"), the images painted on the tent neatly draw together all of the prefigurations of the hero's destiny in order to conclude the poem.

For all his desire to see from a superlunary (and subaquatic) perspective, Alexander remains a human, sublunary, pre-redemptive, and, ultimately, an unredeemed figure. The poet calls upon the audience to see, hear, and even smell Alexander's conquered world. Nevertheless, the conquered world that Alexander himself sees and perceives is a material world available to the corporeal senses that he is only partially able to translate to the figurative sense. What could have been a journey to wisdom is just a journey to sight, consumption, and fame.

Alexander, exemplary in both positive and negative ways, has the intellectual potential to approach divine wisdom as understood by the thirteenth-century poet; but as a pre-Christian figure he is fixed in the material world, immortalized by fame and poetic vision if not by salvation. Alexander can connect the past and his present, but the poet, through his *mester* and all the rhetorical devices he deploys, can connect past, present, and, to a certain extent, future. The poet and thirteenth-century audience, with the gift of typological hindsight, can map the history of salvation onto Alexander's story. Indeed, this is how the poet reconciles the glorification of the pagan hero with his Christian didacticism. Nevertheless, the poet, like Alexander, must rely upon the senses in order to captivate, delight, and instruct his audience. It is significant that the axis of the poem occurs at a moment of heightened sensual stimuli and synaesthesia. The Edenic odour of Babylon reminds audiences of sensual pleasures and hidden meanings, of the need to understand allegorically and the dangers of reading corporeally, fixed on the sensible objects of the pagan Alexander, rather than on the spiritual senses of the clerkly poet.

NOTES

1 All quotations from the *Alexandre* are from *Libro de Alexandre*. Translations into English are from *Book of Alexander*.

2 Ian Michael points to how the description foreshadows Alexander's death by treachery as a thematic connection. Peter Bly and Alan Deyermond suggest Babylon's typological importance in "The Use of *Figura* in the *Libro de Alexandre*," an idea further developed by Marina Scordilis Brownlee in "Pagan and Christian: The Bivalent Hero of the *Libro de Alexandre*." Amaia Arizaleta reads Babylon not only as a figure for canonical narratives, but as a figure or the city of Cuenca, conquered by Alfonso VIII and described in contemporary texts as having been liberated from its "Babylonian submission" in "Le centre introuvable: La Babylone castilliane du *Libro de Alexandre*."

3 I take the term "somaesthetic" from the work of Richard Shusterman. For Shusterman, who argues that the body has all too often been ignored in Western philosophy, somaesthetics returns to the body's role as an "indispensible medium for all perception," in order to bring the body, and all of its workings, to the forefront of discussions of mental processes and aesthetic responses (3).

4 *Oír*, as Pablo Ancos notes, is the primary mode of poetic reception considered by the *Libro de Alexandre*, and by the *mester de clerecía* on the whole (162–4, 315–16).

5 Gordon Rudy remarks that medieval Christian theologians ranked the senses according to their supposed relations to the body: sight and hearing, which seem immaterial, were considered "lofty" and spiritual, while taste and touch, "lowly" and "bodily," reflect the "basically dualist anthropology" that undergirds medieval Christian theology (4).

6 Without entering into the murky waters of attributing authorship or positing a date for composition, it is safe to say that that it is probable that the author had university, clerical, and court connections and composed the *Alexandre* at some point during the first decades of the thirteenth century. For a review of debates about authorship and date, see Cañas's introduction to the *Libro de Alexandre* and Zuwiyya, "The Alexander Tradition in Spain."

7 See also Rudy and Vance.

8 "So then the outer man is endowed with sensation, and with it perceived bodies; and this sensation, as can be readily verified, is divided into five parts, seeing, hearing, smelling, tasting, touching. But it would be too much, and quite unnecessary, to ask all these five senses about what we are looking for [...] So let us use for preference the evidence of the eyes; this is the most excellent of the body's senses, and for all its difference in kind has the greatest affinity to mental vision" (*The Trinity* 304).

9 Bly and Deyermond note that manuscript O of the *Alexandre* renders 88a "ya contava por suya tierra de Babilón" (169). Although the association of Babylon with Babel was commonplace, the effect of the variant is to lessen slightly the typological relationship.

10 See also Arizaleta; Cacho Blecua; Weiss.

11 See also Mary Carruthers's discussion of *painture* and *parole* in *The Book of Memory*.

12 Elder Philosotratus, *Xenia*, provides a good example. See also Shaffer; Nichols.

13 On the *sensus communalis*, see Heller-Roazen. See also Carruthers, *Book of Memory* 78–9.

14 The melon, *budefa*, as Cañas explains, is a "sandía o melón de mala calidad" (612n).

15 For an economic interpretation of this exchange see Pinet, "Political Economy."

16 The description of Babylon in the *Alexandre* amplifies the poet's Old French source, the *Roman de Alexandre*, by expanding the description of spices and precious stones found in Babylon, as Ian Michael observes (202–3).

17 A commentary on Psalm 55 attributed to Jerome reads: "There are two cities in the world: Babylon and Jerusalem. By Babylon is to be understood evil [...] and Jerusalem [...] the chosen soul that does not cease to pray for its enemy." On the traditional exegesis of Babylon see also Biguzzi and Robertson.

18 See Arizaleta, "Le Centre"; Bly and Deyermond; Brownlee; Michael; and Jesús Cañas's notes to this section in the *Libro de Alexandre*. However, to my knowledge, the direct connections between spices, aromas, and Paradise have yet to be noted.

19 Among the enumerated spices, amomum (*anamomo*) and galingale have fallen out of common usage and parlance. According to Isidore, "Amomum is so called because it produces an odor like that of cinnamon. It grows in Syria and Armenia as a shrub producing seeds in clusters like grapes, with a white flower that looks like a violet's, leaves like bryony, and a good scent; it induces sweet sleep" (XVII.viii.11, 349). Andrew Dalby explains that *amomum* often refers to cardamom in classical texts (165). Galingale is a spice related to ginger: "Galingale (*cyperum*) is so called by the Greeks because of its hot quality [...] Its root is like that of a triangular rush, its leaves like a leek's, its roots black or close to the color of olive roots, and it is very odoriferous and sharp. It grows in swamps and empty places. There is said to be another species of galingale that grows in India and is called zinziber ('ginger') in their language" (Isidore XVII.ix.7, 350).

20 Krondl adds that "the idea of an unearthly scent was not unique to Christendom. Persian and Arabic sources also describe a sweet afterlife filled with perfumed plants and food" (13).

21 It is possible that the poet drew upon the *Etymologies* for the section on spices in addition to drawing upon them for his descriptions of the many precious gems found in Babylon. On the source for the lapidary section of the description, see Jesús Cañas's notes to stanzas 1468–92 in the *Libro de Alexandre.*

22 Prudentius's *Hymn for Christmas Day* describes how the earth turned into a garden upon the birth of Christ, "sweet with nectar and nard," where rocks flow with honey, and "fragrant liquor is distilled / from the shriveled trunks of old oaks, / And tamarisks yield ambrosial balsams."

23 Guillaume de Lorris and Jean de Meun (48).

24 In fact, unlike the other senses, which go through a relay station in the brain called the thalamus before getting to the cortex to be processed, the olfactory bulb is directly connected to the temporal lobe and so smell often triggers memory. I am grateful to my colleague Rachel F. Barr for this information.

25 Bly and Deyermond remark, "It is possible that all the references to Babylon in the *Alexandre* would be read by the poet's contemporaries as alluding also to the Tower of Babel. If so, the lengthy description of the city (1460–1533) acquires much greater thematic relevance" (169n).

10 Portuguese Scenes of the Senses, Medieval and Early Modern

JOSIAH BLACKMORE

The Portuguese scenes of the senses that are the focus of this essay cross time and oceans. All of them, in one way or another, are a result of the centuries-long engagement of Portugal with the sea. From the thirteenth century onwards, the sea is a formative aspect of Portuguese literary creativity. This maritime imaginary grows in complexity as the practice of maritime expansion becomes prevalent in the Portuguese national consciousness beginning in the fifteenth century and is especially active in the sixteenth. The senses are a recurring presence in the imaginative and historical realms of lyric and epic poetry in the three-century swathe delimited here. We will see that sensory experience shapes key moments in a literary tradition that ranges from medieval to epic poetry and to the narrative of New World encounter.

Portugal's literary culture of the sea begins properly with the poetry composed in the Galician-Portuguese language and that flourished from the late twelfth century to the first part of the fourteenth. This poetry thrived throughout medieval Iberia, and its practitioners included kings, aristocrats, courtiers, and professional performers. The Galician-Portuguese *cantigas* (songs) include religious poetry, love poetry, and joke and insult poetry. The secular love poetry comprises two main genres: the *cantigas de amigo* (songs of a friend, or lover's songs), characteristically in the voice of a (young) woman, and the *cantigas de amor*, in the voice of a man.[1] The *cantigas de amigo* are of interest here. These *cantigas*, a robust corpus of some 500 compositions, evoke a woman-centred world, alive with sentiment and that often celebrates female comaraderie and solidarity.[2] A number of these *cantigas* turn on the amorous lament of a young woman or girl whose lover (*amigo*) is absent, sometimes overseas. In some poems, the young woman addresses the sea or travels to seaports to await her *amigo*'s return, and in some we find the nautical world of boats and ships.[3] The amorous experiences of young women occupy a significant portion of these lyrics, with a concentration on amorous affliction or the *coyta de amor*. The *coyta* is both a sentimental and a physiological condition: it is the emotional suffering caused by an absent lover and it is a physical condition linked to lovesickness.[4] This corporal dimension of suffering and desire is part of a larger sense of embodiedness that many of the songs promote. For if the *cantigas de amigo* are woman-*voiced* poetry, they are also frequently woman-*bodied* poetry, in which bodies dance, bathe, swim, and travel.

The embodiedness of the female persona, through references to corporal movement and to the physiological aspect of *coyta*, establishes many *cantigas de amigo* as a poetry of bodily sensation. On the basis of the bathing *cantigas*, Maria do Rosário Ferreira argues for a universal and symbolic equation between water and the feminine (51)[5] and contends that in such poems it is possible to identify a feminine desire to fuse with water (50), even as a stylized form of drowning (56). Yet even though youthful love and eroticism are defining characteristics, the poetic vocabulary of the *cantigas de amigo* is restrained and highly connotative and allusional, since, as Rip Cohen notes, "kisses and embraces are nowhere explicitly mentioned" ("In the Beginning" 245). Erotic encounters and yearnings are largely present symbolically, such as the stag (*cervo*), a figure of male sexuality, or water in the form of sea, rivers, and fountains.[6] Water yields erotic power in part through its tactile dimension as a natural element that receives and envelops young, desiring bodies. Let us consider first a *cantiga* by Denis (1261–1325), the Portuguese *rei trovador* (troubadour king):

Levantou s' a velida,
levantou s' <aa> alva,
eno alto,
vai las lavar <a> alva

Levantou s' a louçana,
levantou s' <aa> alva,
e vai lavar delgadas
eno alto,
vai las lavar <a alva>

<E> vai lavar camisas;
levantou s' <aa> alva;
o vento lhas desvia
eno alto,
vai las lavar <a> alva

E vai lavar delgadas;
levantou s' <aa> alva;

o vento lhas levava
eno alto
vai las lavar <a alva>

O vento lhas desvia;
levantou s <aa> alva,
meteu s' <a> alva en ira
eno alto,
vai las lavar <a alva>

O vento lhas levava;
levantou s' <aa> alva;
meteu s' <a> alva en sanha
eno alto,
vai las lavar <a alva> (602)

The fair girl arose,
she arose at dawn,
and she goes to wash her shirts
by the mountain stream:
she goes to wash them at dawn.

The beautiful girl arose,
she arose at dawn,
and she goes to wash her blouses
by the mountain stream:
she goes to wash them at dawn.

And she goes to wash her shirts;
she arose at dawn;
the wind carries them away
by the mountain stream:
she goes to wash them at dawn.

And she goes to wash her blouses;
she arose at dawn;
the wind carries them away
by the mountain stream:
she goes to wash them at dawn.

The wind carries them away;
she arose at dawn;
she became angry at dawn

by the mountain stream:
she goes to wash them at dawn.

The wind carried them away;
she arose at dawn;
she became angry at dawn
by the mountain stream:
she goes to wash them at dawn. (81)[7]

Denis's *cantiga* evokes a world of touch, albeit somewhat indirectly. The *velida* comes into contact with the mountain stream during her matinal laundry task (and perhaps the cool freshness of dawn), and feels the wind that carries off her *camisas*. In the emotional landscape of the poem there is a haptic relationship of the young girl to her surroundings. Denis initially paints a moment of idyllic, daily routine, then introduces a dissonant chord in the fifth strophe with the appearance of *ira* (ire, irritation, pique) as a result of the wind carrying off the clean *camisas*. Most critics who have studied this *cantiga*, on account of this *ira*, find sexual overtones present in it. Helder Macedo reads the *ira* of the young girl as the result of a violent sexual initiation enacted by the "sopro fálico" (phallic gust) of the wind (68).[8] Ferreira offers a slightly different take, suggesting that the song depicts not a scene of violent sexual initiation but one in which the young girl has invited her *amigo* to a tryst, but in the end he does not appear; he is substituted for by the wind, resulting in the girl's *ira* (135, 137). The washing of *camisas* and *delgadas*, items of intimate apparel, adds to the erotic nature of the scene by linking water and sensuality (Corral 87).

Yet there is a further symbolic dimension at work here that underscores the erotics of absence. The emotional centre of the song is the experience of *ira*, a sentiment opposed to the one found in a *cantiga* by Pero de Meogo to which this composition likely responds.[9] Meogo's song, in part, reads:

<Levou's aa alva>, levou s' a velida,
vai lavar cabelos na fontana fria
leda dos amores, dos amores leda
[...]
Vai lavar cabelos na fontana fria;
passou seu amigo, que lhi ben queria
leda dos <amores, dos amores leda>
[...]
Passa seu amigo, que lhi ben queria;
o cervo do monte a augua volvia

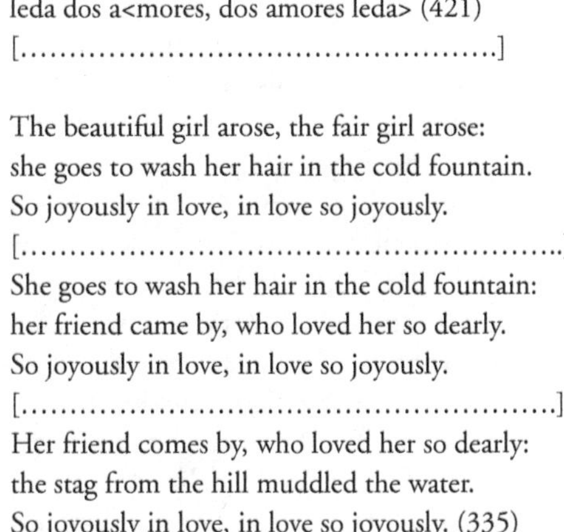

leda dos a<mores, dos amores leda> (421)
[..]

The beautiful girl arose, the fair girl arose:
she goes to wash her hair in the cold fountain.
So joyously in love, in love so joyously.
[..]
She goes to wash her hair in the cold fountain:
her friend came by, who loved her so dearly.
So joyously in love, in love so joyously.
[..]
Her friend comes by, who loved her so dearly:
the stag from the hill muddled the water.
So joyously in love, in love so joyously. (335)

Meogo's *cantiga* establishes the erotic connotation of water with the stag that muddles or stirs it, the same water in which the *velida* washes her hair. The water sexually links the *velida* and the *cervo*.[10] The young woman's happy disposition (which is the predominant sentiment of the poem) is due to the presence of the *amigo* with whom she carnally frolics.[11] The plural and therefore multifaceted *amores* suggests a proliferation of bodily pleasures between *amiga* and *amigo*. Denis's poem, in contradistinction, paints a picture in which the absence of the *amigo* triggers the unhappy experience of *ira*. I want to posit that the reason for the *ira* is not that the wind is an unsatisfactory substitute for the body of an absent lover, as Ferreira has argued, but that a constellation of elements reminds the girl of why her *amigo* is not there: it is because he is overseas. There is a nautical allusion in the form of wind, water, and cloth. The wind that carries off the clean clothing reminds the *velida* of the wind that filled the sails of the ship on which her beloved left, and her response to this unwanted departure and resulting (erotic) solitude is *ira*. In the poetics of Galician-Portuguese lyric, in which an individual poet might depend on a collectively constituted repertoire of vocabulary, ideas, themes, or conceits as part of the referential possibilities of any one composition, the absence of the *amigo* (and the resulting erotic longing) due to sea travel is plausible. *Cantigas* such as Nuno Fernandez Torneol's "Vi eu, mha madr', andar" (130) or Johan Zorro's "El rei de Portugale" (389) are examples.[12] Seafaring permits readings in which (sea) water awakens or intensifies the young woman's desire for her absent friend. Denis's "Levantou s' a velida" depicts an especially acute moment in which a young woman is reminded of her *amigo* who travels over the sea. Interestingly, Macedo finds onomatopoeia in the many occurrences of *l* and *v* in Denis's *cantiga* because of its mimicking of the sound of the wind (66). The aural evocation of the wind places the *amiga*, as well as the audience of the *cantiga* as it was sung, on board a ship as the wind suddenly fills the sails. The mountain breeze reminds the woman of the sea voyage of her *amigo* and the impossibility of consummating her desire.

Denis's and Meogo's *cantigas* are of a set with other compositions that join touch and water in which women swim or bathe. Estevan Coelho sings of this in a poem that begins "Se oj' o meu amigo / soubess', iria migo; / e < n > al rio me vou banhar < e > , / al mare" (207) (If today my friend / knew it, he would come with me: / I will go swimming in the river – in the sea) (103), where swimming, were the *amigo* present, suggests sexual congress. An invitation to swim to women who know the ways of love and in which a rendezvous with the *amigo* will take place is the topic of Martin Codax's "Quantas sabedes amar amigo, / treides comig' a lo mar de Vigo / e banhar nos emos nas ondas" (517) (All of you who know what it is to love a friend, / come with me to the bay of Vigo, / and we shall go swimming in the waves) (211). The presence, hypothetical or otherwise, of the *amigo* inflects swimming with an erotic dimension, so that we might consider immersion as a symbolic or compensatory activity for sexual encounter. Water, especially seawater, is very much a male, erotic presence in many *cantigas de amigo*.

This sex-by-aquatic-proxy may in part be a device by which poets allow a female poetic persona the initiative in amorous adventures.[13] In the seafaring environment of many *cantigas*, it also transforms the woman's body into a ship or vessel whose contact with water is a tactile substitute, through several layers of metonymic removal, for the body of the lover: the water that runs to the sea, which the *amiga* touches in turn, carries the vessel on which the young man is present. The tactility associated with water in this love poetry, in addition to the bodily experience of *coyta*, poetically reflects some medieval formulations of the theory of touch. It was Aristotle (in *De Anima*) who proposed the lasting paradigm of the five senses, and of these senses touch is the most fundamental (Farina 18) but the most difficult to define and locate in the body. Aristotle ambivalently proposes that the organ of touch is both the flesh and something deeper within the body (Farina 20). In "On Sense and Sensible Objects," a section of *Parva naturalia*, the philosopher claims that "the sense organ of both taste and touch is near the heart" (*De Anima* 229). Katie L. Walter notes that Albertus Magnus follows the Aristotelian understanding of touch (and distinguishes flesh from skin) in that "those things perceived by touch are received first by 'the heart, then the flesh, and then the skin'" (122). Touch, then, could be understood as cordial, not cutaneous, and this resonates strongly with the *cantigas* as a poetry of the *cor* or *coraçon*. The heart as an organ of physiological sensation makes a number of the *cantigas* (both the *cantigas de amigo* and the *cantigas de amor*) potentially about tactile experience or touch-driven understandings of love and yearning. The *coytas no coraçon*, so frequently invoked by poets, in addition to being the physiological manifestations of love in terms of cardiac palpitations, can also be understood as a longing for tactile encounter with a present or absent *amigo*, a desire for haptic submission to the beloved.

We move forward now a few centuries, from the sea and streams in and around Portugal to a beach in the New World, a space of encounter revealed by maritime, imperial enterprise. The beach I refer to is along the northeastern coastline of what will come to be known as Brazil. Here, Portuguese seafarers travelling with Pedro Álvares Cabral came face-to-face with New World natives (the Tupi) in late April 1500. The report of this encounter is the subject of the famous *Carta* (letter) of Pero Vaz de Caminha to Manuel I of Portugal, dated 1 May 1500. Scholars regard Caminha's *Carta* as the founding document of Portuguese imperialism in the Americas (much as Columbus's first diary in 1492 established Spanish presence) in what was initially called the Terra da Vera Cruz (Land of the True Cross).[14] In the *Carta*, Caminha presents an exuberant natural world teeming with life, but in the early portion of the document what pricks up our ears is the sound of breakers. Here is how Caminha, in part, describes the initial meeting between the Portuguese landing party (headed by Nicolau Coelho) and the native men on the shore:

> traziam arcos nas maãs esuas seetas. Vijnham todos rrijos perao batel e nicolaao coelho lhes fez sinal que posesem os arcos. e eles os poseram. aly nom pode deles auer fala nẽ entẽdimento que aproueitasse polo mar quebrar na costa [...] e com jsto se volueo aas naaos por seer tarde e nom poder deles auer mais fala por aazo do mar. (99, 101)

> [the natives] had their bows and arrows with them. They came to the boat in a determined manner, and Nicolau Coelho made a sign that they should put down their bows, which they did. There, he was unable to have any conversation or useful understanding with them because of the sea breaking on the shore [...] and with that, the landing party returned to the ships because it was late and because no further communication was possible on account of the sea.[15]

Caminha's reference to the sea as an impediment to communication between Europeans and New World natives is an important dimension of the beach as a primordial scene of encounter between worlds. In fact, throughout the document, the most common space of interaction between Portuguese and Tupi is the beach (*praia*) or sometimes the riverbank (*ribeira*) near the natural port where Cabral's ships are anchored. The beach or shore, an archetypally liminal space where water metamorphoses into land and land into water, is also, in Greg Dening's arguments, a cultural space where categories are made including definitions of "we" and "they"

(*Islands and Beaches* 3). They are "thresholds to some other place [...]. Writing a beach will always be stories of defining moments" (*Beach Crossings* 31). We can use these theoretical postulations about beaches in reading Caminha, given the precedented nature of Cabral's encounter as a defining moment in maritime enterprise and the construction of the categories of "we" and "they" Caminha records in the beach scenes of his *Carta*.

The failed attempt at communication on the beach suggests that Nicolau Coelho – and by extension, the entire Portuguese company – could have understood the natives had it not been for the waves crashing on the beach; the description provides a sort of first sound recording of Brazil, an initial instance of the sonic as a dimension of imperial encounter. To Caminha's (or Coelho's) Portuguese ear, native speech and oceanic sound mix indistinguishably. This aural equivalence seems all the more significant because, apparently, the Portuguese had no problems understanding each other on the same beach. Speech as an auditory phenomenon is a result of both the ear and the mouth; C.M. Woolgar, for example, argues that we can understand speech as one of the "senses of the mouth." Woolgar studies a medieval tradition about the sensorial aspects of speaking that dates back to Aristotle and Constantine the African. One of the tenets for understanding speech as a sense of the mouth derives from a varied body of knowledge linking physiology with intellection, spirituality, and morality, the discipline known as faculty psychology. As Woolgar explains, "The tongue received the influence of the 'animal spirit': it formed speech and told the meaning of the thoughts of the soul" (84). Consequently, the timbre or clarity of the voice revealed much: the clearer voice originated in moral or spiritual rectitude, while the less articulate or hoarse voice indicated a certain baseness. Given the regular emphasis on the perceived openness of the natives to conversion to Christianity throughout Caminha's text, we could read the raw, acoustic mix of human sound and the sea, and the failure or impossibility of *fala*, as an acknowledgment of an inward, indigenous waywardness ripe for discipline and catechistic instruction. Native tongues moved on the beach but revealed nothing, produced no useful *entendimento* or knowledge. Soon after this initial moment of contact, in another encounter on the beach, Caminha reiterates a judgment of native speech as unintelligible: "aly por emtam nom ouue mais fala nẽ emtendimento cõ eles por aberberja deles seer tamanha que se nom emtendia nem ouuja njngẽ" (109) (there, then, it was not possible to speak with them or attain any kind of understanding, since their barbaric chatter was so great that no one could be understood or heard). The meaningless chatter of the natives is a motif in imperial texts of European encounter with non-European others and is a standard stratagem to define the categories of "we" and "they." Here, that distinction opposes a European, linguistic capacity to a senseless, native din. The white noise of the Tupi language – and its manifestation in Caminha as a phenomenon of the shore (recall the deictic "aly" [there] in the quotation above as a means of locating our awareness on the beach) – establishes the beach as a chatterspace, a locale that creates an awareness of an imperative of colonial dominance. In the *Carta* the beach instantiates an acoustemology, or a "world view centered on sound" (Smith 289) in which the sounds of the New World come into contact and contest with the sound of Portuguese as the implicit standard that casts native speech as "berberia."[16] Acoustics are therefore instrumental in cementing a Lusocentric realm over the newly encountered world along the shore, one in which the sounds of the Portuguese language (emanating from Lisbon) were a world of power and culture unto themselves. The situation is comparable to Latin in the Roman Empire in Bruce R. Smith's analysis: "In acoustic terms as well as geographic, one might conceive of the Roman world as a huge circle with Rome as its effective center. The sounds that historically gave that acoustic field its coherence were the phonemes of Latin [...] the Latin language made the [...] circle of sound a single cultural space" (288). The unintelligible sounds of Tupi, like a raw force in nature, invite an acoustic/linguistic act of possession of the Terra da Vera Cruz, a conquest of human sound that is analogous to the conquest of the sea that aurally reverberates along the beach.

The acoustic realm comes into play again in a different context later in the letter. The Portuguese are celebrating Mass on a small island and are listening to a sermon; Caminha notes:

> em quanto esteuemos aamisa e aapregacom seriã na praya out[a] tanta gente pouco mais ou menos como os domtem cõ seus arcos e seetas os quaaes amdauam folgando e olhandonos e asentaramse. e despois dacabada amisa aseẽtados nos aapregaçom aleuantaranse mujtos deles e tanjeram corno ou vozina e comecaram asaltar e dançar huũ pedaço. (113)

> As we were hearing Mass and the sermon, about the same number of people were on the beach as yesterday, and they had their bows and arrows with them. They were relaxing and observing us as they sat. When Mass was over, and as we listened to the sermon, many of them stood up and played horns or shells, leaping and dancing for a short while.

Indigenous music is the second acoustic manifestation of Tupi culture. Music, in fact, serves as a common ground for Luso-Tupi interaction, as the Portuguese will eventually play music with native inhabitants. And, as Richard Cullen Rath maintains, music "bears more than a surface relationship to language" in its system of notes, vocabulary, and syntax (72). Rath's approximation of music and language advocates for music's importance as an acoustic phenomenon within a given cultural sphere. Interestingly, Caminha refrains from making judgments about the quality of indigenous musicianship – it is neither melodious nor cacophonous (like Tupi speech) – because he is more interested in the spontaneous performance during a ceremony of worship. Caminha's juxtaposition of indigenous revelry and the delivery of the sermon is strategic, for it suggests that, although the natives could not understand the words of the sermon, they nonetheless rejoiced while the beachside service was in progress. Their sonorous merrymaking at this particular moments reveals their inbuilt disposition to receive Christian instruction. The natives naturally and without schooling demonstrate an innate understanding of ritual and worship and the symbolic dimensions of music, all made manifest as a response to Christian devotion. The Tupis in this sense speak "correctly" and intelligibly through music, since it is a result of and an accompaniment to Christian liturgy. Caminha further corroborates such an understanding when he later observes that during a Mass, while the Portuguese were taking communion,

> huũ deles homẽ de l ou lb anos ficou aly cõ aqueles que ficaram [...] ajumtaua aqueles que aly ficaram e ajnda chamaua outros. este andando asy antreles falando lhes acenou cõ adedo perao altar e depois mostrou odedo perao ceeo coma que lhes dizia alguũa cousa debem e nos asy otomamos. (143)

> there was a man of fifty or fifty-five years of age who was among the other [natives] who remained [...]. He gathered together those who were there and even called out to others to join them. He was speaking among them, pointing to the altar and then to the sky as if making an important point. That is how we understood his action.

Caminha describes this scene shortly after concluding that "esta jente he boa e de boa sijnprezidade e enpremarsea ligeiramẽte neeles qualq̃r crunho que lhes quiserem dar" (137, 139) (these people are good, of a good simplicity. Any mark we wish to make would be easily imprinted on them). This use of a printing metaphor anticipates a similar observation made half a century later by Manuel da Nóbrega, one of the founding Jesuit missionaries in Brazil, who wrote in one of his letters "[o] converter este gentio hé mui fácil cousa [...] e estão papel em branco para nelles escrever à vontade" (qtd in Villas Bôas 28) (converting these pagans will be very easy [...] they are blank paper on which one can write at will).[17] Luciana Villas Bôas situates Nóbrega's blank paper metaphor within a classical and medieval rhetorical tradition, arguing that it is indicative of a Jesuit desire to imprint Christian texts onto the memories of the natives.[18] Such a memory creation is part of a sensorial process that includes hearing. This explains why, in an early Tupi catechism published in Lisbon, the use of music is recommended as an instructional method (Villas Bôas 34–6). Caminha's use of the printing metaphor establishes at least a basic familiarity with the rhetorical tradition of memory creation, and his regular references to the sonic aspects of native communication and comportment (unintelligible speech or musical ability) suggests that the auditory sense in part structures the imperial perspectives of Caminha and the members of Cabral's fleet. It therefore is a component of the architecture of the ideological perception of the New World.

~

We cross the ocean once more, from the time of Caminha's letter drafted in the first months of the sixteenth century to 1572 and the publication of Luís de Camões's poem *Os Lusíadas*, when for almost a century the Portuguese empire had spanned the Atlantic and Indian Oceans. Readers will recall that the poem narrates the inaugural sea voyage of Vasco da Gama between Portugal and India (Calicut) in 1497–9, a voyage that established the *carreira da Índia* (India voyage) or the maritime trading route between Portugal and the subcontinent. Camões's complex historico-imaginative narrative of Gama's voyage and its place in western, historical consciousness relies necessarily on the maritime world and nautical experience. In Bernhard Klein's assessment, "few other sixteenth-century instances of epic poetry are so heavily invested in the culture of seafaring" (232). This culture of seafaring so pervades the poetic logic and imaginary of Camões's text that there are few stanzas in this ten-canto poem in which some reference to ships, water, or nautical travel is not made. Seafaring is, for Camões, at once an empirical reality and practice of exploration and a literary principle, a *modus cognoscendi* of oceanic travellers and poets, a lens through which real and imagined worlds and experiences are encountered and rendered into narrative.

Near the end of *Os Lusíadas* there occurs an episode that is the culmination of the history and destiny of Portugal as both symbolized and instantiated by the epochal voyage of Vasco da Gama: the episode of the Isle of Love (Ilha dos Amores, or Ilha namorada), a pleasurable and sensual respite afforded to the seafarers on their homeward journey to Portugal (after having reached India, the objective of the expedition) which is partly a celebration of the senses. Immediately preceding the beginning of the lengthy episode itself,[19] Camões writes of the mariners' yearning for home:

> O prazer de chegar à pátria cara
> [.......................................]
> Pera contar a peregrina e rara
> Navegação, os vários céus e gentes,
> Vir a lograr o prémio que ganhara,
> Por tão longos trabalhos e acidentes,
> Cada um tem por gosto tão perfeito
> Que o coração para ele é vaso estreito. (IX.17.i, iii–viii)

What pleasure the dear land to reach once more,
[..]
Strange tales of the far voyage telling o'er,
And every various sky and various race;
There to enjoy the prize, by travail sore
Well-earned 'mid effort and in bitter case;
Men think, when they feel bliss so infinite,
That the heart's chalice is too slight for it.[20]

Camões establishes an ambience of delight and pleasure here ("prazer," "gosto") while he also forges a tight alliance between home, nation, navigation, and narrative as the ultimate desideratum of his Lusitanian seafarers. This alliance is emblematic of Camões's own poetic project, so that the adventurers' pleasure at the prospect of returning home and telling the tale of their maritime wanderings and encounters abroad is fulfilled in *Os Lusíadas*. Yet before reaching home, Venus (the divine patron and champion of the Portuguese on Mount Olympus) prepares an "ínsula divina" (divine isle) in the ocean for the delectation of the Portuguese, a pelagic *locus amoenus*. On this Isle of Love a company of sea nymphs awaits to be the sexual companions of the weary, homeward-bound mariners, and there a banquet will be proffered and Gama will receive the poem's final prophecy from the mouth of Tethys, goddess of the sea.[21] This prophecy spoken by Tethys as she shows Gama a crystalline model of the universe (the *máquina do mundo*) predicts the future presence in the East of Portuguese imperial figures.

Venus prepares the Isle of Love by first ordering Cupid to imbue his "fogo imortal" (immortal flame) into the waters of the sea. The god complies, shooting a barrage of arrows into the water. Consequently,

[...] geme o mar cos tiros;
Dereitas pelas ondas inquietas
Algũas vão, e algũas fazem giros;
Caem as Ninfas, lançam das secretas
Entranhas ardentíssimos sospiros;
Caï qualquer, sem ver o vulto que ama,
Que tanto como a vista pode a fama. (IX.47.ii–viii)

[...] at each shot Ocean gave a groan.
Straight through the waves heaving unquietly,
Some lanced, where others in long curves had flown.
The nymphs fall and aloud their sorrows cry
From their most secret hearts, with burning moan,

Before the faces of their loves they scan,
For Fame can do as much as seeing can.

Cupid eroticizes the ocean, the water and nymphs moaning and roiling with desire. This pronounced aurality of Eros is complemented by the exuberant, sensorial quality of the Isle itself:

Mil árvores estão ao céu subindo,
Com pomos odoríferos e belos;
A laranjeira tem no fruito lindo
A cor que tinha Dafne nos cabelos.
Encosta-se no chão, que está caindo,
A cidreira cos pesos amarelos;
Os fermosos limões ali, cheirando,
Estão virgíneas tetas imitando. (IX.56)

Skyward a thousand fruit-trees tower tall,
Laden with apples odorous and fair.
The orange bears its fruit ambrosial,
Which has the very hue of Daphne's hair.
The citron totters as about to fall
Under the yellow burdens he must bear;
And beauteous lemons breathe out perfume here,
And as they were the breasts of maids appear.

Eros as a force of nature in Camões inheres in the fruit of the trees, a promise of the pleasures the Portuguese are about to enjoy.

The sensual and sexual rewards of the Isle of Love, it is important to remember, are present only in the first portion of the episode and lead to Tethys's prophetic vision, which is, effectively, the close of *Os Lusíadas*. The carnal union of Portuguese mariners with sea nymphs has prompted a number of critical opinions. Camões himself points to fame as the reward of the Isle, leading modern scholars to find differing allegorical and symbolic valences to the island paradise. A. Bartlett Giamatti, for example, contends that the union of Gama and Tethys symbolizes "Portugal's final mastery over the sea" (220), and that the sensual and amorous delights of the Isle convey a satisfaction that itself is the reward of duty (220, 221). João Adolfo Hansen similarly reads the carnal unions as the marriage of Portugal with the sea (184), while Fernando Gil identifies in the Isle the manifestation of a second golden age and the mythological coming into contact with the human (77–8). What these and other scholars have in common is an interest in reconciling the bodily, sensorial aspects of the first part of the episode with a larger cosmological or divine perspective evident in Tethys's prophecy. This is understandable, given that Camões takes great effort to juxtapose and emphasize the body, the senses, and the non-bodily in terms of prophetic vision, a narrative move that begs the question of the allegorical and symbolic dimensions of the island. For nowhere else in *Os Lusíadas* do sound, olfaction, vision, and touch come together in such exuberant concert – the senses, it would seem, highlighted only to be superseded by supernal powers. Carmen Nocentelli has proposed an interpretation that situates the sexual gratification of Portuguese and nymphs within a historical context. Nocentelli maintains that it is not possible to separate the erotic dimensions of the Isle from the poem's imperial subject matter. In this argument the Isle of Love symbolizes not only a politics of marriage between Portuguese explorers and native, eastern women (a practice that was widespread in Portuguese territories overseas), but also coercive, imperial sexual relations between conquerors and the conquered, a conceit that, in literary culture, can be traced back to the abduction of Sabine women in early Rome as transmitted through Ovidian myth. "The Isle of Love [...] is shown to channel desire into a conjugal erotic especially suited to the political requirements of imperial rule in Asia" (60).

If the erotic escapades of the sailors are a fantastically imagined joining of desire and imperial, conjugal politics, this is only one aspect of the Isle in the poetic logic of Camões's epic poem. We should remember that the island is a-cartographic – the poet says only of its location that is is "lá no meio / das águas" (IX.21.ii–iii) (there in the middle / of the sea) – and that it is supernatural in nature (ínsula divina). Camões pointedly removes the Ilha from geographic specificity and, because of its other-worldly nature, from historical time, apart of course from its place in the itinerary of Gama's voyage. Of the identity of the sea nymphs, Camões says simply that they are "aquáticas donzelas," their water-nature being their primary, defining trait. The sexual union of mariners and the aquatic maidens is one, explicit instance of Eros, which is part of the larger scheme of Camões's epic imagery. And water is a privileged component of the human and mythic drama of Eros, the medium of a Portuguese, imperial gnosis of the globe.

It is important to reiterate once again that the exuberant, sensorial delights of the Isle culminate in the prophecy of Tethys. Gama is granted a special knowledge by witnessing the trajectory of a new historical age initiated by his Indian voyage. The prophetic revelation of Tethys is a scene of knowing, and the sensorial and sexual delights of the mariners are evidence of a consummation of a relationship between humans and the natural world, which includes, but is not limited to, the sea. If, by dint of contact with the maidens of Venus and, in Gama's case, with Tethys and a prophetic, Apollonian vision of Portuguese history yet to be enacted, it is possible to read the episode as a "divine ascension of Vasco da Gama and his companions" (Silva 141), there is also a sensorial plenitude that is concomitant with or even causative of a new historical age. While undeniably carnal and corporeal, the island is the site where bodily experience, historical trajectory, and the mythic are brought into unison.

In closing, we might observe that there is something of a sly, ironic aspect to the mariners' dalliance on the Ilha dos Amores. On first sighting, the Portuguese crew simply wanted to make an *aguada*, a stop to replenish their supply of fresh water. The desire *for* water soon became a desire *in* water and, with that, a sating of bodily appetites that allowed this company of seafarers (in the iconic figure of Vasco da Gama) a knowledge of the world glimpsed from the upper spheres of the heavens. This genesis of a new historical age is profoundly oceanic: the maritime world is a locus and symbol of mythopoeisis. In the satisfaction of all the senses, we witness a Portuguese sovereignty over the sublunary world. The senses provide the means, in their ecstatic fulfilment, for the integration of bodily, first-person experience into the forces of the cosmos. These forces are encountered by Gaman ships throughout the globe, an errancy through the water worlds that lap incessantly at the edges of history and myth.

NOTES

1 Most, but not all, of the *cantigas de amigo* are woman-voiced. An example with an unspecified narrator is "Levantou s' a velida," studied below.

2 In the extant manuscript compilations of the Galician-Portuguese lyric, all *cantigas de amigo* are attributed to male authorship. Some scholars, however, posit a native, oral tradition as underlying the origin of some of these *cantigas* (see Cohen, "In the Beginning," for a review of this argument) or a tradition of woman-authored, Sapphic poetry (see Schantz, esp. chap. 5). For the purposes of this essay what is important is the female persona as the presiding consciousness of these compositions, regardless of the sex of the author.

3 These maritime *cantigas de amigo* are sometimes classed generically as *marinhas* or *barcarolas*; for a brief descriptive overview see Jensen, *Portuguese Lyrics* 64–9.

4 For further analysis of this topic, see the studies by Blackmore and Meneses.

5 Beltrán Pepió similarly sees water as a universal symbol of the feminine and fecundity (*O cervo* 15).

6 On the erotic connotations of the *cervo* in a *cantiga* by Pero Meogo, see Asensio 47, 52; Beltran 116–17; Beltrán Pepió, *O cervo* 23–9. Beltran (76, 102–3, 105) recognizes the erotic significance of water, and Ferreira (59) studies the sea as a symbol of love.

7 Citations of the *cantigas de amigo* in this essay are from Cohen, *500 Cantigas d'Amigo* (words or letters in angle brackets are editorial emendations supplied by Cohen), and

English translations are from Jensen, *Medieval Galician-Portuguese Poetry*. Here and below page numbers refer to these editions.

8 Other critics who argue that the wind represents male, sexual advances on the *velida* are Beltrán Pepió, "O vento" 21, 24; Brea 145, 147; Cohen, "Girl in the Dawn" 176; Ferreira 131–2. Cohen differs in that he reads this *cantiga* as a poetic rendering of the Annunciation, so for him the wind is the impregnating wind of the Holy Spirit (179).

9 For arguments proposing a link between Denis's *cantiga* and Pero Meogo's see Beltrán Pepió, "O vento" 8–11; Brea 143–5.

10 The *cervo* is a symbol in Meogo's *cantigas* for the eroticized male.

11 We also find hair washing as a cause of an amorous encounter in Johan Soarez Coelho's "Fui eu, madre, lavar meus cabelos" (Cohen, 174).

12 It also bears remembering that Denis was invested in building the Portuguese navy. He ordered a pine forest to be planted in Leiria to provide timber for ships. Another *cantiga de amigo* by this nautically minded monarch is "Ai flores, ai flores do verde pino," in which the young woman addresses flowering pines and asks for news about her *amigo*. In addition to the blooming pines as part of a western, sylvan imaginary (some aspects of which Joaquim-Francisco Coelho [81–5] explores), the trees possess a privileged knowledge because they will become the planks from which future ships will be built, like the one responsible for carrying away the *amigo*.

13 The *amiga* who swims as a means to connect with her lover stands in contrast to the male-centred imaginings of touch in troubadour lyric studied by Gubbini.

14 Whether Cabral's landing in the New World was accidental or purposeful has long been a matter of debate. Caminha's use of the term *achamento* (finding) suggests an unexpected encounter. The discovery, planned or otherwise, occurred during Cabral's voyage from Lisbon to Calicut.

15 Translations of Caminha's text are mine.

16 On acoustemology as an imperial phenomenon Ana María Ochoa Gautier notes that "Once sound is described and inscribed into verbal description and into writing it becomes a discursive formation that has the potential of creating and mobilizing an acoustic regime of truths, a power-knowledge nexus in which some modes of perception, description, and inscription of sound are more valid than others in the context of unequal power relations" (33).

17 The translation is mine.

18 In *De memoria et reminiscentia*, Aristotle explains that the creation of the phantasm or memory image marks the body in the manner of a stamp or impression (Villas Bôas 31).

19 The Ilha dos Amores episode runs from canto IX, st. 18, to canto X, st. 143.

20 The translation is by Leonard Bacon (Camões *The Lusiads*).

21 For classical precedents to Camões's Isle see Giamatti 216–21.

11 Eucharistic Thought and Imperial Longing in Portugal from Amadeus da Silva's *Apocalypsis Nova* (1502) to António Vieira's *História do Futuro* (1663–1667)

HENRY BERLIN

"What is visibly received in the sacrament, should be eaten and drunk spiritually in truth."
St Augustine, "Sermon" 131 (Lubac 188)

Introduction: Prophecy, Signification, Possession

The independence of the kingdom, later empire, of Portugal was from the beginning sustained by prophecy. It was said that, shortly before the Battle of Ourique in 1139, Portugal's eventual founder, Afonso Henriques, was visited by an old man – an old man he had already seen in dreams. The man promised that Henriques would triumph in the upcoming battle, and that God would favour not only him, but the next sixteen generations of his descendants. He had only to leave camp alone the following night when he heard the hermit's bell; and indeed, upon doing so, Henriques had a vision of Christ on the cross. Kneeling in devotion, he heard the Lord's voice promise him victory in this and other battles. After the battle, the legend continues, he decided that Portugal's flag would bear a cross with five *quinas*, representing both Christ's five wounds and the five Moorish kings defeated at Ourique. In this way prophecy and signification are woven together in Portugal's foundational – albeit legendary – history.

This essay traces one thread of Portugal's prophetic tradition as preoccupations with national integrity became entwined with colonial expansionism, taking as its starting point the *Apocalypsis Nova*, made public for the first time in 1502 and attributed to the Blessed Amadeus Menezes da Silva (c. 1427–82). The *Apocalypsis*, nominally a commentary on Revelation 12, recounts a series of ecstasies or raptures (*rapti*) in which the Portuguese Franciscan – who founded a reformed order, the Amadeites, which grew rapidly throughout Iberia and Italy before being incorporated into the Franciscan Observants in 1568 – is led by the Archangel

Gabriel before an assembly of God, the angels, and the souls of the saints. There, Amadeus is made privy to a series of revelations whose central theme is the imminent arrival of an "Angelic Pastor" who will purify the Church and convert the infidels, inaugurating a lengthy era of peace and concord.

The *Apocalypsis* is not, however, a mere string of prophecies. Rather, Gabriel engages Amadeus in a series of exegetical and theological discussions seemingly independent of the work's prophetic framework. In this essay's first section, I analyse the sixth *raptus*, which deals with the Eucharist. Focusing on passages devoted to the problem this sacrament poses for the senses, I seek to explain how the metaphysical theory of signification underlying Gabriel's account of the Eucharist is deeply relevant to the *Apocalypsis*'s millenarian perspective. If the text as a whole is structured by the question of presence and absence in its ecstatic narrative and messianism, the sixth *raptus* analyses, from Scotist underpinnings, our ability (or inability) to perceive real divine presence in the Eucharist – the confusion provoked, that is, not only by what we see but what we feel, smell, taste, and hear during the sacrament. Despite Christ's real corporeal presence, the accidents of the bread and wine are, Gabriel explains, theologically necessary conventional signs, mediating our perception until Christ's final return and the end of the world. One of my central claims, then, is that the problem of our fallible senses, raised paradigmatically by the Eucharist, appeals to apocalyptic thinkers because, on the one hand, it recalls the imperfection and finitude of the postlapsarian world, and, on the other, it suggests the necessity of interpreting that world and its signs beyond sight, touch, smell, taste, and hearing.

Amadeus's text springs from the Joachimist tradition of prophetic literature, but it stands out for its afterlife in the literature of Portugal's imperial ambitions. Its messianic prophecies were taken up during the sixteenth and early seventeenth centuries by millenarian writers such as Gaspar de Leão, first archbishop of Goa, and the Sebastianist João de Castro, whose respective works, the *Desengano de Perdidos* (1573) and *Aurora da Quinta Monarchia* (1604–5), are the subject of the second section of this essay. Both Leão and Castro emphasize the role of hearing, rather than seeing, in their prophetic approaches to Portugal's history and future, and both draw on the *Apocalypsis* in making Portugal's temporal dominion integral to the broader millenarian picture.

It is in the prophetic writings of the famous preacher, missionary, and diplomat António Vieira, however, that the *Apocalypsis*'s particularly Eucharistic themes return to full prominence. This is especially true, as I will conclude in this essay's third section, in the unfinished but influential *História do Futuro* (c. 1663–7). Here, Vieira predicts the advent of the *Quinto Império*, a new, glorious era of Portuguese history. During this Fifth Empire Christ will return, exerting not just spiritual but temporal control over the entire globe through Portugal's kings.

Vieira's main task in the *História* is to justify the necessity of Christ's temporal (rather than merely spiritual) dominion during this period. In his argument the Portuguese empire comes to occupy a theological place similar to the accidents remaining after transubstantiation in the Eucharist, and, in justifying his argument's exegetical method, Vieira is at pains to identify this prophesied future as the invisible underside of time, *heard but not seen*. Just as Amadeus had heard and recorded pure truth from Gabriel, Vieira privileges hearing in the reception of prophecy. As such, the Eucharistic theories expounded by Amadeus in the *Apocalypsis*, along with the theory of signification they imply and the mystical context in which they are articulated, underlie later prophetic justifications for Portugal's colonial dominion.

The *Apocalypsis Nova*: Mysterious Presence, Mysterious Possession

Amadeus Menezes da Silva was born around 1427 to members of Portugal's high nobility, and he was thus raised at the Avis court (his father, Rui Gomes de Silva, was a counsellor to kings Duarte and Afonso V).[1] After a brief military career, Amadeus entered the Jeronomite monastery in Guadalupe, Spain, around 1450; two years later, however, he would opt to join the Franciscan order, living from that point on in a series of monasteries and eventually gaining the favour of the Sforza family, which aided him in establishing the Amadeite order. He is reported to have been named Pope Sixtus IV's personal confessor, living during this time in a cave near the convent of Saint Peter in Montorio. He died at the church of Santa Maria della Pace in 1482, having spent the last years of his life overseeing the growth of his order.

Readers of the *Apocalypsis Nova* have doubted its attribution to the Blessed Amadeus since the text made its 1502 appearance in Rome, in the possession of the Franciscan Giorgio Benigni Salviati (1445–1520).[2] However, there is no indication that the authors studied in this essay harboured doubts as to the text's authenticity or Amadeus's authorship. Another problem that has arisen frequently in studies of the *Apocalypsis* is the text's coherence. First, the eight raptures are accompanied in most manuscripts by two separate works attributed to Amadeus, the *Sermons of Saint John the Baptist to the Soldiers* and the *Sermons of the Lord*. Second, the material covered in the raptures themselves is very diverse, and explaining the place of the theological doctrine within the prophetic framework has been particularly vexing. The prophecies themselves account for a very small portion of the text, about 2 per cent of the whole (Morisi-Guerra, "Plan" 32), although this did not prevent the Irish Franciscan Luke Wadding from complaining that the coming of the Angelic Pastor is prophesied ad nauseam (Morisi-Guerra, "Plan" 33). The raptures are largely devoted to complex elucidations of Catholic doctrine, mariological doctrine in particular, which are said to constitute the teachings through which the prophesied pope – with the aid of a great king – will reform and unite Christendom. As such, Anna Morisi-Guerra has written that "the *Pastor Angelicus* is [...] to be seen as a theologian. The meaning of his message must therefore be sought in the doctrinal part of the text" ("Plan" 36). Nonetheless, in the same article, Morisi-Guerra refers to the sixth and seventh raptures, on the Eucharist and Trinity, respectively, as "independent treatises" (40), owing to their theological complexity and loose connection to the properly prophetic portion of the text.

To begin to address the *Apocalypsis*'s apparent discontinuity, it should first be noted that the topic of a *renovatio* of the Church under a *Papa Angelicus* is a Joachimist commonplace (Reeves 234), and that the Spiritual Franciscans had identified themselves with Joachim of Fiore's (apocryphal) writings throughout the thirteenth and fourteenth centuries in their struggle to preserve Francis's vows of strict poverty (Phelan 22). The Eucharistic theology of the sixth *raptus*, meanwhile, draws heavily on the writings of the Franciscan philosopher John Duns Scotus, a fact noted with irony by the Flemish Jesuit Cornelius a Lapide, who wrote that the "angelus beati Amadei fuit scotista" ("the Blessed Amadeus's angel was a Scotist"; cited in Meirinhos 334), despite Amadeus's own claims in the *Apocalypsis* to be an untutored *asinus*.[3]

Eucharistic dogma posed two related problems for scholastic theologians such as Scotus. On the one hand, there were the metaphysical questions raised by the belief that Christ's body was *really present* in the consecrated bread, in so many different places at once, while also remaining in impassible glory in heaven.[4] On the other hand, there was the fact that, insofar as the Eucharistic sacrifice was a sacrament, the bread and wine must still *signify*, *despite* the real presence of Christ's body; as Gabriel explains pithily in the *Apocalypsis*, "If it does not signify, it is not a sacrament" (84r).[5] Where these two problems meet is in the questions raised by the easily perceptible accidents that remain in the consecrated bread, subsisting despite the absence of the bread's substance, which, according to the doctrine of transubstantiation, has been replaced by the substance of Christ. Again, as Gabriel explains the problem: "You thus think according to the judgment of your senses that the bread is there after consecration, just as before; but the bread is no longer there; rather, Christ's body is with [the bread's] accidents, in the very same place and at the very same time" (81v–82r). Gabriel summarizes this problem of perception thus: "For just as it is not Christ that you see, smell, taste, touch, and feel, but rather the accidents of the bread and wine beneath which and in which is Christ [...] you thus worship what you neither see nor sense and not what you do see and do sense" (83r).

Scotus's solution to the problem of the accidents is to argue that it is only the *quantity* of the bread that lacks a subject, and the accidents inhere in this quantity; as Richard Cross explains, "the subject of [...] the color, or taste, of the consecrated host is its extension. What we see on the altar is in essence the *size* of the bread and wine" (142–3). And, despite Christ's real presence, it is theologically necessary that we perceive these accidents; Scotus believes, in the words of Marilyn McCord Adams, that "what is at stake in the sacraments is not *natural* signification but the Divinely instituted *conventional* signification by which a sensible sign signifies the really present Body of Christ" (148). Or, in the words of the *Apocalypsis*'s Gabriel: "God can remove the substance of the bread or another substance and what is in its place, nature defines to be the body of Christ: and the accidents define it to be a sacrament" (85v). For the Eucharist as sacrament to fulfil its liturgical function, the accidents must remain, despite their potential to mislead all of the senses at once.

The Scotist account reproduced faithfully in the *Apocalypsis* is thus that of a real but hidden presence revealed by signs that mislead the senses, but are nonetheless theologically necessary and interpretable. From this perspective, I contend, the presence of a Eucharistic treatise in a millenarian text becomes easier to understand, especially when we consider that, among the sacraments, the Eucharist was conventionally held to contain the "fullness of the Gospels," whose truth was considered by many *not* to be definitive, but rather to be that of an "intermediate state between the shadows of long ago and the full light of eternity" (Lubac 193–4). In other words, in a prophetic context, the Eucharist encapsulates the way in which the correct interpretation of signs contributes to the effective exercise of God's will in the teleological unfolding of creation. Central to this prophetic reading of the sacrament, as emphasized by Gabriel's repeated references in the *Apocalypsis* to what is seen *and* sensed (or unseen and unsensed) therein, is the idea that sight is not alone among the senses in its gullibility. Rather, the Eucharist's lesson in signification explicitly invokes the other senses heuristically.

Sacramental signs are thus key mediators between the divine, creation, and the human. This is especially true in Franciscan thought, in which signification had already, at the time the *Apocalypsis* was produced, been linked to deeper questions of ontology and spiritual praxis – particularly in attempts to work out the philosophical underpinnings of sacred poverty. Thus, in a text recently studied by Giorgio Agamben, the thirteenth-century Franciscan theologian Peter John Olivi could ask, "*Quid ponat ius vel dominium?*" (What do law and ownership [or dominion] establish?).[6] Here, Olivi asks whether ownership and royal and priestly jurisdiction add anything real to those who exercise them or to those subject to them; he also asks whether "signification in act adds something real to the substance of signs or the things signified" (Agamben 134). Olivi's somewhat surprising conclusion is that, although ownership, laws, and signs are really effective, they in fact add nothing to worldly substances, operating on the level of existence rather than of essence (Agamben 135). Even more surprisingly, the same is true of the sacraments, which differ from other signs only insofar as their efficacy depends directly on God's will (Delorme 325). To return to the particular case of the Eucharist, the accidents of the bread and wine are indispensable but insubstantial signs that nevertheless – and this is the key point for what follows – allow real dominion to be exercised on earth. And, in an analogous way, worldly jurisdiction and possession are exercised through signification without effecting ontological changes in rulers and owners.

Seemingly arcane theological discussions such as these within Franciscan and broader scholastic thought have given late-medieval philosophy its contemporary reputation for esoteric point-missing. And yet, as Patricia Seed has shown, different understandings of *possession* were at the heart of several critical diplomatic disputes between Portugal and other countries during the first centuries of colonial expansion (8–11, 128–40). Thus, the focus on signification in the *Apocalypsis*'s sixth *raptus*, beyond its immediate Eucharistic context, bears on the *content* of the text's radical prophetic strains as well. It is the prophesied Angelic Pastor, after all, who will understand and interpret the theological material as he ushers in an era of global peace and unity in Christ. And, although the *Apocalypsis*'s prophecies focus geographically on Rome, they nevertheless played a key role in the assimilation of the conquest and evangelization of the New World into Portugal's millenarian world view, as "news and evaluations relating to the progress of Christianity in the Atlantic 'islands' became intermingled with the expectation of the prophesied Angelic Pope" (Prosperi 285).

In the final two sections of this essay, I will consider the legacy of the *Apocalypsis*, and of its Eucharistic material in particular, in the prophetic thought that accompanied Portugal's imperial ambitions and efforts. Millenarian thought in the New World has been associated with the Franciscans, among whom it took on apocalyptic overtones: "Christianity could be global as well as universal. To those of mystical temperament this possibility appeared as a vision which was so blinding and radiant that its fulfillment must inevitably foreshadow the rapidly approaching end of the world" (Phelan 18). It is important to recall, however, that prophetic thought of different kinds took root among the Jesuits as well in the sixteenth century. As early as 1538 the order began to identify references to itself in past prophecies (Reeves 275). St Francis had been identified with the Sixth Angel of the Apocalypse; by 1595 St Ignatius had been hailed as the Fifth (Reeves 276). In Portugal both orders played important roles in the development of colonial thought and policies,[7] and their prophetic tendencies were central to this development, especially after the death of King Sebastian in 1578 and Portugal's subsequent annexation by Spain in 1580 (a point to which I will return in the next section). Especially among the Jesuits (Ricard 363), prophetic interpreters of Revelation and other texts increasingly sought to carve out a central role for Portugal in the temporal reign of Christ that would precede the end times.

Reading the *Apocalypsis* before and after Alcácer Quibir: Gaspar de Leão and João de Castro

The *Apocalypsis*, after it first appeared, circulated regularly throughout Europe, and one copy, brought to Spain sometime after 1528 by Fray Francisco de los Ángeles Quiñones, general minister of the Franciscan Observants, eventually crossed the Atlantic to be copied in Mexico before returning to Spain (Carvalho, "Difusão" 14). Nevertheless, its early influence in Portuguese colonial thought can first be clearly traced in Asia, in Gaspar de Leão's *Desengano de Perdidos*, published in Goa in 1573 by João de Endem. Leão (d. 1576) was the first archbishop of Goa; Eugenio Asensio, in the introduction to his edition of the *Desengano*, notes both the Franciscan and the Joachimist inheritances in the archbishop's thought (XIII; XXII–XXXV). Asensio further identifies the three fundamental sources of the *Desengano* as the humanist Bernardo Pérez de Chinchón (d. 1556), the theologian Alonso de Madrigal (d. 1455), and the Franciscan mystic Hendrik Herp (d. 1477), although only the last two are explicitly cited (LXVIII). It is likely, however, that some of the prophetic material in the first part of the *Desengano*, which predicts both the coming of the Angelic Pope and the defeat of the Turks, is drawn from the *Apocalypsis* (Carvalho, "Achegas" 85–9).

The *Desengano* takes the form of a dialogue between a Christian and a Turk in which the Christian predicts the imminent global triumph of Christendom. In the text's prologue Leão explains his description of kings as "desenganadores" (undeceivers), when others have taken a much more sceptical view of the royal relationship with the truth: "Está a nossa diferença nisto, que os homens falão conforme aos accidentes (por não dizer desordens) que muitas vezes vem nos Reys, & eu trato da substancia delles" (Our difference is in this, that these men speak according to accidents [not to say disorders] that they often see in kings, and I speak of their substance) (3). While there is not necessarily an allusion to the Eucharist here, it is clear that interpreters of prophecy were keenly aware that the accidents of perception could distract from essential (substantial) truths. This scepticism was nevertheless wedded to a belief that the correct perception of signs must point to hidden truths and, crucially, that the correct interpretation of these signs depends on one's historical situation. Thus, in explaining why he is giving new interpretations of prophecies that had already been interpreted many times over, Leão writes that in these mistaken interpretations, in which the facts fail to fit the prophetic text (*não quadrem os casos com a letra*), the misguided exegetes "trabalhão de dar a exposição do que ja tem visto: o que não farião se ells virão o que estaua por vir" (struggle to explain what they have already seen: which they would not do, if they had seen what was to come) (12). For writers such as Leão, the *descobrimentos* represented a watershed not just in Portugal's national (and now imperial) history, but in the interpretation of prophecy – a historical hermeneutic key. It is nevertheless worth noticing that Leão still associates sight with history rather than the future.

Part one of the *Desengano* interprets Revelation 18. The Christian speaker explains to the Turk that the prophecy includes four principal points: that the Moors and their law will be destroyed and how this destruction will occur; the lamentations of the Moorish kings, merchants, and all who sail the "mar dos Estreitos"; the joy of the Christians; and the reasons why God has undone Islam (66). The Christian further explains that the angel of whom John speaks in verse one is Pius V; when John says that this angel will illuminate the earth, it refers to Pius V's deeds, especially at the Council of Trent (67). Meanwhile, the other voice that John hears in verse four[8] must be understood several ways: it refers first to the divine inspiration by which some Moors will be saved (69); second, to the warning the pope will give to the Christians living under Turkish rule (70); and third, to King Sebastian himself, who agreed to marry the king of France's sister on the condition that France abandon its alliance with the Turks (70–1). One can thus see in the *Desengano* the seeds of a millenarian world view in which an Angelic Pope and a Portuguese king – Sebastian himself – usher in, and preside over, the era of Christ's temporal dominion; the coming of this era is revealed not by a vision but by a voice.

Perhaps Leão would not have placed such high hopes in Sebastian if, as he says of his mistaken predecessors, he had seen what was to come. For, as I have alluded to above, the Portuguese king was to disappear, presumably killed, at the Battle of Alcácer Quibir in 1578; soon after, in 1580, Portugal would be annexed by Spain, regaining its independence only in 1640. During this period a movement that has come to be known as Sebastianism – the belief that the king had not died in battle and would return to re-establish Portuguese independence and imperial glory – took root among various sectors of Portugal's political and religious classes.[9] Sebastianism's rise gave new life and urgency to the burgeoning prophetic movement in which Leão had taken part, as exegetes began to examine not only biblical texts but also the prophetic *Trovas* of Gonçalo Annes Bandarra (d. 1556), a cobbler from Trancoso, in northeastern Portugal.[10] It seems, furthermore, that this urgency was very little deterred when, in 1581, the *Apocalypsis*, Bandarra's *Trovas*, and the *Desengano* all were in some form condemned by the Portuguese Inquisition (Carvalho, "Difusão" 17; *Desengano* V).

The most prominent early Sebastianist was João de Castro (d. 1623), grandson of the well-known viceroy of India by the same name.[11] Castro is best known today as a promoter and interpreter of Bandarra's *Trovas*, but he interpreted a wide range of prophetic sources in his attempts, in the words of the editor of his 1604–5 *Aurora da Quinta Monarchia*, to "promote Portugal beyond its borders" (24). In fact, Castro specified in his instructions for the *Aurora*'s printing that its frontispiece should feature a quotation from the *Apocalypsis*: "Cum Magno Pastore Resurget Rex Magnus" (26). The *Aurora* is thus the most relevant of Castro's texts in tracing the *Apocalypsis*'s legacy in Sebastianism's royal millenarism.

In his prologue Castro describes his ideal audience as those whose hopes lie in what is seen not by the eyes of the body, but by those of the spirit (39). Even spiritual sight, however, will not remain the dominant prophetic sense in the *Aurora*. For example, when describing Afonso Henriques's founding vision, Castro emphasizes the aural in Henriques's words: "O Senhor com hu~ suave orgão de voz, que meus indinos ouvidos receberam; me disse: não te appareçi desta maneira pera acresçentar a tua Fe; mas pera corrobar teu coração neste conflicto: e pera estabeleçer sobre firme pedra os prinçios de teu Reyno" (The Lord, with a soft voice, which my unworthy ears received, said to me: I did not appear to you in this way to increase your faith, but to strengthen your heart in this conflict, and to establish on firm rock the beginnings of your kingdom) (45). Castro's retelling of this foundational narrative thus echoes Leão's reading of Revelation 18.4, and as we will see in the next section of this essay, António Vieira will make explicit the relative trustworthiness of hearing as a prophetic sense.

One of the primary texts interpreted by Castro is Nebuchadnezzar's dream from Daniel 2 (again, a text to which Vieira also returned frequently). Nebuchadnezzar had dreamed of a statue with a head of gold, torso of silver, waist of copper, legs of iron, and feet of clay. As Castro explains, any *doutor* who has studied this passage has understood the first four metals to represent the four great monarchies the world had seen: the Assyrians and Chaldeans, the Persians, the Greeks, and the Romans (100–1). Daniel predicts that these monarchies would be succeeded by one great, holy, universal monarchy – clearly, according to Castro, the "Monarchia temporal de toda a terra que ha de ter a Christandade" (temporal monarchy of the entire world that Christendom will have) (101). Castro concedes that this *reyno* must be understood above all spiritually, as universal obedience to Christian law (101). Here, Castro cites Joachim's reading of Daniel 4, in which the abbot states that the whole world will subject itself "antes espiritual que carnalmente" to Christ and Christ's vicar (101). Castro is at pains to clarify, however, that Joachim is not denying the truth of Christ's temporal reign: "Ao qual Abbade, pareçe no modo de fallar, que não foy tão claramente descuberto o mando temporal da Christandade, de que imos fallando; como o Espiritual. Todavia em dizer: 'In spiritu potius, quam in carne': não exclue o primeiro, posto que se assegura no segundo" (It seems, from his way of speaking, that the temporal dominion of Christianity, of which we have been speaking, was not revealed so clearly to this abbot as the spiritual one. However, in saying, "More in spirit, than in flesh," he does not exclude the first, although the second is verified) (102). Just as it is crucial for Castro that the Angelic Pastor be accompanied by a great (Portuguese) king, the Fifth Monarchy must not be purely spiritual, even if it is principally so: a worldly, historical, "accidental" meaning must also be valid.

These questions of spiritual and temporal exegesis are brought to bear on the specific role that Portugal will play in the Fifth Monarchy when, later in the *Aurora*, Castro directly cites the *Apocalypsis*. First, and not insignificantly, he expresses his admiration for the *Apocalypsis*'s "resolução de sutilissimas questões de Theologia" (resolution of very subtle questions of Theology) (397); later on he notes that, although Amadeus wrote in Latin, his style often follows the "Portuguese way of speaking" (400). This emphasis on Amadeus's Portuguese origins is necessary because Castro understands Amadeus as a spiritual prophet who complements the more worldly Bandarra:

> Não deixarei de notar os juizos immensos de Deos em annunçiar as Summas bemaventuranças temporaes per Bandarra Portugues: o qual profetizou mais que nenhu~ outro, assi dellas, como Del Rey Dom Sebastião sua Cabeça. E as summas espirituaes do mesmo tempo, revelou pello Santo Varão Frey Amadeu, outro Portugues: o qual tambem passou todos os mais, nas revellações do Papa Angelico, Cabeça no Espiritual: e dos divinissimos, e innumerabilissimos segredos de nossa Santissima Crença, pera o dito Pontifiçe os repartir pello mundo. (398)

> I will not avoid noting the immense judgments of God in announcing the Great temporal blessings through the Portuguese Bandarra: who prophesied more of them than any other, as of King Sebastian as their Head. And the great spiritual [blessings] at the same time, revealed by the Holy Brother Amadeus, another Portuguese: who also passed on the others, in the revelations of the Angelic Pope, Head of the Spiritual: and of the most holy, innumerable secrets of our Holy Faith, so that the aforesaid Pontiff could spread them throughout the world.

For Castro, spiritual and temporal interpretation, embodied respectively by Amadeus and Bandarra, foretell analogous forms of dominion during the Fifth Monarchy, in which an Angelic Pope and King Sebastian will carry out Christ's reign, exercising the divine will on earth. Castro suggests, that is, a unity of form and content in prophecy as it relates to the Portuguese empire, which, although undoubtedly temporal, will play an indispensable role in the triumph of Christian truth before the end of the world.

For both Leão and Castro, then, the accidents of history, worldly though they are, provide the key to the correct interpretation of prophetic texts. The truth revealed by these texts is, in turn, both spiritual and temporal. Leão, writing at the end of a period of Portuguese expansion, optimistically understands Sebastian to be playing a central role in achieving Christian dominion. For Castro, however, the key is to demonstrate the necessity of a temporal component of Christian dominion and, furthermore, to place a returned Sebastian at its head. Both Leão and Castro emphasize the role of hearing rather than seeing in Sebastianist revelation. As decades passed without Sebastian's return, however, it would fall to the Jesuit António Vieira to theorize most explicitly the practice of prophetic interpretation, the role of the worldly (history and sense perception) therein, and the necessity of Christ's temporal dominion (through Portugal) as a signifier of its spiritual counterpart.

António Vieira's *Sermão do Mandato* and *História do Futuro*: Accidental Dominion

António Vieira (d. 1697) is the best known interpreter of prophecy (he was very careful to clarify that he himself was no prophet) in Portuguese history.[12] He spent much of his life in Brazil, and this fact was important to his exegetic thought: "The New World represented for Vieira not an appendage to the Old but a locus of prophecies that the Portuguese had been providentially chosen to reveal" (T. Cohen 23). At the same time, Vieira maintained an active role in Portuguese politics. Although he was at first an orthodox Sebastianist (in the sense that it was Sebastian himself whose return Vieira expected), João IV came to embody Vieira's hopes for Portugal's future after the restoration of 1640. Indeed, during the reign of João IV (1640–56) Vieira was named, first, as ambassador and, later, as the royal preacher. After the death of João IV, however, Vieira would fall out of royal favour, eventually suffering imprisonment at the hands of the Inquisition, which found his prophetic views to be heretical. It was during this imprisonment that he composed the never finished *História do Futuro*, a text in which Vieira seeks to demonstrate that Portugal will return to imperial glory as the temporal arm of the Quinto Império (essentially synonymous with Castro's *Quinta Monarchia*).[13] Although the *História* was never finished, a plan for the whole work reveals that questions of dominion and possession, similar to those posed by Peter John Olivi in his abovementioned *quaestio*, were to be treated thoroughly. For example, Vieira planned to answer affirmatively the question, "Se no dito Império espiritual e temporal de Cristo se distingue o domínio, posse, exercício?" (Whether in this spiritual and temporal Empire of Christ, dominion, possession, exercise are distinguished?) (28). While Vieira never reached this point in the text, he does analyse the nature of Christ's temporal reign, and it is to this analysis that I will turn, after a brief exposition of Vieira's

Eucharistic thought and the pivotal role of the senses therein, as expounded in his 1650 "Sermão do Mandato."[14]

In this sermon Vieira considers which of Christ's *finezas* (gifts or favours)[15] at the end of his life was the greatest. He first rejects Augustine's view that Christ's death on the cross was the greatest *fineza*, arguing that, because Christ loved humanity more than his own life, it was a greater sacrifice to absent himself from humanity than to die (330). Here, Vieira notes that Christ died with the ease of a typical human leave-taking, whereas he "ausentou-se com todos os accidentes com que os homens costumam morrer" (absented himself with all the accidents with which humans customarily die) (332). In this sense, the accidents of the Passion point the way towards its theological truth.

Continuing to think in terms of presence and absence, Vieira next takes on Aquinas's view that the greatest *fineza* was the sacrament of the Eucharist itself, the fact that Christ "left himself" with us even while absenting himself. But it was a greater *fineza*, Vieira argues, for Christ to forsake the use of his senses during his sacramental presence:

> Que fosse maior fineza o encobrir-se[16] que o deixar-se, provo: O deixar-se foi buscar remedio á ausencia, isso é comodidade: o encobrir-se, foi renunciar os allivios da presença, isso é fineza. Para maior intelligencia desta materia, hemos de suppôr com os theologos, que Christo Senhor nosso no Sacramento do altar, ainda que está alli corporalmente, não tem uso, nem exercicio dos sentidos. Assim como nós não vemos a Christo debaixo daquelles accidentes, assim Christo nos não vê a nós com os olhos corporaes.[17] (335–6)

> That it was a greater gift to veil himself than to remain, I prove: Remaining was seeking a remedy for absence, which is a comfort; veiling himself was to renounce the relief of presence, which is a gift. To better understand this matter, we must suppose with the theologians that Christ our Lord in the Sacrament of the altar, although he is there corporeally, has neither the use nor exercise of his senses. Just as we do not see Christ beneath those accidents, Christ does not see us with his corporeal eyes.

Anticipating the counterargument that because Christ is impassible, he must not suffer his lack of perception during the Eucharist, Vieira answers that, in consecrating the bread during life in such a way that his senses would be veiled during the sacrament, Christ accepted in advance this particular form of suffering (339–42). Alluding to the Song of Songs,[18] Vieira summarizes his view thus:

> Porque encoberto daquella primeira parede, que é a da humanidade, elle via-nos a nós em quanto Deus, posto que nós o não viamos a elle: porém depois que sobre

> aquella parede se pôz a segunda, que é a dos accidentes, nem nós em quanto homem o vêmos a elle, nem elle nos vê a nos. E esta é a fineza cruel e terrivel do amôr, pela qual deixando-se com os homens, se condemnou a não vêr os mesmos por quem se deixou. (343)

> Because veiled by that first wall, which is that of humanity, he, as God, saw us, although we did not see him: however, after the second wall, that of the accidents, was built upon the first, we neither see him as a man, nor does he see us. And this is the cruel and terrible gift of love, by which, remaining among men, he condemned himself not to see the very ones for the sake of whom he remained.

In Vieira's view, then, the accidents' interruption of natural perception – both that of Christ's really present, but veiled, body, and that of our own – is the central fact of the Eucharist. Christ's greatest acts of love are negative, and thus absence and senselessness become the most powerful signs of spiritual presence. Yet Vieira concludes that the greatest *fineza* of all was Christ's command to wash each other's feet, interpreted as a command for neighbourly love (352–9). This exercise of Christ's will over human community is what is most highly signified in the "accidents" of Christ's leave-taking; they are the temporal corollary of the spiritual love that caused Christ to sacrifice the use of his senses during his sacramental presence. Vieira's understanding of the Eucharist thus anticipates his view of Christ's temporal dominion during the Quinto Império whose imminent arrival is so fervently predicted in the *História do Futuro*.

The *História* ranges widely in the texts it interprets, although, as in Castro's *Aurora*, Bandarra and Daniel figure prominently. Vieira also repeatedly emphasizes the importance of Revelation, writing that no one doubts that its prophecies refer to the present day (80) and that many of the *História*'s predictions are drawn directly from it (93). While the *Apocalypsis* is never cited directly, Vieira did write in a 1664 letter – during the *História*'s most active period of composition – that Amadeus's text had recently been "most necessary" to his work (Carvalho, "Difusão" 10n33).

Vieira opens the *História* with an explanation of his general thoughts on prophecy – thoughts in which the senses play an important role, and sight is often at a disadvantage. Time, like the world, has two hemispheres, Vieira explains: the past, "above and visible," and the future, "below and invisible" (45). With sight thus disqualified as a means of perceiving the invisible hemisphere of the future, Vieira writes that, in his *História*, "Ouvirá o Mundo o que nunca viu" (The World will hear what it has never seen) (46). As in Castro's account of Afonso Henriques's encounter with the divine, hearing becomes here a privileged prophetic sense. And, as in the case of Leão, Vieira believed himself to be in a historically privileged position as well, with a clarity granted by living in the "final days of the world" (Jordán 50). The "history" of Vieira's title, he thus explains, is not figurative, neither a hyperbole nor a synecdoche, "it does not call a pygmy a giant, nor an arm a man" (60). Vieira is speaking directly of the world as it is and as it will be: "O mundo de que falo é o mundo, aquele mundo, e naquele sentido em que disse São João [...] 'O Mundo que Deus criou, o Mundo que o não conheceu' [John 1.10], e o Mundo que o há-de conhecer. Quando o não conheceu, negou-lhe o domínio; quando o conhecer, dar-lhe-á a posse" (The World of which I speak is the world, that world, in which sense Saint John said [...] "The World that God made, the World that knew him not," and the World that will know him. When it did not know him, it denied him dominion; when it knows him, it will give him possession) (60).[19] The events foretold by Vieira are thus beyond natural signification, even beyond the figurative language available to humans; only divinely instituted (conventional and prophetic) signification – and its relationship with Christ's dominion, with his possession of the world – is here at play.

Indeed, it is with a discussion of the nature of Christ's *possession* of the world during the Fifth Empire that the *História* – in the incomplete form in which Vieira left it – concludes. Christ's spiritual dominion in no way precludes the temporal, "de modo que um e outro domínio bem pode sem repugnância alguma convir e ajustar-se no mesmo sujeito" (such that one dominion and the other can, without any repugnance, coexist and adjust to one another in the same subject) (287). Furthermore, the spirituality that is opposed to the body is not always the greater (293). In fact, Christ would not have been fully human without his temporal dominion: "Por Cristo ser verdadeiro e inteiro homem, composto não só de espírito, se não de carne, foi muito conveniente que não só tivesse o Império espiritual que pertence às almas, senão também o temporal que é próprio dos corpos" (For Christ to be truly and wholly human, composed not only of spirit, but also of flesh, it was very appropriate that he have not only the spiritual Empire that belongs to souls, but also the temporal one that belongs to bodies) (347).

On the other hand, Vieira asks, why should Christ's dominion during this new era be temporal and not merely spiritual when, as many theologians point out, Christ is humanity's very model of poverty? Vieira's answer takes a form whose structure resembles closely his discussion of the Eucharist: Christ's renunciation of use – a key term in the Franciscan poverty debate studied by Agamben – is even more powerful in light of his temporal dominion (349). But, reply Vieira's proleptic critics, would not the renunciation of dominion itself constitute a still more powerful example (349–50)? Not, says Vieira, if Christ was to be an example to his spiritual vicar:

> Era mais conveniente ao mesmo exemplo do Mundo conservar o domínio sem o uso, que renunciar o uso e mais o domínio; porque Cristo como Mestre e Exemplar da perfeição evangélica, não só devia dar exemplo aos religiosos que professam

> renunciar o domínio dos bens temporais, senão também aos prelados e bispos, e ao supremo bispo e supremo prelado, cujo estado, sendo de maior perfeição, conserva o domínio e administração dos bens e só periga ou pode perigar na imoderação ou excesso do uso deles. Foi logo convenientíssimo que em Cristo se ajuntasse o sumo domínio e o sumo desprezo e abstinência das cousas do Mundo, para que no mesmo exemplar aprendessem os religiosos a mortificação do uso e os prelados a moderação do domínio. (350–1)
>
> It was more convenient for the World's example to maintain dominion without use, than to renounce use and dominion as well; because Christ as Master and Exemplar of evangelical perfection, must give an example not only to the religious who profess to renounce dominion of temporal goods, but also to the prelates and bishops, and to the supreme bishop and supreme prelate, whose state, being of greater perfection, maintains the dominion and administration of goods and can only run the risk of immoderation or excessive use of them. It was therefore extremely convenient that Christ unite the highest dominion and highest disdain for and abstinence from the things of this World, so that in the same example the religious would learn the mortification of use and the prelates, moderation of dominion.

Christ must maintain his temporal dominion, without its use, if he is to be an example to the Angelic Pope. But Christ's will must also be exercised temporally through a great Portuguese king.[20] In the Eucharist Christ is really corporeally present, but his senses are veiled by the accidents of the bread and wine; this constitutes for Vieira a painful but loving sacrifice and, for the tradition on which he is drawing, a necessary element of the sacrament's signifying purpose. In the Quinto Império, as in the Franciscan account of signification, Christ's dominion will be truly effective throughout the globe, yet his presence will be mediated by the pope and the king of Portugal. In Vieira's millenarian view, then, Portuguese imperial dominion is a kind of spiritually necessary accident, signifying a truth whose perception it veils, but whose will it exercises throughout all existence.

The banner of Sebastianism, and of the Quinto Império in particular, would be carried into the twentieth century by none other than Fernando Pessoa. The key feature of Pessoa's Fifth Empire was a union of matter and spirit, of which Sebastian and the Angelic Pope were the symbol: "A aliança de D. Sebastião, Imperador do Mundo, e do Papa Angélico figura esta íntima aliança, esta fusão do material e do espiritual, talvez sem separação. E o próprio Segundo Advento, ou nova incarnação de mesmo Adepto em que outrora Deus projectou o seu Símbolo, ou Filho, não faz senão figurar d'outro modo esta mesma aliança suprema" (The alliance of D. Sebastian, Emperor of the World, and the Angelic Pope figures this intimate alliance, this fusion of the material and the spiritual, perhaps without separation. And the very Second Coming, does nothing else but figure in another way this same supreme alliance) (*Sobre Portugal* 146). Pessoa thus perceived very clearly the intimate alliance between Sebastianist/Joachimist thought, messianism, and signification (figuration) at the heart of the historical imagination of the Portuguese empire. Unlike his predecessors, Pessoa believed that Sebastianism would replace Catholicism as a national religion in the Fifth Empire (179), and that Sebastian's return would occur through metempsychosis (Pessoa's word), the reappearance of the form of Sebastian's soul:

> Quando houverdes criado uma cousa cuja forma seja idêntica à do pensamento de D. Sebastião, D. Sebastião terá regressado, mas não só regressado modo dizendo, mas na sua realidade e presença concreta, posto que não fisicamente pessoal. Um acontecimento é um homem, ou um espírito sob forma impessoal. (196)
>
> When you have created something whose form is identical to that of D. Sebastian's thought, D. Sebastian will have returned, but not only returned in a manner of speaking, but in his reality and concrete presence, although not physically personal. An event is a man, or a spirit under impersonal form.

Historical Portugal's error, for Pessoa, was precisely to have attempted to forge a "material" empire, when a small nation can (and should) achieve only a "Spiritual Empire" (225–6). We can see, then, why he emptied Sebastian's return of its "physically personal" presence. Yet for Portugal to become the Quinto Império, Sebastian must be actually and concretely present in his return. It is for this reason that, in *Mensagem*'s "O Desejado," – in the section of the book titled "Os símbolos" (The Symbols) – the poet would figure the hidden and desired king's return as a New Eucharist:

> Vem, Galaaz com pátria, erguer de novo,
> Mas já no auge da suprema prova,
> A alma penitente do teu povo
> À Eucaristia Nova. (78)
>
> Come, Galahad with a homeland, raise again,
> But now at the height of the supreme trial,
> The penitent soul of your people
> To the New Eucharist.

Pessoa was aware that his call for a purely spiritual Eucharist signifying a purely spiritual empire set him apart from his Sebastianist predecessors. However, as I have sought to show in this essay, the difference does not consist solely in the renunciation of temporal dominion. In the *Apocalypsis Nova* the temporal accidents of the bread and wine draw attention to the sacrament as sign through the fallibility of all five senses, and it is in this connection that Eucharistic doctrine becomes relevant to prophetic practice. While it was the content of the *Apocalypsis*'s prophecies – particularly the prediction that a great king would accompany the Angelic Pastor – to which Gaspar de Leão and João de Castro responded directly, both authors began to explore a privileged role for hearing rather than sight in the interpretation of prophecy. Finally, in the writings of António de Vieira, this methodological privileging of hearing is brought together with a reinvigorated examination of the role of the senses in the Eucharist and of the relationship between the Eucharistic accidents and Portugal's temporal dominion in the *Quinto Império*. An apparently puzzling juxtaposition of theological doctrine and mystical prophecy in the *Apocalypsis Nova* thus gave rise to a rich and varied practice of prophetic interpretation in the Portuguese empire, where signification and territorial dominion had already long been legendarily and foundationally linked.

NOTES

1 Here, I am following the brief biography of Amadeus found in Nelson Novoa (74–5); for a longer biographical study see Sousa Costa.
2 Salviati himself is a popular candidate among modern scholars for authorship of the work (Nelson Novoa 75); another possible author is Cardinal Bernardino López de Carvajal (1456–1523), organizer of the schismatic Council of Pisa in 1511 (Carvalho, "Achegas" 79). On the problem of the text's authorship more broadly see Nelson Novoa (72–6).
3 Specifically, the Eucharistic discussion follows closely Scotus's *Opus Oxoniense* IV.8–13 (Morisi-Guerra, *Ricerche* 70–2). Scotus is explicitly praised twice for his Eucharistic theory in the sixth *raptus* (Meirinhos 335).
4 For a helpful overview of Scotus's answers to these questions see Burr (76–98).
5 I will quote throughout ms. Vat. Lat. 3825, identified by Morisi-Guerra as "one of the earliest codices" ("Plan" 30n8). All translations from the *Apocalypsis* and other texts are my own unless otherwise noted; I am grateful to David Kaufman for clarifying some obscure passages in Amadeus's Latin.
6 For an edition of Olivi's *quaestio*, see Delorme.
7 Tara Alberts has recently shown that the Eucharist was a central element of missionary activities in southeast Asia (137), and that the Jesuits made extensive use of Eucharistic (and penitential) processions in Goa and Malacca (139).

8 "And I heard another voice from heaven, saying, Come out of her, my people, that ye be not partakers of her sins, and that ye receive not of her plagues" (Rev. 18.4).

9 A full account of the roots and history of Sebastianism is beyond the scope of this essay; for an overview of the phenomenon see Besselaar, and for a detailed study of its first two centuries see Hermann. Ironically, Philip II's conquest of Portugal also seems to have provoked a wave of street prophets in Spain (Kagan 88).

10 In a further irony, Bandarra's references to a "redemptory king" known as "O Encoberto" – an epithet that would be applied to the missing Sebastian – seem to have been inspired by the earlier Spanish legend of the "Encubierto" (Jordán 48). These Spanish roots would not prevent Sebastianism from being "converted into a symbol of national redemption" in Portugal at the close of the sixteenth century (Jordán 48).

11 For a brief biography of Castro see Besselaar (71–2); for a list of his major works see *Aurora* (12–13n11).

12 For a brief account of Vieira's general approach to prophecy see Ricard (358–62); a more detailed study can be found in Cantel.

13 Phelan summarizes Vieira's position thus: "In the second coming Christ would not corporeally but only metaphysically return to earth. Christ would reign over the millennial kingdom through his vicars – the king of Portugal in temporal matters and the Pope in the spiritual sphere" (120).

14 This is the sermon to which Sor Juana Inés de la Cruz responded in her well-known "Carta atenagórica."

15 See Brescia 45.

16 Vieira's use of this loaded term – recall that Sebastian was often referred to as "O Encoberto" – should be noted.

17 Sor Juana, in summarizing Vieira's argument (in the process of rejecting it), refers only to the senses categorically rather than to sight in particular: "quedar sin uso de sentidos en ese Sacramento" (420–1).

18 "Look, there he stands behind our wall, gazing in at the windows, looking through the lattice" (Song of Songs 2.9).

19 A similar attitude is to be found in Columbus's prophetic writings, whose language "is figural, but it figures a worldly reality and literal correspondence between that reality as named and as it is envisioned" (Kadir 142).

20 María V. Jordán summarizes this part of Vieira's argument thus: "The union of body and spirit that is Christ would be historically materialized before the end of days as the most worthy example of moral teaching offered to mankind" (51).

12 Festive Soundscapes in Colonial Potosí and Minas Gerais

LISA VOIGT

On his third voyage to the Indies in 1498, Christopher Columbus appealed to various senses in an attempt to entice the people he encountered into peaceful contact with Europeans. Early in the letter describing the voyage, Columbus recounts how a canoe of twenty-four indigenous people approached his ship as it neared mainland South America. The encounter is initially limited to the visual realm, with Columbus first focusing on their weapons, dress, and appearance and then describing his attempts at communication through signs and shiny objects: "Yo ni otro ninguno no los entendíamos, salvo que yo les mandaba hacer señas que se allegasen, y en esto se pasó más de dos horas, y si se llegaban un poco luego se desviaban. Yo les hacía mostrar bacines y otras cosas que lucían, por enamorarlos porque viniesen" (none of us could understand them; I made signs to them, however, to come nearer to us, and more than two hours were spent in this manner, but if by any chance they moved a little nearer, they soon pushed off again. I caused basins and other shining objects to be shown to them to tempt them to come near) (Colón "Narrative," 174; 120). Yet when the natives finally begin to approach, Columbus introduces another sensory realm by ordering the playing of drums: "yo deseaba mucho haber lengua y no tenía ya cosa que me pareciese que era de mostrarles para que viniesen; salvo que hice sobir un tamborín en el castillo de popa que tañasen e unos mancebos que danzasen, *creyendo que se allegarían a ver la fiesta*" (as I was very anxious to speak with them and had nothing else to show them to induce them to approach, I ordered a drum to be played upon the quarter-deck and some of our young men to dance, *believing the Indians would come to see the amusement*) (174; 120; my emphasis). Columbus proposes using the sounds of festivities to bring about greater intercultural proximity, an effort that this essay evaluates in later colonial contexts.

The visual and aural methods of attraction articulated by Columbus are echoed in the *Ordenanzas de S.M. hechas para los nuevos descubrimientos, conquistas y pacificaciones* (Ordinances of His Majesty made for the new discoveries, conquests, and pacifications), issued by Philip II in 1573. In order to preach to those natives who had not yet peacefully accepted "la doctrina cristina" (the Christian doctrine) (184; 28), the ordinances recommend that a nearby, already "pacified" chief lure them to his land "a se holgar o a otra cosa a que los podieren traer" (to amuse themselves or for any other reason that might attract them) (184; 30), until the previously hidden Spanish priests find it safe to emerge and use interpreters to preach. While Columbus lacked such interpreters, his other strategies are emulated in the *Ordenanzas*:

> para que oigan [la doctrina Cristiana] con mas veneracion y admiracion, estén revestidos á lo menos, con albas ó sobre pellices y estolas, y con la cruz en la mano, [...] que la oigan con grandisimo acatamiento y veneracion, para que á su imitacion los infieles se aficionen á ser enseñados; y si *para causar mas admiracion y atencion en los infieles, les pareciera cosa conviniente, podran usar de musica de cantores y de menestriles altos y baxos para que provoquen á los indios á se juntar,* y usen de los otros medios que les pareciere para amansar y pacificar a los indios que estobieren de guerra. (184–5; my emphasis)

> in order that they may be accorded greater respect and admiration they should be wearing at least white vestments, or surplices and stoles, and with the Cross in their hands; [...] and, *should they wish to generate greater admiration and attention among the infidels – and if available – they might use music, by way of singers and high and bass wind instruments, in order to entice the Indians to join them* – and to use other means available that they might think suitable to subdue and pacify belligerent Indians. (29; my emphasis)

The instruments may have changed, with voice and wind instruments replacing Columbus's "tamborín," but the confidence in the ability of music and festivities to entice and pacify hostile natives has not.

By the time the *Ordenanzas* were promulgated, the importance of ceremonial music and dance in many indigenous cultures was well known to Spanish authorities and served to justify such an approach to pacification and evangelization. The Third Provincial Council of Lima (1582–3) affirms that it is "cosa cierta y notoria que esta nacion de yndios se atraen y provocan sobremanera al conoscimiento y veneracion del summo Dios con la[s] cerimonias exteriores y aparatos del culto divino" (a certain and notorious thing that this nation of Indians is especially attracted and provoked [to the] veneration of the supreme God by exterior ceremonies and displays of divine worship) (*Concilios* 1: 374; my trans.). As a result, the council mandates that "procuren mucho los obispos y tambien en su tanto los curas, que todo lo que toca al culto divino se haga con la mayor perfeccion y lustre que puedan, y para este effecto pongan estudio y cuydado en que aya escuela y capilla de cantores y juntamente musica de flautas y chirimias y otros ynstrumentos acomodados en las yglesias" (the bishops as well as the priests (in their realm) must seek greatly to perform the divine service with the greatest perfection and luster that they can, and to achieve this result they must studiously and carefully ensure that there is a school and chapel of singers, and with it music of flutes and shawms and other instruments present in the churches) (*Concilios* 1: 374; my trans.). D.R.M. Irving argues that such attention to "musical display and musical pedagogy" is characteristic of colonial policy in the early modern Spanish empire, part of the "concerted and conceited attempt by dominant ruling groups to effect the integration of subjugated peoples' musical tastes [...] in the hope of achieving some form of social cohesion" (2). Both Irving's *Colonial Counterpoint: Music in Early Modern Manila* and Geoffrey Baker's *Imposing Harmony: Music and Society in Colonial Cuzco* employ musical terminology (counterpoint and harmony) in the literal as well as metaphorical senses in order to describe the ideology and function of sonic hegemony in the Spanish empire. As Baker writes regarding Cuzco, "The imposition of harmony in the Americas was a multifaceted program [...] the incorporation of European music in Cuzco may be seen as an essential part of the process of forging a Hispanic sacred city out of an Inka ceremonial center, an attempt to impose European urban values through sound" (*Imposing Harmony* 30–1).

Despite the continuing reverberations of his pacification strategy, however, Columbus's third letter reveals that the festive performance actually had the inverse effect: "luego que vieron tañer y danzar, todos dejaron los remos y echaron mano a los arcos y los encordaron, y embrazó cada uno su tablachina y comenzaron a tirarnos flechas" (No sooner, however, did they perceive the beating of the drum and the dancing, than they all left their oars, and strung their bows, and each man laying hold of his shield, they commenced discharging their arrows at us) (Colón "Narrative," 174; 120–1). Columbus proceeds to order an attack and the natives quickly retreat; he reports that "nunca más los vide ni a otros en esta isla" (I never saw any more of them or any of the other inhabitants of the island) (174; 121). The cultural miscomprehension at this scene of first encounter goes beyond the difficulty of linguistic communication. The drumbeat and dancing that to Columbus and his men signify friendly festivities, in which everyone is invited to join, mean just the opposite to the natives, who interpret them as signs of war and hostility. In *The Singing of the New World*, Gary Tomlinson cites this episode as his first example of the "fear of the other's singing, dancing, and musical instruments" in the phase of first contact, but unlike his other examples this is not one in which the music was meant to be frightening (169). Rather, the episode speaks more to the lack of transparency of non-verbal, sonic communication: music can misfire and yield just the opposite of what was intended – discord rather than concord. Indeed, the episode challenges the coercive universality that, as Baker writes, lies within the concept of harmony (*Imposing* 30).

This essay attends to both of these sonic dimensions – the harmonic and the discordant – in the festive soundscapes of the mining boomtowns of Potosí, in the Spanish Viceroyalty of Peru, and Mariana, in the Portuguese Captaincy of Minas Gerais, Brazil.[1] The Villa Imperial de Potosí, founded after the discovery of the *Cerro Rico* (Rich Hill) of silver in 1545, came to be one of the world's most populous cities by the early seventeenth century, but its vast silver production had long been in decline by the time the Portuguese struck gold, in the region they came to call "Minas Gerais" (General Mines), at the end of the seventeenth century. In 1745 – exactly 200 years after Potosí's founding – the first town and capital of Minas Gerais, Vila da Nossa Senhora do Riberão do Carmo (originally established in 1711), was renamed the city of Mariana and made the seat of a new diocese. Despite the chronological gap, both Potosí and Mariana were known for opulent baroque festivals that displayed the cities' abundant mineral wealth in and through lavish costumes, floats, triumphal arches, and other ephemeral architecture. Just as extravagant was the amount of money spent on the candles with which the streets were illuminated during the processions; Potosí historian Bartolomé Arzáns de Orsúa y Vela asserts that more money was spent there on white wax in one month than in the great cities of Europe in six months (*Historia* 2: 325). The elaborate descriptions in such accounts sought to recreate the dazzling visual spectacles for readers who did not witness the events. However, the festive soundscape that resonates in their texts is just as worthy of attention.

The music, drumming, and other sounds of festivals are part of what Geoffrey Baker calls the "*la ciudad sonora* or 'sonorous city'" (*Imposing* 22) or "resounding city" ("Resounding" 9), in response to Ángel Rama's influential concept of the "lettered city" to describe the urban elite culture of colonial Latin America. Baker points out that while the verbal and visual dimensions of colonial cities have received the most scholarly attention, the "resounding city" can bring other issues and agencies to the fore. As Baker explains,

> The resounding city was [...] a performative construct that depended, to varying degrees across the New World, on indigenous and/or African participation. [...] In some ways, the resounding city is a more complex structure than its lettered cousin: rather than presenting a pure, Hispanic image of colonial power, it reveals the performance of complex and nuanced cultural negotiations between different social and ethnic groups, often played out via that archetype of baroque culture, the fiesta. ("Resounding" 16)

Baker goes on to point out that the "performative, festive city [...] depended on indigenous and African involvement," and that the "manifold meanings of musical performance reveal [...] urban spaces [...] to be multiply imagined and inflected, contested rather than fixed" (18).

Festivals were thus much more than a tool in the "attempt to impose European urban values through sound" (*Imposing* 30), since they allowed the articulation of other beliefs and agendas. In order to access the contested sounds of festivals, written accounts may be more useful than visual depictions like Melchor Pérez Holguín's *Entry of Archbishop Viceroy Morcillo in Potosí* (1716) (Figure 12.1). Such pictures effectively display the visual diversity that characterized festivals – the different skin tones of participants and observers, or the Inca costumes and paraphernalia worn by the indigenous elite – but narrative descriptions attend more to the contribution of subaltern groups to the festive soundscape.[2]

Potosí

The ceremonial entry of Archbishop Diego Morcillo Rubio de Auñón into Potosí – where he stopped on his way to Lima to assume his new post as interim Viceroy in 1716 – is represented in not one but two narratives, in addition to Holguín's painting. The official, published account, *Aclamación festiva de la muy noble Imperial Villa de Potosí* (Festive acclamation of the very noble Imperial Town of Potosí) (1716), was written by the Augustinian friar Juan de la Torre, who composed the music that was performed during the festivities. Bartolomé Arzáns de Orsúa y Vela also dedicated a chapter to it in his massive history of Potosí, *Historia de la Villa Imperial de Potosí* (History of the Imperial Town of Potosí), which was written in the early eighteenth century (but remained unpublished until 1965). Like Holguín's painting and the *Aclamación festiva* – both of which he may have been aware of, as they coincide in most details – Arzáns's version was written contemporaneously with the events described. Arzáns explicitly acknowledges Juan de la Torre and his *Aclamación festiva* when he describes the solemn entry's music as "compuesto todo ingeniosamente por el reverendo padre maestro fray Juan de la Torre, prior de San Agustín, de quien mucho hemos dicho, y también añado que a petición de la Villa escribió la relación de esta entrada, recibimiento y fiestas de su excelencia para la ciudad de Los Reyes, que quisiera mi corta pluma parte del colmo de la suya para adorno de estos reglones" (all composed ingeniously by the Reverend Father Master Fray Juan de la Torre, prior of St Augustine, of whom we have said a great deal, and I also add that at the petition of the Town he wrote the relation of this entry, reception and festivities for his excellency on his way to the City of the Kings, and my small pen wishes that it reached part of the heights of his for the adornment of these lines) (*Historia* 3: 48).

Figure 12.1. *Entry of Archbishop Viceroy Morcillo in Potosí* by Melchor Pérez Holguín (1716). Museo de América, Madrid.

Figure 12.2. Detail. *Entry of Archbishop Viceroy Morcillo in Potosí* by Melchor Pérez Holguín (1716). Museo de América, Madrid.

The performance of Fray Juan de la Torre's musical compositions is represented in the painting as well as in the texts. The *Aclamación festiva* transcribes the *loas*'s lyrics and describes the music as "sonoros concentos" (sonorous harmonies) (de la Torre 14r), echoing the harmonious social hierarchy that the festival as a whole is supposed to display to the visiting authority. According to Arzáns, this music at least initially drowned out the other sounds of the festival: "entretanto (haciendo pausa la inquieta turba cuyo eco y murmurio resonó en breve espacio) dio principio la armoniosa música dando la bienvenida a su excelencia" (Meanwhile [the murmurings of the restless crowd having momentarily been hushed] sweet music began, offering welcome to His Excellency) (*Historia* 1: 48; 188).[3] In Arzáns's version, the welcome is followed by a *loa* performed by two allegorically dressed children, who are also depicted on Holguín's painting under the triumphal arch on the far right, their mouths open in song (Figure 12.2).[4] Arzáns praises both the "verso muy elegante" ("very elegant verses") and the "admirable dulzura" ("wonderful sweetness") of the *loa* (*Historia* 1: 48).

Figure 12.3. Detail. *Entry of Archbishop Viceroy Morcillo in Potosí* of Melchor Pérez Holguín (1716). Museo de América, Madrid.

The recital of another of Juan de la Torre's compositions in praise of the archbishop-viceroy, also sung by two children representing Europe and America, is similarly lauded by Arzáns for its "gran destreza y melodía" (great skill and sweet melody) and "verso elegantísimo" (most elegant verse), for which it earned the composer "grandes aplausos" (enthusiastic applause) (*Historia* 1: 50; 193).[5] This performance is also depicted on Holguín's canvas (upper right inset), on the float in the corner of the plaza, upon which the archbishop-viceroy gazes while seated in the balcony above (Figure 12.3).

Nevertheless, the songs composed in a European style by Juan de la Torre are not the only music performed for the occasion, as his own account reveals. De la Torre describes the indigenous reception of the archbishop-viceroy as he made his way to Potosí on the day of his official entry:

> Día pues veinte y cinco de Abril, salió su Exc. [...] para la Villa de Potosí, [...] y en el espacio de quatro leguas bien estendidas, que consta su distancia, se vian coronadas

> las cumbres de los peñascos mas altivos, de copioso numero de Indios, que admirados esperavan ver su dueño, matizando de varias banderas, y colores sus alturas, ni era menor la multitud que a la margen del camino real esperaba en varias danzas, repetidos a su usanza con rústicos instrumentos, que si bien podia causar admiración su número crecido, movía a risueña diversion la variedad de sus trages, y figuras, con que cada qual intentava hazer la salva a su Señor [el Arzobispo-Virrey], y mostrar con su sencillo amor su regozijo. (7v–8r)

> On 25 April his Excellency left [...] for the Town of Potosí, [...] and in the space of four long leagues that make up the distance, one could see the peaks of the highest crags crowned with a copious number of Indians, who admiringly waited to see their lord, painting the heights with various flags and colours, nor was the multitude any less who waited on the side of the royal road with various dances, repeated in their manner with rustic instruments, such that if their large number caused admiration, smiling amusement was provoked by the variety of their costumes and figures with which each one tried to salute their lord [the archbishop-viceroy] and demonstrate their joy with their simple love. (My trans.)

Although the indigenous groups' performance of music and dance temporarily displaces the arriving dignitary as the object of admiration, the author circumscribes the meaning of their salute to an expression of adulation for and submission to the archbishop and newly appointed viceroy. Yet it surely meant more than that to the indigenous performers themselves.

Indeed, the repeated references to variety in the flags, music, and dances suggest that a more immediate goal was to display the performers' diverse regional or local identities. The vast majority of indigenous peoples in Potosí were *mita* mining workers, forced to migrate to Potosí on a rotational basis from one of sixteen *capitanías* or provinces, which generally followed the regional divisions that existed in the Inca empire.[6] The festive display appears to be not entirely unfamiliar to Juan de la Torre, since he acknowledges that the dances were performed "a su usanza" (in their manner). Such performances surely have their roots in pre-Hispanic practices in the multi-ethnic Inca empire. Karen Spalding argues that ceremonial songs and dances were "occasions for exhibitions of skill" and a "mark of group membership" and thus a way for *ayllus* (or the larger kinship groups of which they were a part) to compete with one another.[7] Such competitive displays of local identity are evident in the mestizo historian el Inca Garcilaso de la Vega's description of Inca ceremonies in *Comentarios reales de los Incas* (Royal Commentaries of the Incas) (1609). In a chapter dedicated to Inti Raymi, "la fiesta principal del sol" (the main festival of the sun) and the most important one on the Inca calendar, Garcilaso writes, "cada nación venía lo mejor arreada y más bien acompañada que podía, procurando cada uno en su tanto aventajarse de sus vecinos y comarcanos, o de todos, si pudiese" (each nation came as best adorned and accompanied as possible, trying each one to surpass their neighbours and all the others, if they could) (418; my trans.). The continuation of pre-Hispanic festive practices and rivalries during Corpus Christi, whose date nearly coincides with Inti Raymi, explains Viceroy Francisco de Toledo's concern for the proper instruction of *indios*, who, "en la fiesta de Corpus Christi saquen sus andas y danza en cada parroquia y vayan en procesion con su cruz y banderas" (in the feast of Corpus Christi take out their platforms and dance in each parish and go in procession with their cross and flags) (414; my trans.).[8] After verifying that the Indians are not hiding any "idols" under the saints on their platforms, the priest should explain to them in their language, "la razón de aquella fiesta para que la entendian y honren con la veneración que son obligados" (the reason for that festival so that they understand and honour it with the veneration that they are obliged to give) (414; my trans.). Perhaps the indigenous musicians and dancers depicted in de la Torre's account did not (or chose not to) understand the "veneration that they [were] obliged to give" the new viceroy and performed their music and dances for other reasons.

The description of another festival in Arzáns supports the interpretation of indigenous musical performances as expressions of local identities in Potosí. In his account of the celebration of Philip IV's coronation in 1622 Arzáns refers to how *mita* workers performed the dances and music of their place of origin both upon their initial entry into Potosí to perform their labour service and during public festivals. In the midst of the one of the masquerades, Arzáns recounts:

> De allí a breve rato se oye mucho ruido de tiros de pólvora, y cesando vieron entrar hasta 200 indios como cuando vienen a la mita de este rico Cerro cada año, mas esta entrada fue de regocijo y la otra es de mucho llanto. Entraron, pues, con varios instrumentos como de trompetas, cañahuecas y calabazos, todos plateados y encintados, que son los mismos instrumentos con que entran cuando vienen de sus provincias, que si no es muy agradable el sonido de ellos a lo menos no es enfadoso. Traían también unos cañoncitos de plata alternativamente puestos a manera de órgano (que llaman los indios ayarichis) que hacen una suave armonía. (*Historia* 1: 349)

> A little while later a great noise of gunshots was heard, and after it stopped up to 200 Indians were seen to enter, as they do when they come to the *mita* of this rich Cerro each year – but this entry was joyful and the other one is of much weeping. They entered, then, with various instruments like trumpets, panpipes, and gourd drums, all silver-plated and adorned with ribbons, which are the same instruments with which they enter when they come from their provinces – which, even if the sound of them is not very agreeable, at least it is not annoying. They also brought

> some little pipes alternately placed in the manner of a pipe organ (which the Indians call *ayarichis*), which make a soft harmony.

In this account of a jubilant, noisy soundscape of both gunshots and music – which echoes a much more plaintive one, when the *mita* workers arrive to begin their period of forced labour – we can hear Arzáns struggling to make sense of sonic difference. He certainly does not ascribe to it the "admirable dulzura y discreción" (wonderful sweetness and grace) (*Historia* 1: 48) that he attributes to Juan de la Torre's *loas*. However, Arzáns offers more detail – and a more ambiguous appraisal – than de la Torre's allusion to the "rústicos instrumentos" (rustic instruments) in *Aclamación festiva*. Arzáns concedes that while the sound of trumpets, panpipes, and drums is not very agreeable, "a lo menos no es enfadoso" (at least it is not annoying.) He even describes the *ayarichi*, another type of Andean panpipe, as capable of producing "una suave armonía" (a soft harmony).

Arzáns goes on to describe the performers' appearance in a way that corroborates the connection between music, dance, and the expression of ethnic identity: "Venían de 20 en 20 con sus caciques o principales, y todos vestidos a su uso, con ricas camisetas bordadas de oro y perlas" (They came 20 by 20 each with their *caciques* or leaders, all dressed in their manner, with rich shirts embroidered with gold and pearls) (*Historia* 1: 349). Accompanied by their *caciques* – the indigenous leaders charged with delivering mita workers to Potosí – the *indios*' festive entry continues to evoke the more sorrowful one of their arrival to serve in the mita (1: 349). The *caciques*' costume – besides the embroidered shirts, Arzáns highlights the *llautu* or headdress, *ojotas* or sandals, and golden *mascarones* or maskettes on the shoulders, knees, and ankles (1: 349) – bears a close resemblance to those depicted in some of the paintings of Corpus Christi in Cuzco. This costume does not reflect, as Arzáns claims, "[el] modo que vestían los reyes ingas" (the manner that the Inca kings dressed) (1: 349); Carolyn Dean has shown that this is a hybrid colonial product incorporating Inca regalia in order to denote noble, elite status (127–30). Such a costume is on display in the nocturnal masquerade performed for the archbishop-viceroy in 1718, although Arzáns more succinctly describes the appearance of the Inca and his *coyas* or queens, the last figures in the procession, as being of "gran majestad y riqueza de apropiados trajes" (great majesty and richness of the appropriate dress) (*Historia* 3: 50; my trans.). Both the 1622 acclamation of the king and the 1718 entry of the viceroy thus feature representatives of not only Spanish but Inca sovereignty, while other indigenous participants evoke discrete ethnic or local identities through music and dance. That is, rather than signifying the unified subservience of a homogeneous group of "indios" to Spanish figures of authority, the festive performances denote different cultures of origin and statuses, just as they do in pre-Hispanic celebrations in the Inca empire.

Furthermore, in Arzáns's narratives of festivals, indigenous instruments are heard not only on the periphery – the rugged road to Potosí, where the indigenous music and dancing described in *Aclamación festiva* occurred – but also at the centre of the city and the festival. For example, Arzáns depicts the cacophony that ensues when the archbishop-viceroy enters the main church and the soundscape yields to broader participation:

> Llegó su excelencia a la iglesia mayor donde lo recibieron el clero con su vicario y curas y todas las sagradas religiones en comunidad, y la capilla entonó el *Te Deum laudamus.* Las suspendidas campanas de toda la Villa con sus tiples, tenores y contraltos en discordante armonía la atronaron con varios sones, y lo mismo ejecutaban los atabales, tambores, chirimías, clarines y otros sin número instrumentos de los indios, ayudando a la bulla el estruendo militar, la grita y voces. (*Historia* 3: 49)

> His Excellency reached the principal church, where he was received by the clergy with their vicar and priests and members of all the city's religious communities, and the choir sang the *Te Deum laudamus*. The bells hanging in the city's churches, with their soprano, tenor, and contralto voices in discordant harmony, rang out the Te Deum in their respective registers, all echoed by the sound of kettledrums, snaredrums, hornpipes, trumpets, and innumerable other instruments [of] the Indians; and the noise made by the soldiers and the roar of the crowd added to the din. (*Tales* 189–90)

Here the "discordant harmony" reflects the actual discord among the various sectors of Potosí's population – in particular, between the Creole-controlled *cabildo* and the crown-appointed officials (the *corregidor* and the viceroy himself), whom Arzáns criticizes quite pointedly elsewhere in the chapter.[9] The sounds of "innumerable" indigenous instruments also compete with the church bells and choir at this climactic moment of the viceroy's reception – the arrival at the *iglesia mayor* – yielding not a mixture that blends harmoniously, but one in which difference can still be heard. The sonic disharmony can serve to remind us that participation in the ceremonial entry was not united around the single objective of glorifying and demonstrating subservience to the arriving figure of authority.

By including "el estruendo militar, la grita y voces" (the military racket, the shouting and voices) (3: 49) in his account of the entry, Arzáns also shows the festive soundscape to encompass much more than music. Here and in other festivals narrated by Arzáns, the "murmurings of the restless crowd" (*Tales* 188) are not always drowned out by the singing and musical instruments, whether European or indigenous. For example, a 1641 wedding celebration included the performance of a theatrical work, *Prosperidad y ruina de los ingas del Perú* (Prosperity and Ruin of the Incas of Peru), whose plot concludes with the controversial execution of the last Inca sovereign, Tupac Amaru, by Viceroy Toledo (*Historia* 2: 86). Arzáns calls it "muy aplaudida tanto por la nueva de ella cuanto por los verdaderos e inauditos sucesos que en ella se representaron" (highly praised, both for its newness and for the true and unheard of events that were represented in it); the response of the indigenous audience was even more vocal and expressive: "Para los indios fue de mucho sentimiento levantando grandes alaridos conforme se declaraban" (for the Indians it was very sorrowful, and they raised great cries as it was declared) (2: 86–7).

According to Arzáns, similar exclamations had been heard in 1560 when the death of Carlos V was announced in Potosí: "recibieron las noticias con muchas demostraciones de sentimiento, particularmente los indios, pues se señalaron dando grandes alaridos por las calles y plazas, diciendo en su idioma que era muerto su rey, su señor y su Carlos" (they received the news with many demonstrations of sentiment, particularly the Indians, for they stood out by giving great cries in the streets and plazas, saying in their language that their king, their lord and their Carlos was dead) (*Historia* 1: 111). Although Arzáns portrays the Indians' "grandes alaridos" (great cries) as a sign of veneration for the Spanish king, he also points out that the Spanish authorities were nervous about their participation in the funeral procession, "porque no mezclasen en aquel sentimiento algunas ceremonias y supersticiones que en semejantes funciones suelen hacer con sus señores e ingas" (so that they would not mix in that sentiment some ceremonies and superstitions that in similar functions they normally do for their Lords and Incas) (*Historia* 1: 111).[10] Obviously, indigenous participation in ceremonies was not just a means of evangelization and subjugation, since it could lead – as in this case – to interpretations and responses that were not subject to Spanish control. Even during Arzáns's lifetime, the defeated Inca sovereign continued to elicit public demonstrations of sorrow during festivals. When describing Atahuallpa's costume in a 1555 festival, Arzáns alludes to the continuing relevance of this figure to the indigenous population: "hasta en estos tiempos es tenido en mucho de los indios, como lo demuestran cuando ven sus retratos" (even in these times he is highly respected by these Indians, as they demonstrate when they see his portraits) (Historia 1: 99). The "grandes alaridos" (great cries) that Arzáns may have heard on this occasion were just one of the multiple ways that indigenous peoples contributed to the festive soundscapes of Potosí. While more melodious than the "alaridos" to Spanish ears, indigenous singing and instrument-playing may have been equally dissonant in meaning and function, challenging the festivals' expression of harmonious concord and unified reverence for Spanish and Christian authority.

Mariana

Subaltern musical performances also fill the festive soundscape in a ceremonial entry into Mariana, Minas Gerais, in 1745. Nearly three decades after the archbishop-viceroy's entrance into Potosí, the newly designated city of Mariana was made the seat of a new diocese, and Frei Manuel da Cruz – then bishop of the northern province of Maranhão – was appointed as the region's first bishop. The solemn entry of Manuel da Cruz, which finally occurred in 1748, was recorded in an anonymous account published in Lisbon in 1749, entitled *Áureo Throno Episcopal* (Golden Episcopal Throne).[11] In contrast to Potosí, in Minas Gerais it was Africans and their descendants who constituted the vast majority of the mining workforce (mostly as slave labour), and they participated actively in the baroque festive culture of the region, particularly through the institution of black and mulatto lay religious brotherhoods. The best-known and most prestigious of these was the Black Brotherhood of Our Lady of the Rosary, which had sponsored the publication of an earlier festival account in Minas Gerais, Simão Ferreira Machado's *Triunfo Eucharístico* (Eucharistic Triumph) (1734).[12] The celebration of the feast day of Our Lady of the Rosary by this brotherhood involved the coronation of an African king and queen and a procession with music and dancing, which, as Cécile Fromont has shown, have festive precedents in the Central African Kingdom of Kongo.[13]

The Black Brotherhood of the Rosary does not feature prominently in the bishop's entry (though there are allusions to its festive practices, as we will see). What the anonymous author of *Áureo Throno* emphasizes about African participation, instead, is similar to Juan de la Torre's portrayal of the indigenous reception of the archbishop-viceroy in *Aclamación festiva*. The bishop is so universally well loved, the anonymous author writes, "que até os proprios pretos em sinal do seu sincero reconhecimento, e obediencia se tem convocado com galantaria a virem dos Arraiaes de fóra, e de partes distantes, repartidos pelos dias Santos, a trazer cada hum seu esteio de lenha" (that even the blacks, as a sign of their sincere recognition and obedience, have gallantly agreed to come from the mining camps and distant parts, divided according to the saint's days, to bring each one their bundle of wood) (430). The groups divided into "saint's days" may refer to different black and mulatto brotherhoods, named after patron saints and responsible for the celebration of their feast day (besides Our Lady of the Rosary, they included St Benedict, Our Lady of Mercy, Our Lady of Amparo, among others).[14] The anonymous author does not hesitate to offer an interpretation – similar to that of Juan de la Torre – of this festive reception of the bishop:

> E he para admirar o concurso, que se ajunta de cada repartição, entrando pela Cidade formados em duas alas, com bandeiras, tambores, e instrumentos, e cantos

> a seu modo, e se encaminhão ao Palacio de S. Excellencia, e em hum pateo largão a lenha, que em grande quantidade tem conduzido. He inexplicavel o contentamento, que recebem, em S. Excellencia lhes apparecer, a cuja vista se põem todos de joelho debaixo das janellas, e com as mãos levantadas ao Ceo pedem com grandes vivas, e alegrias a benção, que Sua Excellencia lhes dá mandando tambem repartir por todos muitas veronicas de Santos, que elle aceitão com grande devoção. (430–1)

> And one must admire the crowd that gathers from each district, entering the City formed in two wings, with flags, drums, instruments, and songs in their manner, and they direct themselves to the Palace of His Excellency, and on a patio they leave their wood, which they have brought in great quantity. The contentment they receive when His Excellency appears before them is unfathomable, and at his sight they all kneel down under the windows, and with their hands raised to Heaven they ask for a blessing with great shouts of "long live" and "rejoice," which His Excellency gives to them, as well as orders that many images of saints be distributed among them all, which they accept with great devotion. (My trans.)

In this distant antecedent of modern *alas* – the groups within samba schools that parade with the same costumes during Brazil's Carnaval – the blacks render their gift of wood as well as a sonic offering of songs, drums, and shouts to the new bishop. In return, they receive a Christian blessing and images of Catholic devotion. For the author of *Áureo Throno*, this unequal performative exchange serves to demonstrate the triumph of Christianity and the devotion of all sectors of the population to the new bishop.

Other musical performances in the bishop's entry allow for a rather different interpretation. The first triumphal chariot in the procession is pulled by seven masked figures, who

> se occupavão [...] em varias danças, e cantos compostos ao modo dos pretos, que taes representavão nas feições, e cor das mascaras [...]. A mais passava a destreza dos ditos mascaras; porque em outras occasiões formavão gravemente entre si hum Coro de musica, que a solos, e a cheios respondião, e acompahavão o Coro superior. (441–2)

> were occupied with various dances and songs composed in the manner of the blacks, for that is what the features and colour of their masks represented. [...] The skill of these masked figures surpassed all, because on other occasions they gravely formed a musical choir, which the superior Chorus responded to and accompanied with solos and in full chorus. (My trans.)

The description of the chorus seems to refer to the "call-and-response" style of African music, corroborating the songs' identification as "composed in the manner of the blacks."[15] Although the masks hide the identity of the singers, the references to the skill and gravity of the chorus suggest it was more than a farcical, caricatured performance, as in nineteenth-century "blackface."

Áureo Throno attributes more levity to one of the other dances, which was also performed in disguise – but this time by individuals whose African ancestry is clearly identified in the text. The anonymous author calls it a "dança de Carijós, ou gentio da terra" (dance of the Carijó Indians, or natives of the land) but points out that it was actually represented by "onze mulatinhos de idade juvenile" (eleven little mulattos of young age) (454).[16] Dedicating a full paragraph to this dance, *Áureo Throno* describes the young mulattos' appearance – naked from the waist up, with feathered skirts and headdresses as well as ribbons and rattles tied to their arms and legs – and relates how they danced and sang "celebres toadas ao som de tamboril, flautas, e pifaros pastorís tocados por outros Carijós mais adultos" (popular tunes to the sound of tambourines, flutes, and rustic fifes played by other, more adult Carijós) (455; my trans.). *Áureo Throno* highlights the crowd's amusement at the verisimilitude of the performance: "na grosseria natural dos gestos excitavão motivo de grande jocosidade" (the natural coarseness of the gestures provoked great jocularity) (455; my trans.). In contrast to the gravity of the masked figures singing *like* blacks, the mulattos' performance as Indians appears to elicit laughter.

In her study of the Black Brotherhood of the Rosary in Minas Gerais, Elizabeth Kiddy compares the description of the "mulatto Carijós" to some figures in the late eighteenth-century watercolours by the Italian artist and soldier Carlos Julião, which depict the celebration of an African King and Queen on the feast day of Our Lady of the Rosary (Figure 12.4) (131).[17] Julião's musicians do not don the same feathered skirts or arm and leg ornaments, but they do wear feathered headdresses and play tambourines, among other instruments, while their dark, tight shirts evoke the nude trunks of the "mulatto Carijós."[18] Kiddy also points out the resemblance of the Julião images to one of the "congado" groups – known as "caboclos" or "caboclinhos," in reference to their indigenous costume – which accompany the African king and queen in the Rosary festivals in some areas of Minas Gerais today (131).[19] For her part, Cécile Fromont has compared the Julião images to two watercolours that depict ritual performances involving African sovereigns in the Kingdom of Kongo, also created by an Italian artist. Fromont highlights the similarities in terms of the costumes, gestures, and instruments:

> Bringing these images together highlights visual, gestural, and material resonances that give further substance to the central African dimension of the election and festive celebrations of black kings in Brazil. Point by point correspondences in the regalia,

Figure 12.4. "Black King Festival" (c. 1770) by Carlos Julião. In *Riscos illuminados de figurinhos de brancos e negros dos uzos do Rio de Janeiro e Serro do Frio.* Fundação Biblioteca Nacional, Rio de Janeiro, Brazil, Iconografía C.1.2.8.

musical instruments, and choreographies deployed in contemporaneous performances on either side of the Atlantic offer an evocative portrait of cultural continuity. (194)

Just as indigenous Andeans adapted Inca regalia and rituals from pre-Hispanic celebrations in Cuzco to Christian festivals in Potosí, so too did Africans bring performance practices and representations of sovereignty from their places of origin – including the already Christianized Kingdom of Kongo in Central Africa – when they were forcibly relocated to Minas Gerais. In both mining regions it was not only European immigrants who brought their music with them: those who were forced to migrate, whether because of the mita or slavery, also contributed to the festive soundscape with their own traditions.

The performance of the "mulatto Carijós" thus suggests an alternative avenue of interpretation to the one ascribed by the author to the blacks' "gift of wood" – that is, a demonstration of subservience and a confirmation of the triumph of Christianity. Instead, Afro-Brazilian spectators at the bishop's entry may have been reminded of the festive coronation of African sovereigns, performed annually by the Black Brotherhood of the Rosary of Mariana, when viewing the dance of the "mulatto Carijós" as well as the earlier procession of blacks with flags, drums, instruments, and songs "in their manner." Perhaps these performers were even making an intentional allusion to the Rosary festival and its celebration of African sovereignty. In this sense, they may have viewed their participation in the bishop's entry as a proud assertion of a distinct identity and festive tradition – both Christian and African in inspiration – rather than as a sign of comic debasement, misrecognition (of mulattos as Indians), or subservience. But this assertion would be evident to us only if we look past their indigenous (Carijó) disguise and attend to the sounds of their performance. In the case of the mulatto Carijós, the songs and rhythms point even more strongly to their African heritage than their appearance does.

Like the account of Archbishop-Viceroy Morcillo's entry in de la Torre's *Aclamación festiva* and Arzáns's *Historia de la Villa Imperial de Potosí*, *Áureo Throno* certainly privileges visual description of the magnificent costumes, floats, and triumphal arches, which are literally adorned with and symbolically evoke the vast mineral wealth of these towns and regions. In the introduction to his modern edition of *Áureo Throno Episcopal*, Affonso Ávila dedicates a full thirty-page chapter to the "primacy of the visual in the Baroque culture of Minas Gerais" (85; my trans.). Nevertheless, the grandiose festivals in the mining towns of Minas Gerais as well as Potosí sought to impress all of the senses. And while the other senses are readily discriminatory – distinguishing between those who could see the procession from a choice spot on a balcony and those who could not; between those who could feel the rich fabrics of silk and velvet on their skin and those who could not; between those who were invited to the banquets and those who were not – the festive soundscape may have been more egalitarian, less dependent on position and proximity. Yet surely not everyone heard the same thing. Music and festivals may have been understood as an effective means of indoctrinating and acculturating those who were new to the Catholic faith, whether indigenous or African; but the instruments, tunes, and rhythms of musical performances in festivals echoed other traditions and identities and sometimes served other goals.

NOTES

1 I discuss the festivals of colonial Potosí and Minas Gerais more broadly in *Spectacular Wealth*. Some of the following material is adapted from chapters 3 and 4 of that book.

2 Baker makes a similar point in relation to the series of paintings depicting Corpus Christi processions in colonial Cuzco, which feature musicians playing European

instruments and singing polyphony (37–8, 53–5): "The implication of these paintings is that in the context of Corpus Christi in mid-colonial Cuzco, difference was performed visually, through ceremonial dress and headwear, whereas assimilation was performed musically" (*Imposing* 55). Although this "series of paintings tells us nothing [...] about 'traditional' Andean music making," Baker points out, "contemporary chroniclers prove more useful" (39).

3 I cite the translation of a portion of Arzáns's narrative of the entry in *Tales of Potosí*, indicating my amendments with brackets. The painting depicts the "murmurings of the restless crowd" in the speech scrolls of two observers on the bottom foreground of the canvas, to the right of the painter's self-portrait: "Hija pilonga as bisto tal marabilla" (Old girl, have you seen this marvel?), asks the elderly man, whose indigenous female companion responds, "Alucho en cientoitantos años no e bisto grandeza tamaña" (I swear that in 100-some years I have not seen such grandeur). Unless indicated by a citation of *Tales*, all translations from *Historia* are mine.

4 This *loa* is transcribed in *Aclamación festiva* 12r–14r.

5 This *loa* is transcribed in *Aclamación festiva* 20r–25v.

6 Thomas A. Abercrombie describes how the *capitanías*'s basis in pre-Hispanic provinces allowed native lords to "reintegrate" their rule and to preserve some of the festive practices (especially drinking) that were part of mita "pilgrimages" under Inca administration, as Potosí became the "new center of the Andean world" (230–6).

7 Spalding defines *ayllu*, the smallest administrative unit of Andean society, after the household (24), as a "group of kin that held land as a corporate unit" (48). *Ayllus* were nested in larger administrative units, from *pachacas* (groups of 100 households) to *waranqas* (1,000 households) (49).

8 Garcilaso narrates "una pendencia particular que los indios tuvieron en una fiesta de [Corpus Christi]" (a particular quarrel that the Indians had in a festival of Corpus Christi) in Book 8, chapter 1 of the *Historia general del Perú* (General History of Peru) (1617) (2: 785–9); on this interethnic dispute between Incas and Cañaris, which invokes the memory of historical conflict between the groups, see Dean (179–99).

9 For the critique of the *corregidor* and the archbishop-viceroy see Voigt (283–5).

10 For a description of the lamentations, dirges, and sad songs performed in burial ceremonies for lords and Incas see Cobo (250–1).

11 The full title is: *Áureo Throno Episcopal, collocado nas Minas do Ouro, ou Notica breve da Creação do novo Bispado Marianense, da sua felicíssima posse, e pomposa entrada do seu meritíssimo, primeiro Bispo, e da jornada, que fez do Maranhão, o Excellentíssimo, e Reverendíssimo Senhor D. Frei Manoel da Cruz* (Golden Episcopal Throne, established in the Gold Mines, or brief Notice of the Creation of the new Bishopric of Mariana, of the most joyful investiture and pompous entrance of the worthiest first Bishop, and of the journey from Maranhão made by the most Excellent and most Reverend Lord Father Manoel da Cruz). All translations from this text are my own.

12 On the black brotherhoods in Minas Gerais, see Borges, who lists forty-six branches of the Black Brotherhood of the Rosary in Minas Gerais, founded between 1715 and 1820 (225–8). Boschi mentions sixty Rosary chapters, which together represent by far the greatest quantity – 19.31 per cent – of all thirty-three lay brotherhoods in Minas Gerais (187, 195–8).

13 On the festival of Our Lady of the Rosary in Minas Gerais, from colonial times to the present, see Kiddy; on the festive coronation of African sovereigns in Brazil more generally, see Souza.

14 For a list of the black brotherhoods active in Minas Gerais, see Mulvey (277–9); chapters of the Black Brotherhood of the Rosary are by far the most common, but she includes several others.

15 See Tinhorão, 113.

16 *Carijó* was originally designated Guaraní Indian, but later came to denote a person of mixed white and Amerindian blood. John Monteiro points out that at the beginning of the eighteenth century the term acquired a generic sense and could connote "enslaved Indian," deriving from the prevalence of captured Guaranís as a result of the *bandeirantes'* slaving expeditions in São Paulo (166).

17 Julião's images are collected in a portfolio entitled *Riscos iluminados de figurinhos de Brancos e Negros dos Uzos do Rio de Janeiro e Serro do Frio* (Sketches of Figures Illustrating the Customs of Whites and Blacks in Rio de Janeiro and Serro do Frio).

18 For other descriptions of "tight, dark clothing" used to feign nudity in performances of African or indigenous identity see João Sardinha Mimoso, *Relacion de la real tragicomedia* (Relation of Royal Tragicomedy), 57v; Sotério da Silva Ribeiro, *Súmula Triunfal* (Triumphal Summary), 33. In Mimoso's text, which transcribes a play performed for the entry of Philip III into Lisbon in 1619, the description of a Brazilian king's costume closely resembles that of the "mulatto Carijós": "El Brasil sobre un vestido justo de color de negra carne, trahia en la cabeça una guirnalda de plumas de papagayos, ceñiase con un faldon dellas, y en los braços e piernas trahia lo mismo" (With a tight costume the colour of black flesh, Brazil wore a garland of parrot feathers on his head, a skirt of feathers around his waist, and the same thing on his arms and legs) (57v; my trans.).

19 As Kiddy explains, *congados* are the groups that participate in the Rosary festival: "Historically the groups were referred to as the 'ambassadors' to the king of Congo, and today they play an important role in escorting the royalty of the festival to different locations" (260). She glosses *caboclo* or *caboclinho* thus: "The term *caboclo* refers literally to a person with mixed Indian and Portuguese heritage. It can aslo mean a country bumpkin. In Minas Gerais the name refers to one of the congado groups that are found mostly in northern Minas Geras. The dancers and musicians wear headdresses of brightly colored feathers and snap their bows and arrows in syncopated rhythms as they dance" (259).

PART FIVE

Sensing the Urban

13 Celestial Visions and Demonic Touch: García's Inventions in *La verdad sospechosa*

FREDERICK A. DE ARMAS

Don García's many lies and fabrications in Ruiz de Alarcón's *La verdad sospechosa* (*The Truth Can't Be Trusted*)[1] partake of astonishing rhetorical *inventio* as well as pointing to new inventions and ancient techniques.[2] His fictive tales are replete with images that evoke the senses. As the stories are heard, those listening would be struck in particular by the visual and tactile elements. Thus, at least three of the senses are manipulated so as to make the lie seem tangible. Alarcón's play has triggered an ongoing critical debate on the significance of the protagonist's propensity to lie. Throughout the work Don García is repeatedly fashioning a false image of his character and background, his valorous deeds, his amorous exploits, and his love for a woman whose name he confuses with another.[3] The purpose of this essay is to come to a better understanding of the sense and the sensory elements of the lies, arguing that both are related also to the causes of his *inventio*. And indeed, according to Sebastián de Covarrubias, to invent is not only to create something new but has as a secondary meaning to lie.[4]

The wondrous materiality of Garcia's imagined scenes evokes the saturation of all five senses in the urban spaces of seventeenth-century Spain.[5] At court, newness was avidly sought through gossip, ostentation, and even inventions such as new stage machinery in plays and new objects of display – from coaches to personal clocks. As the senses become overloaded, the humours (choleric, melancholic, phlegmatic, and sanguine), the four substances that were believed at the time to be crucial in the health of a person, could easily become deranged through excessive input, and they in turn could affect the senses.[6] The link between inventions, the senses, the four humours, and even the four elements, I will argue, allows us to understand García's excessive, mendacious, and sensory fabrications.[7] The element of fire, connected to García's choleric disposition, exacerbates his imagination and leads him to trick and deceive. It also leads him to imagine fiery things, from the stars in the heavens to the more demonic fires of gunpowder as used in fireworks and pistols.[8] Although his verbal magic seduces through the sense of hearing and creates wonderment, while it seeks to show the brilliance of the sky and of his mind, it also hides the anxieties of viewing a cosmos that no longer conforms to ancient authorities and a self that wills to turn away from sight to the lower senses. In a misguided attempt to balance his body and mind he seeks the opposite of choler, fire, and sight. In Pythagorean and Galenic theories this would involve the humour labelled as melancholy, the element of earth, and the sense of touch. But touch, as he will discover, is also considered the highest of the senses in the new art of fencing. Thus, towards the end of the play, his imagination turns in this direction. A key metaphor in García's world will be the telescope, which turns a brilliant celestial orb into an imperfect and tangible object.

As political and ecclesiastical authorities sought to exercise control through constant vigilance and public punishments, and as elements of material culture attempted to "reinforce" and mirror prevalent ideologies,[9] Alarcón sought to stage the allure of the senses and the ease with which a brilliant mind can move from the celestial to the demonic and from sight to touch. While eccentric subjectivities were countered, as Anthony Cascardi explains, through technologies of self-discipline, a repression directed at the inner self (116–18), Alarcón embraced extreme sensuality; and as "those powers that could act upon the will" (122–3) were labelled as demonic, Alarcón foregrounded a demonic will to fame. Although his defiance appears diabolical, his intent is also magical: to act through words, to make material his illusory magic, and to bring this contagion to others through a sensory overload.[10]

The beginning of the work tells of the heat and dryness of summer and how it affected his journey from Salamanca to Madrid (vv. 3–8). Because he had completed his studies at the university, the quality of dryness is further accentuated, since it was known that excessive reading had a drying influence. These factors seem to point to Don García's having an excess of the choleric humour, which in itself is made up of two qualities: heat and dryness. Although it is possible to see García, as Ricardo Castells has done, as suffering from love melancholy, I believe that these are qualities he seeks in his fabrications to unintentionally balance the humours and elements of his self. I think it appropriate to diagnose García as having the kind of heated or choleric *ingenio* or wit that leads to the prolific imagination and *inventio* of the poet and the artist.[11] Indeed, the subtlety of García's wit is praised repeatedly in the play. Tristán affirms: "Tiene un ingenio excelente / con pensamientos sutiles" (He's got a great imagination, / A wonderful sense of fine detail) (vv. 1237–8), and García is well aware of this trait: "Agora os he menester, / sutilezas de mi ingenio" (Come on, imagination, lend / Me now your finest subtlety) (vv. 1522–3).

Alarcón's play is carefully constructed so as to foreground García's wit or *ingenio* and the *inventio* that echoes it. He is quite vocal about his desires: he has come to court to shine, to be fiery. This desire is in line with the excess of choler. To accomplish his aims, he relies on his disposition towards invention: rather than composing poems or plays, he invents astonishing lies, which transform the world creating brilliant objects that others wish to view or touch as they listen to his amazing words (hearing). Even at the court, a place that is brimming with sensory stimulation, he can arouse *admiratio*. There are a total of ten major lies in the play, four taking place in the first act and four in the last one. The central *jornada* (act) feature only two.[12] Of these ten fabrications, three, one in each act, are of great length and complexity: the illusory banquet, the false marriage, and the imaginary duel. To underline their importance, the play includes them in very lengthy *relaciones* (accounts) where García resorts to the *romance* verse form. I will then focus primarily on these three lies in order to show the brilliance of his fiery *invention*, his use of material inventions, the sensual nature of their appeal, and the move from sight to touch.

At the court García's choleric disposition, filled with brilliance and fire, is contaminated by a location that already is bursting with sensory stimuli and thus furthers his own imbalance. From the start, García's imagination is related to fire, the element that controls him. This fiery brilliance is also encountered in his squire/servant Tristán, who uses it to admonish and teach. It is through the lenses of sight and fire that Tristán views the women at court:

Resplandecen damas bellas
En el cortesano suelo
De la suerte que en el cielo
Resplandecen las estrellas.

Beautiful women are permanent / Fixtures here. Against the fine / Background of the court, they glitter and shine / Like the brightest stars in the firmament (vv. 293–6)

For Alan K.G. Paterson, this is "the art of supercharging reality" as seen at the court (363). Indeed, this type of comparison is found with some frequency in poems and plays of the period.[13] In *La estrella de Sevilla* (The Star of Seville), for example, the king, as he enters the city views the seven women standing in their balconies as the seven Ptolemaic planets.[14] These women, then, are praised as celestial beings, an analogy that was common in the period. Although Tristán's imagination is suffused with vision and brilliance as he turns to the fiery skies, thus echoing his fiery disposition, his analogical thinking is not there to idealize. He actually denigrates the heavenly bodies, since their earthly counterparts are no longer the beautiful women of the court, but courtesans.[15] These verses foreground the opposition between sight and touch, the heavenly vision and the allure of the body/object of desire, which recurs throughout the play. Although Tristán carefully arranges the women/stars by categories, most likely following the inventory found in his memory and a basis for *inventio*, his analogies cast a shadow on the heavens at a time when new discoveries, including the telescope, were casting doubt on the harmony of the spheres, on the perfection of the skies.

Don García, already prone to the fiery, is contaminated by Tristán's astrological usage but begins by making a more commonplace description when he praises Jacinta's "divino resplandor" (what a divine whiteness) (v. 377) as her eyes shoot arrows of love and death. Once again, speech (hearing) brings together fire (sight/splendour) and earth (touch/arrows, albeit metaphorical ones). Tristán amplifies the field of analogy when he describes a carriage in which don García's beloved travels as a "coche del sol" (a coach fit for the sun) (v. 384). García has travelled under the sun all the way from Salamanca, exacerbating his choleric humour, and now he is faced with a sensory image at court that reverberates with his own disposition: a coach or celestial carriage carrying the most beautiful of women. Selecting one of the two, he swears that no other lady at court would shine as brightly, to which Tristán replies: "Mirarlos ya con antojos / que hacen las cosas mayores" (Things always look better than they are / When you look at them through love-tinted glasses) (vv. 403–4). The invention of eyeglasses made objects appear larger and closer. Eyeglasses were first crafted in Venice in the thirteenth century, the ideal place for such a discovery, since the uses of glass have always been one of their trademarks (García Santo-Tomás, "Fortunes" 61). Enrique García Santo-Tomás has shown that they acquired a moral aspect in the literature of the seventeenth century, starting with Boccalini's *Ragguagli di Parnaso* (News-sheet from Parnassus) (1612) and then moving through a number of Spanish works: "In depicting the corrective power of glass, Boccalini thus creates a literary template for an intersection of optics with morals" ("Fortunes" 61). In addition, let us recall that the telescope was not invented until the seventeenth century, when it was thought to turn the eyeglasses towards the heavens. Eyeglasses/telescopes will make the imperfections in the skies reflect human foibles and vice versa.[16] In this instance, Tristán seems to be conflating the two senses of *anteojos*: eyeglasses to see the woman and the telescope to see the sky. We would expect his speech to include a moralistic element, since he had already warned García about courtesans through the use of celestial analogies. But in this case he is simply following the continued analogies between sky and earth, sight and touch. Thus, what seems to the point is that both servant and master are now of one mind in that the eyeglasses or telescope bring the beautiful objects closer. They beckon to be touched.

As Jacinta trips when emerging from her carriage, don García is able to support her by giving her his hand. Once again we are faced with the new sensuousness of the cityscape. Coaches and carriages, as García Santo-Tomas has noted: "ejercen un proceso de desplazamiento y/o sustitución de la arquitectura urbana mediante sus cualidades de decoración, majestuosidad y elevación" (they exert a process of displacement and/or substitution of the urban architecture through qualities of embellishment, majesty, and elevation) (*Espacio urbano* 92). Faced with an urban invention, don García turns to myth. As Atlas he can hold her, since it is not a body that he is touching but the very heavens (v. 439). This moment solidifies in his mind an idealizing and even Neoplatonic view of woman with a notion of corporeality. There is no hint here that celestial bodies can be seen as imperfect through the new sciences. Rather, García revels in aiding and holding the perfect, a new sun.

Since the ladies are standing by a jewellery store and García wants to impress them, he immediately becomes overgenerous.[17] He pretends to be an *indiano* and thus immensely rich.[18] He is very specific about how these riches were obtained, comparing his fortune to the ones that derive from mining: "que al minado Potosí / le quito presunción" (And all my goldmines I despise, / And leave my el Dorado there) (vv. 499–500). Discovered in 1545, these South American silver mines at Potosí (located in what is today northern Bolivia) produced such riches that they became a common expression for extreme wealth or value (Elliott 399). Cervantes, for example, alludes to these mines as a referent to wealth throughout his works.[19] The mines also have several important connotations that can relate to García. Located on top of a rugged and frozen peak in the mountains, the mines required much invention and the labour of thousands of natives who were treated miserably. Many perished in this endeavour, earning the mines the name of "mouth of hell" (de Armas Wilson, *Cervantes* 90). The brilliance of his wealth and of the jewels at the store, images of light and sight, are thus contaminated with the fires of hellish mines (demonic sight) and with the labour of those who bring out the silver (touch). Further invention was needed to refine the silver with the use of mercury. The Fuggers were given the lease of the Almadén mines in Spain so that they could process these riches (de Armas Wilson, *Cervantes* 90). García, then, is not content with holding the heavens. Instead, he becomes a marker for *inventio*, for the hellish connotation of such inventions, and for a New World, a land that had to be invented in the European imaginary.

The confusion of lands, the fact that no such continent was supposed to exist, is followed by a confusion of names (recalling the confusion between India and the Indies). When Tristán asks the coachman for the name of the most beautiful of the women, he is told that she is Lucrecia de Luna. Don García cannot even conceive that the *cochero* (coachman) is naming the other lady, since Lucrecia must be the very sun and the others are mere stars. Thus, he believes he has fallen for Lucrecia de Luna, while in reality his beloved's name is Jacinta. Carolyn Nadeau explains: "García, the symbolic sun god, searches for his complement and twin, Diana, the moon goddess, who appears, not as one might think as his beloved Jacinta, but rather as Lucrecia de Luna whose surname reveals her astrological identity" ("Star-Crossed Love" 65). To this insight I would add that the moon was under scrutiny at this time. In 1610 Galileo had published *Siderius Nuncius* (*Starry Messenger*), wherein, using his telescope, he sought to prove that the moon had a rough surface with mountains much higher than those on earth. In Spain, Benito Daza de Valdés wrote *Uso de los antojos para todo género de vistas* (The Use of Eyeglasses for All Types of Sight) in 1623. He describes the uses of eyeglasses but is much more circumspect about the telescope: "There is not, however, a single mention of Galileo in these pages – Daza may have wanted to avoid upsetting his superiors in the Tribunal – despite the fact that the author quotes entire passages from Galileo" (García Santo-Tomás, "Fortunes" 64). Once again the sight of heavenly bodies is linked to the touch of the corporeal. García's imagination makes his lady like the moon, a celestial object, albeit imperfect. The new cosmology allows him to think that she is approachable, and that touch is not far removed from his desires.

When don García runs into two former friends from Salamanca, don Juan and don Félix, they are in the midst of discussing a mysterious banquet that took place by the river, where a gallant wooed his lady. The main fabrication of Act One, then, has García posing as the mysterious gallant. He begins by describing a site that reflects the sense of touch: the many trees are "olmos" or elms, a signal that love is at hand, since this arboreal figure was used in emblems that show the elm and the vine.[20] The tree (the male) gives strength and supports the vine (the woman) who embraces it. As the lady's carriage appears, the link between earth and sky is once again invoked. She arrives: "dando envidia a las estrellas" (all the stars where dimmed with envy) (v. 690). James F. Burke, who has studied this fabrication in detail, argues that it derives from the Banquet of Sense. Such a banquet contrasts with the Platonic Symposium, where man has the ability to rise above the passions and acquire knowledge of the divine: "It showed how man, through an ever increasing involvement with sensual experience, could descend through the senses until his only concern was the gratification of the lower soul. Through such a fall he would in effect become a beast or an adherent to bestial love" ("'Banquet of Sense'" 52). While the location intimates touch, the description of the banquet per se begins with the highest of senses, sight, and continues with hearing: these two senses are tied to reason and notions of ascent. The other three senses are closer to the animals, and the basest and most sinful is touch. I would add that material inventions intrude upon the symbolic, providing it with a much more alluring and problematic vision.

García begins by regaling the lady with a vision of what appears to be new lights in the heavens. This fabrication derives from a material invention: fireworks.[21] In Spain and the German lands, Charles V had fireworkers in his armies charged with celebrating victories (or creating new explosives), while in England, Elizabeth I appointed her own "Fire Master." In 1533, at the celebrations of Henry VIII's marriage to Anne Boleyn, a fire-spewing dragon dazzled the audience (Chambers 171); and in 1598, as Margaret of Austria travelled from Graz to Valencia to marry Philip III, she was treated to many festivities, including a castle in the air constructed with fireworks (n.p.). Although fireworks also marked her entrance into Madrid, they were by no means so inventive (T. Ruiz 111).[22] Thus, an invention worthy of royalty becomes part of García's poetic *inventio*. The appearance of new lights in the heavens also points to the astronomical debates that were taking place at the time: the appearance of "new stars" (novas/supernovas) in 1572 and 1603. Is García following up on previous astronomical anomalies and showing the breakdown of the fabric of the universe, the breakdown in his own desire for a perfect lady?

As García continues to describe the banquet, he moves to hearing (music), taste (food), smell, and finally touch, as he presents the woman with a jewel in the form of a man pierced by the arrows of love.[23] If the banquet shows that García, through his choleric imagination and subtle wit and invention has created a story worthy of admiration, filled with sensual elements, what is not clear is his motivation. Ricardo Castells vehemently defends García, claiming that his love for Jacinta comes from the higher senses: reason and intellect (97). I would argue that his *inventio* has to do with his desire to shine, given his choleric disposition (sight); with his desire to be heard above all the sounds and gossip at court and thus gain fame (hearing); and even with his hidden desire to possess corporeally (touch).

Soon after the banquet fabrication García reveals some of his innermost thoughts to Tristán. First of all, he believes that to be exalted at court he should make it clear that he is not a country bumpkin who goes around gawking at and admiring surprising events. If his friends are astonished by a banquet, he must not show such a feeling. Thus he utilizes the notion of *nil admirare* so prevalent among the stoics and detailed, for example, in Juan Boscán's *Respuesta a don Diego de Mendoza* (Response to don Diego de Mendoza) (Reichenberger). Borrowing from Horace's sixth epistle, García argues that *nil admirare* comes from observing the universe from above. He completely alters and corrupts this principle, since the wise man would neither lie nor show excessive passion after such a change of perspective. For García, it is simply a strategy to appear superior to others at court.[24]

García further clarifies his ambitions when he affirms that he wants to make a mark on life and does not want to live without being known or heard (v. 857); that would relegate him to being a mere beast (v. 860). Curiously, according to the Counter-Reformation, his imaginative banquet is doing precisely that. He has turned away from a Platonic symposium and has described a banquet that moves from the highest to the lowest senses, thus implying a kind of seduction of the lady that would be corporeal in the end – he is not in love with Jacinta, but is seducing and tricking others through her beauty and the magic of his enchanting fabrications. If anything, he intimates touching the lady. Thus, García is seeking not heavenly truths, but worldly satisfaction. Far from internalizing Counter-Reformation self-control, he revels in excess, albeit of the mind.

But García does not stop here. He goes further in his quest for fame at any cost. He compares his desires to those of Herostratos, who burnt the temple of Diana at Ephesus so as to attain fame. The inhabitants of Ephesus, aggrieved by this crime, forbade the naming of the culprit so that he would not succeed. Despite Ephesian efforts Herostratos is still known, as his deeds are told in ancient and modern texts from Cicero to Cervantes.[25] In recent years one thinker has sought to coin the "Herostratos syndrome" in a book entitled *Terrorism for Self-Glorification*.[26] García, then, seeks to reinforce not the traditional and aristocratic value of fame, but the more modern (albeit with ancient roots) concept of notoriety.[27] To be known, to be spoken of, is what is important – not the context. Thus, he would even burn a sacred temple to achieve fame. The notion of burning can once again be related to the heat of his passions, to his choleric disposition; and the fact that the example he uses is that of the temple of Diana recalls that the woman he thinks he loves is Lucrecia de Luna, in other words Luna/Diana. He would even sacrifice her to gain everlasting fame. His inventions push the strictures of the times towards modernity, much like physical inventions of the period destabilized the authoritative view of the cosmos and the world.

The central fabrication in the second act is equally filled with choleric *inventio*, material inventions, and the fires of fame and destruction. They mix the more commonplace astral images with astounding bits of invention. When his father announces that he has arranged a marriage for him, García comes up with a tale that he is already married. He places the story in Salamanca, so as to ground it in his own experience. Again it is the solar imagery, typical of a choleric, that predominates. In his invented story his attraction to Sancha begins with sight, as her eyes are like "dos soles" (two suns) (v. 1529). He sees her one afternoon and she is in her carriage, which he compares to that of Phaeton, the son of the sun, who fell from the heavens while attempting to drive his father's chariot. In García's image, the Eridanus of mythology becomes the river Tormes in Salamanca. So he is using a truth to lie: he had seen Jacinta/Lucrecia in what he called the carriage of the sun. The transformation from Sol (Sun) to Phaeton also comes from experience, since Jacinta had almost fallen as she got out of her carriage. Now, Sancha

Figure 13.1. Portrait of Cosimo I de Medici. Painting by Maso de San Friano (1560).

becomes a new Phaeton who falls from the sky.[28] The fall comes to represent the expectation to touch.

One night, the gallant is allowed to climb to the heavens of her rooms, but her father returns and asks her to marry another. She equivocates, and he is about to leave when García's timepiece strikes midnight. According to Daniel L. Heiple, the mechanical clock was introduced into homes in the sixteenth century (*Mechanical Imagery* 115). Smaller timepieces that could be carried soon ensued. The oldest depiction is found in a portrait of the Florentine Cosimo I de Medici painted by Maso de San Friano around 1560 (Figure 13.1). Very much like the banquet scene, where material inventions such as fireworks give weight to the poetic invention, here material inventions are also key. In this case they serve to create suspense and signal danger to the lovers.[29] While the watch seems innocuous enough, it surprises them when it strikes midnight. The hour itself was considered a malefic sign, a time for demonic apparitions, and even Cervantes uses it to create fear when the knight and his squire enter El Toboso.[30] As García rushes to give Sancha the timepiece, which her now curious father demands to see, a second accident takes place. On giving it to her, García fires his pistol by mistake.[31] A second invention is thus introduced in this poetic *inventio*, and it too has demonic associations – gunpowder was derided by many as an infernal discovery. It smelled of brimstone or sulphur, thus evoking Satan and his hellish abode. Gunpowder, of course, also is tied to the fireworks of García's first fabrication, Renaissance and seventeenth-century fire-makers often developing powders for spectacles and for warfare. They could be used in dramatic spectacles, in celebrations of victory and peace, and in fierce sieges and bloody wars.[32] The term "pistol," in the fifteenth century, still referred to small, concealed daggers, although firearms had existed in Europe since the previous century. The personal firing weapon slowly developed in Spain during the sixteenth century, acquiring the name of *pistola* or *pistolete* (pistol). Thus, the small individual weapon was still a relatively new invention when it appears in Alarcón. The two material inventions in García's second major lie underline the fiery and unorthodox imagination of this figure. But they also present a meditation on the senses. The clock striking midnight represents a warning to the gallant through the sense of hearing, while the pistol going off calls on sulphur, the sense of smell, which is a second warning. It is as if García's own inventions and imaginings are telling him not to touch, not to make of his beloved Luna a fetish, an object, an imperfection that he can defile.

Could García's invention have gone so far as to imagine a clock mechanism that led a gun to fire? If so, it seems to have misfired in his inventive tale.[33] A malfunctioning clock was often labelled a *reloj desconcertado*.[34] This expression was also applied to a person who acted without reason or decorum. It is as if García is blaming himself for the situation, which is, of course, fictional. García seeks to amaze by breaking with the expected, by becoming a *reloj desconcertado* that surprises all around him.

The third act exhibits the third main lie by Don García. He is now so involved in his fabrications that this one has little purpose and is told to his tutor, Tristán. It is as if he wants him to know that he has mastered the arts of rhetoric to such an extent that his sophistries will be taken for truth. García tells him that he had duelled with Don Juan. While his opponent was at first saved by an Agnus Dei that he was wearing, García's expert swordsmanship eventually led to don Juan's death: the sword opened his head and his brains spilled on the ground (vv. 2714–73). In this tale García is undermining the chivalric qualities of don Juan: since the Middle Ages it was frowned upon to wear relics or amulets, including the *Agnus Dei*, during a duel. At the same time García follows the rules of the new type of fencing, the *destreza matemática* (geometrical fencing). The scientific art of fencing came into vogue with Jerónimo Sánchez de Carranza and was further popularized (with some changes) by his student Luis Pacheco de Narváez in his famous book *Libro de las grandezas de la espada*

(Book of the Greatness of the Sword) as well as in many other treatises.[35] In his description of the imaginary duel García introduces many terms from Pacheco such as "elegí mi medio" (I seek the mean of proportion) (v. 2734) and "grados del perfil" (degrees of profile) (v. 2736). These terms echo the fencing treatise wherein Pacheco underlines mathematical elements such as how far one should be from the opponent, what part of the sword one should use, and so on. Furthermore, Pacheco makes use of the notion that the tip is the feeblest part of the sword, while the further inward you go, the stronger is the power of the weapon. García is quite aware of the weakness of the tip: "vino, tirando una punta: / mas yo por la parte flaca / cogí su espada" (he came thrusting and I took his sword by the weak [end of the blade]) (vv. 2744–6). García's *destreza* (fencing) is such that he wins the duel.

The lengthy description of the duel and the clear use of Pacheco are of importance here, since García seeks to change in the hierarchy of the senses. Pacheco explains that touch is the most important of the senses for the swordsman: "El principal es el tacto, uno de los más principales sentidos del hombre, cuyos efectos en Destreza son milagrosos" (The main is the touch, one of the most important of the senses, whose effects in Fencing are miraculous) (*Libro* 271r). He adds that touch is the most important sense for survival, since: "por parecer de Aristóteles, que cualquier animal, privado del tacto morirá necesariamente: y así mismo que el hombre tiene más cierto el tacto que los otros sentidos" (according to Aristotle, any animal deprived from the sense of touch will necessarily die: likewise, for men the sense of touch is more developed than the any other sense) (*Libro* 271r). Here, Pacheco goes further, claiming that touch is more important than other senses, given that it is the most reliable. Thus, García, echoing Pacheco, could be attempting to demonstrate that the lowest of senses in the Platonic hierarchy can be the highest. Curiously, Pacheco often cites Plato and his translator Marsilio Ficino in order to discuss proportion and number.[36] Through Pacheco and his Platonist citations, García's new tactile "inventions" acquire authority. These inventions are also important, since in his imagination he kills his opponent don Juan and perhaps even deserves to touch/feel the lady of his dreams. García, then, is so carried away by his invention that he swerves from Pacheco, who stresses the Christian side of fencing. For Pacheco, swordsmanship is not the art of killing but the art of being able to kill. Thus, it is best to disarm the opponent rather than to kill.[37] Even though García is using the "newest" invention on how to duel, and even though this invention is highly Christianized, it is important to stress that García is the negative force in this quarrel – his opponent was saved by an Agnus Dei, a sacred object and Christian symbol of sacrifice.[38] This sacramental object was supposed to protect from evil spirits and sudden death. García, in his imagined feat, has triumphed against an apotropaic symbol of the Church. His touch has become deadly and malefic while using, paradoxically, a treatise that asserts that touch is the highest and most reliable of the senses.

But Don García is not quite finished with his demonic inventions. Immediately after he tells this tale, don Juan appears in perfect health. To cover up his lie, García claims that his opponent has been cured by an *ensalmo*. When Tristán questions him, García asserts that he has seen a man whose back and arm were cut and put back together with an *ensalmo*, and that he himself knows this ritual (vv. 2790–9). An *ensalmo*, a potion and prayer used to cure the sick was a practice forbidden by the Church.[39] In his 1538 treatise Pedro Ciruelo, writing against all superstitions, dedicates a whole chapter to the *ensalmadores* who perform these cures. He exhorts those who have suffered wounds and other physical traumas to go to doctors and pharmacists and to pray to God. At no point is the wounded to resort to *ensalmos*, which are of two kinds of words alone and of words and substances (Ciruelo 80). Such words incur the sin of blasphemy, since they obtain their power from the devil. Don García, then, is once again invoking the demonic and heterodox. All his techniques form a spectrum that reveals the range from the most recent technologies to ancient magics.

When Tristán, amazed at what an *ensalmo* can do, asks don García to teach him, the *galán* replies: "Está en diccciones hebraycas, / y si no sabes la lengua, / no has de saber pronunciarlas" (The thing's in Hebrew, I'm afraid, / So if you don't know that, you won't / Know how the incantation's sung) (vv. 2805–7). Don García is delving deep into the forbidden. *Conversos* and *moriscos* were famous for their *ensalmos*,[40] and there were prohibited books containing specific words to be pronounced in Spanish, Latin, Hebrew, or Arabic. García brags that his Hebrew is excellent (he claims to speak ten languages), thus arousing suspicion that he is a New Christian who has reverted to the practices of his ancestors; and all this is in addition to having committed a mortal sin by using ensalmos. Hearing, considered one of the highest senses, is here subverted and used in a lie about a forbidden practice. It is as if García has not heard the clock striking midnight; he has not heard his own inner warnings. García has used the senses to rise above the court, to fabricate greater splendours, to seek new inventions that bring him closer to the heaven of his desires, both the brilliance of airy fame and the woman he seeks to embrace (touch). Although his desires seem boundless, embracing all the senses, he seeks to rule them by placing himself above their hierarchy – sight seems as important as touch. In the end his punishment is suspect, since he will be able have them all, albeit with the "wrong" woman. His final restraint, his acceptance of marriage, is but one more invention, one more way to have what he wants: celestial fame and bodily touch.[41]

In conclusion, the fiery qualities of García's *ingenio* (wit) lead him to a fiery demonic realm. He has the power to deceive, much like the devil, and this power is so brilliant that it can confuse fireworks with the stars, the smell of sulphur with a vision of the heavens. Through the magic of his voice, of sound, he can instil a desire for the lowest of senses, and, although he claims to desire a celestial being, he hides his cravings for forbidden touch. Indeed, he uses the new art of fencing or *destreza* to highlight the importance of touch. García can sound the clock at a demonic hour and join it with a pistol, a suspect invention that smells of devilish matter; most of all, in a new world out of sync, he can blur the distinction between truth and falsehood. Although the forces of containment lead him to marry the "wrong" woman, the text may be saying that this is the correct choice.[42] He will wed Lucrecia de Luna, a celestial body that is no longer idealized in the new cosmology. The moon, like the Lucrecia he has fashioned in his mind, is an imperfect body, as imperfect as the body politic, the court in Madrid. He can embrace woman and court with what he now believes is the most important of senses – touch – one that will not deceive him. The play telescopes the future; it allows us to see the difficult road that leads from the Counter-Reformation to modernity, from authority to will, from Madrid to the New World. In this new world the hierarchy of the senses from high to low will no longer prevail, since highest sight reports that the sun and moon revolve around the earth, and hearing tells of ancient authorities that no longer apply. Touch, on the other hand, is a mode of experimentation, a new *destreza*, and it is here that García succeeds as he imagines the death of his rival while he approaches the changing heavens.

NOTES

1 All translations from *La verdad sospechosa* (*The Truth Can't Be Trusted*) come from the English edition and translation by Dakin Matthews. All translations in the chapter are mine, unless otherwise indicated.

2 In classical rhetoric, *inventio* is the what, or the subject matter, of a speech. It is a key element in how to persuade. So the rhetorician must know a vast amount and choose, from all available material, a subject that would best persuade others. Mary Carruthers foregrounds the double meaning of the word: "The Latin word *inventio* gave rise to two separate words in modern English. One is our word 'invention,' meaning 'the creation of something new' (or at least different) […]. The other modern English word derived from Latin *inventio* is 'inventory.' This word refers to the storage of many diverse materials, but not to random storage […]. Having inventory is a requirement for invention" (*Craft of Thought* 11). García uses the inventory in his mind to create amazing stories, but these stories also include scientific inventions, ancient techniques, and his own invention or a kind of originality.

3 Some scholars see the play as didactic and focus on the lies of the main character and notions of poetic justice (Staves 1972). In a perceptive study Jules Whicker

argues that "it is also a play with an explicit interest in evaluating deceit in moral terms, so that, at its close, don García is unambiguously presented to the audience as the author of his downfall" (*The Plays* 54). He then goes on to evaluate the lies through their literary and moral aspects, showing, for example, that García is more interested in *admiratio* than in verisimilitude. Others, such as Mary Gaylord, point to the unstable nature of García's portrayal: "Throughout the play don García is both a liar and a bungler, the duper and the duped, the liar and the victim" ("Telling of Lies" 226). Another set of critics view the play as an indictment of the society being depicted. Alan K.G. Paterson portrays don García thusly: "With each performance he demonstrates how a system embedded in the old traditions of honour becomes more vulnerable to mockery in the process of being adapted to urban mores" (365). A third group of critics points to the instability of meaning in the text. Robert Fiore, for example, shows that the father's "moral ground" is subverted by his intention to marry his son quickly so that his fault may not be known (1977). A few have attempted to break the constant focus on one topic by turning to astrological and linguistic games (Nadeau "Star-Crossed Love"); by turning to role-playing (A. Paterson); or by pointing to don García's "desire to ornament society with his originality and excellence" (Soons 240). Others focus on the opposition between the oral and the written within the work (Larson; Veeser); on the presence of mimetic desire (Gaylord "Telling of Lies") or on the eccentricities of the protagonist (Weber "La excentricidad"). Don García has been analysed as a figure who is plagued by wrong assumptions (Darst "Hidden Truths); characterized by the humours (Riley); consumed by love melancholy (Castells); or impelled by a quixotic humoral imbalance (de Armas "Burning at Ephesus"). For Barbara Simerka what we have is a problem play.

4 "Algunas veces sinifica mentir, y llamamos invencioneros a los forjadores de mentiras" (Sometimes it means to lie, and we call liars to those who forge lies) (*Tesoro* [1987] 740).

5 Describing the Madrid of Philip IV, Enrique García Santo-Tomás sees it as part of "una nueva sociedad de consumo rendida a los nuevos placeres pero también sometida a miedos y sospechas" (*Espacio urbano* 16).

6 Teresa de Cartagena, for example, equates the four humours with the five senses. When agitated, they produce a sickness of the body and even of the intellect (Seidenpinner-Nuñez 106).

7 On the link between the four humours and the four elements see Rico (*El pequeño mundo del hombre*) and Heninger. The choleric humour is related to fire; the sanguine to air; the phlegmatic to water; and the melancholic to earth.

8 Discussing a chart in Helisaeus Roslinus, *De opera dei creationis seu de mundo hypotheses* (1597), S.K. Heninger shows how the starry heavens with its perfect circles are on top, while at the bottom are "the infernal regions, which encompasses chaos

and Satan. Chaos contains fire, storms, the void, darkness" (159). Thus fiery objects are at both the top and the bottom of the cosmos.

9 On this subject see the collection of essays edited by Anne J. Cruz and Mary Elizabeth Perry.

10 Even though Claydon's assessment emphasizes the ethical dimensions of the play, I very much agree with him that García shows an "almost diabolical defiance of Christian virtue and the authority which represents it" (118).

11 Studying Huarte de San Juan's *Examen de ingenios*, Daniel L. Heiple concludes that three of the main qualities of the humours produce different types of individuals: heat (choler) leads to imagination, poets, artists, inventors; dryness (melancholy) generates philosophers and judges; and coldness brings about a good memory ("Pro-Feminist Reactions" 123).

12 The ten fabrications are as follows:

ACT I
(The initial three "lies for love" told to Jacinta)

1. García has been in love with her for more than a year (v. 483)
2. García is an Indiano (v. 489)
3. García is fabulously wealthy (vv. 498–9)
4. Banquet scene told to don Juan (vv. 665–770)

ACT II

5. Marriage in Salamanca, false tale told to his father don Beltrán (vv. 1522–711)
6. Correction: Banquet was with married woman (to don Juan) (vv. 1788–803)

ACT III

7. Correction: Wife, doña Sancha, is pregnant (to father) (vv. 2238–41)
8. Correction: Name of the wife's father (Diego vs. Pedro) (to father) (vv. 2262–71)
9. Duel with don Juan told to Tristán (vv. 2714–73)
10. Correction: *Ensalmo* (to Tristán) (vv. 2785–809)

13 Comparisons between earth and sky abound in the theatre of Calderón. Góngora takes them to an extreme in his description of the sign of Taurus, the bull that "en campos de zafiro pace estrellas" (comes to azure pastures grazing stars) (v. 6). Indeed, Tristán mentions Taurus as one of three astrological signs that point to infidelity: "y los de cuernos son tres, / Aries, Capricornio y Toro" (that in the zodiac, Capricorn's / Not the only sign that wears the horns, / There's also the Bull and the Ram) (v. 360).

14 For an analysis of the seven women in *La estrella de Sevilla* (The Star of Seville) in terms of the seven planets and Estrella as Saturn see Burke (*La estrella*).

15 Staves perceptively points out: "Tristán is not an ordinary servant [...] but an impoverished gentleman who sought a government post and lacked the money to secure it (517).

16 The invention of spectacles and telescopes led to the proliferation of satirical texts that viewed the foibles of humanity. On this topic and in particular the *occhiale politici* (political lenses) see the important essay by García Santo-Tomás ("Fortunes") in which he focuses on three works: Rodrigo Fernández de Ribera's *Los antojos de mejor vista* (Glasses for Better Sight) (c. 1625), Luis Vélez de Guevara's *El diablo cojuelo* (The Limping Devil) (1641) and Andrés Dávila y Heredia's *Tienda de anteojos políticos* (Political Eyeglasses Shop) (1673).

17 Mary Gaylord emphasizes the placement of the scene at a jewellery store, a place that often satirizes "sentimental idealism reduced to materialism or love turned to greed," thus foregrounding "the question of values and of Value" ("Telling of Lies" 227).

18 García also lies by claiming that he has been at court and in love with Jacinta for one year. This statement is also derivative – Tristán had been speaking of the sun, which takes a year to revolve around the earth.

19 Potosí is mentioned in at least three of Cervantes's plays: *La entretenida* (The Diversion) (vv. 751, 962, 1366, 1746), *Pedro de Urdemalas* (vv. 1459, 2805) and *El rufián dichoso* (The Lucky Ruffian) (v. 165). There are also mentions in *Don Quijote* and the *Persiles*.

20 The image of the embrace of the elm and the vine derives from Catullus's *Carmen* LXI and LXII. The first one deals with the destructive aspects of lust, which kill the tree; while the second eulogizes true love. In Golden Age Spain there are sonnets on the subject by authors such as Lope de Vega, Carrillo y Sotomayor, and Quevedo. The image can also be used to exalt the poet-patron relation (Erdman 591–5).

21 Fireworks made their way to Europe during the thirteenth century, probably brought back by crusaders. They had been known in China and possibly India since the tenth century. Over the centuries, and certainly by the Renaissance, Italians became masters of this art. Yet in the middle of the seventeenth century the Russian ambassador to China exclaims: "They make such fireworks that no one in Europe has ever seen" (Werrett 181).

22 Teofilo Ruiz remarks that the different elements of a princely or royal entry changed little over the years "except in the display of new technical or military knowledge (discharges of artillery, fireworks, harquebus discharges, and the like)" (83).

23 Burke states: "It is difficult to believe that Alarcón is not implying something about García other than that he would be absolutely firm in his love. One has to recall that the entire scene is the product of his imagination" ("'Banquet of Sense'" 55). At the same time Burke claims that García's error is a corrupt imagination: an *ingenio* or wit created by heat (choler), but one that is corrupt and "overwhelms his rational soul" (51). I very much agree with the humoral diagnosis, but I am not convinced that the protagonist is truly in love with Jacinta.

24 Comparing Horace's and Boscán's epistles on the subject, Arnold Reichenberger asserts: "The *Epístolas* [Epistles] show great similarities in structure. Both take up the

nil admirari and the *Beatus ille* theme in the same order" (17). However, for David Darst there is a new element that is not present in Horace and is added by Boscán, the notion that the human being will stop marvelling at things around him when he observes the world from above (*Juan Boscán* 104). A corruption of this principle is also evinced in Calderón's *El pintor de su deshonra* (The Painter of Dishonour) (de Armas, "De jerarquías pictóricas" 217–20).

25 See, for example, Cicero (2.27.69) and Cervantes, *Don Quijote* (2.8.95).

26 See Borowitz (2005).

27 Whicker comes close, but veers away from this conclusion when he states: "the 'reason' or motive for his mendacity is not in fact reason but desire, whose ultimate object, fame, leaves no doubt as to Garcia's arrogance and egotism" (*Plays* 58).

28 He claims that Cupid should not be depicted as fiery, since, on seeing her, he becomes like ice. Rehashing the well-known Petrarchan figure of "icy fire," García foreshadows the many contraries that will prevail in his fabrication.

29 As such, they appear in a number of plays of the period to show the lover's anxieties: In *El burlador de Sevilla* (The Trickster of Seville) Batricio compares his jealousy to a clock; in Lope's *La dama boba* (The Foolish Lady) the moving hand of the clock reflects a change of heart (Heiple, *Mechanical Imagery* 162–3).

30 The chapter begins with a quote from the first line of the ballad of Conde Claros: "Medianoche era de filo" (2.9.99). A series of bad omens are then listed.

31 "Quitémelo yo, y al darle, / quiso la suerte que toquen / a una pistola, que tengo /en la mano, los cordones, / cayó el gatillo, dio fuego (vv. 1620–4) (I reached for it, and was about / To hand it over, when once again / Chance intervened. As I pulled it out, / My pistol tangled in the chain – / I had the pistol out, you see – / The chain caught in the trigger, the gun / Fired as the hammer fell).

32 In 1496 a performance of the *Mystère de la vie de Saint Martin* (The Mystery about the Life of Saint Martin) by André de la Vigne proved the point. An actor who was dressed to play the part of Satan was even carrying some gunpowder for added show. As he readied himself to come up through the trapdoor, his costume caught fire. Although badly burned, he went ahead and played his part. The audience may have wondered if this was an instance of the real devil at work (J. Kelly 85; Enders 62). Even in Shakespeare's *Henry V* we are treated to "devilish canons" (J. Kelly 85); and we all are aware of don Quixote's dislike of these "endemoniados instrumentos de la artillería, a cuyo inventor tengo para mí que en el infierno se le está dando el premio de su diabólica invención" (those devilish engines of artillery, whose inventor I am persuaded is in hell receiving the reward of his diabolical invention (I.38:470–1) (*Don Quixote*, trans. Jarvis).

33 One may wonder at the proximity of clock to pistol. This was a period when automata were being created – figures that moved, impelled by a clockwork mechanism inside. Carlos Alvar and Enrique Fernandez have documented the amazement caused by small

figurines that walked, collected alms, or performed other functions. As early as the sixteenth century these inventions stirred admiration even in the mightiest: "When Charles V abandoned his position at the head of the empire, he retreated to the secluded monastery of Yuste bringing Turriano along as imperial clockmaker. Many testimonies survive of how the most powerful man on earth passed his time tinkering with automata, clocks and another machines" (E. Fernández ms. 17).

34 "Reloj desconcertado llaman al sujeto desordenado en sus acciones o palabras" (A malfunctioning clock refers to someone disorganized in his actions and speech) (Covarrubias [1987] 561).

35 Jerónimo Sánchez de Carranza (1539–1600) wrote *De la Filosofia de las Armas y de su Destreza y la Agresión y Defensa Cristiana* (1569) (Of the Philosophy and Skill of Arms and of Christian Offence and Defence). His book triggered the *destreza* (fencing) school, which was developed by his pupil Luis Pacheco de Narvaez, fencing master to Philip IV. Here, I have cited from his *Libro de las grandezas de la espada* (1600) (Book of the Greatness of the Sword). On the importance of the new school of fencing in *Don Quijote* see Merich.

36 "Como lo dice Marcilio Ficino en el Timeo de Platón" (As Marsilio Ficino points out in Plato's Timaeus) (Pacheco, *Engaño y desengaño* 81v)

37 Pacheco, for example, states "en su mano estará herir o matar cuando quisiere, de lo cual ha de huir, como verdadero cristiano" (*Libro* 270v).

38 The Agnus Dei was a medallion that had wax from the paschal candles and depicted a lamb. The lines read: "Sagrado fue de su vida / un Agnus Dei que llevaba; / que topando en él la punta / hizo dos partes de mi espada (His life was rescued by the / Agnus Dei medal he displayed / Upon his chest, which caught my point, / And snapped in two my thrusting blade) (vv. 2738–41).

39 In a fascinating confession to the Inquisition, Martin de Valenzuela states: "todo esto dixo aquel hombre que me curo, y me encargo que lo dixese muchas vezes sobre la herida, y lo tome de memoria [...] y tuve por cierto que me halle bien de la herida [...] pregunte a aquel hombre que ensalmo era, y me dixo que el sancto ensalmo de Lanchero, del cual muchos años antes tenía yo noticia aunque no avia oydo la forma [...] Esta cura y este *ensalmo* se me hizo en la juris[di]cion del arfobispado del nuevo Reyno de Granada donde vivio y murio el capitan Lanchero que lo llevo a las Yndias que donde dicen que hizo con el dicho ensalmo maravillosas curas" (all this was said by the man that healed me, and then he requested from me to spell the *ensalmo* over my wound many times, and I learned it by heart [...] I had it for the truth since my wound was cured [...] I asked him what type of *ensalmo* it was, and he revealed it was the sacred *ensalmo* of Lanchero, of which I have heard news many years before, although I did not know its composition [...] This cure and this *ensalmo* [were] applied to me at the jurisdiction of the Archbishopric of the Kingdom of Granada, where captain Lanchere, who took the *ensalmo* to the New World, where it has been said he did wonderful cures, lived and died) (de Grey Birch 1: 388).

40 In his treatise on *ensalmos*, Manuel do Valle de Moura, an Inquisitor from Portugal, tells us that they are often performed by a convert, who may appear to embrace the "true" religion but actually preserves some of his older beliefs (Maggi, 2001 65). The *moriscos* had available to them manuscripts containing *ensalmos* such as the *Misceláneo de Salomón* (Salomon's Miscellaneous) (Martínez Ruiz 217–22).

41 Mary Gaylord asserts: "In *La verdad sospechosa* [The Truth Can't be Trusted], as in *La vida es sueño* [Life is a Dream], harmony is made to succeed conflict, not through the redemptive workings of a (figuratively) Natural order [...] but by the forceful, almost violent imposition of restraint" ("Telling of Lies" 24).

42 In this sense my reading is different from Morton's (1974) and Urbina's, who see marriage as part of reintegration in society. My analysis comes closer to Simerka's view of the problem comedy, where the spectator has "doubts concerning the happy ending" (198). However, I do not see García as playing the role of both lover and *figurón*. Rather, he is lover and transgressor. His new bride will allow him to hone his views of society with even more conviction.

14 Motherhood Interrupted: Sensing Birth in Early Modern Spanish Literature

ENRIQUE GARCÍA SANTO-TOMÁS

Pregnant Muses

This essay stems from an interest in the dialogue between early modern Spanish literature and the history of science and technology in the Iberian Peninsula. It is the second instalment in a trilogy of interdisciplinary conversations between Spanish letters and the three most prevalent and published disciplines of the time – astronomy, medicine, and mechanics. This project, which began with what is now a book entitled *La musa refractada: literatura y óptica en la España del Barroco* (Refracted Muse: Literature and Optics in Early Modern Spain), has proven to be a unique opportunity to gain new insights into the past, including what I consider to be a revealing and little-known engagement by its major writers with the discoveries of the so-called Scientific Revolution. If the fertile refracted muse has led me to formulate new questions on optics and fiction, I believe that this newly tackled pregnant muse – this muse that floods the literary field with numerous images of procreation – will allow me to trace undiscovered connections between two not-so-distant discourses, those of literature and obstetrics, in order to better understand the reasons why childbirth became such an appealing topic and a powerful metaphor for the writers of the time. Writing on bearing and nursing allowed Cervantes and his contemporaries to explore the limits of poetic expression as well as to imagine new fictional worlds by crafting a new lexicon and an innovative imagery for what was a daily occurrence in a century that witnessed major demographic transformations.

This early modern dialogue, which resulted in the incorporation of medical elements into fiction as well as the integration of fictional devices in the medical treatises of the time, is an exciting field that offers great hermeneutic potential – the coinage *medical fiction*, in fact, has begun to gain some traction lately in certain academic circles. The medical profession is present in all genres, which, as we know, exploit the humorous side of healers who cure nothing, and who, on occasion, kill the healthy – take, for instance, the Spanish word *matasanos* (quack) in its long genealogy of mistrust. Doctors face all kinds of challenges – including one's honour, as Calderón famously wrote in *El médico de su honra* (The Doctor of His Honour) – although many of these challenges, it is fair to say, define a profession in rapid change that is constantly updating itself through the opening of new markets and the arrival of new matters, new objects, and new ideas to the Iberian Peninsula. Consequently, its public standing, as fiction reminds us time and again, is surrounded by an aura of suspicion that allows for the creation of infamous stock characters in pieces such as Francisco de Quevedo's *El Buscón* (History of the Swindler) and Juan de Zabaleta's *El día de fiesta por la mañana* (Holiday Morning). Surgeons' practices often juxtapose those of *virtuosi* and alchemists in their attempts to achieve the impossible,[1] as they frequently embody popular beliefs, superstitions, and home remedies such as bloodletting, purgatives, and the consumption of controversial imports such as chocolate, clay, pepper, and tobacco. Some of these literary archetypes have already been studied in depth,[2] and therefore I will not delve into them here. Rather, I would like to focus in this essay on other medical agents of the period, such as midwives and wet nurses, for I believe their presence in the fiction of the time unveils a number of concerns related to the status of the husband and the father in the medical realm as symptomatic of the role of men in contemporary society. These minor figures in early modern Spanish fiction make the process of parturition an exciting and compelling object of scholarship, as has already been suggested by historians such as Montserrat Cabré, María Luz López Terrada, and Teresa Ortiz. I am therefore interested in how birthing is abstracted from its material concreteness and rendered as a code for social and gender relations that operated at the centre of numerous medical fictions in the Spain of the baroque.[3] This essay offers some preliminary observations of what I hope will be a large-scope project titled *La musa encinta: alumbramientos ficticios en la España del Barroco* (The Pregnant Muse: Fictional Deliveries in Baroque Spain).

Women in the Middle

Birth attendants were well-known figures in pre-modern Europe, as their skills were orally transmitted by mothers and aunts, monitoring childbirth in what some scholars have considered "an inversion of customary gender hierarchies" and a fostering of "genuine female empowerment" (Paster 165). In Hapsburg Spain women often sought the help of midwives or *madrinas* (matrons), who were highly regarded in their communities, among other things, for their ability to empathize and care (López Terrada, "Medical Pluralism" 11; Enrenreich and English).

Although in general terms it is true that before "childbirth belonged to medicine, it belonged to women" (Wilson 70), in the case of early modern Spain it is generally difficult to pinpoint specific milestones, since midwifery was often in flux and its practices varied geographically. As I have noted elsewhere ("Offspring"), manuals like those of Damián Carbón, *Libro del arte de las comadres y del regimiento de las preñadas y paridas de los niños* (Book of the Art of Midwives and the Management of Women Pregnant with and Newly Delivered of Children) (Mallorca, 1541), Francisco Núñez, *Libro del parto humano en el cual se contienen remedios muy sutiles y usuales para el parto dificultoso de las mujeres* (Book of Human Parturition Containing Very Subtle and Useful Remedies for Difficult Childbirth in Women) (Alcalá, 1580) and Juan Alonso de los Ruyzes de Fonteche, *Diez privilegios para mujeres preñadas* (Ten Privileges for Pregnant Women) (Alcalá, 1606) privileged the role of midwives to perform a number of activities within the domain of the *operatio manualis* (manual delivery) but outside the domain of doctors, in the words of Carbón, "por honestidad" (for the sake of honesty) and "por ser cosas feas" (because these are ugly things).[4] Controversy, in fact, was never out of sight, since the midwife was often believed to belong to the realm of sorcery – as the popular medieval *dictum* said, *cuanto mejor es la bruja, mejor es la matrona* (the better the witch, the better the midwife). To protect itself against witchcraft the Catholic Church demanded that midwives receive a permit from the local bishop, swearing against the use of magic to help women deliver. Aurelia Martín Casares has indicated that

> la llamada caza de brujas desacreditó para siempre a las curanderas, de manera que los hombres empezaron a invadir el último bastión de las sanadoras: la obstetricia. Se elimina a las mujeres y se crea una profesión médica que se estudia en la universidad a la que sólo tenían acceso los hombres. Estos estudios eran no menos supersticiosos que los de las curanderas, por ejemplo: la creencia en los humores, o las sangrías con sanguijuelas. (107)

> The so-called witch-hunt permanently discredited women folk healers, so that men began to invade the final bastion of female healing: obstetrics. Women were eliminated and a medical profession was created that was studied at universities that were only accessible to men. These studies were no less superstitious than those of women folk healers, for example: the belief in humours and bleeding with leeches.[5]

Generally speaking, this is the perception that we inherit in texts of the period such as *La Gitanilla* (The Little Gypsy Girl), in which Preciosa's visit to Don Juan's house ends with the arrival of the *gitana vieja* (old gypsy), who comes from assisting the birth of a neighbour's baby. The secrecy involving the whole episode allows Cervantes to comment on the poor standing of these otherwise instrumental social agents. But what we also get from this encounter between high and low is ultimately a critique of these immoral noblemen, of these *estirados* (braggarts) who in public show nothing but scorn (*nos tienen en poco*), but who on occasion may need the expertise of these same women:

> –Nieta, acaba, que es tarde y hay mucho que hacer y más que decir.
> –Y ¿qué hay, abuela? -preguntó Preciosa-. ¿Hay hijo o hija?
> –Hijo, y muy lindo -respondió la vieja-. Ven, Preciosa, y oirás verdaderas maravillas.
> –¡Plega a Dios que no muera de sobreparto! -dijo Preciosa.
> –Todo se mirará muy bien -replicó la vieja-; cuanto más, que hasta aquí todo ha sido parto derecho, y el infante es como un oro.
> –¿Ha parido alguna señora? -preguntó el padre de Andrés Caballero.
> –Sí, señor -respondió la gitana-, pero ha sido el parto tan secreto, que no le sabe sino Preciosa y yo, y otra persona; y así, no podemos decir quién es.
> –Ni aquí lo queremos saber -dijo uno de los presentes-, pero desdichada de aquella que en vuestras lenguas deposita su secreto, y en vuestra ayuda pone su honra.
> –No todas somos malas -respondió Preciosa-: quizá hay alguna entre nosotras que se precia de secreta y de verdadera, tanto cuanto el hombre más estirado que hay en esta sala; y vámonos, abuela, que aquí nos tienen en poco; pues en verdad que no somos ladronas ni rogamos a nadie. (64)

> "Granddaughter, finish, it's getting late and there is much to do and more to say."
> "So what is it, grandmother?" asked Preciosa. "Is it a boy or girl?"
> "A boy, and very handsome" responded the old woman. "Come, Preciosa, and you will hear true marvels."
> "God grant that she not die from the childbirth!" said Preciosa.
> "Everything will be watched for very well," replied the old woman; "what is more, so far everything has gone right with the birth, and the infant is as good as gold."
> "Has some woman given birth here?" asked the father of Andrés Caballero.
> "Yes, sir" responded the gypsy woman," but the birth has been so secret, that only Preciosa and I know of it, and another person; and as such, we cannot reveal who it is."
> "Nor do we here want to know" said one of those present, "but cursed be she who entrusts such a secret to your tongues, and places their honour under your protection."
> "Not all of us are bad" responded Preciosa: "perhaps there is among us one who is appreciated for discretion and truthfulness, as much as the most haughty man in this room; and let's go, grandmother, for here we are belittled; as truly we are neither thieves nor beholden to anyone."

This *parto derecho* (birth that went well) – as opposed, perhaps, to a few *partos doblados* (complicated births) that we will see later – is a telling detail that speaks of the boundaries of these women, given that female midwives enjoyed a largely unchallenged monopoly through the eighteenth century, at which point male midwives began to push them aside. It was then that childbirth came under the control of surgeons and priests except in cities like Málaga, which had a large Moorish population devoted to this occupation. New institutional practices were then created, as Elixabete Imaz Martínez reminds us:

> A medida que – a partir del siglo XVIII – la medicina fue tomando un interés creciente por todo lo concerniente a la generación de la vida, los médicos fueron asumiendo una mayor responsabilidad en el proceso de parto, desplazando a las comadronas, trasladándolo a los hospitales y relegando a las mujeres a un papel cada vez más pasivo. (101)

> To the extent that – starting in the eighteenth century – medicine was attracting growing interest for everything concerning the generation of life, physicians began assuming a greater responsibility in the process of childbirth, replacing midwives, moving it into hospitals and relegating women to an increasingly passive role.

Childbirth was regulated in 1750 by a royal decree from Ferdinand VI, giving full power back to the *Protomedicato* (Official Board of Physicans) and granting direct licences to women interested in practising this profession, as scholars such as John Tate Lanning, María Luz López Terrada ("Los tribunales"), and Michele Clouse have documented. And although pregnant women of all guises peppered a number of major texts during these decades of formal experimentation, the stakes were always high when motherhood took centre stage, given that royally sanctioned surgeons often competed with midwives for control of the birthing room. With so many historical contingencies surrounding its preparation as well as its outcome, how was the rich and multifaceted sensorial perception of birth captured in fictional forms? How, as the title of this essay announces, was birth *sensed*, perceived in all its complexities? And what do we understand by "interrupted motherhood"?

Birthing Fiction, Fictionalizing Birth

When we think about the bond between mother and child in early modern Spanish fiction, we draw many of the existing examples from the picaresque, both as a young genre flourishing out of harsh conditions and as the voice of a boy chronicling his infancy in an impoverished – and often rural – environment. This union is often depicted from the process of "tearing," or departure (*desgarro*), as Cervantes masterfully put it through a highly visual and tactile image in his exemplary novel

La ilustre fregona (The Illustrious Kitchen Maid) when narrating the vital quest for independence of the young Carriazo, "llevado de una inclinación picaresca" (given to a roguish tendency) (372).[6] But children are also featured in portrayals of the urban milieu, as Iberian cities such as Madrid and Seville experienced in the advent of modernity an unprecedented demographic explosion that changed their appearance for centuries to come. Through etymologies such as *mater*/Madrid the city was conceived as a mother figure that bore, nurtured, and generously welcomed its inhabitants, offering entertainment, solace, and a strong sense of identity that has remained fairly unaltered until today. With the city as a fertile womb, women's bodies and spatial layout thus coalesced in fictional accounts of reproduction in which natural birth was seldom presented neutrally, even if the writer was, as sometimes happened to be the case, a woman.

We know that by the end of the Middle Ages, as Monica Green has argued, "female midwives really only had a monopoly on normal births," as it was considered normative and acceptable "to call in male surgeons in cases of difficult labour" (*Making* x). Touching the woman's body was therefore expected, given that the taboo against male sight and touch of the female genitals was no longer absolute, and, while midwives were still the normative attendants at uncomplicated births throughout western Europe, emergency obstetrics as well as routine gynecological care was considered appropriate work for men (*Making* xii).

If, on the one hand, there was a fairly clear understanding of what a midwife versus a royally sanctioned surgeon could contribute, on the other hand, there was not a defined sense of what – and who – traced that fine line that separated the normative from the exceptional and therefore the legitimacy of male versus female hands when it came to assisting a parturient. And fiction, I argue, took advantage of this constant fluctuation: in order to better reflect on childbirth as a highly charged literary device, I will sketch half a dozen different examples of parturition that reveal the fruitful potential of a motif that, to my surprise, has received little attention in the aesthetic realm. The examples that I will offer belong to different moments in time and reveal pivotal tensions related to the masculinization of women's medicine. In these texts gestation and delivery present a body in limbo, under a transitory state that is resolved only on completion of a process that is at once private and ceremonial, intimate and shared. But what they ultimately show us is that, as the baroque reaches its climax in the last decades of the seventeenth century, the act of parturition becomes a theatrical and ceremonial event in which the lower senses are incorporated as key features of this transformative experience.

The idea of the opened, dissected, or mutilated body has been the object of renewed attention in recent years by scholars such as Jonathan Sawday and Steven Connor, who have highlighted numerous ties between the lettered and the visual.

The baroque fascination with bodies "in transition" – whether in the process of reproduction, evacuation, or putrefaction – is a common theme in Spanish fiction, which sometimes borrowed from masters such as Hans Holbein the Younger and Pieter Brueghel the Elder in their depictions of ritual time and communal space, and from Hieronymus Bosch's oneiric, allegorical, and phantasmagorical visions of mutilated and dismembered beings, not to mention all the body parts that take on a life of their own. Bosch's influence in Spanish literature has been, in fact, widely discussed by critics like Xavier de Salas, James Iffland (1: 128–30; 2: 43–9), Margarita Levisi, and Antonio Sánchez Jiménez (347–74) (and we will discuss it further below), but looking at the numerous images of violent birth one should never discard the influence of northern tastes on southern sensibilities. Entering and exiting narrow passageways, inhabiting occlusive and saturated spaces, and putting to the test the senses in one's skin in pieces such as *The Temptation of St Anthony* and *The Garden of Earthly Delights* are paramount to a poetics and an aesthetics that will be inspirational to baroque writers as the century progresses and cities become, as Vélez de Guevara masterfully put it in *El Diablo Cojuelo* (The Limping Devil), a boiling *puchero humano* (human stew) traversed by those *encochados* who lived inside "their shells." This is a novel, by the way, in which childbirth is chronicled in humorous terms, reflecting a palpable social decline that is felt in daily life, as birthing allows for a meditation on class and gender. Think of the scene in which the cuckolded, suffering *paleto* (bumpkin) attends his woman to see her lover's child being born: "Allí está pariendo doña Fáfula, y don Toribio, su indigno consorte, como si fuera suyo lo que paría, muy oficioso y lastimado; y está el dueño de la obra a pierna suelta en esotro barrio, roncando y descuidado del suceso" (the lady Fáfula is giving birth, and don Toribio, her unworthy consort, as if the offspring were his, is being very obliging and sympathetic; and the owner of the work is out like a light in another neighbourhood, snoring and oblivious to the event) (22). However, the episodes of parturition that we encounter in early modern Spanish literature – starting, for instance, with a few portrayed in Renaissance texts like Francisco Delicado's *La lozana andaluza* (The Lusty Andalusian Woman) – are not limited to the physical realm, as many narratives of the period incorporate childbirth as a metaphor for the laborious effort by which good literature is inspired and written. In some of the most popular genres and modes that we encounter in these two centuries, in fact, we share the awareness that something new is being crafted, that new traditions are replacing obsolete ones, and that this new field – or this new aesthetic expression – is still in its infancy, however promising. Some of these new metaphorical births, like that of the *comedia nueva*, take on a biological imagery when their development is chronicled as if it were that of a child. One can remember the famous image of *mantillas* (swaddling clothes) to reflect on theatre in the sixteenth century, *en estado de mantillas* (still in swaddling clothes) until Lope de Vega arrived with new dramatic formulas. Many of these images belong, as Bryant Creel has noted in an excellent book, to a poetics that includes numerous metaphors of rebirth in a period of merciless competition in the literary field, starting with Lope's famous pen name, *Fénix de los ingenios* (The Phoenix of Wits) – a Lope, by the way, who also wrote "yo me sucedo a mí mismo" (I am my own successor) in his play *Si no vieran las mujeres* (If Only Women Could Not See) (fol. 276v).

As these examples seem to suggest, in this analysis of contemporary mores curiosity allows and limits the construction of the human from the inside out, as it offers ways of access to the female anatomy while placing it in a state of exceptionality: curiosity leads to curiosities, one could argue, in the century of anatomy and anatomists who explore with no small amount of awe the inner workings of the body.[7] But it is here that things get a bit more complicated. Carolyn Nadeau ("Authorizing" 23–5) and Emilie Bergmann remind us that childbirth in most of early modern Europe was conceived as the act not only of parturition, but of lactation as well, for the idea of maternity embraced these two moments as one single continuum. Fray Luis de León had already argued that bearing children could not be uncoupled from raising them – "Es trabajo parir y criar; pero entiendan que es un trabajo hermanado, y que no tienen licencia para dividirlo" (It is work to give birth and raise children; but you must understand that it is a coupled work, and it is not right to divide it) (1987: 165) – and Fray Antonio de Guevara claimed a few years later that a woman became half a mother by giving birth and half a mother by raising her child: "la mujer es media madre por el parir y media madre por el criar" (the woman is half mother for giving birth, and half for raising child) (511).[8] If the female genitals were (almost) un-representable, the female breast, on the other hand, became the site of countless re-creations – a "moralized breast," as Charlene Villaseñor Black has argued. And if Flemish and French painters portrayed the female breast in scenes of lactation in domestic interiors, their southern neighbours, including Spain and Italy, did so in depictions that exploited allegorical readings of the senses: in representations of the so-called Virgen del buen parto (Figure 14.1), in renditions of the biblical episode of the break in the flight to Egypt, in scenes of *Mater lactans* (The mother lactating) and in portrayals on the birth of the Virgin, to which one could add some other less common cases such as José de Ribera's *Magdalena Ventura con su marido* (Magadela Ventura with Her Husband) (Figure 14.2), or Alonso Cano's *San Bernardo y la Virgen* (Saint Bernard and the Virgin).

These ideas of *crianza* (child-rearing) in which sensorial perception is paramount, were incorporated in well-known pieces a few decades later when writers

Figure 14.1 *Retablo de la Virgen del Buen Parto*, Church of San Nicolás de Bari (Valladolid). Attributed to Juan Vela (second half of the sixteenth century).

Figure 14.2 José Ribera, *Magdalena Ventura con su marido.*

such as Miguel de Cervantes and Alonso Jerónimo de Salas Barbadillo commented on the erasure of class distinctions facilitated by children and in particular of "prodigal" sons whose improbable births tied together all the loose ends of the plot(s) and who guaranteed the perpetuation of a new – one could say *exemplary* in the case of Cervantes – family lineage. But in many of these examples motherhood was also interrupted by a number of external agents, prompting the portrayal of what we could here call, following Guevara, "half mothers."

Two of Cervantes's novelas epitomize these views. In *La fuerza de la sangre* (The Power of Blood) the boy Luisico arrives so secretively that the work of the midwife is taken up by his maternal grandmother, who assists her daughter Leocadia in order to protect her honour after an unwanted pregnancy: "llegóse el punto del parto, y con tanto secreto, que aun no se osó fiar de la partera. Usurpando este oficio la madre" (the moment of birth arrived, and with such secrecy, that even confiding in a midwife was risked. This office was usurped by the mother) (312). But the young child, as we know, becomes a public figure who is central to the story, as his grave accident manages to unite two different worlds – those of the victim and the aggressor – thus founding an exemplary family lineage (*ilustre descendencia* [323]) whose reputation is highlighted at the closing of the story. The child is not so much the result but rather the catalyst of a redemptive marriage, as he justifies the union of his parents, not vice versa.

More nuanced and fully developed is the case of *La señora Cornelia*, as the boy situated at the very centre of the story is passed from hand to hand in a series of twists and turns reminiscent of a *comedia de enredo* (bedroom farce). The newborn is the result, as in the case of Luisico, of a secret pregnancy, that of the eighteen-year-old Bolognese beauty Cornelia, but soon after birth he disappears from (her) sight: from her *doncella* Sulpicia's arms he is wrongly transferred to the hands of the Spanish student Juan de Gamboa, who in his nightly stroll is confused by Fabio, the *criado* of the alleged father and the actual target emissary. He is then taken to Don Juan's house and appropriately left in the care of an *ama*, who gives him a bit of honey to make him latch faster (491). He is also changed into a more humble set of swaddling clothes, as preparations are made to leave him "en casa de una partera, que tales siempre suelen dar recado y remedio a semejantes necesidades" (in a midwife's house, as these women always tend to give provision and succour for such needs) (484). But when the baby cries in hunger, the young Cornelia, now too in the house of Don Juan and his housemate Don Antonio, feels compassion for him and asks to have him brought over. Without recognizing the child as her own – the fresh swaddling clothes indicate his origin – she then tries to feed him as if she were a wet nurse. But as Cervantes tells us, something is not quite right: "El niño mamaba, pero no era ansí, porque las recién paridas no pueden dar el pecho" (the boy suckled, but it was not to be, because mothers who've just given birth cannot breastfeed), which prompts Cornelia to lament, "En balde me he mostrado caritativa" (in vain I have shown charity) (492). The breast then becomes a signifier of class: once Cornelia is informed about his true identity, "el ama trujo a quien secretamente y a escuras diese de mamar al niño" (the mistress brought someone secretly and she clandestinely gave her breast to the boy), a "mujer pobre" (a poor woman) (504) who feeds the baby while she rests (497). Then, the three women in charge of the baby's well-being travel with him to the outskirts of Ferrara to find refuge in the house of the *piovano*. At the end of the story, when the young parents finally reunite – not without a number of very theatrical and suspenseful twists – it is the priest who holds the baby with his left arm while energetically blessing them (517). Cervantes's fiction mirrors the historical circumstances surrounding these medical practices, as he is referring to a network of hired wet nurses to breastfeed the poor and the orphaned, the famous "inclusas" (foundling nurses) and "amas de crianza" (child nurses), also called "amas de leche" (milk nurses), in some parts of Spain.[9] There is also a comment on wealth, as these amas freed women from many of their responsibilities, thus allowing them to recover quickly and to have more children, which released them in the process from a duty that was seen as unsuitable for the upper echelons. Although the child's first days of life lay at the centre of the plot, *La señora Cornelia* is more than a tale of motherhood; it is also a novel about all the possible agents that could mediate between mother and child in this reflection on cultural affinities between two different countries: agents of medicine, agents of class, agents of nation. It is Spain, the novel seems to indicate, who nurtures and cares for the defenceless Italians, still in their infancy in a fragmented Peninsula. Touching and tasting – no better exemplified here than in the taste of honey and the shortcomings of the mother's breast – provide a touch of verisimilitude and exemplarity to the development of the plot, along with a note on the pressures of class above all other considerations.

Equally fascinating is the case of Salas Barbadillo's novel *Don Diego de noche* (Don Diego at Night). In the seventh adventure we run into "el caballero del milagro" (the gentleman of the miracle), an acquaintance of Don Diego, who requires his assistance to help him with a thorny issue: he has a secret relationship with a lady of a lower rank who is pregnant and very close to her due date. But the long-awaited arrival cannot take place in his or her home, and therefore he requests Don Diego's help. As preparations reach their final stages, the lady runs out of time, and gives birth in a cemetery:

> le habían tomado los dolores del parto y que, medrosa del rigor de su padre, en cuyas manos perdería la vida, le rogó la llevase consigo donde pudiese parir con mayor seguridad, a cuya petición justa concedió, determinándose a traerla a la casa de don Diego con la luz de aquella linterna, por hacer la noche escura, y que al pasar de aquel

> cementerio le apretaron tan fuertemente los dolores del parto que no pudo proseguir adelante. Y viendo abierto un boquerón del carnero de aquel cementerio, se determinó a meterla dentro. (327)

> the pangs of childbirth had overtaken her and so, fearful of the harshness of her father, in whose hands she would lose her life, she begged to be taken away so that she could give birth more safely, and her fair request was granted, deciding to bring her to the house of don Diego by torch light, as night was darkening, and just as she passed that cementary the labor pains seized her so intensely that she could advance no further. And seeing an unlocked entrance into the graveyard of the cementary, it was decided to put her inside.

The tone and the atmosphere of the episode, which are seminal to the development of the genre in the 1620s and 1630s, share some of the sinister locations depicted by his contemporaries María de Zayas, Francisco de Quevedo, and Juan de Piña. In this case the silence of the night is soon broken by a "Jesús, Jesús" followed by a "Gracias a Dios, esto es hecho" (Thank God, this is done) (328). Nothing else is told about the process. Childbirth is a purely auditory phenomenon, as all we know about the baby is a brief allusion to the decrepitude of his surroundings, "pues era casa de su nacimiento la que a tantos servía de hospedaje mortal. Notable maravilla, que cuando entraba por los umbrales de la vida era viendo los horrores y asombros de la muerte. El primer paso de la vida dio sobre calaveras, juntando su rostro tierno con el duro y disforme de tanto difunto" (so the house of his birth was the one that had provided so many with lodgings in death. A striking marvel, that upon entering through the threshold of life he was seeing the horrors and shocks of death. The first step of life was atop skulls, his tender face joined with the stiffness and grotesquery of so many corpses) (328). The many uses of silence and darkness in these baroque scenes do not need scrutiny, for they have been explored already (García Santo-Tomás *Modernidad*). What I find most interesting, however, is what comes right afterwards: the "caballero del milagro" picks up the newborn, swaddles him in his cape, and takes him "a la casa de una comadre, donde estaba prevenida un ama que le diese leche" (to the house of a midwife, where a nurse was prepared to give him milk), while don Diego remains "con una linterna y la parida" (with a torch and the new mother). Salas situates childbirth in the male domain, as the woman is portrayed as a nameless, faceless vehicle that simply serves to perpetuate the lineage, and whose body must be "repaired" (*reparado*) so she can continue delivering children. The "caballero del milagro," in fact, arranges everything for his woman because he has the means to do so, given that, as Salas tells us, "en esta edad hasta los pechos se alquilan, y aún se venden, y nos venden" (in this age even breasts are for rent, and even for sale, and they sell us) (331), that is, in this age what we now know as "mercenarismo," (mercenarism) or "lactancia asalariada" (salaried lactation) – according to scholars like Mónica Bolúfer – is a fairly common practice. Even all traces of physical pain are removed from the depiction of the parturient; when "el caballero del milagro" leaves the scene with the baby, it is his acquaintance Don Diego, a total stranger to the parturient, who keeps her company in a cemetery with no female companions in sight.

Here Salas is joining a debate that had become one of the most controversial ones in the realm of childhood, not only in Spain, but also in the rest of Europe, given that "as soon as it was offered to a baby other than the mother's own, breast milk became a commercial product that, like any other commodity, varied in quantity, quality, and availability" (Mazzoni 61). Birth is defined as an auditory experience devoid of those sensations – touch, taste, smell – that are more closely associated with the intimate bond between mother and child. Consequently, the transfer of the baby to a new domain that is administered by both the father and a new female agent disrupts and redefines the traditional idea of maternity, so aptly expressed by Carolyn Nadeau and others in the coinage "blood mother / milk mother." If the father is not strictly a "new midwife," he is nevertheless the mediator between two different, but also intertwined domains. This is a role that, as Cristina Mazzoni has argued, has notable epistemological consequences:

> This experiential type of knowing is closely related to the knowing of the pregnant woman herself: Midwives relied heavily on their personal experience of childbirth for their ability to empathize and care. It is therefore not surprising that, along with the invalidation of midwives' knowledge, the pregnant and birthing woman's own knowledge should also have been discredited. (61)

The *night* in *Don Diego de noche* is therefore witness to a joyful creation that is nonetheless stripped from some of its most seminal elements; and the *miraculous* element in the "caballero del milagro," one could also argue, is nothing but an ironic gesture in a male-controlled occurrence. Even in the more subtle case of *La señora Cornelia*, it is up to two strangers from abroad to arrange everything for the proper care of a local baby.

Bursting Decay

I would like to finish this brief itinerary with two final scenes of childbirth that include fascinating examples of sensorial – and sensual – perception. I turn my attention to the writer Francisco Santos (1623–98), whose fiction bore witness to the vital exhaustion of the last third of the century as it made a frequent use of parturition to narrate the miseries of his native Madrid. As María José del

Río reminds us (177–9), Santos wished for an authentic, more traditional way to celebrate local festivities, following an ideology expressed in texts such as Juan de Mariana's *De Spectaculis* (On Spectacles) (1609), Antonio Liñán y Verdugo's *Avisos de la Corte* (News from the Court) (1623) and Remiro de Navarra's *Los peligros de Madrid* (The Dangers of Madrid) (1646). He was inspired by popular emblems when depicting his famous *gigantones*, in particular those of Ripa and Alciato, which were behind many of the so-called *decoraciones efímeras* (ephemeral decorations) of the period (Bernáldez Montalvo). As I have argued already (*Espacio*), his best-known piece *Día y noche de Madrid* (Day and Night in Madrid) is peppered with narratives of birth that allow him to reflect on the moral demise of his surroundings. From the beginning its protagonist Juanillo is portrayed as the tragic result of a violent birth that ends the life of his mother: "sólo a la víbora se le concede esta crueldad, por ser venenoso aborto de la misma fiereza, pues en naciendo, acarrean la muerte a las entrañas que la avivaron [....]. Sólo el mal hijo imita a la víbora o al rayo, que para nacer hace reventar a la nube que le congeló" (only the viper is allowed this cruelty, for being the venomous still birth of this same savagery, as in birth, the organs that gave life are conducted to death [...]. Only the evil son imitates the viper or the bolt of lightening, which in its birth bursts open the cloud that fashioned it) (171). This sentence includes an additional element with which I will close this cursory survey. The image of the bursting cloud is closely related to that of the storm, which appears and reappears in the last decades of the century in novels such as Juan Martínez de Cuéllar's *El desengaño del hombre* (The Disillusionment of Man) (1663). As Santiago Fernández Mosquera has written in a monograph on this motif, storms and hurricanes were as frequent as they were diverse in early modern Spanish fiction in scenes that went back as far as Lucan's *Pharsalia*, Statius's *Thebaid*, and Seneca's theatre, reaching their apogee in the middle decades of the seventeenth century in Calderón's theatre with the use of gunpowder onstage. But as the effects of social and economic decline were deeply felt in Spain in the last thirty years of the century, the storm began to be used for allegorical births that were frequently novelized through carnivalesque features like hyperbole and animalization.[10]

Such is the case of the novel *La Tarasca de parto en el mesón del infierno* (The Tarasque of Childbirth in Hell's Inn) (1672), in which, as I have written elsewhere ("Offspring"), Santos chronicled "las noches de los festivos días de Madrid, que mejor fuera llamarle sueños del Bosco, que si él pintó espantosas sabandijas, más atroces los bosqueja la torpeza de mi pluma" (nights of festivals in Madrid, that would be better called dreams of Bosch, since if he painted frightful vermin, my ungraceful pen sketches them more atrociously) (fol. 2v.).[11] At the start of this novel the signs of the storm, such as thunder, wind, rain, and hail, appear in fierce succession. Its effects are far-reaching, and the destruction caused by the clashing of forces is severe. Darkness, confusion, and the absence of light are central to this cosmic struggle for ascendancy. The Tarasca – or Tarasque – resembles "el retrato del Centauro, si el uno medio caballo y medio hombre, ésta medio demonio y medio mujer" (the portrait of the Centaur, if one is half horse and half man, this is half demon and half woman), and the midwife takes centre stage soon after: "Afuera, a un lado, que viene la comadre doña Fulana al mesón del infierno, a partear la Tarasca del mundo, preñada de los vicios, y en días de parir" (Outdoors, to one side, here comes the midwife lady What's-Her-Name to Hell's inn, birthing the Tarasca of the world, impregnated with vice, and in days of labour). She is the personification of envy, a toothless *vieja* wearing heavy make-up and sporting bright, colourful clothes. But birth also includes a sensory element, this one related to taste, which I find highly original, as its outcome is celebrated with the preparation of chocolate, albeit not any chocolate: the midwife knows her drinks well, as she indicates "con voz melosa" (with a honeyed voice) that "No lo quiero [...] si es de lo que venden en estas tiendecillas, porque tiene cacao Guayaquín, y da hipocondría" (I don't want it [...] if it's what they sell in these little stores, because they have Ecuadorian chocolate, and it causes hypochondria). Her friends at the Inn reply that "Caracas, y S[anto] Domingo es [...] bien lo puede tomar" (it's Caracas, and Santo Domingo [...] she may well take it), offering the toss to the parturient herself: "vaya esa jícara a la parida, que bien la merece" (may this cup of chocolate go to the birth mother, as she deserves it well). It is the American import, in the end, that serves to appease the urges of the European metropolis: "Con esta bulla, y brindis Indiano, se fue apaciguando aquel espantable estruendo" (with this ruckus and toasting from the Indies, the fearful din was pacified) (fols 6v–7r). The context of celebrations in which the senses of hearing and touching become paramount to both actors and witnesses is thus capped with an exercise in taste and smell. Drinking the preferred brand of chocolate completes this comprehensive portrait of urban vices. The depiction of festivities with a New World flavour mirrors what had become a common practice among courtesans as new products from overseas flooded local markets. The process, however, remains incomplete, as there is no lactation immediately after birth, but rather a quick expulsion of these "pieces of hell" propelled by the colossal flood with which the narrative begins. The absence of this final element not only undermines the dignity of the process but also eliminates the positive role assigned to the mother:

> misogyny is legible as discomfort with the fluids and processes of female physiology and [...] with the technical events of birth. In reproduction, the female body was not only different as usual from the male body but different from itself in a way that, at its most dangerous, threatened contamination of self and baby. (Paster 173; see also 181)

Childbirth is therefore located at the very centre of the festivity, subverting medical practices that investigated from an academic perspective every phase and agent involved in it. Santos's novel thus captures a tension that was still absent half a century earlier in Salas's and Cervantes's courtly plots. Madrid has now become a ghoulish, excessive, and hedonistic town in constant growth, but in these processes of reproduction men possess no control whatsoever in the birthing process, as they feel threatened by the figure of the midwife.

These concerns on the suitable roles for father and husband were present in most of Santos's literary output. His time was one in which doctors, theologians, and lawyers had gradually gained ground at the expense of birth attendants, particularly as a result of the debates on the spontaneous abortions and miscarriages that sometimes even took the life of the parturient woman. But there was another concern of a different nature: while paternity prompted men to make sure that all their children really were theirs, parturition involved the intercession of an outside figure like the midwife, who displaced the father to the periphery of events. As we have seen in Salas's novel, this displacement had financial repercussions, for "it was only through controlling this reproductive process that the male's name and property could be transferred from one generation to the next" (Sawday 223).

Beyond these social considerations, birthing is depicted in these pieces as a rich and controversial process that celebrated the role of the senses, saturating human perception by adding new layers of meaning to this pivotal, yet quotidian occurrence. But, as the celebration of life and abundance that it was, birthing also signalled a time of crisis, specifically in those novels that portrayed it as a process of displacements and interruptions. On the one hand, it revealed that manhood and patriarchy were not equated in early modern Spain, as fathers and surgeons were frequently removed from centre stage; on the other hand, it also undermined the autonomy of the female body, in particular of the feeding breast (Villaseñor Black), leaving the parturient, as we saw in the young Cornelia, without the possibility of nursing the newborn. Functions were frequently reassigned, and so it was, in the end, the role of each of the senses. These *alumbramientos barrocos* leave today's reader with a great field of shadows that I find particularly attractive in their aesthetic, political, and philosophical ramifications, as they are transformed into narratives of ownership, loss, and accountability. They fruitfully connect with recent theoretical interventions on these particular questions coming from the history of science (Gélis; Green; Whaley), from cultural and literary studies (Connor; Sawday; Paster), as well as from feminist critics who have specifically written on the subject (Mazzoni; A. Adams; Krier). They expose all the different strands – mythology, hygiene, folklore, and religion, but also anatomy, astrology, and optics – that constituted the fabric of these pieces. Such birth episodes are therefore not only about gender roles and social tensions, but also about Spain and the baroque's self-reflection on its potential for creativity and generation itself.

Claude Larquié lamented a few years ago that "L'histoire de la mise en nourrice en Espagne, à l'époque moderne, et encore mal connue" (the history of wet nursing in Spain, to the modern age, is still little known) (221). However, and as I indicated at the opening of this essay, there was no shortage of surgeons in the Spain of Cervantes, as the dog Berganza reminded us humorously regarding the University of Alcalá: "de cinco mil estudiantes que cursaban aquel año en la Universidad, los dos mil oían medicina" (of the five thousand students studying that year at the University, two thousand took medicine) (544). In the history of early modern curiosity and curiosities, the female breast stands at the crossroads of morals, religion, and aesthetics, and it becomes an indicator of both the versatility and the limits of poetic language. But it can also be read as a metaphor for the country's imperial journey, a journey that had collapsed in Santos's "missing breast" (Schwartz), in his cancerous body, but one that had begun with the curious eye of its founding father Garcilaso de la Vega and the half-seen breast through the lover's open gown:

> Con ansia estrema de mirar qué tiene
> vuestro pecho escondido allá en su centro,
> y ver si a lo de fuera lo de dentro
> en apariencia y ser igual conviene,
> en él puse la vista, mas detiene
> de vuestra hermosura el duro encuentro
> mis ojos, y no pasan tan adentro
> que mirar lo que el alma en sí contiene.
> Y así se quedan tristes en la puerta
> [..] (47)

> with extreme yearning to view what your hidden breast has there in its centre and to see if from what is outside, the inside is equal and agrees in appearance, I set my eyes upon it, and the difficult encounter due to your beauty hinders my eyes, and they do not pass within to look upon what the soul contains in itself. And thus they remain saddened at the doorway.

And thus they remain saddened at the doorway. This breast that is first glimpsed in Garcilaso, then fully revealed in Cervantes, and finally severed by Santos traverses our Spanish Golden Age with heavy medical equipment. Yet, when it comes to its major literary works, its scholarship still is far too divorced from the history of medicine, the scientific discipline with the largest number of published titles at this time. But these are precisely the kinds of dialogues between established areas of knowledge, from which we still know so little, that can open up new fields of inquiry for both cultural scholars and historians of science.[12] The field is ripe for the creation of new disciplinary networks; one can hope that our own curiosity will keep us exploring further so that our insights into the past *do not remain saddened at the doorway.*

NOTES

1 See García Santo-Tomás, "Visiting."
2 See, for example, Simón Palmer; David-Peyre.
3 For a pivotal selection of theoretical readings on the phenomenon of childbirth see Adams; Krier.
4 On the rise of medical fiction in medieval and early modern Spain see, for example, Dangler; Solomon.
5 All translations are my own unless otherwise indicated.
6 I quote from the edition of *Novelas ejemplares* by García López; all subsequent citations from the novelas are from this edition.
7 See the recent studies by Fernández and Skaarup.
8 On the evolution of the role of the mother in sixteenth- and seventeenth-century Spain see Nadeau, "Authorizing"; Moncó Rebello; Morant. For a general survey on medical practices by women in Europe, see the monographic issue of the journal *Dynamis* 19 (1999) entitled "Mujeres y salud: prácticas y saberes."
9 See Larquié; Bolúfer; Chacón Jiménez, Elgarrista Domeque and Fresneda Collado; Whaley.
10 There is an extensive bibliography on the phenomenon of the monstrous birth in Golden Age literature; see, for example, Del Río Parra 46, 59–62, 134; Kirk; Spinks.
11 Melero Jiménez provides a modern edition of the novel; for its connection with the theme of childhood, see Serrano Perdices.
12 See, for example, Sanders.

Bibliography

Abercrombie, Thomas A. *Pathways of Memory and Power: Ethnography and History among an Andean People.* Madison: U of Wisconsin P, 1998.

Ackerman, Diane. *A Natural History of the Senses.* New York: Random House, 1990.

Adams, Alice E. *Reproducing the Womb: Images of Childbirth in Science, Feminist Theory, and Literature.* Ithaca, NY: Cornell UP, 1994.

Adams, John. *Diary and Autobiography: 1777–1780.* Vol. 4. Ed. L.H. Butterfield. Cambridge, MA: Harvard UP, 1961.

Agamben, Giorgio. *The Highest Poverty: Monastic Rules and Form-of-Life.* Trans. Adam Kotsko. Stanford: Stanford UP, 2013.

Aguinaga, Carlos Blanco. "Cervantes y la picaresca: notas sobre dos tipos de realismo." *Nueva Revista de Filología Hispánica*, 11.3/4 (1957): 313–42.

Albala, Ken. *Eating Right in the Renaissance.* Berkeley: U of California P, 2002.

Alberts, Tara. *Conflict and Conversion: Catholicism in Southeast Asia, 1500–1700.* Oxford: Oxford UP, 2013.

Alemán, Mateo. *Guzmán de Alfarache.* 2 vols. Ed. José María Micó. Madrid: Cátedra, 2010.

– *Guzmán de Alfarache.* 5 vols. Ed. Samuel Gili y Gaya. Madrid: Espasa-Calpe, 1962.

Alfonso X. *Primera crónica general: Estoria de España.* Ed. Ramón Menéndez Pidal. Madrid: Bailly-Bailliere, 1906.

– *Siete Partidas.* 3 vols. Madrid: Imprenta Real, 1807.

Alvar, Carlos. "De autómatas y otras maravillas." *Fantasía y literatura en la Edad Media y los Siglos de Oro.* Ed. Nicasio Salvadror Miguel, Santiago López-Rios, and Esther Borrego Gutiérrez. Madrid: Iberoamericana, 2004. 29–54.

Ancos, Pablo. *Transmisión y recepción primarias de la poesía del mester de clerecía.* Valencia: Universitat de València, 2012.

Anderson, Benedict. *Imagined Communities: Reflections on the Origin and Spread of Nationalism.* Rev. ed. New York: Verso, 1991.

Anon. *A briefe discourse of the voyage and entrance of the Queene of Spaine into Italy: With the Triumphes and pomps shewed as well in the Cittyes of Ostia, Ferrara, Mantua, Cremona, Milane, as in other boroughes and townes of Italy. Also the report of the voyage of the Archduke Albert into Almaigne.* London, 1599.

Anon. *Lazarillo de Tormes.* Ed. Joseph A. Ricapito. 11th ed. Madrid: Cátedra, 1983.

Aquinas, Thomas. *Summa Theologica.* Opera omnia. Online ed. Enrique Alarcón. University of Navarra. www.corpusthomisticum.org

– *Summa Theologica.* Trans. Fathers of the English Dominican Province. Raleigh, NC: Hayes Barton, 2006.

Arias, Joan. *Guzmán de Alfarache: The Unrepentant Narrator.* London: Tamesis Books, 1977.

Aristotle. *De anima. De sensu. The Complete Works of Aristotle.* Ed. Jonathan Barnes. Vol. 1. Princeton: Princeton UP, 1984.

– *Metaphysics.* In *The Basic Works of Aristotle.* Ed. Richard McKeon. New York: Random House, 1941.

– *On the Soul, Parva Naturalia, On Breath.* Trans. W.S. Hett. Loeb Classical Library 288. Cambridge: Harvard UP, 1957.

Arizaleta, Amaia. *La Translation d'Alexandre: Recherches sur les structures et les significations du* Libro de Alexandre. Paris: Publication du séminaire d'études médiévales hispaniques, 1999.

– "Le Centre Introuvable: La Babylone Castilliane Du *Libro De Alexandre.*" *La Ville Dans Le Monde Ibérique Et Ibéro-Américain: (Espace, Pouvoir, Memoire).* Actes Du XXVIIe Congrès De La Société Des Hispanistes Français De l'Enseignement Supérieur (Poitiers, 24–26 mars, 1995). Poitiers: La Licorne, 1995. 145–53.

Armistead, Samuel. "La 'furia guerrera' en dos textos épicos." *La tradición épica de las "Mocedades de Rodrigo."* Salamanca: U of Salamanca P, 2000. 69–77.

Arnaud, Emile. *La vie et l'oeuvre de Alonso Jerónimo de Salas Barbadillo: contribution à l'étude du roman en Espagne au début du XVIIe siècle.* 3 vols. Toulouse: U de Toulouse-Le Mirail, 1977.

Arzáns de Orsúa y Vela, Bartolomé. *Historia de la Villa Imperial de Potosí.* Ed. Lewis Hanke and Gunnar Mendoza. Providence, RI: Brown UP, 1965.

– *Tales of Potosí.* Ed. R.C. Padden. Trans. Frances López-Morillas. Providence, RI: Brown UP, 1975.

Asensio, Eugenio. *Poética y realidad en el cancionero peninsular de la Edad Media.* 2nd rev. ed. Madrid: Gredos, 1970.

Astel, Ann W. "A Discerning Smell: Olfaction among the Senses in St Bonaventure's Long Life of St Francis." *Franciscan Studies* 67 (2009): 91–131.

Atchley, E.G.C.F. *A History of the Use of Incense in Divine Worship.* New York: Green, 1909.

Atiles, Joaquín. *Los recursos literarios de Berceo.* Madrid: Gredos, 1964.

Augustine. *The Trinity. The Works of Saint Augustine: A Translation for the 21st Century. Part I: Books.* Ed. John E. Rotelle. Trans. Edmund Hill. Vol. 17. Brooklyn, NY: New City P, 1990.

Áureo Throno Episcopal, collocado nas Minas do Ouro, ou Noticia breve da Creação do novo Bispado Marianense, da sua felicissima posse, e pomposa entrada do seu meritissimo, primeiro Bispo, e da jornada, que fez do Maranhão, o Excellentissimo, e Reverendissimo Senhor D. Fr. Manoel da Cruz. 1749. Rpt in *Resíduos Seiscentistas em Minas: Textos do século do ouro e as projeções do mundo barroco.* Ed. Affonso Ávila. Vol. 2. Belo Horizonte: Centro de Estudos Mineiros, 1967. 335–592.

Ávila, Affonso. "O primado do visual na cultura barroca mineira." *Resíduos Seiscentistas em Minas: Textos do século do ouro e as projeções do mundo barroco.* Ed. Affonso Ávila. Vol. 1. Belo Horizonte: Centro de Estudos Mineiros, 1967. 85–116.

Aylward, E.T. *The Crucible Concept. Thematic and Narrative Patterns in Cervantes's* Novelas ejemplares. Madison, NJ: Farleigh Dickinson UP, 1999.

Bailey, Matthew, ed. and trans. *Las mocedades de Rodrigo. The Youthful Deeds of Rodrigo, the Cid.* Toronto: U of Toronto P, 2007.

Baker, Geoffrey. *Imposing Harmony: Music and Society in Colonial Cuzco.* Durham: Duke UP, 2008.

– "The Resounding City." *Music and Urban Society in Colonial Latin America.* Ed. Geoffrey Baker and Tess Knighton. Cambridge: Cambridge UP, 2011. 1–20.

Baranda, Concepción. "Los lectores del *Dioscórides*: estrategias discursivas del doctor Laguna." *Criticón* 58 (1993): 17–24.

Barbetti, Claire. *Ekphrastic Medieval Visions: A New Discussion in Interarts Theory. The New Middle Ages.* New York: Palgrave Macmillan, 2011.

Barona Vilar, Josep Lluís. *Sobre medicina y filosofía natural en el Renacimiento.* Valencia: Seminari d'estudis sobre la ciencia, 1993.

Beltran, Vicenç. *La poesía tradicional medieval y renacentista: poética antropológica de la lírica oral.* Kassel: Reichenberger, 2009.

Beltrán, Vicente. *O cervo do monte a augua volvia: del simbolismo naturalista en la cantiga de amigo.* El Ferrol: Sociedad de Cultura Valle-Inclán, 1984.

– "O vento lh'as levava: Don Denis y la tradición lírica peninsular." *Bulletin Hispanique* 86.1–2 (1984): 5–25.

Benthien, Claudia. *Skin.* Trans. Thomas Dunlap. New York: Columbia UP, 2002.

Benton, John. "*Trotula*, Women's Problems, and the Professionalization of Medicine in the Middle Ages." *Bulletin of the History of Medicine* 59.1 (1985): 330–53.

Berceo, Gonzalo de. *Milagros de Nuestra Señora.* Ed. Brian Dutton. London: Tamesis Books, 1971.

– *Milagros de Nuestra Señora. Obra Completa.* Ed. Claudio García Tureza. Madrid: Espasa-Calpe, 1992.

– *Milagros de Nuestra Señora.* Ed. E. Michael Gerli. Madrid: Cátedra, 1987.

– *Milagros de Nuestra Señora.* Ed. Fernando Baños. Barcelona: Crítica, 1997.

– *Milagros de Nuestra Señora.* Ed. Michael Gerli. Madrid: Cátedra, 2001.

– *Miracles of Our Lady.* Trans. Richard Terry Mount and Annette Grant Cash. Lexington: U Kentucky P, 1997.

Berg, Walter. *The Thirteen Signs of the Zodiac*. New York: Harper, 1995.

Bergmann, Emilie. "Monstrous Maternity in Fray Antonio de Guevara's *Relox de Príncipes*." *Brave New Worlds: Studies in Spanish Golden Age Literature*. Ed. Edward H. Friedman and Catherine Larson. New Orleans: UP of the South, 1996. 39–49.

Bériou, Nicole, and François-Olivier Touati. *Voluntate Dei leprosus. Les lépreux entre conversion et exclusion aux XIIe et XIIIe siècles*. Spoleto: Centro Italiano di Studi sull'alto Medioevo, 1991.

Bernáldez Montalvo, José María. "Las tarascas de Madrid." *Villa de Madrid* 19.71 (1981): 25–32; 19.72 (1981): 27–32.

Bernard of Clairvaux. *On the Song of Songs IV: The Works of Bernard of Clairvaux*. Cistercian Fathers Series. Trans. Irene Edmonds. Vol. 40. Kalamazoo, MI: Cistercian Publications, 1980.

Besselaar, José van den. *O Sebastianismo – História Sumária*. Lisbon: Instituto de Cultura e Língua Portuguesa, 1987.

Besserman, Lawrence L. *The Legend of Job in the Middle Ages*. Cambridge, MA: Harvard UP, 1979.

Bible. Douay-Rheims version. New York: Benziger, 1941.

Biblia, La, Reina-Valera Antigua (RVA). Bible Gateway. Biblegateway.com.

Biblia Sacra. Iuxta Vulgatam Versionem. Ed. Robert Weber. 4th ed. Stuttgart: Bibelgesellschaft, 1994.

Biguzzi, G. "Is the Babylon of Revelation Rome or Jerusalem?" *Biblica* 87.3 (2006): 371–86.

Blackmore, Josiah. "Melancholy, Passionate Love, and the *Coita d'Amor*." *PMLA* 124.2 (2009): 640–6.

Bloch, David. *Aristotle on Memory and Recollection*. Leiden: Brill, 2007.

Bly, Peter, and Alan Deyermond. "The Use of *Figura* in the *Libro de Alexandre*." *Journal of Medieval and Renaissance Studies* 2 (1972): 151–81.

Boeckl, Christine M. *Images of Leprosy: Disease, Religion, and Politics in European Art*. Kirksville, MO: Truman State UP, 2011.

Bolúfer, Mónica. "La lactancia asalariada en Valencia a finales del siglo XVIII." *Saitabi* 43 (1993): 255–68.

Book of Alexander: Libro de Alexandre. Ed. and trans. Peter Such and Richard Rabone. Oxford: Oxbow Books, 2009.

Boone, Elizabeth Hill, and Walter D. Mignolo, eds. *Writing without Words. Alternative Literacies in Mesoamerica and the Andes*. Durham, NC: Duke UP, 1994.

Borges, Célia Maia. *Escravos e Libertos nas Irmandades do Rosário: Devoção e Solidariedade em Minas Gerais – Séculos XVII e XIX*. Juiz de Fora: Editora UFJF, 2005.

Borges Guerra, M., P. García Moreno, and R. León del Río. "La neuropsicología del renacimiento *Examen de ingenios* de Huarte de San Juan." *Revista Española de Neuropsicología* 1.1 (1999): 67–94.

Borowitz, Albert. *Terrorism for Self-glorification: The Herostratos Syndrome.* Kent, OH: Kent State UP, 2005.

Boschi, Caio. *Os Leigos e o Poder (Irmandades Leigas e Política Colonizadora em Minas Gerais).* São Paulo: Ática, 1986.

Boyd, Stephen. "Cervantes's Exemplary Prologue." *A Companion to Cervantes's* Novelas ejemplares. Ed. Stephen Boyd. London: Támesis, 2005. 47–68.

Brancaforte, Benito. *Guzmán de Alfarache: ¿Conversión o proceso de degradación?* Madison, WI: Hispanic Seminary of Medieval Studies, 1980.

Brea, Mercedes. "*Levantou-s' a velida,* um exemplo de sincretismo harmónico." *Estudos dedicados a Ricardo Carvalho Calero.* Ed. José Luís Rodríguez. Vol. 2. Santiago de Compostela: Universidade de Santiago de Compostela, 2000. 139–51.

Brescia, Pablo A.J. "Towards a New Interpretation of the *Carta atenagórica.*" *Sor Juana & Vieira, trescientos años después.* Ed. K. Josu Bijuesca and Pablo A.J. Brescia. Santa Barbara, CA: Center for Portuguese Studies, 1998. 45–52.

Brownlee, Marina Scordilis. "Pagan and Christian: The Bivalent Hero of the *Libro de Alexandre.*" *Kentucky Romance Quarterly* 30 (1983): 263–70.

Burke, James F. "*La estrella de Sevilla* and the Tradition of Saturnine Melancholy." *Bulletin of Hispanic Studies* 51.2 (1974): 137–56.

– "The 'Banquet of Sense' in *La verdad sospechosa.*" *Hispanic Studies in Honor of Alan Deyermond: A North American Tribute.* Ed. John S. Miletich. Madison: U of Wisconsin P, 1986. 51–6.

Burr, David. "Eucharistic Presence and Conversion in Late Thirteenth-Century Franciscan Thought." *Transactions of the American Philosophical Society* 74.3 (1984): 1–113.

Bynum, Caroline Walker. *Christian Materiality: An Essay on Religion in Late Medieval Europe.* New York: Zone, 2011.

Cabré, Montserrat, and Teresa Ortiz, eds. *Sanadoras, matronas y médicas en Europa, siglos XII–XX.* Barcelona: Icaria, 2001.

Cacho Blecua, Juan Manuel. "La tienda en el *Libro de Alexandre.*" *La lengua y la literatura en tiempos de Alfonso X.* Actas Del Congreso Internacional, Murcia, 5–10 Marzo 1984. Ed. Fernando Carmona and Francisco J. Flores Arroyuelo. Murcia: Universidad de Murcia, Departamento de Literaturas Románicas, 1985. 109–34.

Cahill, Patricia. "The Play of Skin in The Changeling." *postmedieval* 3.4 (2012): 391–406.

Calderón de la Barca, Pedro. *El médico de su honra.* Ed. Jesus Pérez Magallón. Madrid: Cátedra, 2012.

Calero, Francisco. "Dos grandes europeístas españoles del siglo XVI: Luis Vives y Andrés Laguna." *Signa: Revista de la Asociación Española de Semiótica* 8 (1999): 19–35.

Camille, Michael. *Image on the Edge: The Margins of Medieval Art.* Cambridge, MA: Harvard UP, 1992.

Caminha, Pero Vaz de. *A Carta de Pêro Vaz de Caminha.* Ed. Jaime Cortesão. Lisbon: Imprensa Nacional-Casa da Moeda, 1994.

Camões, Luís de. *Os Lusíadas*. Ed. Emanuel Paulo Ramos. Porto: Porto Editora, n.d.

– *The Lusiads*. Trans. Leonard Bacon. New York: Hispanic Society of America, 1950.

Campbell, Neil. "Aquinas' Reasons for the Aesthetic Irrelevance of Tastes and Smells." *British Journal of Aesthetics* 36.2 (2006): 166–76.

Cancionero de Palacio. Ed. Ana María Álvarez Pellitero. Salamanca: Junta de Castilla y León, 1993.

– Ed. Francisca Vendrell de Millás. Barcelona: Consejo Superior de Investigaciones Científicas, 1945.

Cantel, Raymond. *Prophétisme et messianisme dans l'oeuvre d'Antonio Vieira*. Paris: Ediciones hispano-americanas, 1960.

Carroll, Noel. *The Philosophy of Horror, or Paradoxes of the Heart*. New York: Routledge, 1990.

Carruthers, Mary. *The Book of Memory: A Study of Memory in Medieval Culture*. New York: Cambridge UP, 1990.

– *The Book of Memory: A Study of Memory in Medieval Culture*. 2nd ed. New York, Cambridge: Cambridge UP, 2008.

– *The Craft of Thought: Meditation, Rhetoric and the Making of Images, 400–1200*. Cambridge: Cambridge UP, 2000.

Carvalho, José Adriano de Freitas. "Achegas ao Estudo da Influência da *Arbor Vitae Crucifixae* e da *Apocalypsis Nova* no Século XVI em Portugal." *Via spiritus* 1 (1994): 55–109.

– "A difusão da *Apocalypsis Nova* atribuída ao 'Beato' Amadeu da Silva no contexto cultural português da primeira metade do século XVII." *Revista da Faculdade de Letras* 19 (2002): 5–40.

Casas Rigall, Juan. *Agudeza y retórica en la poesía amorosa de cancionero*. Santiago de Compostela: Universidade de Santiago de Compostela, 1995.

Cascardi, Anthony J. *Ideologies of History in the Spanish Golden Age*. University Park, PA: Pennsylvania State UP, 1997.

Castells, Ricardo. "García's Love Melancholy and the Banquet Scene in Ruiz de Alarcón's *La verdad sospechosa*." *Bulletin of the Comediantes* 45 (1993): 93–101.

Castillo, David R. *Baroque Horrors: Roots of the Fantastic in the Age of Curiosities*. Ann Arbor: U of Michigan P, 2010.

Castro, D. João de. *A Aurora da Quinta Monarchia (1604–1605)*. Ed. João Carlos Gonçalves Serafim. Porto: Centro de Investigação Transdisciplinar Cultura, Espaço e Memória, 2011.

Castro, Guillén de. *Las mocedades del Cid*. Ed. Luciano García Lorenzo. Madrid: Cátedra, 1982.

Cavillac, Michel. *Gueux et Marchands dans le* Guzmán de Alfarache *(1599–1604). Romane picaresque et mentalité bourgeoise dans l'Espagne du Siècle d'Or*. Bordeaux: Institut d'etudes ibériques et ibéro-américaines de l'Université de Bordeux, 1983.

Cervantes, Miguel de. *El coloquio de los perros. Novelas ejemplares.* Ed. Harry Sieber. 2 vols. Madrid: Cátedra, 1980.

– "The Dialogue of the Dogs." *Exemplary Novels.* Vol. 4. Trans. John Jones and John Macklin. Ed. B.W. Ife. Warminster, UK: Aris & Phillips, 1992. 85–157.

– *The Divorce Court Judge. Eight Interludes.* Trans. Dawn L. Smith. Ed. Melveena McKendrick. London: Everyman, 1996. 12–20.

– *Don Quijote.* Trans. Burton Raffel. Ed. Diana de Armas Wilson. New York: Norton, 1999.

– *Don Quijote de la Mancha.* Barcelona: Crítica, 1998.

– *Don Quijote de la Mancha.* Ed. John J. Allen. 27th ed. Madrid: Cátedra, 2008.

– *Don Quixote de la Mancha.* Trans. Charles Jarvis. Ed. E.C. Riley. Oxford : Oxford UP, 1992.

– *La española inglesa. Novelas ejemplares.* Ed. Harry Sieber. Vol. 1. 17th ed. Madrid: Cátedra, 1995.

– *La española inglesa. Novelas ejemplares.* Ed. Florencio Sevilla Arroyo and Antonio Rey Hazas. Madrid: Alianza, Centro de Estudios Cervantinos, 1996.

– *Exemplary Novels.* Ed. Roberto García Echevarría. Trans. Edith Grossman. New Haven: Yale UP, 2016.

– *Exemplary Novels II (Novelas ejemplares).* Ed. B.W. Ife. Trans. R.M. Price. Warminster: Aris & Phillips, 1992.

– "The Illustrious Kitchen-Maid." *Exemplary Novels.* Vol. 3. Trans. Michael and Jonathan Thacker. Ed. B.W. Ife. Warminster, England: Aris & Phillips, 1992. 62–135.

– *La ilustre fregona. Novelas ejemplares.* Ed. Harry Sieber. 2 vols. Madrid: Cátedra, 1980.

– *El ingenioso hidalgo don Quijote de la Mancha.* Ed. Luis Andrés Murillo. 2 vols. Madrid: Castalia, 1978.

– *El juez de los divorcios. Entremeses.* Ed. Nicholas Spadacinni. Madrid: Cátedra, 1984.

– *The Jealous Old Man. Eight Interludes.* Trans. Dawn L. Smith. Ed. Melveena McKendrick. London: Everyman, 1996. 131–44.

– *Novelas ejemplares.* Ed. Jorge García López. Barcelona: Crítica, 2001.

– *Novelas ejemplares.* Ed. Juan Bautista Avalle-Arce. 3 vols. Madrid: Castalia, 1982.

– *Teatro completo.* Ed. Florencia Sevilla Arroyo and Antonio Rey Hazas. Barcelona: Planeta, 1987.

– *Los trabajos de Persiles y Sigismunda.* Ed. Juan Bautista-Avalle Arce. Madrid: Castalia, 1985.

– *The Trials of Persiles and Sigismunda.* Trans. Celia Richmond Weller and Clark A. Colahan. Berkeley: U of California P, 1989.

– *El viejo celoso. Entremeses.* Ed. Nicholas Spadacinni. Madrid: Cátedra, 1984.

Chacón Jiménez, Francisco, Rosa Elgarrista Domeque y Rafael Fresneda Collado. "Mercenarismo. ¿Mito o realidad? Análisis del Comportamiento de las amas de cría en el reino de Murcia (siglos XVII–XVIII)." *Enfance abandonnée et société en Europe (XIVe–XXe siècle).* Actes du colloque de Rome (30–31 janvier 1987). Rome: Collection de l'École française de Rome. 405–37.

Chambers, Edmund Kerchever. *The Medieval Stage*. Vol. 2. Oxford: Oxford UP, 1903.

Chaucer, Geoffrey. *Canterbury Tales*. The Riverside Chaucer. Ed. L.D. Benson. 2nd ed. Oxford: Oxford UP, 2008.

Cicero. *De Natura Deorum. Academica*. Trans. and ed. H. Rackham. Cambridge: Harvard UP, 1994.

Ciruelo, Pedro. *Reprouacion de las supersticiones y hechizerias*. Ed. Alva V. Ebersole. Valencia: Albatros-Hispanófila, 1978.

Clarke, Edwin and Kenneth Dewhurst. *An Illustrated History of Brain Function*. Berkeley: U of California P, 1972.

Classen, Constance. *Worlds of Sense: Exploring the Senses in History and across Cultures*. London: Routledge, 1993.

Classen, Constance, David Howes, and Anthony Synnott. *Aroma: The Cultural History of Smell*. London: Routledge, 1994.

Claydon, Ellen. *Juan Ruiz de Alarcón: Baroque Dramatist* Madrid: Castalia, 1970.

Clouse, Michele L. *Medicine, Government, and Public Health in Philip II's Spain: Shared Interests, Competing Authorities*. Burlington, VT: Ashgate, 2011.

Cobo, Bernabé. *Inca Religions and Customs*. Trans. and ed. Roland Hamilton. Austin: U of Texas P, 1990.

Coelho, Joaquim-Francisco. *Letras de Jornal*. Lisbon: Assírio e Alvim, 2010.

Cohen, Rip. "Girl in the Dawn: Textual Criticism and Poetics." *Portuguese Studies* 22.2 (2006): 173–87.

– "In the Beginning Was the Strophe: Origins of the *Cantigas d'Amigo* Revealed!" *Modelo*. Actas do V Colóquio da Secção Portuguesa da Associação Hispânica de Literatura Medieval. Ed. Ana Sofia Laranjinha and José Carlos Ribeiro Miranda. Porto: Faculdade de Letras da Universidade do Porto, 2005. 243–55.

Cohen, Rip, ed. *500 Cantigas d'Amigo*. Porto: Campo das Letras, 2003.

Cohen, Thomas. "Millenarian Themes in the Writings of Antonio Vieira." *Luso-Brazilian Review* 28.1 (1991): 23–46.

Collard, Frank, and Evelyne Samama. *Dents, dentistes et art dentaire: Histoire, practiques et répresentations. Antiquité, Moyen Age, Ancien Régime*. Paris: L'Harmattan, 2012.

Collins, Marsha. "Transgression and Transfiguration in Cervantes's *La española inglesa*." *Cervantes* 16.1 (1996): 54–73.

Colón, Cristóbal. "Carta del Almirante a los Reyes Católicos." *Los cuatro viajes del almirante y su testamento*. Ed. Ignacio B. Anzoátegui. Madrid: Espasa-Calpe, 1946.

– "Narrative of the Voyage which Don Christopher Columbus made the third time that he came to the Indies, when he discovered terra firma, as he sent it to their Majesties from the Island of Hispaniola." *Select Letters of Christopher Columbus, with Other Original Documents Relating to his Four Voyages to the New World*. Trans. and ed. R.H. Major. London: Hakluyt Society, 1870. 108–51.

Concilios Limenses (1551–1772). Ed. Rubén Vargas Ugarte SJ. 3 vols. Lima: Tipografía Peruana, 1951–4.

Connor, Steven. *The Book of Skin*. Ithaca, NY: Cornell UP, 2004.

Corominas, Joan, and José A. Pascual. *Diccionario crítico etimológico castellano e hispánico*. 6 vols. Madrid: Gredos, 1980–91.

Corral, Esther. "Feminine Voices in the Galician-Portuguese *cantigas de amigo*." Trans. Judith R. Cohen with Anne L. Klinck. *Medieval Woman's Song: Cross-Cultural Approaches*. Ed. Anne L. Klinck and Ann Marie Rasmussen. Philadelphia: U of Pennsylvania P, 2002. 81–98.

Covarrubias Orozco, Sebastián de. *Tesoro de la lengua castellana o española*. Madrid: Luís Sánchez, 1611.

– *Tesoro de la lengua Castellana o Española*. Ed. Martín de Riquer. Barcelona: Alta Fulla, 1987.

Crane, Mary Thomas. "Analogy, Metaphor, and the New Science: Cognitive Science and Early Modern Epistemology." *Introduction to Cognitive Cultural Studies*. Ed. Lisa Zunshine. Baltimore: Johns Hopkins UP, 2010. 103–14.

Creel, Bryant. *The Voice of the Phoenix: Metaphors of Death and Rebirth in Classics of the Iberian Renaissance*. Tempe: Arizona Center for Medieval and Renaissance Studies, 2004.

Cross, Richard. *Duns Scotus*. Oxford: Oxford UP, 1999.

Cruz, Anne. "Vindicating the *Vulnerata*: Cádiz and the Circulation of Religious Imagery as Weapons of War." *Material and Symbolic Circulation between Spain and England, 1554–1604*. Aldershot, UK: Ashgate, 2008. 39–60.

Cruz, Anne J., and Mary Elizabeth Perry, eds. *Culture and Control in Counter-Reformation Spain*. Minneapolis: U of Minnesota P, 1992.

Cruz, Sor Juana Inés de la. "Carta atenagórica." *Obras completas, IV. Comedias, sainetes y prosa*. Ed. Alfonso G. Salceda. Mexico City: Fondo de Cultura Económica, 1957. 412– 39.

Curtius, Ernst Robert. *European Literature and the Latin Middle Ages*. Trans. Willard R. Trask. Rpt Princeton: Princeton UP, 2013.

Cuthbert, Edward Godfrey and Frederic Atchley. *A History of the Use of Incense in Divine Worship*. London: Longmans, Green, 1909.

Dalby, Andrew. *Dangerous Tastes: The Story of Spices*. Berkeley: U of California P, 2000.

Dancygier, Barbara. *The Language of Stories: A Cognitive Approach*. Cambridge: Cambridge UP, 2011.

Dangler, Jean. *Mediating Fictions. Literature, Women Healers, and the Go-Between in Medieval and Early Modern Iberia*. Lewisburg, PA: Bucknell UP, 2001.

Danto, Arthur. "Bad Aesthetic Times." *Encounters and Reflections: Art in the Historical Present*. New York: Noonday Press, 1991.

Darnis, Pierre. "'Mucho dejé de escribir, que te escribo': sobre la filosofía velada de Guzmán de Alfarache." *Criticón* 110 (2010): 39–55.

Darst, David. "Hidden Truths and wrong assumptions in *La verdad sospechosa*." *Revista de Estudios Hispánicos* 13 (1979): 439–47.

– *Juan Boscán*. Boston: Twayne, 1978.

David-Peyre, Yvonne. *Le personnage du médecin et la relation médecin-malade dans la littérature ibérique, XVIe et XVIIe siècles*. Paris: Ediciones Iberoamericanas, 1971.

de Armas, Frederick A. "The Burning at Ephesus: Cervantes and Alarcón's *La sospechosa.*" *Studies in Honor of Gilbert Paolini.* Ed. Mercedes Vidal Tibits. Newark, DE: Juan de la Cuesta, 1996. 41–55.

– "De jerarquías pictóricas, planetarias y angélicas en *El pintor de su deshonra.*" *Calderón: Del manuscrito a la escena.* Ed. Frederick A. de Armas and Luciano García Lorenzo. Madrid: Iberoamericana, 2012. 209–26.

– "Heretical Stars: The Politics of Astrology in Cervantes' *La gitanilla* and *La española inglesa.*" *Material and Symbolic Circulation between Spain and England, 1554–1604.* Ed. Anne Cruz. Aldershot, UK: Ashgate, 2008. 89–100.

– *Quixotic Frescoes: Cervantes and Italian Renaissance Art.* Toronto: U of Toronto P, 2006.

de Armas Wilson, Diana. *Cervantes, the Novel and the New World.* Oxford: Oxford UP, 2003.

– "Dream Work in the Cave of Montesinos." *Quixotic Desire: Psychoanalytic Perspectives on Cervantes.* Ithaca, NY: Cornell UP, 1993.

de Fournival, Richard. *Il Bestiario d'amore.* Ed. Francesco Zambon. Parma: Pratiche, 1987.

de Grey Birch, Walter. *Catalogue of a Collection of Original Manuscripts Formerly Belonging to the Holy Office of the Inquisition in the Canary Islands.* 2 vols. Edinburgh: William Blackwood, 1908.

de la Torre, Fray Juan. *Aclamacion festiva de la mvy noble Imperial Villa de Potosi, en la dignifsima promocion del Excmo. Señor Maestro Don Fray Diego Morzillo, Rubio, y Auñón, Obifpo de Nicaragua, y de la Paz, Arçobifpo de las Charcas, al Govierno de eftos Reynos del Perù, por fu Virrey, y Capitan General, y Relacion de fu viage para la Ciudad de Lima.* Lima: Francisco Sobrino, 1716.

Dean, Carolyn. *Inka Bodies and the Body of Christ: Corpus Christi in Colonial Cuzco, Peru.* Durham: Duke UP, 1999.

del Río, María José. "Francisco Santos y su mundo: fiesta popular y política en el Madrid barroco." *Bajtín y la historia de la cultura popular. Cuarenta años de debate.* Ed. Tomás A. Mantecón Movellán. Santander: Universidad de Cantabria, 2008. 175–204.

del Río Parra, Elena. *Una era de monstruos.* Madrid: Iberoamericana, 2003.

Delicado, Francisco. *La lozana andaluza.* Ed. Claude Allaigre. Madrid: Cátedra, 2003.

Delorme, Ferdinand. "Question de P.J. Olivi: 'Quid ponat ius vel dominium' ou encore 'De signis voluntariis.'" *Antonianum* 20.1–4 (1945): 309–30.

Dening, Greg. *Beach Crossings: Voyaging across Times, Cultures, and Self.* Philadelphia: U of Pennsylvania P, 2004.

– *Islands and Beaches: Discourse on a Silent Land: Marquesas 1774-1880.* Honolulu: UP of Hawaii, 1980.

Deyermond, Alan. *Epic Poetry and the Clergy: Studies on the "Mocedades de Rodrigo."* London: Tamesis, 1968.

– "The Sirens, the Unicorn, and the Asp: Sonnets 21, 23, and 26." *Santillana: A Symposium.* Ed. Alan Deyermond. London: Queen Mary and Westfield College, Department of Hispanic Studies, 2000.

Diccionario de autoridades. 3 vols. Madrid: Real Academia Española, 1726. Facs. ed. Madrid: Gredos, 1990.

Diccionario de la lengua española. 300th Anniversary Edition. Madrid: Real Academia Española. http://dle.rae.es/?w=diccionario.

DiLillo, Leonard M. "Moral Purpose in Ruiz de Alarcón's *La verdad sospechosa*." *Hispania* 56 (1973): 254–9.

Dioscórides. *Acerca de la materia medicinal y de los venenos mortíferos*. Trans. and ed. Andrés de Laguna. Antwerp: Casa de Juan Latio, 1555.

Dod, Bernard G. "Aristoteles Latinus." *The Cambridge History of Later Medieval Philosophy*. Ed. Norman Kretzmann, Kenny Anthony, and Jan Pinborg. Cambridge: Cambridge UP, 1988. 43–79.

Domínguez, Julia. "The Janus Hypothesis in *Don Quijote*: Memory and Imagination in Cervantes." *Cognitive Approaches to Early Modern Spanish Literature*. Ed. Isabel Jaén and Julien Simon. New York and Oxford: Oxford UP, 2016. 74–90.

Donahue, Darcy. "Dressing Up and Dressing Down: Clothing and Class Identity in the *Novelas ejemplares*." *Cervantes* 24.1 (2004): 105–18.

Dutton, Brian. *El Cancionero del siglo XV, c. 1360–1520*. 7 vols. Salamanca: Universidad de Salamanca, 1990–6.

Eco, Umberto. *The Role of the Reader: Explorations in the Semiotics of Texts*. Bloomington: Indiana UP, 1979.

Egido, Aurora. "La memoria y el *Quijote*." *Cervantes* 11.1 (1991): 3–44.

Eisenberg, Daniel "La biblioteca de Cervantes. Una reconstrucción." *Studia in Honorem prof. Martín de Riquer*. Vol. 2. Barcelona: Quaderns Crema, 1987. 271–328.

El Saffar, Ruth. "Cervantes and the Imagination." *Cervantes* 6.1 (1986): 81–90.

– *Novel to Romance: A Study of Cervantes'* Novelas ejemplares. Baltimore: Johns Hopkins UP, 1974.

Elliott, J.H. "The Old World and the New Revisited." *America in European Consciousness, 1493–1750*. Ed. Karen Ordahl Kupperman. Chapel Hill: U of North Carolina P, 1995. 391–408.

Enders, Jody. *Death by Drama and Other Medieval Urban Legends*. Chicago: U of Chicago P, 2002.

Enrenreich, Barbara and Deirdre English. *Brujas, comadronas y enfermeras. Historia de las sanadoras*. 3rd ed. Valencia: Cuadernos inacabados, 1988.

Enríquez Gómez, Antonio. *La torre de Babilonia*. Ed. María Teresa de Santos Borreguero. Madrid: Universidad Autónoma de Madrid, 1989.

Erdman, E. George. "The Elm and the Vine: Arboreal Figures in the Golden Age Sonnet." *PMLA* 84.3 (1969): 587–95.

Evans, Suzanne. "The Scent of a Martyr." *Numen* 49 (2002): 193–211.

Farina, Lara. "Wondrous Skins and Tactile Affection: The Blemmye's Touch." *Reading Skin in Medieval Literature and Culture*. Ed. Katie L. Walter. New York: Palgrave Macmillan, 2013. 11–28.

Fauconnier, Gilles, and Mark Turner. "Conceptual Integration and Formal Expression." *Metaphor and Symbolic Activity* 10.3 (1995): 183–203.

– "Conceptual Projection and Middle Spaces." *Department of Cognitive Science Technical Report 9401*. San Diego: University of California, 1994.

– *The Way We Think: Conceptual Blending and the Mind's Hidden Complexities*. New York: Basic, 2002.

Fernández, Enrique. "Baroque Reliquaries and Automata as Representations of Eternal Life." *The Iberoamerican Baroque*. Vol. 1. Ed. Beatriz de Alba Koch. Toronto: U of Toronto P, forthcoming.

Fernández Mosquera, Santiago. *La tormenta en el Siglo de Oro. Variaciones funcionales de un tópico*. Madrid: Iberoamericana, 2006.

Ferreira, Maria do Rosário. *Águas doces, águas salgadas: da funcionalidade dos motivos aquáticos na Cantiga de Amigo*. Porto: Granito, 1999.

Field, Catherine. "'Many Hands Hands': Writing the Self in Early Modern Women's Recipe Books." *Genre and Women's Life Writing in Early Modern England*. Ed. Michelle M. Dowd and Julie Eckerle. Aldershot, UK: Ashgate, 2007. 49–63.

Fiore, Robert L. "The Interaction of Motives and Mores in *La verdad sospechosa*." *Hispanófila* 61 (1977): 513–27.

Flory, David A. *Marian Representations in the Miracle Tales of Thirteenth-Century Spain and France*. Washington, DC: The Catholic U of America P, 2000.

Foley, Augusta E. *Occult Arts and Doctrine in the Theater of Juan Ruiz de Alarcón*. Geneva: Droz, 1972.

Folger, Robert. *Images in Mind: Lovesickness, Spanish Sentimental Fiction and Don Quijote*. Chapel Hill: U of North Carolina P, 2002.

Forcione, Alban K. *Cervantes and the Humanist Vision: A Study of Four* Exemplary Novels. Princeton: Princeton UP, 1982.

Fotherghill-Payne, Louise. "La justicia poética de *La verdad sospechosa*." *Romanische Forschungen* 83 (1971): 588–95.

– "La percepción por la vista y la averiguación por el oído en *El Quijote*." *Aureum Saeculum Hispanum. Festschrift für Hans Flasche zum* 70 (1983): 69–79.

Foucault, Michel. *Madness and Civilization: A History of Insanity in the Age of Reason*. Trans. Richard Howard. Rpt. New York: Vintage, 1988.

Freedman, Paul H. *Out of the East: Spices and the Medieval Imagination*. New Haven: Yale UP, 2008.

Fromont, Cécile. "Dancing for the King of Congo from Early Modern Central Africa to Slavery-Era Brazil." *Colonial Latin American Review* 22.2 (2013): 184–208.

Frye, Northrop. *The Great Code: The Bible and Literature*. New York: Harcourt Brace, 1982.

Funes, Leonardo, with Felipe Tenenbaum, ed. *Las mocedades de Rodrigo*. Woodbridge, UK: Boydell, 2004.

Gaposchkin, Marianne Cecilia. *The Making of Saint Louis: Kingship, Sanctity, and Crusade in the Later Middle Ages*. Ithaca, NY: Cornell UP, 2008.

García Ballester, Luis. *Historia social de la medicina en la España de los siglos XIII al XIV.* Vol 1. Madrid: Akal, 1976.

– *Medicine in a Multicultural Society. Christian, Jewish and Muslim Practitioners in the Spanish Kingdoms, 1222–1610.* Burlington, VT: Ashgate, 2001.

García Barreno, Pedro. "La medicina en *El Quijote* y su entorno." *La ciencia y* El Quijote. Ed. José Manuel Sánchez Ron. Barcelona: Crítica, 2005. 155–79.

García Irigoyen, Javier. *The Spanish Arcadia: Sheep Herding, Pastoral Discourse, and Ethnicity in Early Modern Spain.* Toronto: U of Toronto P, 2014.

García Santo-Tomás, Enrique. *Espacio urbano y creación literaria en el Madrid de Felipe IV.* Madrid: Iberoamericana, 2004.

– "Fortunes of the *Occhiali Politici* in Early Modern Spain: Optics, Vision, Points of View." *PMLA* 124.1 (2009): 59–75.

– *La creación del "Fénix": recepción crítica y formación canónica del teatro de Lope de Vega.* Madrid: Gredos, 2000.

– *La musa refractada: literatura y óptica en la España del Barroco.* Madrid: Iberoamericana, 2014.

– *Modernidad bajo sospecha: Salas Barbadillo y la cultura material del siglo XVII.* Madrid: Consejo Superior de Investigaciones Científicas, 2008.

– "'Offspring of the Mind': Childbirth and its Perils in Early Modern Spanish Literature." *Medical Cultures in the Early Modern Spanish Empire.* Ed. María Luz López Terrada, John D. Slater, and José Pardo Tomás. Aldershot, UK: Ashgate, 2014. 149–66.

– "Visiting the Virtuoso in Early Modern Spain: the Case of Juan de Espina." *Journal of Spanish Cultural Studies* 13.2 (2012): 129–47.

Garcilaso de la Vega, el Inca. *Comentarios reales: La Florida del Inca.* Ed. Mercedes López-Baralt. Madrid: Espasa-Calpe, 2003.

– [1617] 1944. *Historia general del Perú (Segunda parte de los Comentarios reales de los Incas)*, ed. Ángel Rosenblat. 2 vols. Buenos Aires: Emecé.

Gaylord, Mary Malcolm. "Cervantes's Other Fiction." *The Cambridge Companion to Cervantes.* Ed. Anthony J. Cascardi. Cambridge: Cambridge UP, 2002. 100–30.

– "The Telling of Lies of *La verdad sospechosa.*" *Modern Language Notes* 103.2 (1988): 223–8.

Gélis, Jacques. *History of Childbirth: Fertility, Pregnancy and Birth in Early Modern Europe.* Cambridge: Cambridge UP, 1991.

Giamatti, A. Bartlett. *The Earthly Paradise and the Renaissance Epic.* Princeton: Princeton UP, 1966.

Gil, Fernando. "*The Lusiads* Effect." Trans. K. David Jackson. *The Traveling Eye: Retrospection, Vision, and Prophecy in the Portuguese Renaissance.* Fernando Gil and Helder Macedo. Dartmouth, MA: U of Mass. Dartmouth, 2009. 33–85.

Gobry, Ivan. *Saint Francis of Assisi.* San Francisco: Ignatius Press, 2006.

Goldie, Peter. *The Emotions: A Philosophical Exploration.* New York: Clarendon, 2000.

Góngora, Luis de. *Soledades.* Ed. Robert Jammes. Madrid: Castalia, 1994.

González Manjarrés, Miguel Ángel. *Andrés Laguna y el humanismo médico: Estudio filológico.* Valladolid: Junta de Castilla y León, 2000.

Green, Monica. *Making Women's Medicine Masculine: The Rise of Male Authority in Pre-Modern Gynaecology.* Oxford: Oxford UP, 2008.

– "The Possibilities of Literacy and the Limits of Reading: Women and the Gendering of Medical Literacy." *Women's Healthcare in the Medieval West: Texts and Contexts.* Ed. Monica Green. Vol. 7. Burlington, VT: Ashgate. 2000. 1–76.

Green, Otis. "On the Attitude toward the Vulgo in the Spanish Siglo de Oro." *Studies in the Renaissance* 4 (1957): 190–200.

Grieco, Allen J. "Body and Soul." *A Cultural History of Food in the Medieval Age.* Ed. Massimo Montanari. London: Berg, 2012. 143–9.

Gubbini, Gaia. *Tactus, osculum, factum: il senso del tatto e il desiderio nella lirica trobadorica.* Rome: Edizioni Nuova Cultura, 2009.

Guevara, Fray Antonio de. *Relox de Príncipes.* Ed. Emilio Blanco. Madrid: Confres, 1994.

Guiance, Ariel. "En olor de santidad: La caracterización y el alcance de los aromas en la hagiografía medieval." *Edad Media. Revista de Historia* 10 (2009): 131–61.

Guillaume de Lorris, and Jean de Meun. *Le Roman de la Rose.* [1275]. Ed. Michel Zink. Paris: Livre de Poche, 1992.

– *The Romance of the Rose.* Trans. Charles Dahlberg. Princeton: Princeton UP, 1971.

Gumbrecht, Hans Ulrich. Introduction. *Rethinking the Medieval Senses: Heritage, Fascinations, Frames.* Ed. Stephen G. Nichols, Andreas Kablitz, and Alison Calhoun. Baltimore: Johns Hopkins UP, 2008. 1–10.

Halliday, Sam. *Sonic Modernity: Representing Sound in Literature, Culture and the Arts.* Edinburgh: Edinburgh UP, 2013.

Halpern, Cynthia. *The Political Theater of Early Seventeenth-Century Spain with Special Reference to Juan Ruiz de Alarcón.* New York: Peter Lang, 1993.

Hansen, João Adolfo. "A máquina do mundo." *Poetas que pensaram o mundo.* Ed. Adauto Novaes. São Paulo: Companhia das Letras, 2005. 157–97.

Harvey, Elizabeth D. "Introduction: The 'Sense of All Senses.'" *Sensible Flesh: On Touch in Early Modern Culture.* Ed. Elizabeth D. Harvey. Philadelphia: U of Pennsylvania P, 2003. 1–21.

Harvey, E. Ruth. *The Inward Wits.* London: Warburg Institute, University of London, 1975.

Heiple, Daniel L. *Mechanical Imagery in Spanish Golden Age Poetry.* Potomac, MD: Studia Humanitatis, 1983.

– "Pro-Feminist Reactions to Huarte's Misogyny in Lope's *La prueba de las promesas* and María de Zayas' *Novelas amorosas y ejemplares.*" *The Presence of Women in the Spanish Golden Age Drama.* Ed. Anita K. Stoll and Dawn L. Smith. Lewisburg, PA: Bucknell UP, 1993. 121–34.

Heller-Roazen, Daniel. "Common Sense: Greek, Arabic, Latin." *Rethinking the Medieval Senses: Heritage, Fascinations, Frames*. Ed. Stephen G. Nichols, Andreas Kablitz, and Alison Calhoun. Baltimore: Johns Hopkins UP, 2008. 20–30.

Heninger, S.K. *Touches of Sweet Harmony: Pythagorean Cosmology and Renaissance Poetics*. San Marino, CA: Huntington Library, 1974.

Hermann, Jacqueline. *No reino do Desejado: A construção do sebastianismo em Portugal (séculos XVI e XVII)*. São Paulo: Companhia das Letras, 1998.

Hogan, Patrick C. *Cognitive Science, Literature, and the Arts: A Guide for Humanists*. New York: Routledge, 2003.

Holanda, Sérgio Buarque de. *Visão do paraíso: os motivos edênicos no descobrimento e colonização do Brasil*. São Paulo: Companhia das Letras, 2010.

Huarte de San Juan, Juan. *Examen de ingenios para las ciencias*. Ed. Esteban Torre. Barcelona: Textos Universitarios, 1988.

– *Examen de ingenios para las ciencias*. Madrid: Cátedra, 1989.

Huneycutt, Lois L. *Matilda of Scotland: A Study in Medieval Queenship*. Woodbridge, UK: Boydell, 2003.

Iffland, James. *Quevedo and the Grotesque*. 2 vols. London: Tamesis, 1978.

Imaz Martínez, Elixabete. "Mujeres gestantes, madres en gestación. Metáforas de un cuerpo fronterizo". *Política y sociedad* 36 (2001): 97–111.

Irving, D.R.M. *Colonial Counterpoint: Music in Early Modern Manila*. Oxford: Oxford UP, 2010.

Isidore of Seville. *The Etymologies of Isidore of Seville*. Trans. and ed. Stephen A. Barney, W.J. Lewis, J.A. Beach, and Olivier Berghot. Cambridge: Cambridge UP, 2006.

Jablonski, Nina G. *Skin. A Natural History*. Berkeley: U of California P, 2006.

Jaén, Isabel. "Cervantes and the Cognitive Ideas of his Time: Mind and Development in Don Quixote." *Cervantes* 32.1 (2012): 71–98.

Jeannaret, Michel. *A Feast of Words: Banquets and Table Talk in the Renaissance*. Trans. Jeremy Whiteley and Emma Hughes. Chicago: U of Chicago P, 1991.

Jensen, Frede. *The Earliest Portuguese Lyrics*. Odense, Den.: Odense UP, 1978.

– ed. and trans. *Medieval Galician-Portuguese Poetry: An Anthology*. New York: Garland, 1992.

Jerome. *Opera Omnia Hieronymi. Patrologia Latina Database*. Vol. 26. Ed. J.-P. Migne. Ann Arbor, MI: ProQuest, 1996. http://pld.chadwyck.com/.

Johansen, T.K. *Aristotle on the Sense-Organs*. Cambridge: Cambridge UP, 1997.

John of Salisbury. *Policratus*. Ed. and trans. Cary J. Nederman. Cambridge: Cambridge UP, 1990.

Johnson, Carroll B. *Cervantes and the Material World*. Urbana: U of Illinois P, 2000.

– *Inside Guzmán de Alfarache*. Berkeley: U of California P, 1978.

– "*La española inglesa* and the Practice of Literary Production." *Viator* 9 (1988): 377–416.

Jordán, María V. "The Empire of the Future and the Chosen People: Father António Vieira and the Prophetic Tradition in the Hispanic World." *Luso-Brazilian Review* 40.1 (2003): 45–57.

Josa, Lola. *El arte dramático de Juan Ruiz de Alarcón.* Kassel: Reichenberger, 2003.

Jütte, Robert. *A History of the Senses: From Antiquity to Cyberspace.* Cambridge: Polity, 2005.

Kadir, Djelal. *Columbus and the Ends of the Earth: Europe's Prophetic Rhetoric as Conquering Ideology.* Berkeley: U of California P, 1992.

Kagan, Richard L. *Lucrecia's Dreams: Politics and Prophecy in Sixteenth-Century Spain.* Berkeley: U of California P, 1990.

Kelly, Daniel. *Yuck! The Nature and Moral Significance of Disgust.* Cambridge, MA: MIT P, 2011.

Kelly, Jack. *Gunpowder: Alchemy, Bombards and Pyrotechnics. The History of the Explosive that Changed the World.* New York: Basic, 2004.

Kelly, Thomas E., Stephen Knight, and Thomas H. Ohlgren, trans. and ed. *Robin Hood and Other Outlaw Tales.* Kalamazoo, MI: Medieval Institute, 1997.

Kemp, Simon, and Garth J.O. Fletcher. "The Medieval Theory of the Inner Senses." *The American Journal of Psychology.* 106.4 (1993): 559–76.

Kennedy, Ruth Lee. *Studies in Tirso I: The Dramatist and his Competitors, 1620–26.* Chapel Hill: North Carolina Studies in the Romance Languages and Literatures, 1974.

Kerigan, Thomas, and John Hamilton Moore. *Moore's Navigation Improved: Being the Theory and Practice of Finding the Latitude, the Longitude, and the variation of the Compass by the Fixed Stars and Planets.* 2nd ed. London: Baldwin and Cradock, 1835.

Kiddy, Elizabeth W. *Blacks of the Rosary: Memory and History in Minas Gerais, Brazil.* University Park: Penn State UP, 2005.

King, Willard F. *Juan Ruiz de Alarcón: letrado y dramaturgo. Su mundo mexicano y español.* Mexico City: Colegio de México, 1989.

Kirk, Stephanie. "El parto monstruoso: creación artística y reproducción biológica en la obra de Sor Juana Inés de la Cruz." *Revista Iberoamericana* 75 (2009): 417–32.

Klein, Bernhard. "Mapping the Waters: Sea Charts, Navigation, and Camões's *Os Lusíadas.*" *Renaissance Studies* 25 (2010): 228–47.

Korsmeyer, Carolyn. *Savoring Disgust: The Foul and the Fair In Aesthetics.* New York: Oxford UP, 2011.

Krier, Theresa M. *Birth Passages: Maternity and Nostalgia, Antiquity to Shakespeare.* Ithaca, NY: Cornell UP, 2001.

Krondl, Michael. *The Taste of Conquest: The Rise and Fall of the Three Great Cities of Spice.* New York: Ballantine, 2007.

Laguna, Andrés. *Pedacio Dioscorides Anazarbeo, annotado por el doctor Andrés Laguna, medico dignissmio de Julio III, pontífice máximo nuevamente ilustrado, y añadido, demonstrando las figuras de plantas, y animales en estampas finas, y dividido en dos tomos.* Madrid: Alonso Balbas, [1555] 1733.

Lakoff, George, and Mark Johnson. *Philosophy in the Flesh: The Embodied Mind and Its Challenge to Western Thought.* New York: Basic, 1999.

Lanning, John Tate. *The Royal Protomedicato: The Regulation of the Medical Profession in the Spanish Empire.* Durham, NC: Duke UP, 1985.

Larquié, Claude. "Les milieux nourriciers des enfants madrilènes au XVIIe siècle." *Mélanges la Casa de Velázquez* 19 (1983): 221–42.

Larson, Catherine. "Labels and Lies: Names and Don García's World in *La verdad sospechosa.*" *Revista de Estudios Hispánicos* 20.2 (1986): 95–112.

Leão, Gaspar de. *Desengaño de Perdidos.* Ed. Eugenio Asensio. Coimbra: Universidade de Coimbra, 1958.

León, Fray Luis de. *La perfecta casada.* Ed. José López Navarro. Madrid: Ediciones Rialp, 1968.

– *La perfecta casada.* Ed. Mercedes Etreros. Madrid: Taurus, 1987.

Leong, Elaine. "Collecting Knowledge for the Family: Recipes, Gender and Practical Knowledge in the Early Modern English Household." *Centaurus* 55.2 (2013): 81–103.

Levisi, Margarita. "Hieronymus Bosch y los *Sueños* de Francisco de Quevedo." *Filología* 9 (1963): 163–200.

Ley, Charles David, trans. "The Discovery of Brazil. 1500." *Portuguese Voyages, 1498–1663.* Ed. Charles David Ley. London: Phoenix Press, 2000. 39–59.

Libro de Alexandre. Ed. Cañas, Jesús. 4th ed. Madrid: Cátedra, 2003.

Lida de Malkiel, Rosa María. *La idea de la fama en la Edad Media castellana.* México: Fondo de Cultura Económica, 1983.

Livro de receptas de pivetes, pastilhas e vvas perfumadas y conserbas. Madrid, 1462.

Lobera de Avila, Luis. *El Vanquete de nobles cavalleros.* 1530. Rpt. Chicago: U of Chicago P, 1991.

López, Fray Domingo. *Talentos del Superior. Symbolos en los cinco sentidos corporales.* Granada: Imprenta de la S.S. Trinidad, 1717.

López de Ayala, Pero. *Rimado de Palacio.* Ed. Germán Orduña. Madrid: Castalia, 1987.

López-Muñoz, Francisco, Cecilio Álamo, and Pilar García-García. "'Than All the Herbs Described by Dioscorides ...': The Traces of Andrés Laguna in the Works of Cervantes." *Pharmacy in History* 49.3 (2007): 489–501.

López Pinciano, Alonso. *Filosofía antigua poética.* Valladolid, Sp.: Rodríguez, 1894.

López Piñero, José María. *Ciencia y técnica en la sociedad española de los siglos XVI y XVII.* Barcelona: Labor, 1979.

López Piñero, José María, and Francisco Calero. *Los temas polémicos de la medicina renacentista: las Controversias (1556), de Francisco Valles y la medicina renacentista.* Madrid: Consejo Superior de Investigaciones Científicas, 1988.

López Terrada, María Luz. "Medical Pluralism in the Iberian Kingdoms: The Control of Extra-academic Practitioners in Valencia." *Health and Medicine in Hapsburg Spain: Agents, Practices, Representations.* Ed. Teresa Huguet-Termes, Jon Arrizabalaga, and Harold J. Cook. Medical History, Supplement 29. London: The Wellcome Trust Centre for the History of Medicine at UCL, 2009. 7–25.

– "Los tribunales del protomedicato y el protoalbeiterato." *Historia de la ciencia y de la técnica en la corona de Castilla. Siglos XVI y XVII*. Ed. José María López Piñero. Salamanca: Junta de Castilla y León, 2002. 107–25.

Lorenzo, Javier. "'En blanco y sin figura': Prologue, Portrait, and Signature in Cervantes' *Novelas ejemplares*." *Letras hispanas* 2.2 (2005): 86–101.

Lubac, Henri Cardinal de. Corpus Mysticum*: The Eucharist and the Church in the Middle Ages*. Trans. Gemma Simmonds with Richard Price and Christopher Stephens. Ed. Laurence Paul Hemming and Susan Frank Parsons. Notre Dame, IN: U of Notre Dame P, 2006.

Lucas, A. "Cosmetics, Perfumes and Incense in Ancient Egypt." *Journal of Egyptian Archaeology* 16.1 (1930): 41–53.

Macedo, Helder. "Uma cantiga de Dom Dinis." *Do cancioneiro de amigo*. Ed. Stephen Reckert and Helder Macedo. 3rd ed. Lisbon: Assírio e Alvim, 1996. 59–70.

Machado, Simão Ferreira. *Triunfo Eucharístico, Exemplar da Christandade Lusitana na pública exaltaçaõ da Fé na solemne Trasladaçaõ do Divinissimo Sacramento da Igreja da Senhora do Rosario, para hum novo Templo da Senhora do Pilar em Villa Rica, Corte da Capitania das Minas.* In *Resíduos Seiscentistas em Minas: Textos do século do ouro e as projeções do mundo barroco*. Ed. Affonso Ávila. Vol. 1. Belo Horizonte, Braz.: Centro de Estudos Mineiros, 1967.

Macpherson, Ian. "*The 'Invenciones y letras' of the* Cancionero general." Papers of the Medieval Hispanic Research Seminar, 9. London: Department of Hispanic Studies, Queen Mary and Westfield College, 1999.

Maggi, Armando. *Satan's Rhetoric: A Study of Renaissance Demonology*. Chicago: U of Chicago P, 2001.

Magner, Lois N. *A History of Medicine*. New York: Marcel Dekker, 1992.

Majid, Asifa, and Stephen C. Levinson. "The Senses in Language and Culture." *Senses & Society* 6.1 (2011): 5–18.

Mancing, Howard. "Embodied Cognition, Theory of Mind, and Narrative Technique in *Don Quijote*." Paper presented at the National Cervantes Symposium, April 2014, Chicago.

Manuel, Juan. *El Conde Lucanor*. Ed. Ian Michael. Madrid: Castalia, 1984.

Marcombe, David. *Leper Knights: The Order of St. Lazarus of Jerusalem in England, c. 1150–1544*. Woodbridge, UK: Boydell, 2003.

Márquez de Villanueva, Francisco. "'Nasçer y morir como bestias' (criptojudaísmo y criptoaverroísmo)." *Los judaizantes en Europa y la literatura del Siglo de Oro*. Ed. Fernando Díaz Esteban. Madrid: Letrúmero, 1994. 273–93.

Martín Casares, Aurelia. "La hechicería en la Andalucía moderna: ¿una forma de poder de las mujeres?". *Pautas históricas de sociabilidad femenina: rituales y modelos de representación*. Ed. M. Nash, M.J. De la Pascua y G. Espigado Tocino. Cádiz: Universidad, 1999. 101–11.

Martínez Crespo, Alicia. *Manual de mugeres en el qual se contienen muchas y diversas reçeutas muy buenas*. Salamanca: Ediciones Universidad, 1995.

Martínez de Cuéllar, Juan. *Desengaño del hombre*. Andrés García de la Iglesia, Juan Martín Merinero, 1663.

Martínez-Góngora, Mar. "Un unicornio en la corte de una reina virgen: 'Ginecocracia' y ansiedades masculinas en 'La española inglesa.'" *Cervantes* 20.1 (2000): 27–46.

Martínez Ruiz, Juan. "Ensalmos curativos del manuscrito árabe *Misceláneo de Salomón* de Ocaña (Toledo) en el marco de convivencia de las Tres Culturas." II Congreso Internacional "Encuentro de las Tres Culturas" (Toledo, 3–6 de octubre 1983). Toledo: Ayuntamiento de Toledo, 1985. 217–22.

Matthews, Dakin, trans. *The Truth Can't Be Trusted.* By Juan Ruiz de Alarcón. New Orleans: UP of the South, 1998.

Mazzoni, Cristina. *Maternal Impressions: Pregnancy and Childbirth in Literature and Theory*. Ithaca, NY: Cornell UP, 2002.

McCord Adams, Marilyn. *Some Later Medieval Theories of the Eucharist: Thomas Aquinas, Giles of Rome, Duns Scotus, and William Ockham*. Oxford: Oxford UP, 2010.

McGann, Jerome. *The Textual Condition*. Princeton: Princeton UP, 1991.

McKim-Smith, Gridley, and Marcia Welles. "Material Girls – and Boys: Dressing Up in Cervantes." *Cervantes* 24.1 (2004): 65–104.

Meirinhos, José Francisco. "Escotistas portugueses dos séculos XIV e XV." *João Duns Scotus (1308–2008). Homenagem dos scotistas lusófonos*. Ed. Luís Alberto De Boni et al. Porto Alegre: EST, 2008. 330–47.

Melero Jiménez, Elisa Isabel. *La tarasca de parto en el mesón del infierno, y días de fiesta por la noche. Su autor Francisco Santos, criado del Rey Nuestro Señor, y natural de Madrid. Dedicada a Juan Díaz Rodero*. Edición y estudio de los preliminares y del libro primero. Presentado en el Departamento de Filología Hispánica, Facultad de Filosofía y Letras, de la Universidad de Extremadura, el día 25 de septiembre de 2004.

Meneses, Paulo. "Fenomenologia da morte-por-amor: do influxo das teorias médicas antigo-medievais na actividade poética trovadoresca." *Estudos dedicados a Ricardo Carvalho Calero*. Ed. José Luís Rodríguez. Vol. 2. Santiago de Compostela: Universidade de Santiago de Compostela, 2000. 491–506.

Mercado, Luis. *El libro de la peste*. Ed. Nicasio Mariscal. Madrid: Julio Cosano, 1921.

Merich, Stefano de. "La presencia del *Libro de la filosofía de las armas* de Carranza en el *Quijote* de 1615." *Cervantes* 27.2 (2007): 155–80.

Michael, Ian. *The Treatment of Classical Material in the* Libro de Alexandre. Manchester: U of Manchester P, 1970.

Micó, José María. "Introducción." *Guzmán de Alfarache*, by Mateo Alemán. Ed. José María Micó. Cátedra: Madrid, 1987. 15–75.

Miller, William Ian. *The Anatomy of Disgust*. Cambridge, MA: Harvard UP, 1997.

Mimoso, João Sardinha. *Relación de la real tragicomedia con que los padres de la Compañia de Iesus en su Colegio de S. Anton de Lisboa recibieron a la Magestad Catolica de Felipe II de Portugal, y de su entrada en este Reino, con lo que se hizo en las Villas, Ciudades en que entró*. Lisbon: Jorge Rodrigues, 1620.

Moncó Rebollo, Beatriz. "Demonio y mujeres: historia de una transgresión." *El Diablo en la Edad Moderna*. Ed. María Tausiet and James S. Amelang. Madrid: Marcial Pons, 2004. 187–210.

– *Mujer y demonio: una pareja barroca*. Madrid: Instituto de Sociología Aplicada, 1989.

Montaner, Alberto. "Rodrigo y el gafo." *El Cid, de la materia épica a las crónicas caballerescas*. Actas del congreso internacional "IX Centenario de la muerte del Cid." Ed. Carlos Alvar, Georges Martin, and Fernando Gómez Redondo. Alcalá de Henares, Sp.: Alcalá de Henares UP, 2002. 121–79.

Monteiro, John. *Negros da Terra: Índios e Bandeirantes nas Origens de São Paulo*. São Paulo: Editora Schwarcz, 1994.

Morant, Isabel. *Discursos de la vida buena: matrimonio, mujer y sexualidad en la literatura humanista*. Madrid: Cátedra, 2002.

Morisi-Guerra, Anna. "The *Apocalypsis Nova*: A Plan for Reform." *Prophetic Rome in the High Renaissance Period: Essays*. Ed. Marjorie Reeves. Oxford: Oxford UP, 1992. 27–50.

– Apocalypsis Nova*: Ricerche sull'origine e la formazione del testo dello pseudo-Amadeo*. Rome: Istituto Storico Italiano per il Medio Evo, 1970.

Morton, John G. "Alarcón's *La verdad sospechosa*: Meaning and Didacticism." *Bulletin of the Comediantes* 26 (1974): 51–7.

Mulvey, Patricia. "Black Brothers and Sisters: Membership in the Black Lay Brotherhoods of Colonial Brazil." *Luso-Brazilian Review* 17.2 (1980): 253–79.

Munro, Jill M. *Spikenard and Saffron: The Imagery of the Song of Songs*. Sheffield, UK: Sheffield Academic Press, 1995.

Nadeau, Carolyn. "Authorizing the Wife/Mother in Sixteenth-century Advice Manuals." *Women in the Discourse of Early Modern Spain*. Ed. Joan Cammarata. Gainesville: U of Florida P, 2003. 19–34.

– "Blood Mother/Milk Mother: Breastfeeding, the Family, and the State in Antonio de Guevara's *Relox de Príncipes* (*Dial of Princes*)." *Hispanic Review* 69.2 (2001): 153–74.

– "Star-Crossed Love: Spheres of Reality in Ruiz de Alarcón's *La verdad sospechosa*." *A Star-Crossed Golden Age: Myth and the Spanish Comedia*. Ed. Frederick A. de Armas. Lewisburg, PA: Bucknell UP, 1998. 62–73.

Nalbantian, Suzanne. *Memory in Literature. From Rousseau to Neuroscience*. New York: Palgrave, 2002.

Nelson Novoa, James W. "Imagination as Exegesis in the *Apocalypsis Nova* Attributed to Blessed Amadeus da Silva." *Faith and Fantasy in the Renaissance: Texts, Images, and Religious Practices*. Ed. Olga Zorzi Pugliese and Ethan Matt Kavaler. Toronto: Centre for Reformation and Renaissance Studies, 2009. 71–83.

Nichols, Stephen G. "Seeing Food: An Anthropology of Ekphrasis, and Still Life in Classical and Medieval Examples." *Modern Language Notes* 106.4 (1991): 818–51.

Nobre, Kia. "El cerebro construye la realidad." Entrevista realizada por Eduardo Punset en el programa Redes, RTVE. http://www.rtve.es/television/20111027/cerebro-construye-realidad/471391.shtml.

Nocentelli, Carmen. *Empires of Love: Europe, Asia, and the Making of Early Modern Identity*. Philadelphia: U of Pennsylvania P, 2013.

Nordenfalk, Carl. "The Five Senses in Late Medieval and Renaissance Art." *Journal of the Warburg and Courtauld Institutes* 48 (1985): 1–22.

Noreña, Carlos G. *Juan Luis Vives*. The Hague: Martinus Nijhoff, 1970.

Núñez de Oria, Francisco. *Regimento y aviso de sanidad: que trata de todos los géneros de alimentos y del regimento della*. Medina del Campo: Francisco del Canto, Pedro Landry y Ambrosio du Port, 1586.

Ochoa Gautier, Ana María. *Aurality: Listening and Knowledge in Nineteenth-Century Colombia*. Durham, NC: Duke UP, 2014.

Octavio de Toledo, José María. "Visión de Filiberto." *Zeitschrift für Romanische Philologie* 2 (1878): 40–69.

Odo of Cluny. *The Life of Gerald of Aurillac*. Trans. and ed. Gerard Sitwell. London: Sheed & Ward, 1958.

Olid Guerrero, Eduardo. "The Machiavellian In-Betweeness of Cervantes's Elizabeth I." *Cervantes* 33.1 (2013): 45–80.

Oliván Santaliestra, Laura and Rafaella Pilo. "Recetario en busca de dueño: perfumería, medicina y confitería en la casa del VII Duque de Montalto (1635–1666)." *Cuadernos de historia moderna* 37 (2012): 103–25.

"Ordenanzas de S. M. hechas para los nuevos descubrimientos, conquistas y pacificaciones (Año de 1573)." *Colección de documentos inéditos relativos al descubrimiento, conquista y organización de las antiguas posesiones españolas de América y Oceania*. Ed. Joaquín Feancisco Pacheco, Francisco de Cárdenas y Espejo, and Luis Torres de Mendoza. Vol. 16. Madrid: Imprenta del Hospicio, 1871. 142–87.

Ordinances for the Discovery, New Settlement and Pacification of the Indies. Trans. Axel I. Mundigo and Anna Mercedes Mundigo. *Hispanic Urban Planning in North America*. Ed. Daniel J. Garr. New York: Garland, 1991. 3–33.

Ortega, Francisco. "Excessive Friendships: Face-to-Face and Play in Caminha's 'Letter to the King' (1500)." *Chasqui: revista de literatura latinoamericana* 34 (2005): 7–41.

Ortiz, Teresa. From Hegemony to Subordination: Midwives in Early Modern Spain." *The Art of Midwifery: Early Modern Midwives in Europe*. Ed. Hilary Marland. London: Routledge, 1993. 99–106.

– "La educación de las matronas en la Europa Moderna: ¿liberación o subordinación?" *De leer a escribir: la educación de las mujeres, ¿libertad o subordinación?* Ed. Cristina Segura Graiño. Granada: Asociación Cultural Al-Mudayna, 1996. 155–70.

Oxford Latin Dictionary. Ed. P.G.W. Glare. Oxford: Clarendon, 1996.

Pacheco de Narváez, Luis. *Engaño y desengaño de los errores que se han querido introducir en la destreza de las armas. A don Pedro Mexía de Tovar y Paz. Por don Luis Pacheco de Narváez*. Madrid: Emprenta del Reyno, 1635.

– *Libro de las grandezas de la espada*. Madrid: Los herederos de Iuan Iñiguez de Lequerica en la imprenta del Licẽciado Varez de Castro, 1600.

Palma, José Alberto, and Fermín Palma. "Neurology and *Don Quixote*." *European Neurology* 68 (2012): 246–57.

Palmer, Richard. "In Bad Odour: Smell and its Significance from Antiquity to the Seventeenth Century." *Medicine and the Five Senses*. Ed. W.F. Bynum and Roy Porters. Cambridge: Cambridge UP, 1993.

Paniagua, Juan Antonio. "Introducción." Alonso de Santa Cruz. *Sobre la melancolía. Diagnóstico y curación de los afectos melancólicos*. Pamplona: Universidad de Navarra, 2005. 13–22.

Parker, Alan, Alan Marshall, and Elliott Kastner. *Angel Heart*. United States: Carolco International N.V., Winkast Film Productions, and Union, 1987.

Parker, Alexander A. *Literature and the Delinquent: The Picaresque Novel in Spain and Europe, 1599–1753*. Edinburgh: Edinburgh UP, 1967.

– *The Philosophy of Love in Spanish Literature*. Edinburgh: Edinburgh UP, 1985.

Pascual-Argente, Clara. ""El cabdal sepulcro": Word and Image in the *Libro de Alexandre*." *La corónica* 38.2 (2010): 71–98.

Paster, Gail Kern. *The Body Embarrassed: Drama and the Disciplines of Shame in Early Modern England*. Ithaca, NY: Cornell UP, 1993.

Paterson, Alan K.G. "Reversal and Multiple Role-Playing in Alarcón's *La verdad sospechosa*." *Bulletin of Hispanic Studies* 61 (1984): 361–8.

Paterson, Mark. *The Senses of Touch: Haptics, Affects and Technologies*. New York: Berg, 2007.

Pérez Samper, María de los Ángeles. "Los recetarios de mujeres y para mujeres. Sobre la conversación y transmisión de los saberes domésticos en la época moderna." *Cuadernos de historia moderna* 19 (1997): 121–54.

Peset, José Luis. "Melancólicos e inocentes: la enfermedad mental entre el Renacimiento y el Barroco." *La ciencia y* El Quijote. Ed. José Manuel Sánchez Ron. Barcelona: Crítica, 2005. 181–8.

Pessoa, Fernando. *Mensagem*. Ed. David Mourão-Ferreira. Lisbon: Babel, 2010.

– *Sobre Portugal: Introdução ao problema nacional*. Ed. Maria Isabel Rocheta, Maria Paula Morão, and Joel Serrão. Lisbon: Ática, 1978.

Phelan, John Leddy. *The Millennial Kingdom of the Franciscans in the New World*. Berkeley: U of California P, 1970.

Philostratus, Philostratus, and Callistratus. *Imagines*. Trans. Arthur Fairbanks. Cambridge, MA: Harvard UP, 2000.

Pinet, Simone. "'Será todo en cabo a un lugar': Cartografías del *Libro de Alexandre*." *Actes Del X Congres International De l'Associació Hispànica de Literatura Medieval*. Ed. Rafael Alemany, Josep Lluís Martos, and Josep Miquel Manzanaro i Blasco. Alicante: Institut Interuniversitari de Filologia Valenciana, 2005. 1321–34.

– "Toward a Political Economy of the *Libro De Alexandre*." *Diacritics* 36.3–4 (2006): 44–63.

Plato. *Republic*. Trans. David J. Vaughan and John L. Davies. Cambridge: Cambridge UP / Macmillan, 1852.

Pollard, Tanya. "Enclosing the Body: Tudor Conceptions of Skin." *Companion to Tudor Literature*, ed. Kent Cartwright. Hoboken: Wiley-Blackwell, 2010. 111–22.

Porter, Jess, et al. "Mechanisms of Scent-Tracking in Humans," *Nature Neuroscience* 10.1 (2007): 27–9.

Prescott, John. *Taste Matters: Why We Like the Foods We Do*. London: Reaktion, 2012.

Prosperi, Adriano. "New Heaven and New Earth: Prophecy and Propaganda at the Time of the Discovery and Conquest of the Americas." *Prophetic Rome in the High Renaissance Period*. Ed. Marjorie Reeves. Oxford: Clarendon, 1992. 279–303.

Prudentius. *The Poems of Prudentius: A New Translation*. Trans. M. Clemet Eagan. Vol. 43. Washington, DC: Catholic UP, 1962.

Quevedo, Francisco de. *La vida del Buscón*. Madrid: Cátedra. 1981.

– "Vieras que con yeso blanqueaban (553)." *Fundación Francisco de Quevedo*. Web. 21 May 2014.

Quintero, María Cristina. "The Body of a Weak and Feeble Woman: Courting Isabel in Antonio Coello's *El conde de Sex*." *Material and Symbolic Circulation between Spain and England, 1554–1604*. Aldershot, UK: Ashgate, 2008. 71–86.

Rallo Gruss, Asunción. "Las misceláneas: conformación y desarrollo de un género renacentista." *Edad de Oro* 3 (1984): 159–80.

Ramírez Santacruz, Francisco. *El diagnóstico de la humanidad por Mateo Alemán: el discurso médico del Guzmán de Alfarache*. Potomac, MD: Scripta Humanistica, 2005.

Rath, Richard Cullen. *How Early America Sounded*. Ithaca, NY: Cornell UP, 2003.

Rawcliffe, Carole. *Leprosy in Medieval England*. Woodbridge, UK: Boydell, 2006.

Receptas experimentadas para diversas cosas. Madrid: National Library of Spain, n.d.

Recetas y memorias para guisados, confituras, olores, aguas, afeites, adobos de guantes, ungüentos y medicinas para muchas enfermedades. Madrid: National Library of Spain, n.d.

Reeves, Marjorie. *The Influence of Prophecy in the Later Middle Ages: A Study in Joachimism*. Notre Dame, IN: U of Notre Dame P, 1993.

Reichenberger, Arnold. "Boscán's Epístola a Mendoza." *Hispanic Review* 17 (1949): 1–17.

Ribbans, Geoffrey. "Lying in the Structure of *La verdad sospechosa*." *Studies in Spanish Literature of the Golden Age Presented to Edward M. Wilson*. Ed. R.O. Jones. London: Tamesis, 1973. 193–216.

Ribeiro, Sotério da Silva. "*Súmula Triunfal da nova e grande celebridade e invicto mártir são Gonçalo Garcia*." In *Movimento Academicista no Brasil, 1641–1820/22*. Ed. José Aderaldo Castello. Vol. 3, Tomo 2. São Paulo: Conselho Estadual de Cultura, 1969. 11–105.

Ricapito, Joseph. *Cervantes's* Novelas ejemplares: *Between History and Creativity*. West Lafayette, IN: Purdue UP, 1996.

Ricard, Robert. "Prophecy and Messianism in the Works of Antonio Vieira." *The Americas* 17.4. (1961): 357–68.

Richards, Jennifer. "Introduction. Classical and Early Modern Ideas of Memory." *Theories of Memory*. Ed. Michael Rossington and Anne Whitehead. Edinburgh: Edinburgh UP, 2007. 20–4.

Rico, Francisco. *El pequeño mundo del hombre: Varia fortuna de una idea en las literaturas españolas*. Madrid: Castalia, 1970.

– *La novela picaresca española*. Vol. 1. Barcelona: Planeta, 1970.

– "*Un penacho de penas*: de algunas invenciones y letras de caballeros." *Textos y contextos: Estudios sobre la poesía española del siglo XV*. Barcelona: Editorial Crítica, 1990. 189–230.

– "Unas coplas de Jorge Manrique y las fiestas de Valladolid en 1428." *Textos y contextos: Estudios sobre la poesía española del siglo XV*. Barcelona: Editorial Crítica, 1990. 169–87.

Riera, Juan. *Vida y obra de Luis Mercado*. Salamanca: Universidad de Salamanca, 1968.

Riley, E.C. "Alarcón's *Mentiroso* in the Light of Contemporary Theory of Character." *Hispanic Studies in Honour of I. González Llubera*. Ed. Frank Pierce. Oxford: Oxford UP, 1959. 287–97.

Rivlin, Robert, and Karen Gravelle. *Deciphering the Senses: The Expanding World of Human Perception*. New York: Simon, 1984.

Robertson, D.W. "The Doctrine of Charity in Mediaeval Literary Gardens: A Topical Approach through Symbolism and Allegory." *Speculum* 26.1 (1951): 24–94.

Roch, Martin, and M. Van Uytfanghe. *L'intelligence d'un dens: Odeurs miraculeuses et odorat dans l'Occident du haut Moyen Âge (ve–viii siècles)*. Turnhout: Brepols, 2009.

Rorty, Amélie, ed. *Explaining Emotions*. Berkeley: U of California P, 1980.

Rosenwein, Barbara H. *Emotional Communities in the Early Middle Ages*. Ithaca: Cornell UP, 2006.

Rothenberger, David J. "The Marian Symbolism of Spring, ca. 1200-ca. 1500: Two Case Studies." *Journal of the American Musicological Society* 59.2 (2006): 319–98.

Rozin, Paul, Jonathan Haidt, and Clark R. McCauley. "Disgust." *Handbook of Emotions*. Ed. Michael Lewis and Jeannette M. Haviland. New York: Guilford, 1993. 575–94.

Rudy, Gordon. *The Mystical Language of Sensation in the Later Middle Ages*. New York: Routledge, 2002.

Ruiz, Juan. *Libro de buen amor*. Ed. G.B. Gybbon-Monypenny. Madrid: Castalia, 1988.

Ruiz, Teofilo F. *A King Travels. Festive Traditions in Late Medieval and Early Modern Spain*. Princeton: Princeton UP, 2012.

Ruiz de Alarcón, Juan. *La verdad sospechosa*. Ed. Alva V. Ebersole. Madrid: Cátedra, 1982.

Salas, Xavier de. *El Bosco en la literatura española*. Barcelona: J. Sabater, 1943.

Salas Barbadillo, Alonso de. *Don Diego de noche*. Ed. Enrique García Santo-Tomás. Madrid: Cátedra, 2013.

San Roque, Lila, K.H. Kendrick, E. Norcliffe, P. Brown, R. Defina, M. Dingemanse, T. Dirksmeyer, N.J. Enfield, S. Floyd, J. Hammond, G. Rossi, S. Tufvesson, S. Van Putten, and A. Majid, "Vision verbs dominate in conversation across cultures, but the ranking of non-visual verbs varies." *Cognitive Linguistics* 26.1 (2015) 31–60.

Sánchez, Francisco J. *Lectura y representación: Análisis cultural de las* Novelas ejemplares *de Cervantes*. New York: Peter Lang, 1993.

Sánchez Jiménez, Antonio. *El pincel y el Fénix: pintura y literatura en la obra de Lope de Vega Carpio*. Madrid: Iberoamericana, 2011.

Sanders, Julie. "Midwifery and the New Science in the Seventeenth Century: Language, Print, and the Theater." *At the Borders of the Human: Beasts, Bodies, and Natural Philosophy in the Early Modern Period.* Ed. Erica Fudge, Ruth Gilbert, and Susan Wiseman. New York: Palgrave, 2002. 74–90.

Sanmartín Bastida, Rebeca. *La comida visionaria: Formas de alimentación en el discurso carismático femenino del siglo XVI*. London: Critical, Cultural and Communications Press, 2015.

Santos, Francisco. *Día y noche de Madrid. Obras selectas*. Ed. Milagros Navarro Pérez. 2 vols. Madrid: Instituto de Estudios Madrileños, 1976.

– *La Tarasca de parto en el Mesón del Infierno y días de fiesta por la noche*. Madrid: Domingo García Morrás, 1672.

San Pedro, Diego de. *Cárcel de Amor*. Ed. Keith Whinnom. Madrid: Castalia, 1972.

Sawday, Jonathan. *The Body Emblazoned: Dissection and the Human Body in Renaissance Culture*. London: Routledge, 1995.

Schantz, Maria Lima. *A Feminist Interpretation of the Galician-Portuguese* Cantigas de Amigo. Lewiston, NY: Edwin Mellen, 2004.

Schoenfeldt, Michael C. *Bodies and Selves in Early Modern England.* Cambridge: Cambridge UP, 1999.

Schmitz, Ryan. "Cervantes's Language of the Heart in the *Novelas ejemplares* and *Don Quixote*." *Cervantes* 32.2 (2012): 171–95.

Seed, Patricia. *Ceremonies of Possession in Europe's Conquest of the New World, 1492–1640.* Cambridge: Cambridge UP, 1995.

Seidenpinner-Nuñez, Dayle. *The Writings of Teresa de Cartagena*. Woodbridge, UK: Boydell & Brewer, 1998.

Serrano Perdices, Laura. "*La Tarasca de Parto*: Mayas, moralistas e infancia en el Madrid del siglo XVII." *Las edades de las mujeres*. Ed. Pilar Pérez Cantó and Margarita Ortega López. Madrid: Universidad Autónoma de Madrid, 2002. 81–93.

Serre, Michel. *Les Cinq sens. Philosophie des corps mêlées-1*. Paris: Bernard Grasset, 1985.

Shaffer, Diana. "Ekphrasis and the Rhetoric of Viewing in Philostratus's Imaginary Museum." *Philosophy and Rhetoric* 31.4 (1998): 303–16.

Shaarup, Bjørn Okholm. *Anatomy and Anatomists in Early Modern Spain*. New York: Routledge, 2015.

Shepherd, Gordon. *Neurogastronomy: How the Brain Creates Flavor and Why it Matters*. New York: Columbia UP, 2012.

Shepherd, Odell. *The Lore of the Unicorn*. New York: Avenel, 1982.

Shusterman, Richard. *Thinking through the Body: Essays in Somaesthetics*. New York: Cambridge UP, 2012.

Silva, Amadeus da. *Apocalypsis Nova*. Ms. Vat. Lat. 3825. Vatican Library.

Silva, Vítor Manuel de Aguiar e. *Camões: labirintos e fascínios*. Lisbon: Cotovia, 1994.

Silva y Arteaga, Alonso de. *Tardes de Quaresma repartidas en veinte y tres tratados*. Salamanca, 1702.

Simerka, Barbara. "Dramatic and Discursive Genres: *La verdad sospechosa* as Problem Comedy and Marriage Treatise." *El Arte Nuevo de Estudiar Comedias: Literary Theory and Golden Age Drama*. Ed. Barbara Simerka. Lewisburg, PA: Bucknell UP, 1997. 187–205.

Simón Palmer, María del Carmen. "Hipócrates y Galeno en el teatro del Siglo de Oro." *Tes Philies Tade Dora: Miscelánea léxica en memoria de Conchita Serrano*. Madrid: CSIC, 1999. 523–34.

Smith, Bruce R. *The Acoustic World of Early Modern England: Attending to the O-Factor*. Chicago: U of Chicago P, 1999.

Sobejano, Gonzalo. "De Alemán a Cervantes: Monólogo y diálogo." *Homenaje al Profesor Muñoz Cortes*. Ed. Francisco Sabater García. Murcia: Universidad de Murcia, Facultad de Filosofía y Letras, 1977. 713–29.

Solomon, Michael. *Fictions of Well-Being. Sickly Readers and Vernacular Medical Writing in Late Medieval and Early Modern Spain*. Philadelphia: U of Pennsylvania P, 2010.

Soons, Alan. "La verdad sospechosa in its Epoch." *Critical Essays on the Life and Works of Juan Ruiz de Alarcón*. Ed. James A. Parr. Madrid: Editorial Dos Continentes, 1972. 239–45.

Sousa Costa, António Domingues de. *Studio critico e documenti inediti sulla vita del Beato Amadeo da Silva nel quinto centenario della morte*. Rome: Pontificium Athanaeum Anthonianum, 1985.

Souza, Marina de Mello e. *Reis Negros no Brasil Escravista: História da Festa de Coroação de Rei Congo*. Belo Horizonte, Braz.: Editora UFMG, 2002.

Spalding, Karen. *Huarochirí: An Andean Society under Inca and Spanish Rule*. Stanford: Stanford UP, 1984.

Spiegel, Gabrielle M. "Paradoxes of the Senses." *Rethinking the Medieval Senses: Heritage, Fascinations, Frames*. Ed. Stephen G. Nichols, Andreas Kablitz, and Alison Calhoun. Baltimore: Johns Hopkins UP, 2008. 186–93.

Spinks, Jennifer S. *Monstrous Births and Visual Culture in Sixteenth-Century Germany: Religious Cultures in the Early Modern World*. London: Pickering & Chatto, 2009.

Staves, S. "Liars and Lying in Alarcón, Corneille and Steele." *Revue de Literature comparée* 46.4 (1972): 514–27.

Stoops, Rosa María. "Elizabeth I of England as Mercurian Monarch in Miguel de Cervantes' *La española inglesa*." *Bulletin of Spanish Studies* 88.2 (2011): 177–97.

Summers, David. *The Judgement of Sense: Renaissance Naturalism and the Rise of Aesthetics*. Cambridge: Cambridge UP, 1990.

Surtz, Ronald. "Auto de los Reyes Magos." *Teatro medieval castellano*. Madrid: Taurus, 1983. 13–18.

Tato, Cleofé. *Vida y obra de Pedro de Santa Fe*. Noia, Spain: Toxosoutos Editorial, 2000.

Temkin, Owsei. *Galenism; Rise and Decline of a Medical Philosophy.* Ithaca, NY: Cornell UP, 1973.

"Tierra sellada." *Museo de la farmacia hispana.* Universidad Complutense Madrid. Web. 23 May 2014.

Tiez, Joan Anne. *A Thousand Years of Sweet. A Semantic and Cultural Study.* Frankfurt: Peter Lang, 2001.

Tinhorão, José Ramos. *As Festas no Brasil Colonial.* São Paulo: Editora 34 Ltda, 2000.

Toledo, Francisco de. *Disposiciones gubernativas para el Virreinato del Perú, 1569–1574.* Ed. Justina Sarabia Viejo. 2 vols. Seville: Escuela de Estudios Hispanopamericanos, 1986.

Tomlinson, Gary. *The Singing of the New World: Indigenous Voice in the Era of European Contact.* Cambridge: Cambridge UP, 2007.

Torres, Isabel. "Now You See it, Now You ... See it Again? The Dynamics of Doubling in *La española inglesa.*" *A Companion to Cervantes's* Novelas ejemplares. Ed. Stephen Boyd. London: Támesis, 2005. 115–33.

Touati, François-Olivier. "Contagion and Leprosy: Myth, Ideas and Evolution in Medieval Minds and Societies." *Contagion: Perspectives from Pre-Modern Societies.* Ed. Larence I. Conrad and Dominik Wujuastyk. Burlington, VT: Ashgate, 2000. 179–202.

Tulving, Endel. *Elements of Episodic Memory.* Oxford: Clarendon, 1983.

– "Episodic Memory: From Mind to Brain." *Annual Review of Psychology* 53 (2002): 1–25.

Turner, Mark. *The Literary Mind: The Origins of Thought and Language.* New York: Oxford UP, 1996.

Urbina, Eduardo. "La razón de más fuerza: Triple juego en *La verdad sospechosa.*" *Hispania* 70 (1987): 724–30.

Vaíllo, Carlos. "La novela picaresca y otras formas narrativas." *Historia y crítica de la literatura española: Siglos de Oro.* Ed. Bruce Wardropper. Barcelona: Editorial Crítica, 1983. 448–67.

Vallés, Francisco. *Tratado de las aguas destiladas, pesos, y medidas de que los boticarios deuen vsar, por nueua ordenança, y mandato de su Majestad, y su Real Consejo.* Madrid: Luis Sanchez, 1592.

Van De Mieroop, Marc. "Reading Babylon." *American Journal of Archeology* 107 (2003): 257–75.

Vance, Eugene. "Seeing God: Augustine, Sensation, and the Mind's Eye." *Rethinking the Medieval Senses: Heritage, Fascinations, Frames.* Ed. Stephen G. Nichols, Andreas Kablitz, and Alison Calhoun. Baltimore: Johns Hopkins UP, 2008. 13–29.

Veeser, Harold. "'That Dangerous Supplement': *La verdad sospechosa* and the Literacy of Speech Situation." *Things Done with Words: Speech Acts in Hispanic Drama.* Proceedings of the 1984 Stony Brook Seminar. Ed. Elias L. Rivers. Newark, DE: Juan de la Cuesta, 1986. 51–71.

Vega, Garcilaso de la. *Obra poética.* Bienvenido Morros, ed. Barcelona: Crítica, 1995.

Vega, Félix Lope de. *Si no vieran las mujeres. La Vega del Parnaso*. Madrid: Imprenta del Reino, 1637.

Vélez de Guevara, Luis. *El Diablo Cojuelo*. Ed. Ramón Valdés. Barcelona: Crítica, 1999.

Vieira, António. *História do Futuro*. Ed. Maria Leonor Carvalhão Buescu. Lisbon: Imprena Nacional – Casa da Moeda, 1982.

– "Sermão do Mandato: Prégado em Lisboa, na Capella Real, no Anno de 1650." *Obras Completas do Padre António Vieira: Sermões*. Vol. 4. Ed. Gonçalo Alves. Lisbon: Lello & Irmão, 1907. 327–59.

Villas Bôas, Luciana. "Arte da memória e escrita dos primeiros jesuítas no Brasil." *Estudios portugueses y brasileños* 11 (2011): 25–38.

Villaseñor Black, Charlene. "The Moralized Breast in Early Modern Spain." *The Material Culture of Sex, Procreation, and Marriage in Early Modern Europe*. Ed. Anne L. McClanan and Karen Rosoff Encarnación. New York: Palgrave, 2002. 191–219.

Villegas, Alonso de. *Flos sanctorum e historia general, en que se escriven las vidas de los santos*. Rpt Madrid: Gonçález de Reyes, 1675.

Vinge, Louise. *The Five Senses: Studies in a Literary Tradition*. Lund, Swed.: Liber Läromedel, 1975.

Vitry, Jacques de. *The Life of Marie d'Oignies*. Trans. and ed. M.H. King and M. Marsolais. Toronto: Peregrina, 1994.

Vives, Juan Luis. *De anima et vita*. Ed. Mario Sancipriano. Latin and Italian ed. Padua: Gregoriana Editrice, 1974.

– *El alma y la vida*. Valencia: Biblioteca Valenciana Digital, 1992.

– *The Passions of the Soul: The Third Book of* De Anima et Vita. Trans. Carlos Noreña. Lewiston, NY: Edwin Mellen, 1990.

– *Tratado del alma*. Trans. José Ontañón. Madrid: Ediciones de la lectura, 1916.

Vogt-Spira, Gregor. "Senses, Imagination, and Literature: Some Epistemological Considerations." *Rethinking the Medieval Senses: Heritage, Fascinations, Frames*. Ed. Stephen G. Nichols, Andreas Kablitz, and Alison Calhoun. Baltimore: Johns Hopkins UP, 2008. 51–72.

Voigt, Lisa. "Spectacular Wealth: Baroque Festivals and Creole Consciousness in Colonial Mining Towns of Brazil and Peru." *Creole Subjects in the Colonial Americas: Empires, Texts, Identities*. Ed. Ralph Bauer and José Antonio Mazzotti. Chapel Hill: U of North Carolina P, 2009. 265–90.

– *Spectacular Wealth: The Festivals of Colonial South American Mining Towns*. Austin: U Texas P, 2016.

Wagschal, Steven. *The Literature of Jealousy in the Age of Cervantes*. Columbia: U of Missouri P, 2006.

– "The Smellscape of Don Quixote: A Cognitive Approach." *Cervantes:* 32.1 (2012): 125–62.

Walsh, John K. "Religious Motifs in the Early Spanish Epic." *Revista Hispánica Moderna* 36.4 (1971): 165–70.

Walter, Katie L. "The Form of the Formless: Medieval Taxonomies of Skin, Flesh, and the Human." *Reading Skin in Medieval Literature and Culture.* Ed. Katie L. Walter. New York: Palgrave Macmillan, 2013. 119–39.

Warner, Marina. *Alone of all her Sex. The Myth and the Cult of the Virgin Mary.* New York: Knopf, 1976.

Watt, I. *Myths of Modern Individualism. Faust, Don Quixote, Don Juan, Robinson Crusoe,* Cambridge: Cambridge UP, 1996.

Weber, Alison. "La excentricidad y la norma en dos comedias de Ruiz de Alarcón." *Actas del Sexto Congreso de la Asociación Internacional de Hispanistas.* Ed. Alan M. Gordon and Evelyn Rugg. Toronto: U of Toronto P and Paul Malak, 1980. 783–5.

– "Santa Teresa, Demonologist." *Culture and Control in Counter-Reformation Spain.* Ed. Anne J. Cruz and Mary Elizabeth Perry. Minneapolis: U of Minnesota P, 1992. 171–95.

Weiss, Julian. *The* Mester de Clerecía*: Intellectuals and Ideologies in Thirteenth-Century Castile.* Woodbridge, UK: Tamesis, 2006.

Werrett, Simon. *Fireworks: Pyrotechnic Arts and Sciences in European History.* Chicago: U of Chicago P, 2010.

Whaley, Leigh. *Women and the Practice of Medical Care in Early Modern Europe, 1400–1800.* Houndmills, UK: Palgrave Macmillan, 2011.

Whicker, Jules. "Devilish Artifice: Changing Attitudes to Firearms in the Spanish Golden Age." *Bulletin of Hispanic Studies* 77.4 (2000): 527–50.

– *The Plays of Juan Ruiz de Alarcón.* London: Tamesis, 2003.

Wilson, Adrian. "The Ceremony of Childbirth and its Interpretation." *Women as Mothers in Pre-industrial England: Essays in Memory of Dorothy McLaren.* Ed. Valerie Fildes. London: Routledge, 1990. 68–107.

Wishart, Trevor. *On Sonic Art.* New York: Routledge, 1996.

Wolfson, Harry. "The Internal Senses in Latin, Arabic, and Hebrew Philosophic Texts." *Harvard Theological Review* 28.2 (1935): 69–133.

Woolgar, C.M. *The Senses in Late Medieval England.* New Haven: Yale UP, 2006.

Yates, Frances. *The Art of Memory.* Chicago: U of Chicago P, 2001.

Zabaleta, Juan de. *El día de fiesta por la mañana y por la tarde.* Ed. Cristóbal Cuevas. Madrid: Castalia, 1983.

Zayas, María de. "La fuerza del amor." *Novelas amorosas y ejemplares.* Ed. Julián Olivares. 2nd corr. ed. Madrid: Cátedra, 2004.

– "La inocencia castigada." *Desengaños amorosos.* Ed. Alicia Yllera. 6th ed. Madrid: Cátedra, 2006.

– "Innocence Punished." *The Disenchantments of Love: A Translation of the* Desengaños amorosos. Trans. H. Patsy Boyer. Albany: SUNY P, 1997. 175–201.

– "The Power of Love." *The Enchantments of Love: Amorous and Exemplary Novels.* Trans. H. Patsy Boyer. Berkeley: U of California P, 1990. 159–81.

– "Tarde llega el desengaño." *Desengaños amorosos.* Ed. Alicia Yllera. 6th ed. Madrid: Cátedra, 2006.

– "Too Late Undeceived." *The Disenchantments of Love: A Translation of the* Desengaños amorosos. Trans. H. Patsy Boyer. Albany: SUNY Press, 1997. 139–64.

Ziegler, Philip. *The Black Death.* New York: Harper Torchbooks, 1969.

Zink, Michel. "The Place of the Senses." *Rethinking the Medieval Senses: Heritage, Fascination, Frames.* Ed. Stephen G. Nichols, Andreas Kablitz, and Alison Calhoun. Baltimore: Johns Hopkins UP, 2008. 93–101.

Zunshine, Lisa. "Introduction: What Is Cognitive Cultural Studies?" *Introduction to Cognitive Cultural Studies.* Ed. Lisa Zunshine. Baltimore: Johns Hopkins UP, 2010. 1–33.

Zuwiyya, Z. David. "The Alexander Tradition in Spain." *A Companion to Alexander in the Middle Ages.* Ed. Z. David Zuwiyya. Leiden: Brill, 2011. 231–53.

Contributors

Henry Berlin, Assistant Professor of Spanish, SUNY Buffalo. He studies medieval literature, theology, and political thought in Castilian, Catalan, and Portuguese, and his articles have appeared in *La corónica*, *Medieval Encounters*, the *Journal of Medieval Iberian Studies*, and *Hispanic Review*.

Josiah Blackmore, Nancy Clark Smith Professor of the Language and Literature of Portugal, Harvard University. He specializes in the literature and culture of medieval and early modern Portugal, with an emphasis on the writings of maritime expansion. Author of *Moorings: Portuguese Expansion and the Writing of Africa* (2009; selected as a *Choice* Outstanding Academic Title) and *Manifest Perdition: Shipwreck Narrative and the Disruption of Empire* (2002). He co-edited *Queer Iberia* (1999) and edited the re-release of Charles R. Boxer's *The Tragic History of the Sea* (2001) and the *Songs of António Botto* (2010).

Frederick A. de Armas, Andrew W. Mellon Distinguished Service Professor in the Humanities, Spanish Literature, and Comparative Literature, University of Chicago. He focuses on Renaissance and early modern Spanish literature, often from a comparative perspective. He is the author of numerous books and edited volumes, the most recent of which include: *Cervantes, Raphael and the Classics* (1998); *European Literary Careers: The Author from Antiquity to the Renaissance* (2002); *Writing for the Eyes in the Spanish Golden Age* (2004); *Ekphrasis in the Age of Cervantes* (2005); *Quixotic Frescoes: Cervantes and Italian Renaissance Art* (2006); *Hacia la tragedia áurea* (2008) *Ovid in the Age of Cervantes* (2010); *Calderón: del manuscrito a la escena* (2011); *Objects of Culture in the Literature of Imperial Spain* (2013); and *Don Quixote among the Saracens: Clashes of Civilizations and Literary Genres* (2011). The last book was recognized by the PROSE Award in Literature, honourable mention. De Armas has been the recipient of several NEH fellowships and has served as president of the Cervantes Society of America.

Julia Domínguez, Associate Professor of Spanish, Iowa State University. Her primary area of research is the impact of Miguel de Cervantes and Hispanic picaresque fiction through contemporaneous theories of cognitive mapping, space and cartography; taking into account themes of travel, transculturation, and psychology. She is the editor of the volume *Cervantes in Perspective* (Iberoamericana/Vervuert 2013). Her current book project is entitled *Imaginary Cartographies: The Creation of Utopian Spaces in the Age of Discovery.*

Emily Francomano, Associate Professor of Spanish, Georgetown University. Her research has focused on the sentimental novel, the medieval love poetry, religious writing, and romance in Catalan, French, and Spanish. She is the author of *Wisdom and Her Lovers in Medieval and Early Modern Hispanic Literature* (Palgrave 2008), and the editor of *Three Spanish Querelle Texts, by Pere Torrellas and Juan de Flores. A Bilingual Edition and Study* (Victoria University in the University of Toronto, Centre for Reformation and Renaissance Studies, 2013). She was the recipient of the Modern Language Association, Division of Medieval Spanish Language and Literature's John K. Walsh Prize (2001).

Robert K. Fritz, Assistant Professor, Murray State University, where he began in Fall 2017. He completed his doctorate at Indiana University Bloomington in 2017. In his dissertation, "Pedro Mexía and the Dialogics of Curiosity," he analyses the works of sixteenth-century author Pedro Mexía through the lens of Bakhtinian dialogism to argue that Mexía transformed the notion of curiosity into a discursive tool for redefining Spanish readers' relationship with nature and knowledge.

Enrique García Santo-Tomás, Frank P. Casa Collegiate Professor of Spanish, University of Michigan. He studies the history of science and technology as it relates to literature and has published numerous monographs, critical editions and edited collections, including *La musa refractada: literatura y óptica en la España del Barroco* (2014), *Modernidad bajo sospecha: Salas Barbadillo y la cultura material del siglo XVII* (2008), *Espacio urbano y creación literaria en el Madrid de Felipe IV* (2004) and *La creación del 'Fénix': recepción crítica y formación canónica del teatro de Lope de Vega* (2000). Among other accolades, he was awarded the Guggenheim Fellowship (2007) and won the "William Riley Parker Prize for an Outstanding Article in *PMLA*" (2009).

Charles Victor Ganelin, Professor Emeritus of Spanish, Miami University of Ohio. His book-length studies include an edition of Andrés de Claramonte's *La infelice Dorotea* (Tamesis, 1988), *Rewriting Theatre: The Refundición and the Nineteenth-century Theatre* (Bucknell UP, 1994), and a co-edited collection of essays, *The Golden Age* Comedia: *Text, Theory and Performance* (Purdue UP, 1994).

E. Michael Gerli, Commonwealth Professor of Spanish, University of Virginia. The latest of his thirteen books, *Celestina and the Ends of Desire* (Toronto UP, 2011) was awarded the Modern Language Association of America's Katherine Singer Kovacs Prize for an outstanding book published in English or Spanish in the field of Latin American and Spanish literatures and cultures. He is also a recipient of the *Hispanic Review*'s Edwin B. Williams Prize (1981) and the Modern Language Association's Division of Medieval Spanish Language and Literature's John K. Walsh Prize (1997).

Ryan D. Giles, Associate Professor of Spanish, Indiana University Bloomington. His research focuses on medieval and Renaissance parody and satire, sanctity, theology and popular devotion, and intersections between early Iberian literatures and material culture. He is the author of *The Laughter of the Saints: Parodies of Holiness in Late Medieval and Renaissance Spain* (U of Toronto P, 2009), and is now completing a book on textual amulets in Spanish literature and culture, from the thirteenth to the seventeenth century. He was the recipient of the Modern Language Association's Division of Medieval Spanish Language and Literature's John K. Walsh Prize (2008).

Carolyn A. Nadeau, Byron S. Tucci Professor of Spanish, Illinois Wesleyan University. Her research focuses on food representation in sixteenth-century and seventeenth-century Spanish literature and her most recent book, *Food Matters: Alonso Quijano's Diet and the Discourse of Early Modern Food in Spain* (U Toronto P, 2015) contextualizes the shifts in Spain's gastronomic history at many levels of society and in the process explores the evolving social and cultural identity of early modern Spain. She has also published on the role of wife and mother in early modern advice manuals, mythological female figures in the *comedia*, and on questions of literary continuation and cultural authority in early modern Spain.

Victor Rodríguez-Pereira, Doctoral Candidate, Indiana University Bloomington. He is currently writing his dissertation on representations of monsters and the monstrous in medieval Iberia, with an emphasis on early chivalric literature.

Lisa Voigt, Associate Professor of Spanish and Portuguese, The Ohio State University. Her work centers on colonial Latin American literature and culture, addressing transatlantic and comparative issues, such as captivity and shipwreck narratives in the Spanish and Portuguese empires, *mestizo* historiography, and Baroque festivals. She is the author of *Writing Captivity in the Early Modern Atlantic: Circulations of Knowledge and Authority in the Iberian and English Imperial Worlds* (Omohundro Institute of Early American History and Culture/U of North Carolina P, 2009), for which she won the Modern Language Association's Katherine Singer Kovacs Prize. She is currently working on a book project entitled, "Spectacular Wealth: Power and Participation in the Festivals of Colonial Potosí and Minas Gerais."

Steven Wagschal, Associate Professor of Spanish, Affiliated Faculty Member of Cognitive Science, Caribbean and Latin American Studies, and Renaissance Studies, Chair of Spanish and Portuguese at Indiana University Bloomington. His research focuses on early modern Spanish literary texts as these intersect with art history, philosophy and cognitive studies. He is the author of *The Literature of Jealousy in the Age of Cervantes* (Missouri UP, 2006) and editor of *Peribáñez y el Comendador de Ocaña* by Lope de Vega (Cervantes, 2004). His monograph on animal cognition from a cognitive historicist perspective, *Minding Animals in the Old and New Worlds*, is forthcoming from U Toronto P.

Index

TORONTO IBERIC

1 Anthony J. Cascardi, *Cervantes, Literature, and the Discourse of Politics*
2 Jessica A. Boon, *The Mystical Science of the Soul: Medieval Cognition in Bernardino de Laredo's Recollection Method*
3 Susan Byrne, *Law and History in Cervantes' Don Quixote*
4 Mary E. Barnard and Frederick A. de Armas (eds), *Objects of Culture in the Literature of Imperial Spain*
5 Nil Santiáñez, *Topographies of Fascism: Habitus, Space, and Writing in Twentieth-Century Spain*
6 Nelson Orringer, *Lorca in Tune with Falla: Literary and Musical Interludes*
7 Ana M. Gómez-Bravo, *Textual Agency: Writing Culture and Social Networks in Fifteenth-Century Spain*
8 Javier Irigoyen-García, *The Spanish Arcadia: Sheep Herding, Pastoral Discourse, and Ethnicity in Early Modern Spain*
9 Stephanie Sieburth, *Survival Songs: Conchita Piquer's* Coplas *and Franco's Regime of Terror*
10 Christine Arkinstall, *Spanish Female Writers and the Freethinking Press, 1879–1926*
11 Margaret Boyle, *Unruly Women: Performance, Penitence, and Punishment in Early Modern Spain*

12 Evelina Gužauskytė, *Christopher Columbus's Naming in the* diarios *of the Four Voyages (1492–1504): A Discourse of Negotiation*
13 Mary E. Barnard, *Garcilaso de la Vega and the Material Culture of Renaissance Europe*
14 William Viestenz, *By the Grace of God: Francoist Spain and the Sacred Roots of Political Imagination*
15 Michael Scham, Lector Ludens*: The Representation of Games and Play in* Cervantes
16 Stephen Rupp, *Heroic Forms: Cervantes and the Literature of War*
17 Enrique Fernandez, *Anxieties of Interiority and Dissection in Early Modern Spain*
18 Susan Byrne, *Ficino in Spain*
19 Patricia M. Keller, *Ghostly Landscapes: Film, Photography, and the Aesthetics of Haunting in Contemporary Spanish Culture*
20 Carolyn A. Nadeau, *Food Matters: Alonso Quijano's Diet and the Discourse of Food in Early Modern Spain*
21 Cristian Berco, *From Body to Community: Venereal Disease and Society in Baroque Spain*
22 Elizabeth R. Wright, *The Epic of Juan Latino: Dilemmas of Race and Religion in Renaissance Spain*
23 Ryan D. Giles, *Inscribed Power: Amulets and Magic in Early Spanish Literature*
24 Jorge Pérez, *Confessional Cinema: Religion, Film, and Modernity in Spain's Development Years (1960–1975)*
25 Juan Ramon Resina, *Josep Pla: Life Seen in the Form of Articles*
26 Javier Irigoyen-Garcia, *Moors Dressed as Moors: Clothing, Social Distinction, and Ethnicity in Early Modern Iberia*
27 Jean Dangler, *Edging Towards Iberia*
28 Ryan D. Giles and Steven Wagschal (eds): *Beyond Sight: Engaging the Senses in Iberian Literatures and Cultures, 1200–1750*

www.ingramcontent.com/pod-product-compliance
Lightning Source LLC
LaVergne TN
LVHW090148080826
844660LV00013B/721/J

* 9 7 8 1 4 8 7 5 0 0 0 3 0 *